The Old West in
Fact and Film

# The Old West in
# Fact and Film

## *History Versus Hollywood*

JEREMY AGNEW

McFarland & Company, Inc., Publishers

*Jefferson, North Carolina, and London*

LIBRARY OF CONGRESS CATALOGUING-IN-PUBLICATION DATA

Agnew, Jeremy.
The Old West in fact and film : history versus Hollywood / Jeremy Agnew.
p.     cm.
Includes bibliographical references and index.

**ISBN 978-0-7864-6888-1**
softcover : acid free paper ∞

1. Western films — United States — History and criticism.
2. West (U.S.) — In motion pictures.
3. Motion pictures and history.
I. Title.
PN1995.9.W4A52 2012      791.43'65878—dc23      2012038741

BRITISH LIBRARY CATALOGUING DATA ARE AVAILABLE

On the cover: The Denver & Silverton Narrow Gauge Railroad
has appeared in many Westerns, including *Denver and Rio Grande*
(1952) and *Butch Cassidy and the Sundance Kid* (1969). The railway
also operates in the summer as a tourist ride from Durango to Silverton,
Colorado (author's collection); ornaments © 2012 clipart.com

Manufactured in the United States of America

*McFarland & Company, Inc., Publishers
Box 611, Jefferson, North Carolina 28640
www.mcfarlandpub.com*

For Ron: from one old Western
movie buff to another

# Contents

# Preface

*"Westerns are nothing but American swashbucklers. They concern knights and crusaders, pirates and racketeers, except they are in a more familiar setting."* — Actor Audie Murphy[1]

Movie audiences have long carried on a love affair with the mythical American Wild West. Western movies are escapist entertainment of the best kind. They hark back to the days of the American frontier, when men were men who lived by a code of rough justice, and problems were simply and quickly resolved with fists and guns. Their hero is a lone, rugged individual who is bold, decisive, and ready to right all wrongs. He has persistence, courage, determination, and incredible skill with a gun.

Before focusing on what this book on Westerns is, I am going to start with several comments on what it is not. First, this is not a book of criticism on Western film. I am not a film critic and I don't intend to be one in this book. Edward Dmytryk, in a book on film directing, mentioned a classic example of divergent critical opinions when he noted, "Some years ago MGM produced one of Hollywood's greatest films, *Doctor Zhivago*. The nation's leading news weeklies, *Time* and *Newsweek*, reviewed it. One considered it a truly great film, the other saw it as the decade's disaster."[2] If intelligent, sophisticated, and knowledgeable critics such as these have very diverse opinions, far be it from me to offer mine.

At best, film criticism is a highly subjective field, and film critics vary widely in their opinions. For example, George Fenin and William Everson wrote that "*Butch Cassidy and the Sundance Kid* is undoubtedly one of the most articulate, original, and above all modern Westerns ever made."[3] On the other hand, the opinion of Brian Garfield was that "*Butch Cassidy* [is] really quite ordinary: excellently made but [it] added little to what already existed in the genre."[4] He added, "It seems merely a modern colorful reshaping with a pair of bemused and essentially pathetic characters," and went on to say, "Certainly the film is not merely as sincere or important an effort as the contemporaneous *The Wild Bunch*."[5] Perhaps a more objective footnote to these opinions is that *Butch Cassidy and the Sundance Kid* (1969) won four Academy Awards: best script, best cinematography, best musical score, and best song. It was also nominated for best direction and best film, though it did not win in either of these categories.

For the reader seeking critical commentary on Western movies, there are many books that cover the entire genre, as well as specific films. Readers wishing to study criticism of the Western film in depth might wish to start with books such as Nachbar, Donath, and Foran's *Western Films 2: An Annotated Critical Bibliography from 1974 to 1987*.

Likewise, this book is not an attempt to analyze specific Western movies, to analyze the genre, or to analyze filmmakers' intent. It is not my place to analyze movies and theorize

1

what the director intended. A movie should stand or fall by what is viewed on the screen. It is also not unknown for critics to read more into a movie than the makers originally intended.

Nor is this book, strictly speaking, going to be a history of film, though film history is included to place the evolution of the Western film into perspective with the history of the real West. Instead, my intent is to compare what is presented in Western movies to the Old West. I write about the history of the American West, and what I intend to do in this book is to relate the reality of the Old West to the way that it has been portrayed on the silver screen. In other words, I intend to look at Westerns from the perspective of history.

My method in writing this book will follow two converging (one hopes) paths. One path is to retell some of the history of the Old West that commonly appears in Westerns. This will place the people and events seen in movies into their proper perspective in history. The other pathway is to present enough of the history of making Western films that the reader can place a particular film or period into the timeline of the evolution of Westerns and see how this has influenced the process of making these films.

In some movies the portrayal of the Old West is quite accurate. In others, the reality of the Old West bears little relationship to the filmed version. Furthermore, while incidents that appear in some movies, such as the multiple hangings in *Hang 'Em High* (1968), must seem like incredible fiction to the viewer, many of them were true. Rather than criticisms, then, I will present facts and observations, illustrated by examples from only a selected few of the thousands of Western films that have been made, and the reader can decide how this affects his or her enjoyment of a particular movie. Lack of historical accuracy does not necessarily make inaccurate movies bad or not enjoyable to watch. Western films should be viewed as an entertainment form and a dramatic narrative, not as a history lesson.

Some critics have expressed concern about Hollywood's distortion of the history of the Old West and the failure of Western films to reproduce it accurately.[6] However, Western movies are about legends and heroes, not necessarily about reality. An example of questionable history from a non–Western film is John Ford's *7 Women* (1966), which tells the story of a group of dedicated missionaries in China in 1935. As the movie progresses, the audience sees that the white characters are racist and show contempt for the Chinese, which is historically inaccurate. Among other areas where the movie strays from reality are having the Chinese characters speak the wrong languages, and Mongolians played by a Ukrainian (Mike Mazurki) and a black (Woody Strode). Ford did not intend to depict his version of China as being historically accurate. Instead, he was telling a story.[7] Ford has been quoted as saying, "Do you want good history or a good movie?"[8]

Though not everybody agrees with this opinion, in my view, Western movies should reflect the sentiments echoed at the end of *The Man Who Shot Liberty Valance* (1962) by the editor of the *Shinbone Star*, Maxwell Scott (Carleton Young), who declares: "This is the West, sir. When the legend becomes fact, print the legend." Western movies are all about legends.

I hasten to add that, regardless of criticisms, one of my favorite types of movie is the Western, and it remains so in spite of any shortcomings in accuracy. Any perceived criticisms in this book are intended to relate to the myths and factual errors in Western movies versus the reality of the Old West, not to the art form of the cinema. Though some readers may think that I am being overly picky about minor points, I have the greatest respect and love for Western movies, even with their imperfections.

I grew up with Westerns in the 1950s, strongly influenced by my grandfather and his taste in movies. Twice a week he took our entire family to a matinee double-bill at one of our five local movie theaters, one of which in that era was sure to be showing an "A" and a "B" Western. Unfortunately for my early moviegoing career, my grandfather was a country doctor and held an open clinic every day in the late afternoon, so at five o'clock we all had to rise up and leave the theater, no matter where the resolution of the plot was in the movie. This made for many unintended cliff-hangers for the family, as we often never found out what happened at the end. As a result, I did not know how the plots of many Westerns turned out until I was much older and could watch them again without this restriction.

Western movies still apparently offer a fascination for young boys. While on a recent trip in Utah I took my seven-year-old grandson to see *Fort Dobbs* (1958) at a retrospective showing of old Western movies. A little to my surprise, in this day of comic-book super-heroes in super-action movies, he absolutely loved it, and when we returned home he burrowed into my collection of old Roy Rogers movies and has repeatedly watched them all.

For the purposes of this book I have chosen to retain the convention of Hollywood in the 1940s and 1950s by using the generic name of "Indians" for Native American tribes. I had several reasons for doing this and intend no disrespect by the use of this name to any who prefer a different terminology. One reason is that Hollywood's conception of "Indians" was generally a nameless, faceless caricature of Native American peoples that existed in a movie to attack a wagon train or a patrol of soldiers and be shot down in large numbers. Secondly, most of the "Indian" roles were played by white actors, and their actions were not necessarily consistent with Native American tribes and the specific peoples portrayed. Another reason is that "Indians" is the popular name used by countless children who grew up playing "cowboys-and-Indians," not the more cumbersome "cowboys-and-Native-Americans." Finally, even the current politically-correct name of "Native American" is changing, as some tribes prefer to be called "First Nation."

As a final note, when writing about what has happened in the past, it is sometimes difficult to cull errors from facts in source materials. Unfortunately, there is often a maze of dissenting information to choose from. Even contemporary accounts in local newspapers often contain conflicting information and errors of fact. Typically the greater the detail sought, the more suspect the correctness of the information and the more controversy among historians about whose theory is correct. The worst example I found was a book about Doc Holliday that was allegedly admitted to be a hoax by the author, an Arizona historian, who should have known better.[9] To my mind this puts the rest of this particular author's writings in the suspect category. As an example of errors in primary source material, one contemporary story in the *Denver Tribune-Republican* called Doc Holladay — note the misspelling — a rustler, a member of the Earp gang, and the killer of a dozen or more men in Arizona history. None of these statements is correct.[10]

In this book, therefore, I have tried to confine myself to facts that are considered authentic by a majority of historians. I have done my best to verify everything presented here, but ultimately I have to take the blame for any mistakes that may have ended up in this narrative.

# Chronology

HOW THE OLD WEST BLENDED INTO WESTERN MOVIES

| | |
|---|---|
| 1821 | The Santa Fe Trail from St. Louis to Santa Fe, New Mexico, becomes the first trade route to "the West." |
| 1835 | Samuel Colt patents several improved features for a new, reliable design of revolver. |
| 1841 | The first small parties of pioneer families journey to the Northwest. |
| 1846 | Start of the war with Mexico. |
| 1848 | Discovery of gold at Sutter's Mill in California; end of the war with Mexico adds vast areas of California, New Mexico, and other land in the West to the United States. |
| 1849 | Transcontinental rush of Forty-Niners to the California gold camps. |
| 1851 | Introduction of the .36 caliber Colt Model 1851 Navy revolver. |
| 1854 | The Grattan Massacre in Wyoming initiates war with the Plains Indians for the next thirty-six years. |
| 1858 | Development of the Henry lever-action repeating rifle. |
| 1859 | Major gold rushes to Central City, Colorado, and Virginia City, Nevada. |
| 1860 | First transcontinental mail deliveries via the Pony Express; introduction of the .44 caliber Colt Model 1860 Army revolver; start of the Apache Wars, led by Mangas Coloradas and Cochise, in Arizona and New Mexico; gold rushes to Idaho and Montana. |
| 1861 | Start of the Civil War between the Union and the Confederacy; completion of the transcontinental telegraph; end of the Pony Express. |
| 1865 | End of the Civil War; start of mass migration from the East to colonize The West. |
| 1866 | The first major herds of cattle are driven from Texas to railheads in Kansas. |
| 1869 | Meeting of the Central Pacific and the Union Pacific at Promontory, Utah, completes the first transcontinental railroad from the East to California. |
| 1870 | Beginning of the worst years of war between the U.S. army and the Plains Indian tribes. |
| 1873 | Introduction of self-contained .45-caliber brass cartridges, Colt's single-action (SA) Model P (The Peacemaker), and the Winchester Model 1873 repeating rifle. |
| 1876 | General George Armstrong Custer and his troops are annihilated at the Battle of the Little Bighorn in Montana. |

| | |
|---|---|
| 1877 | Discovery of silver in southern New Mexico Territory (which later becomes south-central Arizona) starts a mining rush that creates the town of Tombstone. |
| 1880 | Boom in silver mining in Leadville makes it the largest city in Colorado after Denver. |
| 1881 | Notorious gunfight takes place at the O.K. Corral in Tombstone, Arizona. |
| 1883 | Showman Col. W.F. Cody organizes *Buffalo Bill's Wild West*. |
| 1885 | The essential end of the cattle drives from Texas and the decline of the Kansas cattle towns. |
| 1886 | Surrender of Geronimo ends the Apache War in Arizona. |
| 1889 | George Eastman develops the first flexible transparent film that will be used for motion pictures; introduction of Colt's Model 1889 double-action (DA) revolver. |
| 1890 | End of the Indian Wars after the battle at Wounded Knee, South Dakota, between the U.S. army and the Sioux Indians; gold discovered on the west side of Pikes Peak in central Colorado results in the boomtown of Cripple Creek, the last great gold rush in the continental United States. |
| 1891 | Edison's assistant W.K.L. Dickson develops the Kinetoscope, an early type of peep show machine that uses a continuous loop of film to view moving images. |
| 1895 | First public showings in Europe of movies of short subjects. |
| 1896 | First public presentation of Edison's Vitascope movie projector at Koster and Bial's Music Hall in New York. |
| 1897 | Start of the Klondike Gold Rush, the last of the great gold rushes, and a boom in mining in Dawson in the Yukon Territory; short silent movies become popular in vaudeville houses. |
| 1899 | Female outlaw Pearl Hart robs one of the last passenger stagecoaches in Arizona; Edison's short movie *Cripple Creek Bar-Room Scene* becomes the first identifiable "Western." |
| 1900 | Frenchman George Méliès develops the first movie special effects, such as slow-motion, fades, dissolves, and double exposures. |
| 1901 | Butch Cassidy and the Wild Bunch still robbing trains in Montana. |
| 1903 | *The Great Train Robbery*, the first "sophisticated" Western movie, is filmed in New Jersey. |
| 1905 | First "nickelodeon" movie theater, named because it cost a nickel, is opened in Pittsburgh by John Harris and Harry Davis. |
| 1906 | Selig Polyscope Company films the first movie at an authentic Western location in Colorado; the introduction of the high-powered mercury-vapor light allows producers to film indoors instead of depending on sunlight. |
| 1908 | Filmmaker Max Aronson creates in himself the first recognizable Western movie star, "Broncho Billy" Anderson, in *Broncho Billy and the Baby*. |
| 1915 | Nickelodeons give way to larger theaters showing longer feature films. |
| 1917 | Col. W.F. Cody dies in Denver, Colorado. |
| 1918 | *The Gulf Between* is the first movie to be filmed with the primitive two-color process by Technicolor. |
| 1922 | Formation of the Motion Picture Producers and Distributors of America (the MPPDA, later called the "Hays Office") to impose general principles of morality on Hollywood. |

1925 Western star William S. Hart bows out of motion pictures with *Tumbleweeds*, a story about the Cherokee Strip land rush.

1926 *Don Juan* is the first movie to use recorded sound (music and sound effects only, no dialogue).

1927 Warner Bros. releases *The Jazz Singer*, the first sound movie to use recorded music and lip-synced dialogue.

1934 Joseph Breen heads up the Production Code Administration (PCA) to impose tighter censorship of morals in movies.

1935 Gene Autry stars in *The Phantom Empire*, his first successful singing Western serial.

1939 Improved Technicolor process used for *Gone with the Wind*; John Ford's *Stagecoach* establishes Monument Valley as an iconic symbol of "the Movie West."

1946 Universal Studios ends B-Western production.

1950 United Artists releases the last of its B-Western films.

1953 Columbia Pictures stops making Gene Autry Westerns; 20th Century–Fox introduces CinemaScope, which shows movies in a wide-screen format.

1954 Paramount introduces VistaVision, which uses 35mm film exposed horizontally to create a wider screen and better picture quality; cowboy star Rex Allen appears in *Phantom Stallion*, the last of the singing Westerns.

1968 The production code is abandoned in favor of the Motion Picture Association of America rating system, and Hollywood returns to more adult themes.

# Chapter One

# Setting the Stage

Most Hollywood Westerns are traditionally set in the time period that starts after the end of the American Civil War and ends before the turn of the twentieth century. These years were a time of rapid population expansion into the western United States that turned it into a place of social upheaval, which made a setting for stories of the Old West that was ideal for tales of rugged individuals, and the trials and tribulations they faced in taming the land. What are generally considered to be the classic cowboy Western movies, then, are presumed to take place between about 1865 and 1895, which is the period that coincided with the real Old West.

There are, of course, many exceptions to this time-span. *The Good, the Bad, and the Ugly* (1966), for example, is set *during* the Civil War and uses the war as an important part of the film's background. The prolog to *The Outlaw Josey Wales* (1976) starts during the Civil War, then the majority of the story takes place right after the end of the war. *The Professionals* (1966), *The Shootist* (1976), and *Tom Horn* (1980), to use other examples, are set after 1900. *Big Jake* (1971) is set in 1909. *Bite the Bullet* (1975) is set in 1906 and *The Wild Bunch* (1969) in 1913. *How the West Was Won* (1962) covers the entire sweep of the expansion of the West, from pioneers journeying westwards from Ohio in the 1840s to the arrival of law and order in Arizona, which was the last of the territories in the West to receive statehood in 1912. Some "Westerns" are set in an even more modern time period — for example, *Monte Walsh* (1970) and *The Rounders* (1965).

After the end of the conflict that was the American Civil War, thousands of men were left with no trade or profession. Many moved to the West to start again. This included men seeking a new life, men looking for adventure, ex-soldiers with no occupations, deserters, men who were out of work, and many who had lost families and homes. These emigrants became the settlers, cowboys, gamblers, prospectors, lawmen, miners, loggers, and railroad workers who populated the West. The lure of the Western Frontier also attracted thieves, pickpockets, bandits, and assorted criminals. Among them were men who had developed a taste for fighting during the war and wanted to continue shooting, killing, and looting. To accomplish this goal, many of them carried weapons left over from the war.

Men headed for the West commonly carried a firearm for self-protection. Though multi-shot pocket revolvers had been available since 1837, the demand for revolvers for personal protection skyrocketed when hopeful prospectors flocked to California in the early 1850s at the beginning of the gold strikes. Firearms manufacturer Samuel Colt claimed that the real expansion of his business of supplying revolvers to the masses came after the Civil War, as thousands of emigrants setting out for the West armed themselves for protection against bandits, wild animals, and native tribes. One concern for many was potential danger from unknown fellow travelers encountered during the journey and after their arrival in the West.

In reality, there was not just one "West" but many, as specific geographic areas of the West were influenced by their regional characteristics, which created differing lifestyles. Texas and its roaming herds of wild cattle, for example, created the cowboy and the great cattle drives. The Pacific Northwest and its trees spawned loggers and the timber industry. The Rocky Mountains and the Sierra Nevada Mountains attracted gold and silver miners to rich mineral deposits, and the prairies of Nebraska and Kansas became the home of settlers and farmers.

Accompanying this assorted collection of individuals pouring into Western towns was an increase in gunfights, saloon brawls, and vigilante actions. Shootings, cattle and horse rustling, and robbery were common, but so also were the lesser crimes of embezzlement, petty theft, fraud, forgery, and arson. Much of the lawbreaking involved minor crimes, such as drunkenness, fights, assaults, disorderly conduct, and petty theft. Men with an independent pioneering spirit often settled arguments the fastest and easiest way they knew by reaching for their revolvers.

In order to place the make-believe world of Western movies into a historical context, the rest of this chapter (and the next) contains an outline of a chronological sequence of some of the events that occurred in the real West. This is not intended to be a comprehensive history of the Old West, but will highlight some of the important events that sparked many of the stories and plots that have appeared in Westerns. To supplement this, the chronology at the front of this book will help place events shown in Western movies in their proper perspective in the real West.

The commonest fault in Western movies is probably anachronism, where an event is shown in a movie before it actually happened, or something is shown in use before it was invented. An example of this occurs in *The Rare Breed* (1966), which was set in 1884 but starts with scenes of bull-dogging, which was the forerunner of the modern rodeo event of steer-wrestling. In reality, the sport of bull-dogging did not became a rodeo event until the 1930s. The original technique has been generally attributed to cowboy Bill Pickett, who discovered in 1903 that he could subdue a steer by biting it on its upper lip.

## Westward Expansion

The origins of "the West" date back to 1803 and the purchase by President Thomas Jefferson of 909,000 square miles of the Louisiana Territory from France for a little over $23 million. In 1800, knowledge of the West was vague. There were only sketchy rumors of mountain ranges, large rivers, and various lakes. Nobody knew if anybody lived in this land, though there were reports of tribes of wild savages out there somewhere. Expeditions under Meriwether Lewis and William Clark in 1804 and 1806, and Zebulon Pike in 1805–1807, were intended to map, explore, and record details about these new uncharted areas west of the Mississippi.

Westward expansion into this vast unknown land started well before the beginning of the American Civil War in 1861. A few hardy missionaries had trickled west to California and Oregon as far back as 1836, but even by 1840 the number of Americans in Oregon was still less than two hundred. These emigrants found that the vast reaches of territory between the Mississippi and the West Coast were mostly empty, populated by only a few bands of

In 1803, at the time of the Louisiana Purchase, "the West" was a vast unmapped land with only vague rumors of towering mountain ranges, fast-flowing rivers, and uncharted deserts. Many of these scenic natural wonders were later used as locations for filming Western movies, such as the majestic Teton Mountains seen here, which were used as the backdrop for *Shane* (1953).

nomadic Native Americans and some white mountain men who were trapping beaver for their fur and trading with the local natives.

For the purposes of this book, it is appropriate at this point to jump forward and look at the emergence of the West of the 1840s and 1850s that became the cinematic West of the 1870s and 1880s.

In the early 1840s the land west of the Mississippi was mostly unsettled and still mostly unexplored. There was a thin strip of population in California that sprawled down the lower half of the Pacific Coast and consisted of a string of missions and small settlements that had been colonized as part of the northward expansion of Mexico. The people who lived there farmed, raised cattle, and traded tallow and cowhides for manufactured goods with visiting American ships, which took the leather skins back to the factories of New England to make saddles, boots, shoes, and belts.

These California ranchos and their cattle industry were the origin of the first cowboys, who were known as *vaqueros*, from the Spanish word *vaca* (cow). Much of the clothing and many of the terms used by later American cowboys originated with these Mexican cowhands. For example, their name *vaquero* was later Americanized to become "buckaroo."

California and Oregon were rumored to be a paradise for emigrants, and the siren call was heeded by many from the East. In the spring of 1841 a small group of fifty-four men, five women, and ten children decided to brave the unknown and started from Kansas for the Northwest. Half of them made it to the Willamette Valley of Oregon, and the other half ended up in California. After their success, others followed, and the major expansion of the West was underway. In 1850 alone, 55,000 people made the journey to the West Coast.

The settlers started in either St. Joseph or Independence, Missouri, and made their way to Fort Laramie in Wyoming through the empty space that would later become Nebraska. They crossed the Rocky Mountains over South Pass, in today's southern Wyoming, because the Colorado Rockies were too difficult a barrier for wagon trains to cross. Close to the western border of Wyoming the trail split. One major route, the California Trail, veered south to Sacramento and the gold fields of California. The other route, the Oregon Trail, headed northwest to the Columbia River and then traveled down the fertile Willamette River Valley to the area of today's Portland, Oregon.

Whether the destination was the Pacific Northwest or California, the two thousand–mile journey from Independence, Missouri, lasted about five months. The wagon trains traveled at anywhere from eight or ten miles a day, to perhaps twenty on a really good day. The trip required great courage and was full of hardships. Narcissa Whitman, for example, reported only being able to do laundry three times from the start of the journey until her party reached Fort Laramie.[1]

Most of the journey of these hardy pioneers was spent walking alongside the family wagon or cart. The alternative was to ride and be constantly bounced up and down on the hard seat of a prairie schooner, named because the wagon's high canopy of canvas cloth supported on wooden hoops made it look like a ship sailing on a sea of grass. The journey west by wagon train has been immortalized in movies such as *Wagon Master* (1950), and the subsequent television series, *Wagon Train*, that was based on it. *Wagon Train* ran from 1957 to 1965 for 284 episodes and dramatized the trials and tribulations of a wagon train from Missouri to California during 1870s. Actor Ward Bond, who starred in the original *Wagon Master* (1950), played wagon-boss Major Seth Adams.

Those who could not complete the journey west for some reason often just stopped and settled wherever they happened to be. Not many movies have been made about these pioneers because their life was not glamorous. Homesteading and farming was a life of almost constant toil. Women spent their days cooking, knitting, sewing, raising children and, when the need arose, working alongside their husbands in the fields. Dreams of a comfortable home on the prairie were often replaced by a small, dark, dank earth house made from blocks of sod cut out of the ground and stacked up to form walls.

## The Rush for Gold

Increased tension with Mexico over the annexation of Texas, and Mexico's refusal to sell land to the United States, led to a declaration of war between the two countries on January 13, 1846. After sixteen months of fighting, the United States and Mexico signed the peace treaty of Guadalupe Hidalgo in 1848 that ceded 500,000 square miles of what would become California, Nevada, Utah, Arizona, and parts of New Mexico and Colorado to the United States in exchange for $15 million. In 1853 the Gadsden Purchase of thirty thousand additional square miles of the New Mexico Territory brought the borders of the United States to their present position.

The major settlement of this new West took place between 1850 and 1890. Interestingly, though, it was not the cowboy of movie fame who opened up the West—it was the gold miner. The miner's role in drawing settlers to the West has not always been fully appreciated, but for every cowboy there were a hundred miners. Various gold rushes in the West induced over four million people to move to and settle in the West between 1849 and 1900.

The first major gold rush that helped settle the West had its origins when laborers constructing a water-powered sawmill by the American River in northern California found a few pieces of gold in the millrace on a January day in 1848. The 100,000 or more men who rushed to the settlement that became known as Sutter's Mill were known as Forty-Niners—because the year was 1849.

The news of Sutter's Mill and the subsequent gold fever electrified the nation. Men in the East scrambled for the limited number of berths on ships that made the six-month journey around Cape Horn and up the west side of South America. The alternative was to sail to Chagres in Panama, where passengers had to make the overland journey to Panama City and hope to catch a north-bound ship to San Francisco, which was the closest jumping-off

Contrary to popular opinion, it was the miner, not the cowboy, who settled the West. After the initial gold rush to California in 1849, prospectors spread out all over the West, hoping to find riches in streams, rivers, and likely-looking hillsides. The image of the grizzled prospector and his burro are common in pulp novels and Westerns (Glenn Kinnaman Colorado and Western History Collection).

point for the gold fields. Eventually the number of men who arrived to dig for gold in California in 1849 was estimated at between 60,000 and 100,000.[2]

Even after the difficulties of reaching the California coast and San Francisco, it was still another discouraging hundred miles or so to the gold fields on the western side of the Sierra Nevada Mountains. Many men, however, felt it worthwhile to make the arduous trek. The population of California quickly grew from 20,000 to more than 100,000, and by 1852 a special census showed more than 223,000 residents. But, also by 1852, most of the easily-accessible surface gold had been worked out. The individual miner was unlikely now to make an easy fortune, as the remaining gold had to be dug, blasted, or hosed out of the ground in large-scale operations that required the resources of large corporations.

The California gold fields stretched for about two hundred miles along the west side of the Sierra Nevada Mountains, from the Feather River in the north to the Mariposa River in the south.[3] Mining camps with exotic names, such as Red Dog, Hangtown, Rich Bar, and Poker Flat, sprang up wherever flecks of gold shone in the sand and gravel of the rushing streams. One lump of gold found at the mining camp of Sonora weighed an amazing twenty-eight pounds. *Paint Your Wagon* (1969) depicts the colorful development of the founding, and eventual collapse, of one such fictional camp — perversely named No Name City — after a chance discovery of gold by farmers headed west creates a ramshackle town. On the other hand, this surface gold was usually quickly worked out, as shown in *How the West Was Won* (1962) when Lillith Prescott (Debbie Reynolds) and tinhorn gambler Cleve Van Valen (Gregory Peck) go to California to claim her gold mine and find that the entire diggings have been abandoned because the gold had only occurred in a small pocket. Total worth: $4,200.

Some of the odder elements of *Paint Your Wagon* (1969), such as the bullfight, were based on fact. Bullfights were an early form of entertainment left over from when California was still a part of Mexico. One of several bullfights staged in the West was a "Mexican" bullfight held in Virginia City, Montana, in October of 1864. It featured some local Mexicans as "bullfighters" and some mean-looking "bulls" that were actually harmless oxen used for pulling wagons. The "bullfighters" didn't like the looks of the "bulls," however, and the heralded fight never took place.

The cattle town of Dodge City, Kansas, put on a bullfight in the spring of 1884. In spite of severe criticism, an estimated three thousand eager spectators showed up on the day of the event to see one bull killed in a rather crude manner, while the other four bulls refused to fight.

Two promoters put on a bullfight in Gillett, Colorado, in 1895. Feelings ran high between those who wanted the bullfight and those who opposed it. One bull was dispatched after a rather weak performance; then the local sheriff appeared and arrested the promoters and bullfighters for cruelty to animals, and threw them all in jail. The organizer went bankrupt and skipped town.

In spite of this type of spectacle, gold miners, from a movie perspective, are not very glamorous characters. Despite their importance to history, digging placer gold out of the earth and shoveling it into a sluice-box or other mining device was dirty, monotonous, back-breaking work with not much to look forward to in the way of relaxation.[4] As Ben Rumson (Lee Marvin) put it at the primitive burial service at the beginning of *Paint Your Wagon* (1969) after Partner's brother is killed in a wagon accident, "He ain't gonna have to suffer through the scurvy, the dysentery, the spotted fever, the cholera, the ague. Not to mention them other maladies contracted in the consort with low women."

The work of hard-rock mining for gold and silver was dangerous, noisy, and took place deep underground. Miners worked in a cave-like atmosphere of dust and dirt, or they worked in mills and smelters that spewed out a deadly pall of poisonous chemicals that hung in black clouds over the mining towns. This was not the stuff of legends, and, as a result, the life of a miner never appealed to movie audiences as much as the wide open spaces inhabited by the cowboy.

Mining, however, *has* been used as a background for movie plots. *Pale Rider* (1985) features a device called a hydraulic monitor, which used a high-pressure spray of water, like a giant fire hose, to blast dirt out of the earth and into sluice boxes to wash it and recover the gold.[5] Though not a film about mining, *Mackenna's Gold* (1969) was based on the concept of a hidden canyon bursting with gold. In the prologue to the movie, the narrator mentions the "Lost Adams" as an example of nebulous lost caches of gold. Adams was indeed a real prospector. In 1864 he and several companions found what has been described as a walled canyon with a flowing stream full of gold nuggets as big as acorns. The canyon was located in west-central New Mexico, somewhere near the Arizona border. One of the group reportedly found a nugget as big as a chicken's egg. After gathering several sacks of gold, most of the party were killed and scalped by Apaches. Adams himself only just escaped with his life. Adams and others later returned to where he thought the canyon was, but nobody could ever find the canyon full of fabulous treasure again.[6]

Though small amounts of gold had been found in the Colorado mountains as early as 1806, it wasn't until 1858 that gold was found in paying quantities to the west of Denver, starting a gold rush to the Rockies. In 1859 a rich strike in Nevada created the Comstock mines and the town of Virginia City. Over the next fifteen years or so, rich strikes of gold and silver were made in, among others, Bannack, Montana; Virginia City, Montana; Leadville, Colorado; Tombstone, Arizona; and Deadwood, South Dakota. Gold or silver was eventually found in almost all of the Western states, attracting hordes of would-be miners to the West.

The gold and silver mining towns that quickly sprang up near strikes to supply the miners' needs produced an almost instant concentration of people and buildings. Because of the speed at which many of these mining towns developed, the mining camps of the West boomed in an almost carnival atmosphere. Law and order were often left behind, and vice of all types was rampant. In some of the larger mining camps that developed into established towns, such as Creede, Deadwood, Tombstone, and Leadville, murder, mayhem, and gunplay often broke the peace, making them ideal settings for movie plots.

## Stagecoaches

Stagecoaches carried mail and valuables in their strongbox, and, along with the possible loot to be taken from the passengers, this made a target that outlaws could not resist. Stagecoaches always seem to be a favorite target of robbers in B-Westerns, and indeed they were just as attractive to criminals in real life. In 1908 a lone gunman robbed sixteen successive stagecoaches full of tourists in Yellowstone National Park in Wyoming and made off with their valuables.[7] To guard against robbery, most stagecoaches and express companies employed armed guards with double-barreled shotguns to accompany their shipments.

Stagecoach lines started to appear in the West in the early 1850s as a convenient method of shipping people, gold, and freight to, from, and around the mining camps of California. This service was provided by small stage companies that served local routes.

Even after the completion of the transcontinental railroad, stagecoaches were often the only method of transportation to remote areas in the West. However, they and their passengers were easy targets for bandits, and hold-ups were common. This Concord stagecoach is guarded by five armed soldiers riding on top, with a corporal in command (National Archives).

Transportation was also required on a national level. Travel in the East was fairly easy, as it was covered by a network of railroads, but the rail lines did not extend to the West Coast. When gold was discovered in California, the two main ways to reach the gold camps were to either trek across the vast expanse of uncharted territory that made up the West or take the perilous sea route around Cape Horn to San Francisco. Mail had to take the same route and took an average of eighty days to be carried around the Horn. The only choice for sending mail to the interior was via a mail route by coach from Independence to Salt Lake City that opened in 1850, and was extended on from Salt Lake City to San Francisco in 1851. Mail delivery to the rest of the West was erratic and chancy.

The need to send mail quickly from the East to the West Coast resulted in the postmaster general letting a contract in 1857 to expressman John Butterfield for a coast-to-coast mail route by stagecoach. The mail contract specified delivery from the St. Louis post office in Missouri to San Francisco in twenty-five days. To meet the terms of the contract, Butterfield built a network of 165 stage stations across the country, where horses were changed and passengers could get a meal. To make the 2,800-mile journey on time, the stages had to travel an average of 112 miles a day, bouncing along primitive tracks by night as well as by day. The more remote stage stations were subject to frequent Indian attacks, as often depicted in Westerns.

As rivalries and competition came and went, the stage and freight companies of Russell,

Majors & Waddell, Butterfield Overland Stage Company, Holladay Overland Mail & Express Company, and Wells, Fargo & Company became household names. Smaller stagecoach lines eventually connected from the main routes to almost all parts of the West.

The transportation and express company that attracted the most attention from robbers was Wells, Fargo & Company. The company was founded by Henry Wells and William G. Fargo, both of whom had been previously involved in various express companies in the East. In 1852 they saw the need for an express company to service the California gold rush and formed Wells, Fargo & Company, with their first office in San Francisco. Wells Fargo specialized in the private delivery of letters and parcels, and the shipment of gold and coins, but also offered banking services, such as the purchase of gold dust and bullion, and the payment of bank notes and bills of exchange.

Wells Fargo guaranteed delivery of shipments of money, jewelry, gold, perishable foods (such as oysters and butter, surprisingly), any other valuables, and even guaranteed the safety of women and children traveling alone over its stagecoach system. By the mid–1860s, Wells, Fargo & Company owned the richest banks and was the West's largest express company, with 196 branch offices. The company essentially controlled the long-distance stage and mail service between the Missouri River and the Pacific Coast.

Money and other valuables were stored in a strong-box carried under the driver's seat at the front of the stage. To make the box harder to steal, it weighed between 100 and 150 pounds when fully loaded with gold bullion and coins (or about as much as a man could carry from the office to the stagecoach). Depending on the particular contents, the box might be worth as much as $10,000.

Additional defense for the strong-box was provided by an express messenger who was usually armed with a double-barreled shotgun or a repeating rifle. If a very valuable shipment was being made, several guards might ride the stagecoach, both inside as well as on top with the driver. One of their best weapons was a 10-gauge or 12-gauge shotgun with a shortened barrel.[8] Wells Fargo guards also used special carbines with barrels shortened to fifteen inches in order to make them easier to maneuver and aim in close situations.

The first holdups of stagecoaches did not net much money, but Wells Fargo robberies continued to increase in frequency and in the size of losses. Between 1870 and 1884 the company was the target of 378 robberies and attempted holdups. Of these, 313 were aimed directly at Wells Fargo stagecoaches. Remarkably, in spite of all these robbery attempts, only four stagecoach drivers and two Wells Fargo guards were killed. The bandits did not fare as well. In the same time period, sixteen robbers were killed and seven lynched.

Stagecoach robberies started in the 1850s when the express business was just emerging, then increased in the 1860s, and peaked in the 1870s and 1880s. Stagecoach robberies became so frequent that Wells Fargo created its own detective force to track down robbers and bandits. The company's unofficial motto was "Wells Fargo never forgets." Stagecoach robberies declined in the 1890s when currency and other valuables were more commonly shipped by train.

## The Pony Express

Twenty-five days to cross the country by stagecoach in the late 1850s was soon considered to be too slow for mail delivery. In April 1860 a new type of mail service reduced the delivery time for a letter from St. Joseph, Missouri, to San Francisco to only ten days.

This was the famous Pony Express, an enterprise that was the brainchild of the giant freighting firm of Russell, Majors & Waddell. The Pony Express covered its route of almost two thousand miles carrying letters at the rate of $5 for a half-ounce. Though the price was steep, it could not possibly cover expenses. The company hoped that if they could prove that the scheme was feasible, they would win a huge government subsidy — perhaps as much as a million dollars. During its eighteen-month lifetime, the Pony Express had the impressive record of carrying 34,753 pieces of mail with only one sack lost.[9]

The Pony Express system consisted of 190 relay stations. Riders mounted a fresh horse every ten to fifteen miles, spending about two minutes on the changeover, and rode for seventy-five miles before the riders were changed. The company preferred small men as riders to save weight, and, because of the hazardous nature of the country they rode through, advertised for daring young men. The company preferred them to be orphans, as marauding Indians and bad weather were constant hazards along the route.

The origin of the Pony Express was featured in *Pony Express* (1953). The plot credited Buffalo Bill Cody (Charlton Heston) as one of the major characters pioneering the route. Unfortunately for historical accuracy, it is questionable whether Buffalo Bill ever even rode for the Pony Express.[10]

## The Telegraph

Even while the Pony Express was galloping its way across the country, another technological innovation, the trans-continental telegraph, was blazing a pathway close behind it. The first coast-to-coast telegram was sent in October of 1861 from California Chief Justice Stephen Field to assure President Lincoln that California would continue to be loyal to the Union. The story of the western expansion of the telegraph was dramatized in *Western Union* (1941).

When the wires from east and west finally met at Salt Lake City on October 24, 1861, the Pony Express was doomed. The company continued to provide limited service to some outlying areas, but by November 20 the last rider had handed in his mailbag. Without their federal subsidy, the firm of Russell, Majors & Waddell was also doomed. They went bankrupt the next year.

## The Civil War

The Civil War that wracked the country from 1861 to 1865 was fought primarily in the East. As a result, most of the federal troops in the West were withdrawn from their posts and sent to fight in the conflict. These soldiers of the regular army were replaced by volunteers who were charged with guarding the Western frontier against marauding Indians.

At one point the Confederacy eyed the rich gold fields of Colorado as a tempting source of money to finance their cause. To try to capture Colorado, General Henry Sibley marched troops into southern New Mexico and defeated the garrison at Fort Craig. He then turned towards Fort Union, north of Santa Fe, which was all that stood between him and conquest of the West. Pro-Union volunteer troops and Confederate forces clashed at Glorieta Pass, southwest of Fort Union, on March 28, 1862. A group of the volunteers was able to infiltrate Confederate lines and destroy all their horses and supply wagons. With

Ghost towns that were left behind by the pioneers dotted the West and were ideal for filming Westerns at authentic locations. Filmmakers often incorporated existing ghost towns into Westerns instead of building sets. When it was in better condition, this old building on the main street of the little town of Mogollon in southwest New Mexico was featured in several scenes from *My Name Is Nobody* (1973), which starred Henry Fonda and Terence Hill.

their supplies gone, Sibley and his men were forced to retreat back to Texas, thus ending any further Confederate threat to the West.

The major impact of the Civil War on the West was to come in 1865 after the war was over and a major wave of emigration to the West took place. When hostilities ceased, many young soldiers were discharged from both armies without a job or much of a future. The economy of the South was in shambles. The North was suffering from an economic depression, and most of the men who fought in the war were out of the military and seeking jobs. Tired by four years of civil war, many people in the East were eager to emigrate and start new lives in the West. As a result, many of them were lured westward by the promise of a new existence, a life of independence, and a place to make a new start. Wide open spaces with land for the taking, opportunities in mining, cattle, and railroading, gold supposedly by the handful, and the freedom of living off the land were part of the romanticized aura that surrounded the West.

One of the factors that helped promote westward expansion was the Homestead Act, signed into law by President Lincoln in May 1862. Under this legislation, any family could homestead up to 160 acres of surveyed public land. After building a house or making other improvements, and living on the land for five years, males over twenty-one years of age and women who were heads of families could apply for and receive full title to the land for a $10 fee. This government scheme to boost settlement of the western frontier was so successful that nearly 2,500,000 acres of public land in the West were claimed during the first four years after the signing of the act.

The early years primarily filled the West with adventure-seeking single young men because heavy manual labor was generally required to homestead in the West. Wives and sweethearts were often left back in the East while the men pursued dreams of wealth and fortune in the West, with the promise that they would return to collect their women or would send for their families to join them when they struck it rich.

## The Transcontinental Railroad

Along with stagecoaches and banks, a favorite target for bandits — both real and the movie type — were railroad trains. One of the first train robberies occurred in July 1873 when Jesse James and his gang derailed a Chicago, Rock Island and Pacific Railroad train near Council Bluffs, Iowa. They escaped with $2,000.

The first sophisticated Western, *The Great Train Robbery* (1903), was about robbing a train. Railroading played a major part in other Westerns, such as *Dodge City* (1939) and *Denver and Rio Grande* (1952). Trains also played an important part in the plots of movies such as *Cat Ballou* (1965), *Butch Cassidy and the Sundance Kid* (1969), and *Breakheart Pass* (1976).

In 1860, approximately 31,000 miles of railroad covered the East like a spider's web, but none of these rail lines extended west of the Mississippi. With the growing importance of the Pacific Coast, it became essential to have a direct transcontinental line that connected the East to California. Starting in 1853, four possible routes were surveyed but quickly discarded, a primary reason being the lack of a practical route over the Rocky Mountains and the Sierra Nevada Mountains.

President Lincoln signed the Pacific Railroad Act that authorized the building of a transcontinental railroad on July 1, 1862.[11] The bill authorized the Central Pacific Railroad to build eastwards from San Francisco into Nevada, and the Union Pacific to build west from Omaha, Nebraska, to meet it. In return, the two railroads were to receive large land grants alongside the tracks and loan bonds to cover the construction.

The stakes for building the railroad were high. The initial railroad bill awarded each railroad ten alternating sections of land (6,400 acres) per mile close to the railroad right-of-way. This land would later be sold to settlers by the railroad at a vast profit. In addition to the free land, the railroads would receive $16,000 per mile in flat country, $32,000 per mile in the foothills, and $64,000 per mile when crossing the Rocky Mountains and the Sierra Nevada Mountains. The size of the land grants was later doubled, and the railroads eventually received nineteen million acres of public land. Other incentives were stock issues and various government grants. The prize was great and the potential profits immense.

By the end of 1865, however, progress had been slow. In 1866 the Union Pacific hired General Grenville Dodge — already an experienced railroad builder — as chief engineer, and brothers Jack and Dan Casement to lay the track. Under Jack Casement's direction, a virtual production line of engineers and workers surveyed the route, graded the right-of-way, laid the rails, and ballasted the track. A twenty-two-car work train followed the newly-laid track with supplies, water, sleeping cars, a kitchen, and all the other support services required to keep the continual process going.

The Union Pacific benefited from the flood of men in the East who were discharged from the army after the Civil War. Though progress improved with this increased labor force, an unexpected obstacle was the Native Americans who lived along the route. These tribes realized that the coming of the railroad would mean an influx of white men and were not happy about it. As a result, survey crews and track-layers had to carry rifles to ward off attacks.

Among the problems that Casement had to deal with was the flood of undesirables who were attracted by the railroad. As the Union Pacific Railroad pushed its tracks to the west, it spawned mobile end-of-the-track settlements (nicknamed "hell-on-wheels" towns) that catered to the earthy recreational desires of the railroad construction workers. Saloons and brothels were the mainstays of these towns, attracting hordes of gamblers, saloonkeepers, con-men, thieves, pimps, and prostitutes. These portable towns were noted for brawling, gambling, boozing, wild women, and frequent homicides. They often contained saloons and bar girls like those seen in *Breakheart Pass* (1976). Every sixty miles or so, one of these temporary towns sprang to life for a short while, then disappeared when the railroad and its workers moved on. Fights and killings occurred almost daily in these towns, and nearly all the men went about armed. Later, after the completion of the railroad, some of these tent cities remained alongside the railroad to eventually become towns, such as North Platte, Julesburg, Cheyenne, and Laramie.

On the other side of the Sierra Nevada Mountains, the Central Pacific, under construction boss James Strobridge, was also struggling to lay track as fast as it could in order to reap the benefits of land grants and loans. Their difficulties were of a more physical nature, which included rockslides, avalanches, and bitterly cold temperatures. A greater problem was keeping enough men on the job. The booming gold fields of California and Nevada offered premium wages for workers of all kinds and enticed men with the even more alluring prospect of finding a fortune in gold. As a result, the Central Pacific found that many men signed on to work merely to gain transportation to the end of the railroad line, and then immediately quit and took off for the gold camps.

As the railroad penetrated higher into the Sierra Nevada Mountains, the work became more dangerous and many of the workers were reluctant to expose themselves to risk. Strobridge finally tried hiring a group of unskilled Chinese laborers from San Francisco and Sacramento. To everyone's amazement they turned out to be excellent workers who swung picks and shovels with a might that belied their small frames. Strobridge hired as many Chinese as he could recruit, eventually importing workers directly from China when he couldn't find enough in California. Even so, progress was slow because of the difficult terrain. The Central Pacific laid only fifty-one miles of track during the first twenty-six months. The Union Pacific, on the other hand, laid 260 miles of track across the prairie during one eight-month period in 1866.

Hell-on-wheels towns were not a problem for the Central Pacific, partly because Strobridge would not tolerate the loose women, gamblers, and whiskey that followed the Union Pacific, and partly because his Chinese laborers did not have much use for whiskey or bawdy women. Another reason was financial. A large part of the workers' wages went to pay off the fees for their travel from the Orient. Many of them were saving money to eventually return to their families in China.

The more track the two railroads laid, the more land grants and loans each one received. So when they raced towards each other in central Utah, the two continued to survey past each other for at least a hundred miles because no meeting place had been formally specified.

After pressure from the government to stop building track that went nowhere, Promontory, Utah, seventy miles northwest of Salt Lake City, was agreed upon for the meeting place for the two lines. The last spike was driven on May 10, 1869, at Promontory, connecting the two railroads and providing a ribbon of steel from Omaha to Sacramento. After the transcontinental route was established, other railroads soon spread across the West, bringing settlers, taking back goods and cattle, and moving freight from town to town. The epic story of the struggle to connect the two coasts has been told in movies such as *The Iron Horse* (1924) and *Union Pacific* (1939).

Not all the women associated with the railroad were of the shady variety. Some of the best were the Harvey Girls, who waited on tables in restaurants along the railroad. Before dining cars became standard on railroads, periodic train stops allowed passengers to grab a bite to eat while the engine took on coal and water. The food was often old, cold, and greasy, and the coffee was lukewarm. Seeing a business opportunity, Frederick Harvey built a chain of restaurants along the Atchison, Topeka & Santa Fe railroad that served quality food at moderate prices in clean, pleasant surroundings. His cleverest innovation, however, turned out to be his waitresses. The waitresses in Harvey's restaurants were young and pretty, and were required to be "of good character." Fred Harvey's good food and quality service became famous, but so did his girls, and an estimated five thousand of them eventually married local ranchers, miners, and businessmen. Harvey later built a chain of hotels that offered luxurious accommodations along the Santa Fe railroad line. Harvey's story has been immortalized in the entertaining musical *The Harvey Girls* (1946).

The coming of the railroad had far-reaching implications for the West. Eventually the Santa Fe connected to the Southern Pacific to create a second transcontinental line in 1881. The Northern Pacific connected from Duluth, Minnesota, to Portland, Oregon, and the Great Northern paralleled the Canadian border on a similar route.

These transcontinental railroads brought settlers to the plains in droves, it provided mobility for the army to rapidly deploy troops to areas of Indian conflict, and it brought buffalo hunters to hunt the buffalo almost to extinction. All three of these greatly impacted the Native American tribes of the Great Plains and essentially crushed their last resistance to the whites.

### Train Robberies

Activities that usually required the efforts of several men and many guns acting together included horse stealing, cattle rustling, and holding up banks and trains. One hold-up of the Southern Pacific railroad in 1887 earned the robbers $200,000 in bonds and $40,000 in cash. Stagecoaches were also easier to hold up if more than one robber was involved. Some of the more famous gangs that carried out these activities were Jesse James and his followers, the Younger Brothers, and Butch Cassidy's Wild Bunch.

Butch Cassidy and the Wild Bunch robbed a train near Wilcox, Wyoming, on June 2, 1889. As there were no reciprocal pursuit laws at the time, bandits had only to cross a state line to escape pursuers. On June 29, 1900, the Wild Bunch robbed a Union Pacific train near Tipton, Wyoming, and rode off with $55,000. They robbed a Great Northern Railroad train near Wagner, Montana, on July 3, 1901, and made off with $40,000. During all these robberies, Cassidy claimed that he never killed a man.

A favorite technique of train robbers, seen both in the movies and in real life, was to blow up the railroad tracks to derail the train. A simpler approach was to place a few trees or railroad ties across the track to block it, as was done in *Denver and Rio Grande* (1952). Once the train had stopped, the bandits could scramble into the coaches and rob the passengers and express car.

Another favorite ploy was for robbers to jump onto the train when it slowed down for a curve or if it stopped for water at an isolated tank. Several members of the gang would confront the engineer and fireman at gunpoint while the others robbed the passengers. Then all of the outlaws would mount horses held by another gang member and make their escape. This real-life technique was shown in *The Great Train Robbery* (1903) to great acclaim by audiences.

One factor that frequently defeated the plans of train robbers was that the express messenger — the man responsible for the money in the express car — usually did not know the combination to the main safe. For security reasons, this might be known only to the senior station agent along the route. Because the safe often contained thousands of dollars, robbers resorted to crude safe-cracking techniques to get at the contents. The usual method was to pour black powder into the cracks around the door of the safe, light a fuse, and retreat in a hurry. The resulting explosion, however, often damaged not only the safe, but also the safe's contents and the entire express car, as happened in the 1899 train robbery by Butch Cassidy near Wilcox, Wyoming. At times this crude method resulted in contents that were unusable or a safe damaged so much that it could not be opened at all. This was shown in *Butch Cassidy and the Sundance Kid* (1969). In the early 1890s, dynamite and nitroglycerine were used instead of black powder, with even more devastating results.

To protect their property and shipments, railroad companies hired gunmen with vague titles, such as "railroad detective," to track down and punish actual and would-be train robbers.

## Towns and Settlers

Many fictional towns in the Westerns seem to have no purpose for their existence, except, perhaps, to provide a bank to be robbed. The population seems to consist of old geezers who sit and drink in a saloon. At night the same saloon comes alive with cowboys who drink and gamble, with an occasional gunfight or stage show with dancing girls to break the monotony.

Movie images to the contrary, most towns had some sort of law and order. Local businessmen did not want anarchy in their towns affecting their businesses, so they were quick to appoint lawmen and pass ordinances against unlawful behavior. The presence of churches, schools, and settlers quickly tamed the wilder elements.

Real towns of the West were founded on mining, lumbering, or ranching. The development of these real towns followed a more organized pattern. First of all, a town had to have an initial reason to be founded, and, secondly, it had to have a strong economic base in order to survive. The West is full of ghost towns for which the first was present but not the second.

In the mountainous West, the initial reason for founding a town was often a gold strike. As a result, a mining camp soon contained a secondary population of people who provided support services. Storekeepers, grocers, butchers, blacksmiths, hardware stores, and other supply merchants followed the miners to cater to their needs. In this way a successful camp that may have been started by only a few miners soon mushroomed into a bustling town

Early Western mining camps or towns in the Rocky Mountains consisted of motley collections of log and frame buildings. This is Garnet, Montana, which at one time boasted thirteen saloons. Garnet's bust was as fast as its boom, and the population dropped from approximately 1,000 residents in 1898 to only 150 in 1910.

that sold food, clothing, and any other necessary supplies to miners in the surrounding area. On the plains and prairies, similar towns were founded as supply centers where ranchers and farmers could obtain supplies. Cattle towns, such as Abilene, flourished as combination cattle and railroad towns for shipping beef from the cattle drives.

Along with the basics of food and shelter, miners, cowboys, and other single men wanted access to liquor, gambling, and women. Drinking, gambling, and womanizing in a saloon were considered to be the healthy pursuits and methods of relaxation for the active, young male population. These demands were rapidly filled by saloons and bawdy houses that mushroomed in the booming frontier towns. So, as well as the miners and businessmen, the camps were soon filled with a large floating population of gamblers, saloon-keepers, thieves, con-men, and loose women, all of whom saw their own opportunity to relieve the miners of some of their gold. Not unusual was the town of Arland, Wyoming, which was built to supply local cowboys with whiskey and women. The town consisted of a dance-hall, a brothel, a store, and the local post office. Perhaps it was not much different than the small town seen in *Shane* (1953).

The success of a town related to its longevity. If the gold continued to flow in a mining area, the town prospered. If the strike turned out to be short-lived, as many were, the people would drift away, and the town would become deserted. As long as the cattle trade was successful, the cattle towns flourished; then they declined when the railroad moved on or the cattle trade disappeared.

Typical of the smaller towns that sprang up due to mining was Garnet, a booming, log-cabin mining town in Montana. The town had four stores, four hotels, three livery stables, two barber shops, a school, a doctor's office — and thirteen saloons. The town grew rapidly until about 1905 when the mining gave out. Its decline was as rapid as its growth, and the population dropped from approximately 1,000 residents in 1898 to only 150 in 1910.

### Boot Hill

"Boot Hill" was a common name in early towns for the local cemetery that was often the last resting place for gunfighters who died violent deaths by being knifed, shot, or lynched. The name was supposedly given to these graveyards because most of the men who were buried there died violently in a gunfight with their boots on, rather than dying at home in bed with their boots off. In reality, these graveyards also held the bodies of men and women who died from old age, smallpox, diphtheria, typhoid and other diseases, or were buried in pauper's graves.

Hays City claims to have the first cemetery in Kansas to be named Boot Hill. More than eighty people were buried there between 1867 and 1874, many of them the victims of violent deaths. Lawmen, lawmakers, and ordinary citizens were buried alongside cut-throats, murderers, prostitutes, and thieves. Though this may have been the first Boot Hill, two other cemeteries vie for the title of the most famous. One was in Dodge City, Kansas; the other in Tombstone, Arizona.

Boot Hill in Dodge City was a hill just northwest of the saloons and bordellos that lined Front Street, which was the main street. The cemetery was first used in 1872 for the poor, the drifters, and the unidentified, though not many people were buried there. In 1879 the bodies buried in Boot Hill were moved to a new five-acre cemetery named Prairie Grove, situated to the northeast of Dodge City. The old Boot Hill cemetery became the location of a new schoolhouse. In 1947 the original Boot Hill was rebuilt and became a tourist attraction, with new gravestones and headboards that sported catchy inscriptions similar to those found in Tombstone and other tourist "Boot Hills" across the West. Some of the epitaphs seen today were invented, while others were borrowed from similar cemeteries in other parts of the West.

Boot Hill in Tombstone, Arizona (also known in early records simply as Tombstone Cemetery), was opened as a burial site in 1879. This Boot Hill was reconstructed for Tombstone's Helldorado Festival, an annual celebration of Tombstone's wild and wooly history.[12] Like its namesake in Dodge City, many of the graves were re-marked with new headstones and catchy sayings that were "invented" or borrowed from other tourist "Boot Hills" across the West.

## The End of the "Old West"

Exactly when the era of the Old West ended is debatable, and has been argued in several ways by different eminent historians. Some claim that by 1890 the American frontier as a western boundary had disappeared, and settlement of the Western states was complete. Other historians argue that the Old West came to an end in 1890 after the battle at Wounded Knee, South Dakota, ended the Indian Wars on the Plains. Yet others argue that the Old West ceased to exist in 1912 when Arizona and New Mexico became the last territories to receive statehood.

Whichever yardstick one uses, it can certainly be said that by 1900 the major settlement of the frontier had taken place. By 1900 the number of states west of the Mississippi had increased to seventeen, and the earlier unsettled wilderness of the American West had ceased to exist. Towns dotted the raw frontier of only a few decades earlier, and much of the West was characterized by areas of mining, farming, logging, and cattle ranching.

From the perspective of Western movies and their gunfighting heros, cowboy "Teddy Blue" Abbott, who lived through this period, noted one particular aspect of the passing of the West when he said, "Along about the nineties a lot of people out here began to quiet down and start leaving off their guns. The country was getting so thickly settled then and the houses was so close together they figured they didn't need them any more. But I wouldn't give mine up. A six-shooter's an awful lot of company."[13]

*Chapter Two*

# Cowboys and Their Cows

One of the enduring legendary characters in the development of the Western frontier, and the one most often identified with Western movies, is the cowboy. The cowboy of the movies has been embodied — somewhat inaccurately — as the uniquely American personality who pioneered the West. The cowboy of the silver screen is depicted as a rugged individualist who's ever ready to help a lady in distress, to join a posse to hunt down rustlers, to draw his gun like lightning to avenge an insult, and to right every wrong. In reality, cowboys were common laborers who worked with cattle. They were dirty and dusty, and those participating in the great cattle drives spent three months on the trail wearing the same clothes.

The life of a cowboy as an itinerant hired hand was not glamorous. In *Bite the Bullet* (1975), Mister (Ben Johnson) reflects on his life as a cowboy just before he dies and sums it up like this: "You know saddle tramps. They sign on, drive the beef a thousand miles, make your mark, draw your pay, and move on to the next ranch. Another roundup. Another drive. Hired, fired, and move on." His only family is his horse.

In reality, the role of the cowboy in opening and settling the West was small, and the men themselves were usually vagrants. In spite of this, there was an air of romance about cowboys and "the West" in the late 1800s, and many boys and young men from the East fantasized about becoming a cowboy and participating in the cattle drives across the West. This was the dream of hotel desk-clerk Frank Harris (Jack Lemmon) in *Cowboy* (1958).

In reality, the legendary cattle drives that are often the subject of cowboy movies lasted for only fifteen years, from 1866 to about 1881. However, the romance and glamour associated with the cowboy during that short time resulted in the image of these men becoming established in American folklore and their lifestyle stirring the imagination of people around the world. Cowboys were glamorized in dime novels by lurid descriptions of riding the open range and the job they did driving cattle. Various aspects of the legend, such as the descriptions of men in high-heeled boots and large Stetson hats carrying loaded guns about their daily business, drinking and carousing all night, and goading each other into gunfights on the main streets of Western towns, amazed and fascinated the readers of Eastern newspapers and illustrated periodicals. This image was dutifully expanded, fictionalized, and promoted by authors of dime novels. As a more recent author has commented, "They enlarged the myth of the Texas cowboy till it seemed he settled every argument, no matter how trifling, with gunplay."[1]

When motion pictures became widespread, they also solidified the wild-and-wooly image of the cowboy as directors and producers depicted these actions on the screen. This created some confusion among the moviegoing public between the heroes of movie and pulp fiction and real people — particularly if the story told the exaggerated exploits of a real

Western individual, such as Buffalo Bill Cody or Kit Carson. Many of the audience assumed that the stars of Western movies were genuine cowboys and gunfighters.

## The Coming of the Cattle

The cattle trade that spawned the cowboy started in the grasslands and river valleys of southeast Texas. Cattle that had drifted away from Spanish explorers and missionaries in the early 1800s mingled with cows and bulls that escaped from Mexican and American settlers to produce the characteristic longhorns of the Westerns. These cattle were well-named, as some had horns that measured more than five feet from tip to tip.

During the 1840s and 1850s some of these cattle were rounded up and driven to New Orleans, Kansas City, and the gold camps in California, but the long distances involved, the low price of beef at the time, and the difficulties of driving cattle across the country limited these efforts. During the Civil War the round-ups and cattle drives slowed to a

The longhorn cattle from Texas that formed the foundation of the cattle business were well-named because their horns could span up to seven feet from tip to tip. These hardy cattle were able to thrive so well in the brush country of southern Texas that there were an estimated five million or so running loose at the end of the Civil War. Worth only $3 or $4 a head in Texas, these cattle could sell for up to $40 a head at the slaughterhouses of Chicago and Kansas City.

trickle, so these hardy, rangy longhorns were left alone to prosper and multiply in the brush country of south Texas until by 1865 there were an estimated five million or so roaming wild.

Following the Civil War, depressed economic conditions in the South and an increased demand for beef in the Northeast gave several entrepreneurs the idea of rounding up some of these wild cattle and selling them. Cows worth only $3 or $4 a head in Texas could be sold for up to $40 a head in Chicago or Kansas City. The problem was that the cattle had to be driven a long way north to Kansas or Missouri, which contained the nearest railheads for shipment to the East.

In 1866 several thousand wild Texas longhorns were rounded up and driven up the Sedalia Trail to the railhead of the Missouri Pacific Railroad at Sedalia, Missouri. The route was long and dangerous, and contained hazards such as hostile Indians and dangerous river crossings with quicksand and deep water. Grazing and water were often questionable, and many cattle died of starvation or thirst before reaching the railhead.

One of the first entrepreneurs to form an organized cattle drive was Charles Goodnight. Goodnight went into partnership with cattleman Oliver Loving and set out for the gold fields of Colorado in 1866 with two thousand cattle and eighteen cowboys. In doing so they pioneered a route that would eventually be named the Goodnight-Loving Trail. When they reached the Navajo Indian reservation at Bosque Redondo in New Mexico, the Navajos were so short of food that the government bought all the steers in the herd to feed them. Goodnight took the cows and calves further north to Colorado where he sold all the rest of them. The two men decided to reinvest the profits in another drive, and Loving returned to Texas to gather more cattle. As he traveled north again with a new herd, he was wounded during a skirmish with a hostile group of raiding Comanches and later died from an infection due to his injuries. Goodnight continued in the cattle business, eventually building a prosperous empire from beef.

The first of the cattle drives consisted of full-blooded Texas longhorns. Due the creature's wild heritage, the meat of the longhorn was generally lean, tough, and stringy, and the animals were slow to gain their full weight. To achieve the greater weight, better meat, and milder disposition of domestic breeds, yet still retain the stamina and resilience of the longhorn, cattlemen soon started to crossbreed the longhorn with cattle imported from Europe. Another benefit to this was that raising polled (hornless) domestic cattle avoided the dangers and handling problems of the longhorns. This transition was dramatized in *The Rare Breed* (1966), in which a cowboy attempted to show that cattle breeds on the Texas range could be improved by using a new type of bull from Britain.

On the receiving end of the first cattle business was Joseph McCoy, a twenty-nine-year-old livestock trader from Springfield, Illinois, who figured that he also could profit from Texas cattle. He bought 250 acres of land at the edge of the little settlement of Abilene, Kansas, not far from the end of the tracks of the Union Pacific Railway Company. There he built a huge stockyard and shipping depot.

The first cattle went out on the railroad from Abilene on September 5, 1867. By the time the cattle season was over, 35,000 cattle had been shipped. In 1868 the number of cattle shipped grew to 75,000, and in 1871 to 700,000. These increasing numbers were partly due to the expansion of the railroad system, which in turn stimulated the growth of the cattle industry. The cowboys who herded the cattle received a nickname of "cowpoke" or "cowpuncher" from the long, metal-tipped poles that they used to prod cattle in and out of the cattle pens and railcars.

Not all the cattle that were driven to Kansas were shipped out on the railroad. Some herds were what were called "through cattle." They were driven up the same trails from Texas, but instead of going to Chicago by railroad they were driven through Kansas to fatten on the northern ranges of Montana, Wyoming, and the Dakotas.

The appearance and growth of the cattle towns was rapid, but their disappearance came just as fast. During the 1870s, Kansas slowly turned into an agricultural state, and barbed-wire fences (nicknamed "the Devil's Rope") started to close off much of the land to cattle drives. Another major factor in the decline of the cattle drives was that Texas steers brought with them splenic fever, also known as "Texas fever" or "Spanish fever," a disease spread by the ticks that were carried on Texas longhorns. The longhorns were essentially immune to the disease, but it was deadly to local domestic cattle. Herds arriving from Texas during the winter were safe because the cold killed off the ticks, but in summer the herds carried live ticks and the active disease. Though the disease problem had been known for some years, increased settlement and more cattle arriving during the 1870s made the problem worse for local cattlemen. The final factor in the decline of the great cattle drives was that the railroads eventually extended their tracks to the south, thus making direct shipment of cattle from Texas by rail possible without driving them to Kansas. By 1880 the great cattle drives were essentially over.

By the early 1880s, settlers had built fences around all the open pasture land, and the old cattle trails had been plowed up. The decline became final in 1885 when a Kansas state law banned the importation of Texas cattle and their shipment by rail across the state.

## Cowboys and the Great Cattle Drives

The men who accomplished the task of driving the cattle and, by doing so, entered American folklore and the movies were the cowboys. The classic film about cowboys and cattle drives is *Red River* (1948), even though the movie was set in 1865, two years before cattle drives actually arrived in Abilene. One Western that vividly shows that life on the cattle trail was not as glamorous as it was made out to be was *Cowboy* (1958), which was based on *Reminiscences of a Cowboy* by real-life cowboy Frank Harris.

Most cowboys were young and single, between eighteen and twenty-eight years of age, with the typical age being around twenty-four. The physical nature of the job and the hardships of the trail were generally too strenuous for older men. Most of the men were relatively small, because a tall or overweight cowboy would quickly wear out a horse. Each cowboy used two or more horses a day that were supplied from a herd that accompanied the drive.

In spite of the glamour heaped on cowboys by the movies and dime novels, driving cows was not a glamorous business. The cowboys had to endure clouds of dust that were raised by the herd, questionable food cooked over a campfire, water that might come from muddy streams polluted by horses and cattle, and fierce prairie storms that could spook the cattle. Other drawbacks for young men were no liquor and a lack of women.

Driving cattle was dangerous work. The herd might be attacked by Indians, the cows might stampede, a cowboy might be injured by being thrown from his horse, or he might be drowned during a river crossing. Most of the time the herd was far from towns and any assistance, so a sick or injured cowboy was on his own to recover — or not. There were also the dangers of ever-present cattle rustlers and raiding guerrilla bands left over from the Civil War.

In *Cowboy* (1958), Tom Reese (Glenn Ford) describes the supposed idyllic life out on the trail when he says, "Lying out there under the stars, listening to the boys singing around the campfire. And your faithful old horse standing there, grazing at the grass by your side." He looks knowingly at Frank Harris (Jack Lemmon) and says, "You know, I'll bet you like horses." When Harris agrees, Reese stares at him angrily. "Well, you're an idiot. Do you know what the trail is really like? Dust storms all day, cloudbursts all night. Man's gotta be a fool to want that kind of life. And all that hogwash about horses. The loyalty of the horse. The intelligence of the horse. You know a horse has a brain just about the size of a walnut? They're mean, they're treacherous, and they're stupid. No sensible man loves a horse. He tolerates the filthy animals because riding's better than walking." He continues with his opinion that cows are "miserable, slab-sided flea-bags."

Other movie cowboys have about the same opinion. In *The Cowboys* (1972), Wil Andersen (John Wayne), describing cows, says, "You're dealing with the dumbest, orneriest critter on God's green earth. A cow's nothing but a lot of trouble tied up in a leather bag." After reflecting a moment, he adds, "Horses ain't much better."

The herd moved at anywhere from ten to fifteen miles each day, which allowed the cows time to graze as they moved. Thus the drive north from Texas to the railheads in Kansas typically took three or four months. The ratio of cowboys to cattle was normally one cowboy to every 100 to 150 cattle, with a trail herd consisting of anywhere from 1,500 to 3,000 head. The cattle were high strung and temperamental. Stampedes were a constant danger and might be started by a distant clap of thunder, the howl of a coyote, a darting jackrabbit, a galloping horse, or a sudden shout. To soothe nervous cattle, the drovers often sang softly to them at night to reassure them.

While the cattle drive lasted, the work was hard and the wages were low. The typical working day for a cowboy on the trail was about eighteen hours, every day of the week. The men were up before dawn and spent all day herding cattle, then bedded down on the ground at night with only a blanket for cover and a saddle for a pillow. After a few hours of sleep, and maybe a few hours of night watch, it was time to start the routine all over again.

The men earned from $25 to $40 a month, plus food. They were paid off at the end of the three-month drive, thus earning them about $100 for the whole trip. It is small wonder that it has been claimed that only about a third of the cowboys who headed north with a herd of cattle were willing to repeat the trip.

One of the most important things on the trail was the cook and his mobile kingdom, the chuckwagon. The invention of the chuckwagon has been credited to Charles Goodnight, who modified a surplus army wagon for his 1866 cattle drive to hold food, dishes, cookware, tools, lanterns, branding irons, medicine, bedrolls, spare clothing, and all the many other items required to feed and support the cowboys during the cattle drive. A hinged worktable dropped down at the back of the chuckwagon to create a storage and work space for food and its preparation. A large wooden barrel was attached to the side of the wagon for water storage in case the trail crossed a long dry section.

The trail boss managing a herd had to be tough and ruthless to get the job done and keep the cowboys in line. This is reflected in the attitude of Reese (Glenn Ford) in *Cowboy* (1958). Trail bosses purposely kept their cowboys away from towns along the route north because they figured that if the men started carousing, the cows would probably never reach the end of the drive. After several months of no liquor, no women, questionable food, hard work, and no relaxation or entertainment, the cowboys were ready to carouse in any town

The development of the chuckwagon to feed cowboys on a cattle drive has been attributed to cattleman Charles Goodnight in 1866. The fold-down door at the rear doubled as a work table for the cook, as seen here. Cubbyholes above the work surface were used to store food and utensils. A barrel for drinking water was strapped to the side of the wagon and tools were slung underneath. The wagon also carried the cowboys' bedrolls and spare clothing.

that happened to be at the end of the trail. After the cattle drive was over, the saloons, gambling houses, and brothels provided whiskey, women, and the rowdy times that the cowboys were looking for. One Wichita newspaper commented that "the cattle season has not yet fully set in, but there is a rush of gamblers and harlots who are 'lying in wait' for the game which will soon begin to come up from the south."[2] Flush with money accumulated from the drive, the cowboys were ready to sample all the pleasures offered by the dance halls and bawdy houses. As another newspaper put it, "They drink, swear, and fight; and life with them is a round of boisterous gaiety and indulgence in sensual pleasure."[3]

Not all cowboys spent their time on cattle drives. When the round-up and cattle drive season was over, many cowboys worked on ranches. Their tasks included feeding the cattle in winter, rounding them up, branding them, and providing simple veterinary care. As well as tending the cattle, the cowboys' job included castrating steers (this produced better meat) and de-horning them to prevent injuries both to other cattle and to the cowboys. Other chores around the ranch were installing and maintaining fences, upkeep of the ranch buildings, cutting firewood, digging wells, maintaining water supplies, and keeping stock ponds free of ice in the winter.

## The Cattle Towns

The settlements founded in response to the cattle drives only lasted as cattle towns for three or four years each. While they lasted, however, the Kansas towns of Abilene, Wichita, Dodge City, Newton, and Ellsworth were everything that Western movies have led audiences to believe. Drinking, gambling, prostitution, fighting, and killing became part of the cowboy's way of life when they came to town. As would be expected, drinking, gambling, and prostitution were also the major causes of violence in the cattle towns. Surprisingly, the towns didn't consider this to be all bad, as taxes and license fees on all three helped pay for the town's municipal services, such as the police force. Saloon women and gamblers typically paid business "fees" of from $5 to $10 a month, and bordellos and saloons paid from $10 to $20.

The cattle season in most towns ran from May to September. The residents of the cattle towns viewed the cowboys with mixed emotions. Most considered the men and their actions to be lawless, profane, and vulgar. On the other hand, the merchants did not want to discourage the cowboys and the herds because they brought business and money into the town. Opinions of cowboys and their wild ways ranged from that espoused in *Illustrated Weekly*, which claimed in 1883 that "they are foul-mouthed, blasphemous, drunken, lecherous, [and] utterly corrupt,"[4] to *Harper's Weekly* opining in 1886 that "cow-boys are a whole-souled, large-hearted, generous class of fellows."[5]

Among activities that were not popular with saloon owners were giving beer to horses (replicated in *Bite the Bullet* [1975]), shooting at the saloon's oil lamps (*Gunfight at the O.K. Corral* [1957]), and shooting at signs and lights up and down the main streets. Another was riding into a saloon (at the beginning of *Destry Rides Again* [1939]) a cowboy rides his horse into a saloon). Guns fired purely for noise were supposed to be shot into the air or at the ground. Pointing the barrel in any other direction might, and sometimes did, result in unplanned and unexpected injuries to bystanders. This is the basis of the plot in *Lawman* (1971), in which a group of celebrating cowboys shoot up a town and accidentally kill an old man.

The residents of the towns in the cattle trade did not like their towns to be called "cowtowns," which was a somewhat derogatory name that came into use in the 1880s. They preferred the name "cattle town."

## Abilene (1867–1872)[6]

Abilene was the first of the wild cattle towns. Each year its population swelled as the cowboys from the cattle drives hit the end of the trail. In the spring of 1871, for example, the permanent population of the town consisted of about five hundred residents. By summer, the population had increased to an estimated four thousand to seven thousand people. Many of these were the cowboys who arrived with the cattle drives, but the rest of the increase was due to prostitutes, gamblers, bandits, and con-men who came to prey on the cowboys.

The "tax" on gamblers was between $5 and $10 a month, and gambling halls paid $20 a month. When municipal revenue was low, additional "fines" that ranged up to $75 were sometimes imposed. Lawman Bat Masterson expressed the opinion that the principal and best-paying industry in Abilene was gambling, and noted that the potential for taxation was enormous.

The red light district in Abilene was filled with saloons and gambling houses that were in operation twenty-four hours a day when the cattle season was in full swing. The red light district contained two hundred to three hundred women, and thirty wooden buildings with from ten to twenty rooms each. Most of the girls worked in shifts to accommodate the twenty-four-hour demands of the cowboys.

The image of saloons and gambling shown in Western movies is not totally inaccurate for Abilene. The wealthy Texas cattlemen spent their time at high-class saloons like the Alamo on Cedar Street, where gambling never stopped and the orchestra played twenty-four hours a day. Saloons in cattle towns often had names such as Alamo, Houston, or Lone Star to draw in the Texas cowboys by appealing to their patriotic leanings. The Alamo fit the movie image of an ornate bar backed by a huge mirror, gambling tables, paintings of nude women on the wall, and glass doors that never closed. Connecting the back of the saloon to a nearby brothel was a wooden boardwalk so that customers sneaking between the two wouldn't sink into the mud. Regular cowboys, with less money to spend, went to the Applejack Saloon, where whiskey sold for 50 cents a shot and, for those who could afford it, a bottle of champagne went for $12.

A continuing problem for Abilene was how to encourage the cowboys to spend their money yet still keep them under some semblance of control. The concern for the townspeople was that if the cowboys were offended they could easily take their business somewhere else. But by the spring of 1870, even the citizens of Abilene felt they had put up with enough, and the town passed strict laws against gambling, fighting, and prostitution to try and control the saloons and brothels. Brothels were restricted to an area on the southeast edge of town known as McCoy's Addition — or, more popularly, the Devil's Half-Acre — which was a concentrated area of gambling, drinking, and bawdy women. If cowboys attempted to go up to the "decent" part of town, they were liable to be arrested.

For the summer of 1870 the town also hired a tough lawman, Thomas "Bear River" Smith, an Irish ex-policeman from New York, as marshal to enforce the laws. If Smith couldn't settle matters peacefully by talking with a lawbreaker, he would hit the man with his fists. For several months he was able to keep the rowdy cowboys in check, and the town was generally quiet until Smith was killed in November. He was shot in the lung and then almost decapitated with an axe while trying to arrest a man named Andrew McConnell for murder. In *Destry Rides Again* (1939), Destry (James Stewart) cleans up the town of Bottleneck with his fists, like Tom Smith, but is luckier and survives.

The next year, in April of 1871, Abilene appointed Wild Bill Hickok as town marshal. He was another strong enforcer of the law and generally managed to keep the peace. One unfortunate incident occurred while he was marshal, however. He started a heated argument with former saloon-keeper Phil Coe and shot him, then, in the resulting confusion, inadvertently shot his own deputy. At the end of the year the town council decided that they did not need Hickok any longer and discharged him as marshal.

Like the towns that followed it, Abilene's life as a cattle town lasted for only a few years. By 1872 the town had become antagonistic towards the cattle trade, and the citizens finally asked the Texans to take their herds and their business elsewhere. Efforts at moral clean-up continued as Abilene banned prostitutes from saloons and raised saloon license fees to $500. The results were as expected. By the spring of 1873, 80 percent of the businesses in town had closed and many of the residents had left. As the end of the railroad tracks moved further south and west to meet the cattle drives, the shipping depot moved with it, and Abilene sank back into obscurity.

The early days of Abilene were supposedly portrayed in *Abilene Town* (1946). The general theme of the movie is that the residents are uneasy over the raucous antics of the cowboys arriving at the end of a drive. The town is in a state of transition as settlers are moving in, which creates conflicts with the cattlemen. Marshal Dan Brown (Randolph Scott) tries to

The working conditions for real cowboys on a cattle drive were not easy. They worked from before sunup to after sundown, constantly tending cattle, for a wage of about $30 a month. No wonder they were ready to "bust out" and have a good time when they reached a town at the end of the drive. Here a group of cowboys are rounding up and branding cattle on the giant XIT ranch in Texas around 1904 (Library of Congress).

keep the peace, while the county sheriff (Edgar Buchanan) tries to stay on the sidelines. In a typical case of gun-anachronism, Marshal Brown uses a Colt Peacemaker, even though the movie is set in 1870.

## Newton (1871–1872)

Like other cattle towns, Newton, Kansas, experienced a meteoric rise and fall. Newton was founded in March of 1871, and the Atchison, Topeka & Santa Fe Railroad arrived in July. Approximately 350,000 head of cattle were shipped from Newton in 1872; however, this was Newton's first and last season as an important cattle-shipping center. Entertainment for the cowboys was provided by a thriving brothel district called Hide Park, which had multiple dance halls, saloons, and gambling establishments.

One of Newton's claims to fame — or infamy, depending on the viewpoint — was a gory event that became known as "Newton's General Massacre." Like the later shootout at the O.K. Corral in Tombstone, this was one of the few gunfights that consisted of sustained shooting and the deaths of multiple participants. The gunfight, which took place in Tuttle's Dance Hall early on the morning of August 20, 1873, was the result of a long-standing grudge between a Texas cowboy and the man who had shot a friend of his. The fight started when cowboy Hugh Anderson marched into the dance hall, pulled a gun, and shot Mike McCluskie in the neck. Several other cowboys drew their guns in response and also started shooting. When the gunfire stopped, five men were dead or dying, including several bystanders. Anderson survived only to be shot and killed two years later by McCluskie's brother.

## Ellsworth (1871–1875)

While Abilene was fading as a cattle town, most of the business had already moved to Ellsworth, sixty miles southwest of Abilene. Ellsworth was founded in 1867. By 1872, Ellsworth and Wichita combined had shipped 350,000 head of cattle.

The red light district in Ellsworth was called Scragtown or Nauchville, and it was all that moviegoers could imagine. As one example, this was the location for the incident of "Lady Godiva of the Plains." A local lady of the night named Prairie Rose supposedly accepted a wager that she would walk (or ride, depending on the version of the story) down the main street of Ellsworth in broad daylight without any clothes. She may have had nothing on, but she carried two loaded pistols to shoot anyone who looked her way. As she had a reputation as an excellent shot, this version of Godiva did not have to shoot anyone.[7]

The rest of Ellsworth was about as bad when the cowboys were in town. A reporter described what he saw as he walked down the street in 1872 like this: "Last Saturday evening about seven o'clock as I was walking down the street from supper, I heard three shots fired and saw a man rush out of a saloon and up the street with a six-shooter in each hand, he ran about half a block and fell, but immediately got up and went into another saloon; shortly after he entered two more shots were fired."[8]

## Wichita (1872–1877)

Wichita was founded in 1870, though the railroad didn't arrive on a branch line from Newton until 1872 to turn it into a cattle town. By the time the Santa Fe arrived in Wichita, it was already pushing its main line west from Newton to Dodge City so that it could meet its government obligations and profit from free land grants. Thus, Wichita was doomed as a cattle town before it even really started. Nevertheless, over 70,000 head of cattle were shipped in 1872. Wichita's last year for a major cattle drive was 1875.

Unusual for a cattle town, gambling was illegal in Wichita, though it operated full blast in Delano, the red light district just across the river from the town. The toughest place was owned by "Mag" Woods, who had an equally tough reputation.

Wyatt Earp served as a policeman in Wichita during 1875 and 1876, though by that time Wichita's wild days as a cattle town were declining. Delano was reported to be Earp's favorite part of town during the time he spent in Wichita, and Bessie Earp, the wife of Wyatt's older brother James, operated a bawdy house there. Doc Holliday's mistress, "Big Nose" Kate, worked in Bessie's house before she and Doc went to Tombstone in 1880. The routine fine for bawdy women in Wichita was $8 a month, plus $2 for court costs. The fee for selling whiskey was $25 a month. In August of 1873, a typical month, money raised from fines on prostitutes and liquor licenses contributed around $1,000 to the city revenues.[9]

The town was highlighted in the movie *Wichita* (1955), with Joel McCrea as Wyatt Earp.

## Dodge City (1876–1885)

Dodge City was one of the last great cattle towns and was sometimes called the Queen of Cowtowns. In 1883 over 75,000 cattle were shipped.

Dodge City was originally named Buffalo City when it was founded in 1872 as a collection of crude shacks, stores, and saloons for buffalo hunters. The town was founded five miles west of Fort Dodge, which was erected in 1865 to house soldiers patrolling against hostile Indians. The post office soon changed the name of the town to Dodge City because Kansas already had a town named Buffalo City.

When the train and the cattle drives arrived in Dodge, the tracks of the Atchison, Topeka & Santa Fe railroad ran down the center of Front Street, which was seventy-five yards wide to accommodate the railroad right-of-way. The railroad track formed an imaginary line called the Deadline that divided the town. North of The Deadline were the more refined saloons, gambling halls, and drinking places, such as the Alamo, the Long Branch, the Saratoga, and the Alhambra. South of the Deadline was the red light district and the wilder watering holes, an area that consisted of low-class saloons, dance halls, brothels, and variety theaters. These were places such as the Varieties Dance Hall (later renamed the Green Front Saloon) and the Lady Gay dance hall. In September of 1877 the *Sentinel* of nearby Hays City said, "Dodge City is dull at the present time, and the town is relapsing into morality. At this writing there are only seventeen saloons and dance houses, sixty prostitutes, thirty gamblers and eighty cowboys in the entire town."[10]

The cowboys and other undesirables were supposed to stay south of the Deadline. Wyatt Earp recalled, "Below the Dead Line, as far as the marshal's force was concerned, almost anything went, and a man could get away with gunplay if he wasn't too careless with lead. North of the railroad, gun-toting was justification for shooting on sight, if an officer was so inclined, and meant certain arrest. Any attempt to hurrah stores, gambling houses, or saloons along the Plaza was good for a night in the calaboose."[11] In *Gunfight at the O.K. Corral* (1957), after a ruckus at the town dance, the mayor tells cattleman Shanghai Pierce to get his men "south of the Deadline."

Wyatt Earp served for brief periods as a policeman and later as an assistant marshal in Dodge City. These duties as part-time peace officer occupied his daytime. At night he dealt faro in the Long Branch saloon. This was one of the best saloons in Dodge City and featured the owner, Chalkley "Chalk" Beeson, on the violin with a four-piece orchestra that played in the main barroom during the peak summer business hours. The Long Branch was unusual for a cattle town in that bar-girls and dancing were not allowed on the premises.

During the 1870s the town marshal of a busy Kansas cattle town such as Dodge City might make as much as $150 a month during the summer months, when cattle buyers and the cowboys were in town. In winter, when the cattle were gone, his pay might be reduced to $50 to $75 dollars a month, as there was not as much to do. When Wyatt Earp served as assistant town marshal in Dodge City, typical monthly "fines" were $5 for a gambler, $10 for a prostitute, and $50 for a liquor dealer. The law officers earned additional pay of $2.50 for each arrest of a minor lawbreaker and $10 for arresting a wanted criminal.

In December of 1875 an ordinance was passed in Dodge City to restrict the carrying of firearms. Hotels, corrals, stores, saloons, and gambling places had racks for visitors to check their weapons as soon as they arrived in town. Many cowboys hated to check their guns, so they wore them anyway, in spite of the ordinances. However, even if a cowboy did check his visible gun, he might have a derringer as a back-up weapon hidden in a vest pocket or in a boot, so the fights and shootings continued, even with regulations in place. On July 16, 1878, for example, Deputy U.S. Marshal Harry McCarty was in the Long Branch saloon when a drunken cowboy grabbed his gun and shot him. A bystander shot the drunk, but McCarty bled to death.

Dodge City has always been popular with moviemakers, and has been used as the typical example of a wild cattle town. *Dodge City* (1939), set in 1872 (which would actually have been before the real boom years), cast Errol Flynn as a fictional marshal on the order of Wyatt Earp cleaning up Dodge City by putting in gun restrictions and the other ordinances later enacted by real lawmen. The early portion of *Gunfight at the O.K. Corral* (1957) shows a quieter Dodge City after Wyatt Earp has "tamed" the town, before he takes off for Tombstone.

Dodge City had such a reputation that it was said that in 1872 the town saw thirty killings, when the town only had a population of five hundred. The truth was considerably different, as there appears to have been only about fifteen homicides between 1877 and 1885.[12]

## The Range Wars

As well as fights in the cattle towns, fighting took place out on the open range. Range wars and fights between neighboring cattlemen, as well as cattle barons and adjoining small ranchers and farmers, over land, cattle, grazing rights, and control of water are another common plot in Westerns. *Open Range* (2004) tells the story of a clash between a ruthless cattle baron and a group of men grazing their cattle on the open range in 1882. The climax of the movie is a protracted, gore-laden shoot-out. Range wars like this actually happened. The best-known examples of these bloody fights were the Lincoln County War, which took place in New Mexico in 1878, and the similar Johnson County Cattle War that occurred in Wyoming in 1889.

### Lincoln County, New Mexico

The Lincoln County War involved killings, ambushes, and bloodshed on both sides. The apparent cause was a conflict over grazing land and water rights, but a deeper cause of the war was the dispute between two large business corporations. Three businessmen, Lawrence Murphy, James Dolan, and Emil Fritz, owned a large general store called The House in Lincoln, New Mexico. Through this they controlled the beef and grain contracts at nearby Fort Stanton. In 1877, English business investor John Henry Tunstall opened his own competing store across the street in Lincoln. His business partners were cattle baron John Chisum, who wanted to break Murphy and Dolan's cattle supply monopoly, and attorney Alexander A. McSween, a young lawyer who was looking for a business opportunity.

Like other feuds, this one simmered until February 18, 1878, when a group of armed gunmen claiming to be a posse stopped Tunstall and some of his men while he was driving between Lincoln and Roswell, New Mexico. The outcome was that Tunstall was shot off his wagon.

A group of men on the other side of the feud, including Billy the Kid, who was working for Tunstall at the time, formed themselves into a quasi-legal posse and called themselves "the Regulators." This group of men with questionable authority caught up with Tunstall's alleged murderers and captured them. Three of the captives were later shot and killed, supposedly as they were trying to escape. Subsequent shootings and killings between the Dolan

Filmmakers have always liked to incorporate the scenic backdrops of America's national parks into Westerns. This is the ghost town of Grafton, which was originally settled in 1861. The mountains in the background are part of Zion National Park. The combination schoolhouse and church on the left was built in 1866. The adobe house on the right was built by Alonzo Russell in 1862 and lived in by him until 1910. Grafton is notable today for being a major filming location for *Butch Cassidy and the Sundance Kid* (1969).

gunmen and the Regulators included the murders of Lincoln County Sheriff William Brady, his deputy, and one of the posse members.

The climax to the Lincoln County War was a pitched gun battle that started in the middle of Lincoln on July 14, 1878, and turned into a siege of McSween's house that lasted for the next five days. The new sheriff, George W. Peppin, called in the U.S. army, who threatened to shell the McSween men with a nine-pounder mountain howitzer if they didn't surrender. Seeing this formidable firepower, most of the defendants sneaked out of the house. On July 19 the remaining men escaped through a hail of gunfire after the building was set on fire. McSween was shot down by the waiting posse as soon as he stepped outside. This final act of violence marked the end of the Lincoln County War.

The story of this notorious Lincoln County conflict has been retold in *Young Guns* (1988). Another version of the fight is given in *Chisum* (1970), which tells the story more as a personal feud between John Chisum (John Wayne) and Murphy (Forrest Tucker). This film generally follows historical fact, while adding extraneous fictional characters to make a better plot, but alters the final shootout and resolution, as Chisum rides to the rescue and resolves the cattle war when he fights it out with Murphy.

### Johnson County, Wyoming

The Johnson County Cattle War, which erupted in 1889, was a similarly vicious range war. It had its beginning when the Wyoming Stock Growers Association tried to stem the growing influx of what they called "nesters," a catch-all term for settlers, homesteaders, and small ranchers who were fencing off open range lands. Suspicions were that some of them were rustling stray calves from the open range. In retaliation, the influential cattlemen had a law called the "Maverick Act" passed by the Wyoming legislature. This law made any stray, unbranded calf on the open range the property of the cattleman's association.

This action created a problem for two of the local residents, Ellen (usually called "Ella") Watson, who homesteaded a small ranch in the Sweetwater Valley in 1886, and her boyfriend James Averell (sometimes spelled Averill), who owned a nearby store and saloon. They came into conflict with Albert Bothwell, who had previously used their land as a pasture for his cattle. He was also trying to create a new town that would be named after him. From there the story becomes murky. As part of the conflict, Watson was accused of trading her favors with some of the local cowboys for a calf or two. This supposedly left her with a small herd of cattle stolen by the cowboys from their employers. Additional historical research, however, has shown that Watson may have bought her herd legitimately but was poor about keeping paper records.[13] Whichever was the case, Watson had a small herd of cattle, the origin of which could not be conclusively proven. There was no evidence that her boyfriend, Averell, was involved in any rustling. There is evidence that she married Averell in May of 1886.[14]

Six of the local stockmen used the questionable origins of Watson's cattle as an excuse to kidnap Averell and Watson on July 20, 1889, to allegedly take them to Rawlins, Wyoming, to charge them with cattle rustling. The captors soon showed their real intent, however, and lynched both of them from a cottonwood tree. At this point the *Cheyenne Daily Sun*—either intentionally or inadvertently—mis-identified Ellen Watson as prostitute Kate Maxwell and gave Watson the nickname of "Cattle Kate Maxwell" because of the cattle she had supposedly taken in trade.[15] The real Maxwell lived in the area and had previously been involved in bawdy houses in Cheyenne, Denver, and Dodge City. The paper printed a retraction the next day, but it was too late, and the legend of "Cattle Kate" has gone down as such in history.

Hanging a woman was rare in the West, and the lynching was soon notorious across the country. Several men from the lynching party were arrested, but none of them were convicted. In spite of numerous attempts to bring the vigilante hangmen to justice, witnesses either disappeared or refused to testify, and the case was never satisfactorily resolved.

The double lynching of Averell and Watson caused the other small ranchers to stand up to the Stock Growers Association, and a full-scale cattle war broke out on the Sweetwater Range. In 1892 the leading cattlemen tried to run off some of the small ranchers who they felt were rustling their cattle by organizing a group called the "Regulators"—made up of hard-core gunslingers—to hunt down supposed cattle rustlers. On April 5, 1892, a special Union Pacific train loaded with nineteen cattlemen, five "range detectives," and twenty-one hired gunmen, along with horses, guns, and supplies, set out for Caspar, Wyoming, intending to invade Johnson County and clear out any suspected cattle thieves.

The small ranchers fought back, and blood was shed on both sides. Finally, acting-governor Amos Barber stepped in and arranged for U.S. cavalry troops to arrest the Regulators and end the fighting. Legal wrangling and the disappearance of key witnesses resulted in the entire case against the Regulators evaporating, and none of them were ever prosecuted.

The best-known example of the retelling of the Johnson County War was *Heaven's Gate* (1980). Unfortunately the story became a bit lost in the extravagance of the production, resulting in, as one critic rather unkindly put it, "an epic that fairly boggles the mind in its excess and incoherence."[16] Cattle Kate/Ella Watson (Isabelle Huppert) is cast as a prostitute and is shot at the end of the movie while Averill (Kris Kristofferson) is trying to rescue her. Watson dies and Averill lives on in this movie world, contrary to the facts.

## Sheep Wars

Another cause of violent range wars was the introduction of sheep to the West. Cattlemen tried to eliminate sheep from cattle-grazing ranges all over the western states because they felt that sheep grazed the grass down to ground-level (thus not leaving any for their cattle), trampled the roots, polluted streams and watering holes for cattle, and left an odor in the soil that was offensive to horses and cattle. As a result, angry cattlemen often tried to get rid of sheep by shooting them, clubbing them, burning them, or poisoning them. One of the nastier techniques used by cattlemen was called "rimrocking," in which a herd of sheep was deliberately driven over a cliff to kill them all.

Encounters between cattlemen and sheepherders could become violent. At the beginning of *Big Jake* (1971), several cowboys are in the process of hanging a sheep farmer in order to get his sheep off the range. This type of encounter was not unheard of in the real West. The area around Hahns Peak, Colorado, for example, was the scene of a real range war between cattlemen and sheepmen.[17] Today both co-exist, and both animals can be found grazing in the area.

The storylines of cattle-versus-sheep conflicts, such as that seen in *The Sheepman* (1958), had their roots in real events like the infamous Graham-Tewksbury feud, which started in Pleasant Valley, near Globe, Arizona. The Grahams were cattlemen, as originally were the Tewksburys. The Graham-Tewksbury feud between the two families exploded when John Tewksbury introduced sheep into the valley early in 1887. During the sheep feud, cattle rustling and horse theft increased as local rustlers and gunmen saw this as an opportunity for their own profit and joined the activities. Even though the sheep were gone after only a few months, antagonism between the two families continued. Ambushes, fights, and shootings eventually resulted in twenty-five deaths. The feud didn't end until 1892 when John Graham was shot by Edwin Tewksbury. Tewksbury was tried for murder but was eventually acquitted on a technicality.

Similar range wars erupted all over the West when farmers — derisively called "sod-busters" — fenced off lands and open range that cattle barons had previously illegally grabbed for their own use. Cattlemen secretly banded together to cut the fences at night, resulting in skirmishes and open shooting between the two sides as both legal and illegal fences were destroyed.

## Cowboys as Gunfighters

Gunfighting by cowboys has been romanticized on the silver screen, and cowboys are shown as the primary gunfighters of the West. Cowboys, however, were not professional gunfighters; they herded cattle for a living. Conversely, professional gunfighters did not become cowboys — unless perhaps they were temporarily hiding from the law. Professional gunfighters could sell their skills as gunmen to become town marshals or range detectives for much more money than they could make by herding cows.

There was also the matter of mind-set. As Marshal Maddox (Burt Lancaster) explains to one of the other characters in *Lawman* (1971), the difference between a lawman and a cowman is that the lawman is a killer of men and the cowman isn't.

Cowboys often had a rowdy nature and frequently carried guns, which was a combination that led to gunplay and injuries. The *Dodge City Times* once said, "A gay and festive Texas boy, like all true sons of the Lone Star State, loves to fondle and practice with his revolver in the open air. It pleases his ear to hear the sound of this deadly weapon."

Cowboys also wore guns as a type of fashion accessory when going to town or when dressing up to impress a girl on a date. Western etiquette dictated that even though a cowboy did not have to remove his hat inside a house or at the dinner table, he was supposed to remove his gun when entering someone else's house or when sitting down to a meal.

Cowboys were not lawless and dangerous gunmen, they were generally just young men trying to have a good time. But they did carry guns, and the combination of weapons and liquor could be a lethal one, both for other cowboys and for innocent bystanders and towns-people. After a little too much to drink, many cowboys imagined themselves to be fast guns with a tough streak to back up what they considered to be their excellent shooting skills. Cowboys tended to create some of their own image themselves. Author Jack Weston commented that "the cowboys' style was partly a deliberate imitation of how the public saw them ... and cowboys would defiantly and defensively justify that image by exaggeration, live up to the reputation, and even go beyond what the public expected. They would take advantage of their wild public image to scare hell out of people."[19]

Most of the guns that the cowboys carried were full-sized revolvers of large caliber, typically Colt single-action revolvers, such as the Peacemaker. To reinforce their tough image, cowboys generally did not use their fists to fight. They considered fighting with fists to be demeaning and preferred to use a revolver or knife.

To their disadvantage, most cowboys were not as good with their guns as they thought they were. In August 1888 in New Mexico, rancher John Good and five companions confronted five men whom he suspected of murdering his son. Both sides opened fire, but, though more than a hundred shots were fired, the only casualties were two horses killed and one wounded.[18]

Driving cows along the trail did not allow cowboys to spend the countless hours of target practice needed to develop and maintain the shooting skills of professional gunmen. Occasionally trying to do so could prove unfortunate, as in the case of a man named LaGrange who accidentally shot himself in the leg in June of 1880 while practicing his fast draw in Bodie, California. Cowboys also did not have the money required to purchase and continually shoot up boxes of ammunition in practice.

It is interesting to note that cowboys, as amateur gunfighters, were often quick to draw their guns, but in many cases it was solely to back up male posturing and bravado. Opponents might simply wave their guns around while swearing at each other and making threatening remarks. They did not always immediately shoot to kill, as a professional man-killer would. Cowboys' confrontations might instead end with a punch in the face and a black eye.

In spite of this, the primary cause of death in the Kansas cattle towns was from a gunshot. Most of the killings were the result of personal quarrels between cowboys rather than cowboys being shot by law officers. The circumstances were usually not those of a movie gunfight in which two opponents faced each other down on the street, and face-to-face showdowns were not always the outcome of a grudge fight. Less than one-third of the victims of these killings shot back, and many of them were not even armed.

Though violence arose naturally out of drinking, gambling, and prostitution, later accounts have exaggerated the violence of the cowboy's rowdy celebrations, and not as many men were killed in the cattle towns as Western legend has claimed. According to contemporary cattle town newspapers, a total of only forty-five documented killings took place in the combined Kansas towns of Abilene, Caldwell, Dodge City, Ellsworth, and Wichita during the height of the great cattle drives between 1870 and 1885.[20]

Most trail bosses bringing a herd up from Texas would not allow their cowboys to carry their guns while on a cattle drive. Very few cowboys carried even a rifle. The extra weight of the rifle and scabbard hanging on the side of the horse could quickly cause saddle sores, a condition to be avoided on a long cattle drive when the horse was the cowboy's only transportation. Another danger was that the rifle butt could become tangled in a rider's reins or stirrups, or in a bush. If the cowboy was galloping at high speed after an escaping steer, the results could be disastrous.

There were several similar reasons for not wearing a revolver on a cattle drive. One was that the continued chafing of a gun-belt rubbing against the cowboy's waist would produce irritation during constant riding, and such a raw spot could easily become infected. For the same reason, a cowboy rarely wore a belt or suspenders while on a cattle drive, instead holding his pants up with a tight fit around the waist. On a more practical level, a gun-belt or holster could easily snag on brush or a steer's horns while riding through heavy brush, unseat the rider, and cause the cowboy to undergo a crippling fall from his horse.

Another reason for not wearing a gun was to prevent fights between the men from turning deadly. Cattleman Charles Goodnight had a rule that if a man was found guilty of shooting another of his men, the shooter would be tried. If he was found guilty, he would be hung from the nearest tree. The rule must have been effective because, while Goodnight enforced it, not one of his men was shot on the trail.

Cowboys on a cattle drive typically stowed their revolver in their bedroll and stored it in the chuckwagon. In *The Cowboys* (1972), Wil Andersen (John Wayne) takes all the boys' guns and says he will lock them up in the chuckwagon. He tells the young cowboys to solve any differences between them by butting heads.

There were, however, situations where the wearing of a gun on the trail was necessary. One of these exceptions was when a personal enemy might be gunning for a cowboy and might show up unexpectedly. Other instances that called for wearing a gun were during travel in country where Indians were present or if there was the possibility of a confrontation with cattle rustlers.

Cowboys not on a drive but working on a ranch might carry a gun to kill rattlesnakes that were common on the prairie, to put an injured horse or steer out of its misery, or for self-defense in town. A cowboy would typically carry a rifle in the back country on a ranch in case he had a potentially-dangerous encounter with a bear, a mountain lion, a wolf, or a coyote. A cowboy might also carry a gun to hunt for antelope, deer, or a jackrabbit to bring back to camp for fresh meat. However, if he did, the gun was more often a rifle or a shotgun than a handgun. A rifle would be more useful to shoot an antelope at long distances on the open prairie, and a shotgun was more likely to hit a rabbit than a revolver.

Even when cowboys did carry guns at work, there were relatively few shooting deaths. Cowboys on the trail were more likely to die from accidentally falling off their horses and breaking their necks, or from getting a foot tangled in a rope or stirrup and being dragged

This cowboy, photographed around 1888 in the Dakota Territory, is wearing a revolver in a holster and carrying a rifle in a scabbard, unlike cowboys on many cattle drives. When riding out on the open range, cowboys could use these guns for protection against snakes or wild animals, to defend against rustlers and hostile Indians, or to finish off an injured steer or horse (Library of Congress).

to death, than they were from being killed in a gunfight. Other ways that cowboys died on the trail were being killed in stampedes, gored by a crazed steer, or killed by a bolt of lightning. Another risk was being drowned while driving the herd across a river or in a flash flood.

In 1882 a movement started among several ranch owners to completely disarm cowboys working on their ranches. The intent was to remove distractions and potential shooting conflicts from the workplace. The idea was that cowboys should tend to the cattle, and lawmen should enforce the law. In March of 1882 a resolution was passed at the Stockmen's Convention in Caldwell, Kansas, to stop cowboys from carrying guns. The same concept spread quickly to Wyoming and Texas.

*Chapter Three*

# The Magic Begins

Western movies date from shortly before the turn of the nineteenth century. As the Old West of reality was drawing to a close and disappearing into the early 1900s, motion pictures started to emerge as a popular form of entertainment. By 1910, twenty percent of all U.S. film releases were Westerns.[1] From 1910 through the end of the 1950s, about twenty-five percent of all the films produced by Hollywood were Westerns.[2] In the seventy-five years between 1910 and 1985, estimates place the number of Western movies made at over four thousand.[3]

Just as there was not one "West," there has not been just one "Western." The look, style, and content of Western movies have changed over the years to reflect the fickle tastes of their audience and the growing sophistication of filmmakers. An understanding of how and why Western movies have evolved and changed will set the background for better understanding their content.

## The First Films

Some of the first showings of projected moving images occurred as early as 1895, when Max Skladanowsky in Berlin and the Lumière Brothers in Paris presented public showings of short subjects. These first films were shown as novelties that made entertaining additions to variety programs in vaudeville houses. Many of these early "films," which only lasted a minute or two, showed common, everyday occurrences, such as the arrival of a train in a station, a horse race, breaking down a wall, a gondola ride in Venice, or a baby eating breakfast. Some of these "movies" were simply visual recordings of static outdoor scenes. Others were merely moving pictures that recorded existing vaudeville acts.

The first identifiable "Western" was a very short movie named *Cripple Creek Bar-Room Scene* (1899), made by the Edison Manufacturing Company and directed by Thomas Edison's assistant W.K.L. (William Kennedy Laurie) Dickson. Not long enough really to even be called a movie, this was more of a short vignette that lasted slightly less than a minute. The film starts with several stock Western characters, who are dressed as a cowboy, a miner, and a gambler, sitting at a table playing cards in a saloon, presumably in the gold-mining town of Cripple Creek, Colorado.[4] A drunk lurches in through a door and starts a fight with one of the patrons who is sitting by the bar minding his own business. The homely female bartender throws them both out of the door, then dusts off her hands with satisfaction and treats the remaining patrons to a drink.[5]

As movies became popular in vaudeville houses, their length expanded and became

One of the earliest movie stars to combine high-action Westerns with a show-business image was Tom Mix (shown here in a publicity still as Jim Logan for the silent movie *Mr. Logan, U.S.A.* in 1918), whose flamboyant acting style and flashy clothing started the trend that led to the singing cowboy movie stars of the 1930s and 1940s (Library of Congress).

fixed at the typical length of a vaudeville act, or around ten minutes. This became "one reel" of film. As movies became even more popular, they broke free from vaudeville theaters and were shown in dedicated buildings that were equipped with seats, a screen, and a movie projector. By 1908, estimates are that there were somewhere between eight thousand and ten thousand of these "nickelodeons," which received their name because the cost of admission was a nickel.[6] By 1928 the number of these "movie theaters" in the U.S. had increased to approximately 20,500.[7]

Early short movies like *Cripple Creek Bar-Room Scene* (1899) were filmed from a single point of view, with a fixed camera position and the camera recording the action as it took place. As the popularity of movies increased and filming techniques matured, directors turned increasingly towards telling stories in their films. One of the more sophisticated films to utilize changing camera angles and editing to tell the story and carry it forward was *The Great Train Robbery* (1903), a Western filmed by director Edwin S. Porter for the Edison Company. Though not the first fictional story to use advanced techniques, this picture employed them to great advantage. The exteriors of a real train (from the Delaware and Lackawanna Railroad) were filmed near Dover, New Jersey.[8] Even though completely unconnected to the rest of the plot, the dramatic image of actor Justus Barnes shooting his gun six times at the camera from a double-action revolver at the end (or at the beginning, if the exhibitor preferred) created a stir in the theaters when it was shown. The running time of the movie was eleven minutes, or about one reel; and it was made at a cost of $150.[9] The supposed reality portrayed in this moving picture sparked a great interest in Westerns and the West among the moviegoing public.

Following the Edison Company's success with *The Great Train Robbery* (1903), other companies hurried to jump on the band wagon with their own Westerns. The Selig Polyscope Company, for example, made *Tracked by Bloodhounds; or, Lynching at Cripple Creek* (1904) and *The Hold-Up of the Leadville Stage* (1904). According to Selig documents, *Tracked by Bloodhounds* was actually filmed on location in Cripple Creek, Colorado, though *The Hold-Up of the Leadville Stage* was shot in nearby Colorado Springs, Colorado. Like *The Great Train Robbery*, these were essentially crime movies set in the West.

Ironically, at the time that Western crime movies like these were starting to become a popular form of entertainment, real crime on the Western frontier was still taking place. On July 3, 1901, for example, Butch Cassidy and his Wild Bunch robbed a Great Northern Railroad train near Wagner, Montana, and escaped with $40,000.

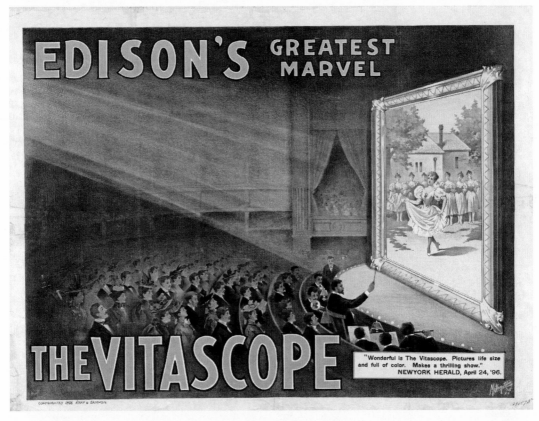

The development of a practical method of projecting moving pictures onto a screen, instead of viewing them individually through the eyepieces of a peep-show machine, ushered in a new era of entertainment. The Vitascope was an early film projector that was first used commercially in Koster & Bial's Music Hall in New York City in 1896. Early short movies presented in vaudeville houses were so popular that dedicated buildings for showing movies rapidly became the new rage for entertainment (Library of Congress).

In the early 1900s, fact and legend blurred in several movies. In 1908 the Oklahoma Mutoscene Company made *The Bank Robbery*, directed by William "Bill" Tilghman. Tilghman had previously been a deputy sheriff, the town marshal of Dodge City from 1884 to 1886, and then chief of police of Oklahoma City. Tilghman also produced and appeared in *The Passing of the Oklahoma Outlaws* (1915).

*The Bank Robbery* (1908) featured Al Jennings as one of the train robbers. Jennings was a real outlaw who had robbed trains and was only released from prison just prior to making the movie. Jennings later went on to star in several silent Westerns, but his portrayals were too grim and realistic at the time for audiences who wanted flamboyant stars, so these movies and their star generally did not do well. Al Jennings later produced *The Lady of the Dugout* (1918), which was supposedly based on his career as a former outlaw and bank robber.[10]

Another real-life robber who appeared in movies was Emmett Dalton. Dalton was a train and bank robber who served time for his crimes and then reformed. In 1920 he moved to Los Angeles, where he wrote movie screenplays, became a technical consultant to Western moviemakers, and even performed in a few bit parts.

One of the minor players who acted in the earlier *The Great Train Robbery* (1903) was Gilbert Max Aronson, who would later become known as Western star "Broncho Billy" Anderson. Aronson had previously acted as an extra in Shakespearean plays, but he was more interested in the production side of the camera. Aronson joined the Edison Company in 1902 because he was not able to land serious acting roles. He wanted to be in movies so badly that he talked his way into *The Great Train Robbery* (1903) by saying that he was born on a horse and could ride like a Texas Ranger.[11] As a result, director Edwin Porter cast him in several roles in the film. Aronson was one of the train robbers, a railroad passenger from the train who was shot during the robbery, and the dude who has his feet shot at in the dancehall scene. In reality, Aronson knew so little about horses that he tried to mount his horse from the wrong side. The animal didn't like it and threw him off, and Aronson had to walk back to the studio.[12]

Aronson still wanted to work his way into movie production, so he moved to Vitagraph to make Westerns. He worked there for a while but left when the owners refused to let him buy into the company. In 1906 he went to Chicago and met William Selig, who hired him and put him to work making films for the Selig Polyscope Company.

William N. Selig was a Chicago-based film manufacturer who had formerly been an entertainer, both as a magician and a minstrel-show performer. In 1895 he saw the potential of Edison's movies, so in 1897 he established the Selig Polyscope Company to make films and distribute them to vaudeville houses. Like other early filmmakers, many of his movies consisted of scenic landscapes, news events, and documentaries of interesting aspects of the industrial world.

To expand his output, Selig made arrangements with Denver photographer Harry Buckwalter to make Westerns that combined the spectacular landscapes of the West with stories of crime and violence. Buckwalter was a commercial photographer who had worked as a reporter and photographer for the *Rocky Mountain News* in the 1890s and had also made movies of rodeos, Indian dances, and scenic attractions to promote railroad travel.[13] Aronson persuaded Selig to let him go to Colorado to work with Buckwalter on Westerns. Selig was not happy with the unenthusiastic response to Aronson's early Western films, so he stopped Aronson from making more.[14]

Around the same time, George K. Spoor, a Chicago-based film distributor and Selig's rival, was overwhelmed by the demand for films. In May of 1907 Spoor and Aronson formed their own film manufacturing company. The partnership was named Essanay Film Company, the "Ess" for Spoor and the "Ay" for Anderson. The company initially made comedy films, then decided to make Westerns, which were very popular at the time. When Aronson couldn't find the type of actor he was hoping for, he cast himself as the star, changed his name, and returned to acting. The result was *Broncho Billy and the Baby* (1908). To everyone's surprise — including Aronson's — he was immensely popular as an actor and thus became the first recognizable Western cowboy film star as "Bronco Billy" Anderson. Partly as a result of Anderson's success, cowboys became a popular subject of single reel movies in the late 1900s and 1910s. Most of these simple short films consisted of setting up an initial conflict situation, such as a bank or train robbery, which then led into a chase sequence and finished with a fight at the end.

## The Industry Matures

The popularity of Anderson's Western movies peaked in the mid–1910s, then Broncho Billy faded away into the proverbial sunset. The next decade, from about 1910 to 1920 was dominated by the movies of William S. Hart, who rode the Western landscapes with his favorite horse Fritz.[15] Hart tried to inject realism and moralistic messages into his movies, and used real-life law officers Bat Masterson and Wyatt Earp as consultants to achieve this.[16] The fact that they were both still alive to lend their first-hand knowledge of the Old West to the motion picture industry again illustrates the overlap of the real West and the movie West.

At the time when William Surrey Hart was at his peak making popular Western movies, the type of crimes depicted in the Westerns were still happening in reality. On February 9, 1916, William "Wild Bill" Carlisle, armed with a loaded six-gun, robbed a Union Pacific train that had just left Green River, Wyoming, taking the passengers' valuables at gunpoint. He was chased by a special train that contained a posse of lawmen who were inspired by a reward of $1,000 for the outlaw's capture — dead or alive. They didn't catch him, and Carlisle robbed the Union Pacific again on April 21. In a fit of remorse, he surrendered to Marshal Bill Hayes and was sentenced to life imprisonment in the state penitentiary in Rawlings, Wyoming. In the best Old West tradition, he escaped in a crate of shirts and was the subject of another manhunt. He was finally recaptured and spent nineteen years in prison before being pardoned in 1936.[17]

As late as 1923, a Southern Pacific Railroad train was blown up near Siskiyou, Oregon, and a mail clerk and three trainmen were killed during a robbery carried out by Roy, Ray, and Hugh Autremont from Eugene.

In the end, Hart's quest for authenticity backfired. His studio felt that his pictures were becoming old-fashioned, and wanted him to give up control of his productions and become more like his flashy cowboy-star competitors. Hart refused to compromise and decided instead to withdraw from pictures. Hart and his sister Mary Ellen retreated to their elaborate ten thousand square-foot mansion at Horseshoe Ranch, which sat on three hundred acres in the Tehachapi Foothills outside Los Angeles.[18]

In the early 1920s the dominant type of Western was the "series Western," which was also called the "program Western" or simply a "programmer." This type of movie consisted of a popular actor playing a character in a series of movies. Contemporary audiences wanted and expected horseback chases, shoot-em-ups, extended fights, realistic stunts, rugged scenery, and a familiar cowboy star — and they didn't want this formula changed. The big cowboy stars of the 1920s, such as Tom Mix, Hoot Gibson, Buck Jones, Harry Carey, Ken Maynard, Tim McCoy, and Bob Steele, all appeared in programmers. Most of them appeared in seven or eight of these programmers each year, and most of them continued making this type of movie into the 1930s.

In the early to mid–1910s, New York theater owners had predicted the need for longer and better movies to keep their rapidly-growing audiences happy. As a result, in the 1920s the length of motion pictures grew from a single reel to multiple reels. The programmers typically ran from four to six reels, or about forty to sixty minutes. These movies were also often disparagingly called "oaters" or "horse operas."

The programmers were made on a small budget by small independent studios, such as Universal and Monogram, and consisted primarily of plenty of action held together by a minimal plot. They featured multiple fist fights and gunplay while the hero solved a crime, such as a robbery or a murder. The plots were also usually full of horse-related scenes, such as fast-riding horse chases, with both factions shooting at each other as they rode furiously across back lots and studio ranches. The stars of the programmers often used their real first

Rugged cowboy star William S. Hart popularized the image of the good badman. One of his Westerns that used this theme was *Hell's Hinges* (1916). The story revolves around a gunfighter who is hired to run a minister out of a sinful town but falls for the reverend's sister instead. He decides to change his ways and ends up burning down the town. The movie was considered so important that it was added to the National Film Registry at the Library of Congress (Library of Congress).

names but usually changed their last names for each picture. Some, though, such as Buck Jones, and later Gene Autry, Roy Rogers, Bill Elliott, and Sunset Carson, kept their name intact from picture to picture.

In the 1920s one of the prominent Western movie stars on the rise was Thomas Edwin "Tom" Mix. In contrast to Hart's gritty realism, Tom Mix was a showman who possessed a flamboyant acting style and specialized in flashy thrills-and-chills entertainment. Like many of the others who broke into Westerns, Mix had previously been a performer in the *Miller Bros. 101 Ranch Wild West Show* at their dude ranch in Oklahoma. While there he had taught himself good horsemanship and roping techniques. These skills helped him when he started making films with the Selig Polyscope Company in 1909, and later as a cowboy star for Fox Studios (which later became 20th Century–Fox) in 1917 and at Mascot in the early 1930s. Mix performed his own stunts (often spectacular ones) with his horse Tony, who was known as "the Wonder Horse." Performers lured from Wild West shows were appealing to film directors and producers who were trying to create lots of action shots, because they could be counted on to perform daring stunts they had learned during their arena performances.

Mix didn't use his guns much in his movies but preferred daring hand-to-hand fist fights with the bad guys in perilous situations, such as on top of a speeding train or at the edge of a cliff. Mix dressed in elaborate costumes in his pictures and projected the image of a clean-cut hero who never smoked, drank, gambled, or swore. With his easygoing screen presence he was the popular forerunner of the singing cowboys of the 1930s.

Tom Mix's wife, Olive, summed up the contemporary Western genre when she described their simplistic plots by saying, "They consisted of plenty of action, a simple plot, a very white hero, an impossibly incorrigible villain, a number of dangerous schemes to be foiled, and a helpless heroine to be rescued at the last moment."[19] Movies about train robberies were still an obsession with filmmakers, and Tom Mix filmed *The Great K&A Train Robbery* in scenic Glenwood Canyon in the Colorado mountains in 1926.

In 1935 Mix purchased and performed in a combination circus and Wild West show that he named the *Tom Mix Circus and Wild West*. His timing, however, was bad. The stock market crash of 1929 had created personal financial difficulties for him, which took a toll on the show and on Mix. At the same time, public tastes were moving towards the singing cowboy stars, and Mix was not able to generate much interest in either his live show or his re-entry into movies. A lack of ready cash among the general public for entertainment during the depression, combined with difficulty performing stunts due to Mix's advancing age, put his career into a general downslide. Mix died in a car accident in Arizona on October 12, 1940.

Though Hart and Mix dominated Western films for the remainder of the silent film period, several other notable actors and movie characters appeared in the Westerns of the 1920s. One popular Western actor in the 1920s was Buck Jones, born Charles Fredrick Gebhart in Vincennes, Indiana, in 1891. Like many other cowboy stars, Jones had worked at the Miller Brothers 101 Ranch in Oklahoma in their Wild West show before he signed up to make Westerns with Fox in 1920. Buck Jones continued to be a popular star of Westerns until 1942, when he was trapped and died in a fire at a burning nightclub in Boston, Massachusetts.

## Singing Cowboys

The 1920s were a period of transition for the movie cowboy, who went from the realism of the cowboy as portrayed by William S. Hart to the stylized type of cowboy of Tom Mix, who had less and less to do with cows and tended more towards being a mythic adventurer. By the end of the 1920s, audiences started to tire of the formula of the programmers and wanted something new. Seeking to keep his movie audiences and keep them happy, cowboy star Ken Maynard decided to use the new medium of sound, which was perfected towards the end of the decade, to make a singing picture. In doing so, Maynard paved the way for the singing cowboys of the 1930s.

Maynard was another actor whose experience with Wild West shows helped him perform his own stunts in his pictures. He starred in several Western movies made by First National, which merged in 1929 with Warner Bros., who then immediately stopped making Westerns.[20] So Maynard moved over to Universal Pictures and made *Sons of the Saddle* (1930), in which he sang two Western songs.[21] His new singing career wasn't received with much enthusiasm by audiences, or even his studio, but he kept on trying.

Maynard made a breakthrough in 1934 when he moved to Mascot Pictures and made *In Old Santa Fe* (1934). Nat Levine, the head of Mascot, planned the picture specifically for Maynard, and signed George Hayes, a veteran character actor, as Maynard's sidekick. Hayes used the name "Windy Halliday" early in his film career before settling later on "Gabby" Hayes due to studio copyright restrictions. The film used contemporary settings that included horse racing and a dude ranch. As part of the plot, Gene Autry, an established radio personality and singing cowboy with several recorded hits to his name, was added to sing and serve as the caller at a square dance. Autry's real-life radio sidekick Smiley Burnette was part of the backup group.

Autry and Burnette were given bit parts in Maynard's next action serial, which was called *Mystery Mountain* (1934). After a subsequent dispute with Levine, Maynard left Mascot.[22] Levine already had another twelve-part serial, called *The Phantom Empire*, ready to go, but after Maynard's departure he was left with no leading man.

At the same time, tentative links were being forged to the music recording industry. In October of 1930 an entrepreneur named Herbert J. Yates had purchased the American Record Company (ARC). ARC distributed records under several labels, sometimes selling the same song on different labels at different prices to different markets, which was a common practice at the time. ARC was a leading supplier of hillbilly records to rural areas, which was a popular market for this type of music. In 1934, ARC acquired the Columbia and Brunswick record labels, and with them the young singing hillbilly cowboy named Gene Autry.[23]

Yates also owned Consolidated Film Industries, a laboratory that developed film and processed optical effects for several independent Hollywood studios. Along with processing film, Yates provided financing to several of the studios he did business with. One of them was Mascot Pictures, owned by Nat Levine.

Levine went to Yates for financing, and Gene Autry's records were selling well at ARC. The result of this combination was that Yates recommended Autry to Levine as a singing cowboy for *The Phantom Empire* because Yates wanted to boost cross-promotion between songs and films in order to sell more records. So Levine gave the lead part to Autry and promoted him as a singer and radio star in the film.

As a result, Gene Autry and the other singing cowboys who went on to dominate the Westerns of the late 1930s and early 1940s developed out of a convenient marriage between the music recording industry and Hollywood movies. Cowboy songs were used in movies and were closely tied to the commercial music industry, so that each promoted the other. As one example, in *The Phantom Empire* (1935) Autry and "the boys" suddenly sing the song "That Silver-Haired Daddy of Mine" for no apparent reason connected to the plot. It makes sense when one realizes that that particular song was one of Autry's first recording hits and singing it in this movie helped promote record sales.

Not everybody was happy with this new type of Western. Of Autry's *Gaucho Serenade* (1940), for example, a disgruntled critic for *Variety* said, "First horse is not mounted until forty-four minutes have passed; first fist is not flung until fifty minutes had passed; first gun is not fired until fifty-six minutes have passed. What manner of Western is this?"[24] Though not totally accurate, this critic's point is well-taken in that this offering is somewhat light on traditional cowboy action and long on song.

## Cowboy Songs

Real cowboys did indeed sing, and their songs were an outgrowth of a lack of available activities in the evening around the campfire after a hard day of herding cattle. This was one of their few forms of entertainment on the trail or in the bunkhouse back at the ranch. Cowboys would also sing while drinking in saloons as part of the camaraderie and for the entertainment of their friends. The authentic cowboy's impromptu concerts, however, were never on the level of the singing cowboys in the movies of the 1930s and 1940s. Due to the limitations of transporting musical instruments on a horse on the trail, accompaniment for real cowboys was more on the order of a harmonica or Jew's harp that could be conveniently carried in a saddle bag than the guitars and banjos of the movie cowboys. At a stretch, a fiddle could perhaps be wrapped in a bedroll or carried on the chuckwagon.

Real cowboy songs tended to be modified versions of traditional folk songs or ballads that arrived with immigrants from England or Ireland. The ever-popular song "Streets of Laredo," for example, was a song that was modified and cleaned up by cowboys from an old English 16th-century street song called "The Unfortunate Rake," about a young man dying from syphilis. Unlike the songs of the movies cowboys, not all the campfire and saloon songs of the cowboy were nice, clean entertainment. Guy Logsdon at the University of Tucson has claimed that many of these songs contained bawdy material, some of them even being obscene.[25]

## Down on Poverty Row

Starting in the 1930s, entertainment at a movie theater typically offered two features (an A-feature and a B-feature), a cartoon, a newsreel, and previews of coming attractions, along with prize giveaways and various promotions. This practice continued through the 1960s and into the 1970s before economic pressures reduced a night at the movies to only the main feature and trailers for upcoming movies.

An A-Western had the full backing and promotional efforts of the studio that produced it. The B-Western was a low-budget film that played on the lower, or "B," half of the double bill after the major, or "A," feature. A-films typically rented for a percentage of the box-office gross. B-films typically rented at a flat rate. During the 1930s, about fifty films were made that could be called A-Westerns, but more than a thousand B-Westerns were produced in the United States.[26] The growth in the number of B-Westerns was due in part to Hollywood's desire to provide the entertainment value of Westerns, but also to a reluctance to finance big-budget A-Westerns.

During the 1930s the programmers evolved into B-Westerns, which included the singing cowboys. B-Westerns, which continued through the 1930s, the 1940s, and into the 1950s, were shorter than A-Western films, seldom running more than seventy minutes and usually just about an hour. The budgets of B-Westerns were typically only about $15,000, and the films had shooting schedules of days instead of weeks. For this reason B-Westerns were also thought of as Budget Westerns, because they were cheaply made, often contained production errors and inconsistencies, and did not allow any time in the shooting schedule for retakes.

Most B-Westerns in the 1930s were made on black-and-white film with very low budgets by independent Hollywood studios, which gradually gave rise to the name "Poverty Row." Some of the so-called Poverty Row studios who made Westerns were Puritan, Mascot, Victory, PRC, Monogram, Resolute, and Spectrum Pictures.[27] The production of these films was like an assembly line. The directors of B-Westerns kept the action going continuously, often with very little rehearsal. To save money, they filmed from sunup to sundown.

As often as possible, many of these low-budget studios recycled their plots, used stock footage, and included long shots from earlier movies where the faces were unidentifiable.

One of Mascot's specialties was serials. Serial Westerns, also known as "movie serials" and "film serials," were shown as part of a Saturday morning or matinee show for younger viewers. Serials were typically made in "chapters," or episodes, of twelve parts. Each chapter consisted of two reels (about twenty minutes) of plot, plus a trailer for the next part. Each episode of the serial ended with a "cliffhanger"—a perilous situation from which the hero apparently had no escape. Typical cliffhangers consisted of the hero engaging in a fistfight in the back of a wagon as it careens out of control towards a cliff edge, or as he is about to be run over by a train or cattle stampede. As a result, the juvenile audience had to attend the theater on the next Saturday to see how the hero escaped from his predicament.

Villains in serials had sinister, melodramatic names, such as the Scorpion, the Ghost, the Wasp, the Mask, the Dragon, the Whispering Shadow, the Spider, and the Rattler. As well as Westerns, science fiction serials were popular, such as *Flash Gordon*, made at Universal in 1936, and *Buck Rogers*, made at Universal in 1939. Columbia, Republic, and Universal churned out so many serials that they made up about one-third of the studios' outputs. Republic had so many serial plots that involved creeping through dark tunnels that they even had a permanent standing cave set. The production of serials peaked in the early 1940s.

The king of the B-Westerns was Republic Pictures. Republic grew out of Consolidated Film Industries, the film processing company owned by Herbert J. Yates. In March 1935 Yates merged Consolidated with two of his film clients who had unpaid processing bills, Monogram and Majestic, to form Republic Pictures.[28] This merger brought Monogram's leading contract player, John Wayne, to Republic.

In the spring of 1935 Republic absorbed the Poverty Row companies Chesterfield and Liberty. Yates then merged Republic and Mascot Pictures, which was producing inexpensive B-Westerns. Yates was head of the studio, but he retained Nat Levine from Mascot as head of production. Economy was still the watchword. Early Gene Autry pictures made by Mascot cost about $12,000 to make.[29]

Upon Republic's merger with Mascot, Gene Autry's Mascot contract was transferred to Republic, where he became one of their consistent box-office stars. Republic's top Western films were split between Autry and previous Monogram star John Wayne. Compared to other Poverty Row studios, Republic produced consistently better movies and had a good distribution system.

### John Wayne

One actor from B-Westerns in the 1930s who did not make it as a singing cowboy was John Wayne. After making many Poverty Row Westerns, Wayne appeared as the character "Singin' Sandy" Saunders, a secret agent of the U.S. Treasury, in *Riders of Destiny* (1933), made by Lone Star Productions and released by Monogram. Wayne walked into the final shoot-out softly singing a ballad. This unusual concept for a Western didn't make much of an impact on the moviegoing public.

Wayne's voice was not considered suitable for a singing part, so his songs were dubbed in by another singing cowboy, Smith Ballew.[30] Ballew later denied this, but Hollywood insiders have claimed that he was indeed the singer.[31] Wayne didn't care much about being a singing cowboy, so this was his first and last attempt at the genre, though he went on to make fifteen more "oaters" for Lone Star Productions and Monogram.

John Wayne was born in 1907 in Winterset, Iowa, as Marion Robert Morrison.[32] His mother changed his name to Marion Michael Morrison so that his younger brother (five years later) could be called Robert.[33] As Marion, Morrison went to the University of Southern California on a football scholarship. In the summer he worked at Fox as a props man, moving furniture and props from set to set. Eventually he was cast in small parts in films. He went on to act in serial Westerns at Mascot, Columbia, and Warner Bros. In his last movie, *The Shootist* (1976), Wayne played aging gunfighter J.B. Books, who was dying of cancer, foreshadowing the time three years later when Wayne would ironically do the same.

Director Howard Hawks, who directed Wayne in some of his most popular movies, once said, "I just don't see how you can make a good Western without Wayne."[34]

## Gene Autry

One of the most popular of the singing cowboy stars was Gene Autry. Born Orvon Grover Autry in 1907[35] in Texas, he grew up in Oklahoma. From childhood he had enjoyed playing the guitar and singing as an amateur entertainer. In 1923, at age fifteen, he sang for three months in the traveling Fields Brothers Medicine Show to entertain the audience before the pitchman touted various pills and ointments, and a patent medicine called "Fields' Pain Annihilator."[36] To provide a steadier income, Autry went to work for the St. Louis and San Francisco Railroad, where he was employed as a telegraph operator from 1923 to 1932.

Autry went to New York City in 1928 and auditioned singing hillbilly music for several record labels. For this he used the professional name of Gene Autry. Unfortunately, he didn't generate much enthusiasm. He persevered and tried again in 1929. This time he had more success and started to record for Columbia Phonograph Company.

In the early 1930s Gene took a job at radio station WLS in Chicago, singing on a regular program as a radio entertainer. In 1933, needing a sidekick, he added Lester Alvin Burnette to the show. Burnette was a radio personality, songwriter, entertainer, and comedian at a small radio station in rural Illinois, where he called himself "Mr. Smiley." This stage name was later shortened to "Smiley" Burnette.

Autry's first starring movie role was in the twelve-part serial made by Mascot called *The Phantom Empire* (1935), which blended traditional cowboy action with singing and science-fiction.[37] The basic plot was thin, as the hero, radio entertainer Gene Autry, lives at Radio Ranch and has to make a live broadcast every afternoon at two o'clock or he could lose the radio contract and the ranch. Burnette provided comic relief— for example, singing a novelty song called "Uncle Noah's Ark," complete with barnyard noises. As part of his act, Burnette could croak out some of the words to his songs like a frog, so he was given the movie name of Frog Millhouse, a name that he used during his years with Republic.

As part of the improbable plot of *The Phantom Empire*, a bizarre futuristic world called Murania, ruled by a powerful and glamorous queen named Tika, exists deep beneath the surface of the earth — and coincidentally right under Radio Ranch. This advanced science-fiction civilization, unknown and unsuspected by the guests and staff of Radio Ranch, uses television screens, ray guns, and robots. It also features warriors on horses brandishing swords and spears who periodically appear near Radio Ranch from under a false rock that covers the entrance to their underground world. To complicate the plot, nefarious businessmen and scientists want to take over the ranch so they can mine radium underneath it. The action is set within a modern timeframe and features airplanes, tear gas, radio, and a high-speed elevator from Murania to the surface. A cliff-hanger ending to each chapter of the serial leaves the movie audience wondering if Gene will make it back to the ranch in time to do his daily broadcast.

The screenplay for *The Phantom Empire* (1935) was written by Wallace McDonald, Gerald Geraghty, and Hy Freedman. The bizarre nature of the plot may be more understandable given that McDonald claimed that the idea came to him while he was under the influence of laughing gas at the dentist.[38]

Peculiar as the plot of *The Phantom Empire* was, the serial was a great success, particularly among rural audiences. The popularity of the science fiction aspects of the film—and the money it brought in—may have influenced Universal's decision to later make *Flash Gordon* (1936) and *Buck Rogers* (1939).

After *The Phantom Empire* (1935), Autry went on to star in *Tumbling Tumbleweeds* (1935) and a subsequent string of very successful singing movies set in the West. Singing Westerns blossomed as a distinct movie form at Republic Pictures, and the studio prospered financially as Autry's pictures gained in popularity. The singing Western promoted the image of the Romantic West, with yodeling cowboys, beautiful heroines in distress, and the hero overcoming villains across a background of a West filled with scenic prairies, plains, mountains, and deserts.

Gene's horse Champion received credit for the first time in *Melody Trail* (1935). Over the next thirty years, Gene owned six different horses named Champion. Three appeared in movies, and the others were trained for Autry's personal appearances, tours, and rodeo performances.

Gene Autry's early films were set in the 1930s, and featured contemporary society and technology. The Autry movies developed into a formula that included trains, trucks, and powerful cars, crooked politicians, night clubs, dude ranches, airplanes, and radio stations. But they also included traditional elements of the Old West, such as horses, six-shooters, and stagecoaches. Purists and critics found this combination to be laughable and ridiculous, and their opinion was that the Western should be set in the era of the Wild West. The public disagreed, and the films—along with their star—became a huge success.

Gene was often cast as a singer, musician, or radio personality to promote his songs. He was billed as "the Singing Cowboy" and played his roles using his own name. He wore the standard Western film clothes for the singing cowboy era—tight pants, ostentatious boots, and colorful shirts decorated with piping, embroidery, and smile pockets. He maintained a large Western wardrobe, most of which was custom tailored for him by specialty tailors Rodeo Ben, Turk, and Nudie, who catered to the movie cowboys. Autry always dressed in Western style to maintain his image.

Gene's pictures have been dubbed "ranch romances," or even musicals, rather than traditional "shoot-'em-ups," as he was always ready to croon a song or two to his leading lady.[39] However, because a large part of his movie audience tended to be small boys who didn't particularly care for mushy stuff, the romantic embraces were kept to a minimum. Because of the audience of youngsters, Autry kept to a strict set of rules of upright behavior in his movies that was outlined in his Cowboy Code (see sidebar). Indeed, though the cowboy stars of the 1930s were only acting in their movies, the lines between their films and reality became blurred and their audiences expected them to live up to their screen images as clean-cut heroes who led real lives in the West.

In 1936, Republic and Autry entered into the first of several contract disputes. Autry claimed that Republic was underpaying him while they made large profits from his films. It is certainly true that Autry was very popular, and the flood of Autry films were the main source of Republic's success and revenue. For example, Republic released seven new Gene Autry musical Westerns in 1936 alone. The titles were *Red River Valley* (March), *Comin' Round the Mountain* (April), *The Singing Cowboy* (May), *Guns and Guitars* (June), *Oh, Susanna!* (August), *The Big Show* (November), and *The Old Corral* (December).[40] When Mascot originally hired Autry, they paid him $75 per week. When Republic took over his contract, they increased this to $100 per week. This particular dispute was resolved by increasing Autry's salary to $2,000 for each picture.[41]

Another odd musical contribution to the Western genre was Gene Autry's *Round-Up Time in Texas* (1937). In this curious "Western," which was actually set in Africa rather than the American West, Gene's screen brother Tex has found a diamond mine and needs horses to work the mine, so Gene and Smiley Burnette have the task of transporting a herd to

---

### Gene Autry's Cowboy Code

1. The cowboy must never shoot first, hit a smaller man, or take unfair advantage.
2. He must never go back on his word, or a trust confided in him.
3. He must always tells the truth.
4. He must be gentle with children, the elderly, and animals.
5. He must not advocate or possess racially or religiously intolerant ideas.
6. He must help people in distress.
7. He must be a good worker.
8. He must keep himself clean in thought, speech, action, and personal habits.
9. He must respect women, parents, and his nation's laws.
10. A cowboy is a patriot.

(From Autry, *Back in the Saddle Again*, 184.)

---

Durban, South Africa. As the plot thickens, Tex's claim is jumped by the bad guys, and Gene is arrested by the police as a criminal diamond buyer. Gene and Smiley go through various adventures to set everything right, including a jail escape and capture by native tribesmen. As part of the comic relief, Burnette, playing his standard sidekick character of Frog Millhouse, disguises himself with soot from the outside of an old cooking pot and appears as a medicine man to cure the son of the tribal chief. The modern African setting includes airplanes and short wave radio, motorcycles and armored cars. The African setting for what was essentially a "Western" movie was developed to exploit the popularity of the contemporary Tarzan movies with Johnny Weissmuller in the title role. Gene's film even used some stock footage from old Tarzan movies.[42]

In 1938 Autry entered into another contract dispute with Republic. Autry was earning $5,000 a film at the time but wanted $15,000. Republic refused.[43] When Autry walked out during the dispute, Republic promoted a newcomer named Roy Rogers to be their star of musical Westerns, the first of which was *Under Western Stars* (1938). Autry's dispute was settled later that year, with his earnings increasing to $6,000 per picture and his contract eventually escalating to $10,000 per picture.[44] To put this in perspective, fellow Western star Buck Jones was at the time making $16,500 for each of his pictures.[45] Buck Jones' films typically cost $50,000 to $75,000 to make.[46] After Republic's dispute with Autry was settled, the studio continued to put Roy Rogers in low-budget period Westerns, where he played roles such as Billy the Kid and Wild Bill Hickok.

In addition to being a popular movie star, Gene Autry had meanwhile also branched out into the role of an astute businessman. Autry's extensive business holdings eventually included luxury hotels, broadcasting stations, music publishing businesses, the California Angels American League baseball team, real estate, a liquor distributorship, oil wells, a flying school, and several ranches that raised rodeo stock. In 1953 he bought the 125-acre former Monogram movie ranch in Newhall, California, and renamed it Melody Ranch.[47] As well as living there, he used the ranch as a location for filming several television series that were made by his Flying A production company.

### Roy Rogers

Roy Rogers, Republic's successor to singing cowboy roles, was born Leonard Franklin Slye on November 5, 1911, in Cincinnati, Ohio. In 1930 his family moved to California. He enjoyed music and singing, and persuaded his friends Bob Nolan and Tim Spencer to join him to form the Pioneer Trio singing group. The three played guitars and sang close-harmony vocals. By 1934 the group was working as staff musicians at radio station KFWB in Los Angeles. That same year they also signed a recording contract with Decca Records. The group expanded to become the Sons of the Pioneers when they were joined by Hugh Farr on fiddle and his brother Karl Farr on guitar.

Singing movie cowboys in Westerns were starting to become popular at the time, and the Sons of the Pioneers' radio exposure led to an opportunity to appear as a musical group in small parts in low-budget Western movies. They appeared in singing parts (with Rogers appearing under his real name of Leonard Slye) in movies such as *Tumbling Tumbleweeds* (1935), *Gallant Defender* (1935), and *Rhythm on the Range* (1936). In Gene Autry's *The Old Corral* (1936), Roy played the part of an outlaw. As part of the plot, Gene had a brief fistfight with Roy and forced him to sing a song. By the next year, Rogers was under contract to Republic and appeared in *Wild Horse Rodeo* (1937) under the stage name of Dick Weston.

When Gene Autry's 1938 contract dispute started with Republic, the studio groomed Rogers as a possible replacement for Autry. Republic starred Rogers in *Under Western Stars* (1938), which was successful enough that Republic continued to use him in Westerns. After appearing in several movies as Dick Weston, Leonard Slye legally changed his name to Roy Rogers in 1942.[48] Between 1938 and 1951 Rogers starred in eighty-three Westerns made by Republic. Unlike Gene Autry, who played parts in movies under his own name, Rogers was written into early scripts as different characters. He was Billy the Kid in *Billy the Kid Returns* (1938), Wild Bill Hickok in *Young Bill Hickok* (1940), Buffalo Bill Cody in *Young Buffalo Bill* (1940), and the Arizona Kid in *The Arizona Kid* (1939). In the early 1940s the writers at Republic changed this trend and he appeared under his own name as Roy Rogers. Roy's popularity throughout his career was boosted by his horse Trigger, who was billed immediately below Rogers, and above all the other supporting actors, as the "Smartest Horse in the Movies."[49]

Similar to Gene Autry films, Roy Rogers movies featured contemporary settings. Typical of the Rogers films is *Bells of Coronado* (1950), which involves tracking nuclear fuel that is being stolen by evil saboteurs for "some foreign country." The movie starts with a wagonload — *not* a truckload — of uranium being hijacked by a group of men on horseback with six-guns. Even with the modern addition of Geiger counters, spies, truth drugs, and airplanes, most of the movie involves horseback chases, blazing six-guns, and daring stunts. Roy, as an employee of the local electric company, wears two six-shooters and rides Trigger.

Autry enlisted in the Army Air Corp in 1942 and served the rest of World War II as a flight officer piloting cargo planes with the Air Transport Command. When Autry joined the military, Republic increased the budget of Rogers' movies and promoted him under the title of "King of the Cowboys."[50] His popularity grew until he actually surpassed Autry as the leading Western movie star. After the war, Autry returned for a while to Republic, then went to Columbia studios. In all, Autry made ninety-three Westerns, fifty-six of them before he enlisted.

With the demise of the B-Westerns in the mid–1950s, both Autry and Rogers went to television with their own shows and presented to new audiences versions of their older movies edited for a television time slot. Both also endorsed personalized lines of children's promotional items, including watches, cameras, cowboy and cowgirl outfits, lunch boxes, comic books, and record albums.

One of the non-singing Western stars of the 1930s was William Boyd as Hopalong Cassidy. The original Hopalong Cassidy, who appeared in a series of novels by Clarence E. Mulford, was known as Bill Cassidy. In Mulford's vision, Cassidy was a red-haired, scruffy, hard-drinking, smoking, cursing cowboy who first appeared in the novel *Hopalong Cassidy*

The boulder-strewn Alabama Hills and the Sierra Nevada Mountains, just west of Lone Pine, California, have formed the backdrop for many Westerns, from serials to major features. The Sierras, with Mount Whitney in the center of this photograph, stood in for the Old West, India, The Far East — and even Africa. The likes of Hopalong Cassidy, Gene Autry, and Roy Rogers were frequently filmed galloping across the sandy dirt roads of Movie Flats in the foreground.

in 1910. Actor Boyd put a different interpretation on Cassidy for movie audiences. Boyd first performed as the character in *Hop-a-Long Cassidy* (1935). In his movies, which lasted from the mid–1930s to the 1950s, Boyd was neat and clean-shaven, wore black or dark blue outfits, was silver-haired, drank sarsaparilla instead of alcohol, and didn't smoke.[51] He was polite, clean-living, and square-dealing. As the movie series progressed into television, Boyd as Cassidy was involved in fewer shootouts and fights. But Boyd's version of Hopalong Cassidy is the one that has been remembered, while the characteristics of Mulford's original book character have been forgotten.

B-Westerns and many of their programmer actors continued to be popular into the 1940s, with new cowboy stars, such as Sunset Carson, Johnny Mack Brown, and William "Wild Bill" Elliott adding to the roster. Rex Allen was the last of the B-Western singing cowboys, and the last of the singing Westerns is generally considered to be his *Phantom Stallion* (1954).

Singing cowboys were parodied in *Rustlers' Rhapsody* (1985). The hero Rex O'Herlihan (Tom Berenger) wears a dazzling all-white outfit, including hat, boots, and gunbelt. He never draws his gun first and only shoots bad guys in the hand. He even practices by shooting at wooden cutouts of hands holding guns. Stereotyped characters in the movie are the town drunk, the evil cattle baron, and the prostitute with a heart of gold.

## The Demise of the B-Western

Moviegoing and the Westerns continued to be immensely popular in the 1940s. In 1947 movie theaters sold an estimated eighty-seven million tickets weekly.[52]

Plots of Western movies in the 1930s and 1940s were generally simple, with heroic good defeating obvious bad guys, and often with singing cowboy heroes yodeling their way across the range. Typical of the non-singing B-Westerns was *Wild Horse Mesa* (1947), which starred Tim Holt. The plot was that of a standard oater, based on the 1928 Zane Grey novel of the same name. Tim Holt plays a horse rancher who helps his neighbor round up a herd of wild horses. As the movie unfolds, Holt's character falls in love with the neighbor's daughter, the father is killed by the villain, and Holt is falsely accused of the murder. At the end, however, the villain gets his just desserts as he is stomped by a wild horse, and Holt gets the girl.

As the 1940s moved into the 1950s, this type of B-Western started to disappear. Paramount stopped making B-Westerns in 1941; Universal Pictures did the same in 1946; and United Artists released their last B-western in 1950. Columbia Pictures discontinued Gene Autry Westerns in 1953 and Westerns in general in 1956.[53] Republic stopped making B-Westerns in 1955. MGM hadn't made a B-Western since 1929.

One of the reasons for the demise of the B-Western was simply that many of the Western movie stars were aging and stopped making action films. Another was that cowboy movies, such as those of Gene Autry and Roy Rogers, were available free on television. Faced with the increasing competition from television, many small-town theaters started to close.

In the early 1950s the major studios still controlled the industry. In the 1950s, however, a new type of Western appeared, with the studios using brilliant Technicolor instead of the black-and-white film stock of the 1930s and 1940s. Actors such as Randolph Scott, Glenn Ford, Audie Murphy, Robert Taylor, Rory Calhoun, Richard Widmark, Joel McCrea,

William Holden, Sterling Hayden, and others appeared in high-quality Westerns made by Warner Bros., Columbia, Paramount, Universal, and the other major studios. These films were not quite up to the standards of the A-Westerns that starred John Wayne or Gary Cooper, but were certainly well above the traditional B-Westerns of the 1940s in budget, scripts, production standards, acting, and overall quality. Big-budget A-Western movies, which were at one time a mainstay of Hollywood, came relatively few and far between.

Many of the actors in this new form of Western were established popular stars in Hollywood who had aged gracefully but were no longer believable in "pretty-boy" and romantic leading-man roles. Consequently, they turned to Westerns. Their mature, rugged — indeed, in some cases craggy — looks made them ideal for these films. Even actors such as James Stewart and John Wayne aged into more mature Western roles.

In an attempt to recapture the audiences that they were losing to television, the studios added all sorts of gimmicks to Westerns, mostly without much success. One example was three-dimensional viewing (3-D), which was employed for Westerns such as *Taza, Son of Cochise* (1954), *Hondo* (1953), and *Devil's Canyon* (1953). These were filmed with visual effects such as arrows, fists, knives, and galloping horses aimed straight out of the screen at the audience for shock value.

Another gimmick was to make the screen picture bigger. The biggest was Cinerama, a three-camera wrap-around screen process introduced in 1962, which was used for *How the West Was Won* (1962) and *Custer of the West* (1968). Another attempt at increasing the size of the projected picture was the Todd-AO process, which used 70 mm film instead of standard 35 mm film to create a wide-screen effect. Paramount introduced a similar concept called VistaVision, which put the 35 mm film onto its side in order to create a bigger image, but unfortunately required a special projector to show the film. Movie theaters were reluctant to purchase new VistaVision projectors, and only about twenty theaters made the necessary modifications. For this reason VistaVision was not a commercial success and Paramount made its last VistaVision film, a Western named *One-Eyed Jacks*, in 1961.[54]

In 1953, 20th Century–Fox introduced a more successful attempt to impress audiences who were becoming used to the small screen of television. This was CinemaScope, a wide-screen process designed to entice people back into movie theaters as television was stealing them away. This process used a lens to optically compress the width of a scene when it was put on film, and then another lens on the projector that expanded the film back to its normal proportions on the screen. CinemaScope, as opposed to the VistaVision process, did not require a special projector.

## On Into the Fifties

By 1950, audience tastes were changing again. The oaters of the 1940s, in which heroes were always good and villains were all bad, were considered too simplistic. As a result, Hollywood scriptwriters in the 1950s tackled more complex and innovative plots, included adult themes, and explored more complex characters. This era created such notable films as *High Noon* (1952), starring Gary Cooper and directed by Fred Zinnemann; and the trio of films *Winchester '73* (1950), *The Naked Spur* (1953), and *The Man from Laramie* (1955), all starring James Stewart and directed by Anthony Mann. Movies such as these were responsible for a renewed interest in the Western in the 1950s and 1960s. Even these movies, however, still relied on a plot with action scenes and then a climactic shootout at the end for the resolution.

Such scenes included saloon brawls, fist fights, horse chases, and violent shootouts. A popular theme that incorporated all these elements is that of defending the weak and the helpless, such as in the plot of *The Magnificent Seven* (1960).

Other changes were looming. In the 1950s changes inside the film industry altered how Westerns were made and the way in which they were produced.

Two major factors affected the motion picture business. One started in the early 1900s, when New York film distributors and nickelodeon operators wanted to increase their supply of films and at the same time increase their profits. To achieve this, some early film exhibitors, such as Marcus Loew, Adolph Zukor, and William Fox, expanded into film production in order to supply themselves with more movies. Loew founded what eventually became MGM, Zukor's company later became Paramount, and Fox Studios eventually became 20th Century–Fox.

By 1938, eight major studios dominated the film industry: Paramount Pictures, Metro-Goldwyn-Mayer, 20th Century–Fox, Warner Bros., RKO, Universal, Columbia, and United Artists. By the end of the 1940s the major studios controlled large chains of theaters and operated distribution channels that supplied other theaters. On May 3, 1948, after a protracted anti-trust suit, the United States Supreme Court decided that operating film manufacturing and exhibition together constituted a monopoly. So the court ordered the major studios to sell off their profitable chains of movie theaters. The theaters made up 93 percent of the movie industry's investment, as opposed to only 5 percent for actual movie production.[55]

The conglomeration of manufacturing, distribution, and exhibition had worked well in the past for the industry. Now, without guaranteed distribution in the studios' own theaters, some films were not profitable. As a result, this shake-up of the system cut revenue at the studios, resulting in a corresponding reduction of movie production — including Westerns. In 1948, 25 percent of all the films produced by major studios were Westerns. By 1964 this had dropped to about 7½ percent.[56]

The second factor that depressed the movie industry — both literally and figuratively — was the growth of the popularity of television. As film production costs rose and profits fell, studios scrambled for ways to bring back profits.

During the 1950s, pressure also came on the major studios from independent filmmakers who had started to make and distribute movies outside the conventional studio system. In turn, this led to more filming on location, away from Hollywood, and further depressed moviemaking at the major studios. An added benefit for audiences from the increase in location filming of Westerns, however, was more realism in the final film than could be obtained by shooting indoors on a sound stage or on a studio back lot.

## The New Breed

By the late 1960s and early 1970s, films in general, and Western movies in particular, contained more violence. The Italian-made so-called "Spaghetti Westerns," such as *A Fistful of Dollars* (1964), *For a Few Dollars More* (1965), and *The Good, the Bad and the Ugly* (1966), along with the two hundred or so offshoots that they spawned, upped the level of violence. The mayhem and body count kept creeping higher and higher. *A Fistful of Dollars* (1964) showed a brutal beating (with screen make-up to match) of the Man-with-No-Name (Clint Eastwood) by Ramon's henchman from the Rojo gang. As a result, American-made movies started to follow this trend of added violence. The beginning of *Big Jake* (1971), for example, contains a violent, blood-spattered raid on the McCandles ranch as a gang arrives to kidnap Big Jake's grandson.

The severe beating of Tuco (Eli Wallach) in the Confederate POW camp in *The Good, the Bad and the Ugly* (1966) showed blood dripping all over the place, as the POW camp sergeant Angel Eyes (Lee Van Cleef) tries to get information from Tuco about some buried treasure. In *Once Upon a Time in the West* (1968) the entire McBain family is shot onscreen in cold blood, including the father, two sons, and the daughter. *The Wild Bunch* (1969) ends with five long minutes of violent carnage as seemingly everybody in sight is shot, knifed, machine-gunned, or blown up.

Along with added violence, this new type of movie changed the protagonist into an anti-hero. In *High Plains Drifter* (1973), the Stranger (Clint Eastwood) rides silently into town and, within the first few minutes, shoots three bullying thugs and then has his way on a pile of hay in a barn with a woman who runs into him on the street, dragging her there while swigging from a whiskey bottle. These were not the good deeds outlined in the Cowboy Code of the flashy singing cowboy of the 1930s. As Hollywood was well aware from the pre–Code days of the 1920s, however, sex and violence sell well. But perhaps nothing is really new. The plotting of *High Plains Drifter* (1973), about a town that has gone so bad that it can only be consigned to the flames of Hell, is not unlike the plot of William S. Hart's *Hell's Hinges* (1916).

Brutal beatings, shootings, and violence continued to characterize later movies. *The Shootist* (1976) and *Open Range* (2004) contains graphic scenes of violent shootouts. *Bad Girls* (1994) builds up to a violent, blood-spattered shootout at the end.

A comparison of the 1957 and 2007 versions of *3:10 to Yuma* shows how movies changed to offer less characterization and more action. The basic plot remains the same, as farmer/rancher Dan Evans takes outlaw Ben Wade to meet the 3:10 P.M. train to the territorial prison in Yuma, Arizona. But audiences of 2007 expected and demanded more action and violence, so the 2007 version is not as talky as the 1957 version, which was more about the tension between the two men. At the end of the 1957 version, Evans and Wade both make it to the train unscathed, while bullets zip around them as they run. After they reach the train through a hail of bullets, Wade grins and says that he has broken out of Yuma prison before. In the darker 2007 version, Evans is killed at the last moment as they reach the train; then Wade grabs a gun and shoots the remaining members of his own gang in a final blood-bath. He then boards the train, also planning to break out of Yuma. Similarly, the 2010 version of *True Grit* was more graphic in terms of violence than the 1969 version.

## Television

The ability of the major studios to make Western movies on a budget and yet still make a profit had been under intense pressure since the early 1950s, as television grew to become the popular American medium for free entertainment. In 1946 approximately 90 million movie theater tickets were sold in the U.S. each week. By 1960 this had dropped to 40 million tickets, a drop that was attributed directly to television. By 1969 ticket sales had sunk to only 15 million. [57]

Television was able to command a large audience. As production costs rose and profits fell, the studios looked at television and considered the opportunity to supply a new form of serial Western — in a weekly format. In the 1950s and 1960s the major studios relented, went into television production, and opened their libraries of old Western films to the late show.

Westerns on television started in the late 1940s with the reworking of B-Westerns into a shorter format to suit the constraints of television. Most of them tended to be half-hour programs, though many were later extended to a full hour. Gene Autry created *The Gene Autry Show*, which ran from 1950 to 1956 for 91 episodes. Roy Rogers did the same and created *The Roy Rogers Show*, which ran from 1951 to 1957 for 100 episodes. In the television series, Roy's real-life wife, Dale Evans, operated a diner in Mineral City, with Pat Brady as the cook who drove a cantankerous jeep called Nellybelle.

Actor William Boyd purchased the rights to his Hopalong Cassidy movies and re-edited them for a shorter time slot on television. He then started filming new episodes, thus creating a very popular — and financially successful — television series that lasted for 99 episodes between 1949 and 1951. Similarly, the Lone Ranger galloped across the small screen on his horse Silver for 221 episodes between 1949 and 1965.

As a result, Westerns didn't die among loyal viewers, but reappeared in a changed format; and television embraced the Western with new adventures of cowboy heroes. By the fall of 1957 there were more than twenty-five Western series on TV.[58] During the 1957–58 television season, seven of the top ten shows were Westerns.[59] At the peak, in 1959, twenty-six Western programs were broadcast on prime-time television.

As the 1950s faded into the 1960s, Westerns on television moved towards more adult themes in original programs such as *Gunsmoke* and *Have Gun Will Travel*. Success bred clones, as Warner Bros. cranked out *Cheyenne, Maverick, Sugarfoot, Lawman, Bronco,* and *Colt .45*. Not all were historically accurate. In *The Texan*, which ran from 1958 to 1960 for eighty episodes, actor Rory Calhoun played Bill Longley, an ex-gunfighter who helped people in distress in Texas in the 1870s. The series took certain liberties with the facts. The real William Preston "Wild Bill" Longley was a multiple murderer who was hung on October 11, 1878, in Giddings, Texas.

## Chapter Four

# Flickering Images; or,
# How Did They Do That?

In the beginning days of the movies, in the early 1900s, one-reel Westerns were cranked out in a few days at a single location. There was no real script, and the director improvised as he filmed. Plots came from stories and magazines, or were "borrowed" from plays, often with blatant disregard for copyright ownership.[1]

By contrast, when the Cinerama epic *How the West Was Won* (1962) was filmed, the scope of the production was so great that it required the talent of three veteran directors — John Ford, Henry Hathaway, and George Marshall — and four directors of photography to complete it. Even with these combined talents, the film took about ten months to shoot.[2] Seventy-five percent of the production was filmed on location in such diverse places as the Ohio River Valley, the Black Hills of South Dakota, the Uncompahgre National Forest and the Gunnison River in Colorado, the Sierra Nevada Mountains of California, and Monument Valley in Utah. This movie would have taken literally years to film with only one director and one cinematographer.

So how do Western movies get started, what is their basis in history, and how have they evolved since their faltering beginnings?[3]

## Scripting a Movie

The first step in making a Western comes when the producer has an idea for a film he wants to make or is assigned by a particular studio to make a specific movie. In the heyday of making Western movies — between about 1940 and 1955 — control of filmmaking was in the hands of the big studios. A major studio making a particular movie chose the script, set the budget, and assigned to the project actors, producers, directors, and other production people already on their staff. When the movie was completed, the studio distributed and promoted the final film.

The blueprint for the production was the script. It contained the dialogue and the breakdown of individual camera shots, and specified such miscellaneous requirements as sound effects, lighting, locations, costumes, and props to be used.

Producer Thomas Ince has been credited as the first filmmaker to use a written script to organize the actors and scenes. Ince made Westerns on a production-line basis, and to improve the efficiency of production he had all aspects of the film written down. This allowed him to relinquish the day-to-day production to others while he still retained control over the project. This also resulted in a more disciplined method for making movies than the previous free-wheeling methods.

There are essentially five basic sources for film scripts for Westerns: novels, short stories, magazine articles, theatrical plays, and original screenplays. Novels and original screenplays are the usual sources for Western scripts, because they allow the freedom for plenty of outdoor action to be written into the scenario. These sources tend to be fiction and present the same type of drama and conflicts as most novels, except that they are set in the early American West. They merely use the history and setting of the West as a background for conflicts and their resolution.

Novels have always been good sources for Western scripts. John Ford's *Cheyenne Autumn* (1964), for example, was based on Willa Cather's novel of the same name. *Hallelujah Trail* (1965) was based on a novel by Bill Gulick; *5 Card Stud* (1968) was adapted from a novel by Ray Gaulden; *The War Wagon* (1967) was from the novel *Badman* by Clair Huffaker; *Shane* (1953) came from a book by Jack Schaeffer; *Dances with Wolves* (1990) was from a novel by Michael Blake; and *The Searchers* (1956) was based on a novel by Alan LeMay. *The Professionals* (1966) was based on *A Mule for the Marquesa* by Frank O'Rourke. The two versions of *True Grit* (1969 and 2010) were based on a book written by Charles Portis. Even suitable novels, though, typically have to be shortened or adapted to make a script for the screen. The visual and time limitations of a 100-minute Western usually do not allow for the level of character development seen in novels.

Ideas for scripts can come from unusual sources. *Sergeants 3* (1962), for example, was a version of Rudyard Kipling's story about Gunga Din and India that was transformed into a script about the cavalry and a young man who wants to enlist. Ironically, the 1939 version of the action-adventure film *Gunga Din* was photographed in the Alabama Hills, the classic location for filming Westerns just below Mt. Whitney in California.

Non-fiction books have also been used as sources for screenplays. The movie *Cowboy*

Screenplays for Westerns have come from books, short stories, magazine articles, and dime novels. Some of the early plots were lifted straight from their sources without much regard for copyright ownership. This poster from 1910 was an advertisement for a story that contained all the ingredients for a good Western melodrama—a stirring adventure in a mountain setting, a villainous Indian, and a swooning heroine to be protected by the hero (Library of Congress).

(1958), for instance, was based on Frank Harris' anecdotal *Reminiscences of a Cowboy. Tom Horn* (1980) was based on *Life of Tom Horn Government Scout and Interpreter, Written by Himself.*

The use of a short story as a basis for a screenplay creates a very different problem than that of adapting a novel. Short stories are difficult to adapt for the screen because they are so short. A short story cannot develop much more than one character due to the limited length of the format, whereas a movie needs to develop various sides to several characters and often include several themes at the same time.

Magazine articles have been widely employed as the basis for scripts by Hollywood Westerns. John Ford's movie *Stagecoach* (1939) was based on a short story by Ernest Haycox called *Stage to Lordsburg* that was published in *Collier's* magazine in 1936. This, in turn, was loosely related to the short story *Boule de Suif* (English translation: "Ball of Tallow") by French author Guy de Maupassant. *High Noon* (1952) was based on a magazine story *The Tin Star* by John W. Cunningham. *Gunfight at the O.K. Corral* (1957) was "suggested" (as the screen credits obliquely put it) by an article by George Scullin, though it was heavily influenced by the book *Wyatt Earp: Frontier Marshal* by Stuart Lake. *The Man from Laramie* (1955) came from a story in the *Saturday Evening Post* by Thomas T. Flynn.

The movies of director John Ford's so-called "Cavalry Trilogy," which consists of *Fort Apache* (1948), *She Wore a Yellow Ribbon* (1949), and *Rio Grande* (1950), were based on stories by James Warner Bellah that appeared originally in the *Saturday Evening Post. Fort Apache* (1948) was based on Bellah's "Massacre," *She Wore a Yellow Ribbon* (1949) on the story "War Party," and *Rio Grande* (1950) on "Mission with No Record."

Though occasionally adapted, theatrical plays tend to be unsuitable for Western movie scripts, which are typically set outdoors. Plays are written specifically for production on the stage and tend to be limited in their possibilities for outdoor action, such as horse chases, which is the stock-in-trade of Westerns. There are, of course, exceptions that have made it to the screen, such as *Paint Your Wagon* (1969), which was originally a 1948 stage musical by Alan Jay Lerner and Frederick Loewe, and Rogers and Hammerstein's *Annie Get Your Gun* (1950). The stage versions of both of these, however, were extensively modified and adapted to make them into outdoor movies.

One additional category that is not always apparent as a source of movie scripts is other movies. With suitable modifications, other movies may be the inspiration for further screenplays. Director John Sturges once candidly said to journalist Michael Munn during an interview, "We play a game in the business called Rip-off. You see what makes money and you follow it up with something you hope will repeat its success."[4] The Japanese action film *The Seven Samurai* (1954), directed by Akira Kurosawa, for instance, was adapted into *The Magnificent Seven* (1960).

*A Fistful of Dollars* (1964), as another example, was freely adapted by Sergio Leone (who used the pseudonym of Bob Robertson) from another Japanese samurai film by Akira Kurosawa, *Yojimbo* (1961). The non–Western movie *Last Man Standing* (1996) updated the same plot to 1930s Chicago gang warfare in a small town in Texas. *Pale Rider* (1985) owes elements of its plot to *Shane* (1953).

Also in this category would be satires of the genre. A plot very similar to *The Magnificent Seven* (1960), for example, appears in ¡*Three Amigos!* (1986), in which three Western movie stars from the silent film era in 1916 mistakenly go to help a Mexican village that is being terrorized by a Mexican bandit named El Guapo.[5] The same type of plot device was used in *Hollywood Cowboy* (1937), where Western movie star Jeffery Carson (George

O'Brien) finds himself accidentally involved in a real range war. As part of the broad satire in *¡Three Amigos!* (1986), the three movie stars use white makeup and perform in a very melodramatic acting style when they are playing the parts of actors, which was just how it was done.[6]

Westerns became so stereotyped that they left themselves open to ridicule. *The Villain* (1979) goes so far as to make fun of the hero, the villain, the girl, and the Indians. Other efforts included comedy Westerns such as *The Sheriff of Fractured Jaw* (1959), which parodied all manner of clichés. The politically-incorrect (in today's terms) *Blazing Saddles* (1974) probably couldn't be made today, but it makes fun of many of the conventions of 1950s movies and includes the famous cowboy "post-bean" scene around the campfire.

## The Classic Western Screen Plots

Western author Frank Gruber, himself the author of many movie screenplays, claimed that there were seven basic plots for Westerns.[7] Gruber knew that there were other plots but felt that they were essentially founded on these fundamental situations and then embellished, expanded, reversed, or given some special twist. Avid watchers of Westerns can perhaps think of more, or perhaps variations, of these same basic themes.

### The Cavalry Versus the Indians

This is the basis for innumerable plots, from the serious, such as *Fort Apache* (1948) and *Escape from Fort Bravo* (1953), to a lighter, more humorous look at life in the cavalry in *Hallelujah Trail* (1965).

### Transportation

This includes trains, such as the building of the transcontinental railroad in *Union Pacific* (1939), and the trials and tribulations of smaller railroad lines, such as in *Denver and Rio Grande* (1952). This category includes other forms of transportation, such as that seen in *Stagecoach* (1939), or uses a background of stagecoaches, such as the plot device of the fight over ownership of a stagecoach line seen in *Rough Night in Jericho* (1967). The plot of *Albuquerque* (1948) revolves around two freighting companies fighting over ore transportation from gold mines. Another form of transportation is the focus of *Pony Express* (1953), as Buffalo Bill and Wild Bill Hickok start the famous pony express — even though the plot was historically inaccurate.

### Homesteaders and Squatters in Conflict with the Local Land Baron

Numerous variations of this theme have appeared in such films as *The Sheepman* (1958), *Saddle the Wind* (1958), and *Chisum* (1970). *Tom Horn* (1980) is the story of one of the "range detectives" employed by the Wyoming Stock Growers Association to protect their members' stock, crops, and other property from bandits, thieves, and outlaws. The classic example of this type of plot would, of course, be *Shane* (1953), in which a range war starts when the local cattlemen do not want squatters (farmers) fencing in what they consider *their* land and water.

*The Dedicated Lawman Who Fights Off Local Outlaws*

The undisputed classic example of this is *High Noon* (1952).[8]

*Outlaws*

Many outlaws have been idolized and turned into almost saintly characters by both the dime novels and well-meaning but inaccurate movies. Examples are *Jesse James* (1939), *The Outlaw Josey Wales* (1976), and *Butch Cassidy and the Sundance Kid* (1969).

*Revenge*

This is an all-encompassing category, and a type of story that is ripe for conflicts and violence. This category would include *The Bravados* (1958) and *Last Train from Gun Hill* (1959). The basis for *The Searchers* (1956) is vengeance, as well as the lengthy search to get back the two girls who were kidnapped by Indians. *Unforgiven* (1992) is all about revenge for the uncalled-for killing of William Munny's friend.

*The Empire Builder Who Wants to Run Everybody Else Off the Land*

*Chisum* (1970), *El Dorado* (1967), and *The Sons of Katie Elder* (1965)[9] are but a few examples of Westerns with this theme.

## The Director

After an initial script is written, it usually goes through various rewrites, either by the original writer or by another writer who provides a different slant to the ideas. At this point real history may become involved, as further research on the initial script may be performed via history books, magazine articles, period newspapers, or through a historical consultant.

After the shooting script is revised and approved, the director has the responsibility for transforming the story and script into a coherent film. He chooses the sets and locations, arranges the shooting plan, and directs the actors. He works closely with the producer on business and budgetary aspects, and with the scriptwriter on dialogue, which often has to be rewritten on the fly as the production progresses. During the golden age of the Westerns — from the 1930s to the 1960s — the director was busy directing. He generally did not pick the location, the budget, or the stars. He did not write the script and rarely edited the final movie. After the 1960s and the breakup of the old studio system, directors often exerted more creative control over their movies and were involved in all aspects of the production.

Some directors have a definite vision of the final film. They shoot very little extra film and mentally "edit" their vision of the plot in the camera as they shoot. John Ford liked to work in this manner. Others, such as George Stevens when filming *Shane* (1953), shoot extensive footage, often filming the same scene from different angles. When Stevens was editing *Shane*, he knew that he had excess material and used this to craft his vision of the story.[10]

When filming *High Noon* (1952), director Fred Zinneman used black-and-white film stock because he wanted the final movie to look like a newsreel.[11] Competent cameramen can put much of the mood of a film into a black-and-white movie. In the late 1980s, many black-and-white Western movies were colorized for showing on network television.[12] Some purists did not like this "improvement," as they perceived that it changed the feel and look of the films. Many filmmakers also protested.

Planning a movie, particularly an outdoor-oriented film like a Western, is like assembling a jigsaw puzzle and involves juggling various elements such as location, weather, night shots, the schedules of actors with other commitments, and the rental costs of a location or movie ranch. Scenes in movies are typically shot out of sequence in order to make the most efficient use of expensive stars, sets, and locations. For example, an expensive star might only be available for a short period of time between other commitments, so his or her scenes may all be filmed together. Or an expensive location or a prop like a steam train may have to be rented, so it is more economical to film all the scenes together that involve that location or with that prop to save money. In addition, all the action has to be planned (called "blocking" in film lingo), whether it is riding a horse or walking across a room and sitting down.

Outdoor locations for Westerns can be difficult for planning purposes because of changing seasons and possible bad weather, such as snow or rain. For example, some shots may

All the major studios owned movie ranches outside Hollywood where they filmed horse and stagecoach chases. Scenes in "towns" were usually shot on Western streets built on studio back lots. Countless heroes and villains raced their horses down this street and around the corner at this Western set on the Paramount Movie Ranch, located west of Los Angeles in the Santa Monica Mountains. Many shoot-'em-ups and shoot-'em-downs took place here on the main street during the heyday of B-Westerns.

be filmed when trees are budding, but earlier shots that appear later in the movie may be filmed when the trees are still bare. Filming in the outdoors can also be difficult because of changing light during the day and in different seasons. As filmmaker Tom Reilly succinctly put it, "Shoot in flat light" (i.e. total cloud cover) so that the editor can later easily match shots.[13]

As scenes in movies are typically shot out of sequence, meticulous planning is vital to maintain continuity, or the matching of one shot to the next one throughout a particular sequence. One example would be a scene shot at an outdoor location where an actor walks through a door into a building from the outside. If the next shot is inside, showing him coming onto a studio set, the two scenes have to be carefully matched. The outside and inside shots may be filmed weeks apart, but to match the two the actor has to have the same clothes in the same state of wear, be carrying the same props, and have the same makeup and hair length. Making this happen is the job of the continuity crew. Correct continuity is particularly important in fight scenes in Westerns, where torn clothing, make-up "bruises," and movie blood all have to match throughout the sequence.

A glaring example of loss of continuity occurred in *5 Card Stud* (1968). In one shot, Van Morgan (Dean Martin) is standing in his hotel room with nothing in his hands, talking to bartender Little George (Yaphet Kotto). But in the next shot he is halfway through smoking a cigarette. As another example in the same movie, when the Rev. Jonathan Rudd (Robert Mitchum) is practicing shooting bottles and cans, he uses a double-action revolver in one shot, but in the next shot replaces a single-action gun in his holster.

Viewers with sharp eyes may notice that during the fight between Frenchy (Marlene Dietrich) and Lily Belle/Mrs. Callahan (Una Merkel) in the saloon in *Destry Rides Again* (1939), Frenchie apparently changes the type of stockings she is wearing from shot to shot during the sequence. She starts out in seamed black stockings held up by garters, then changes to opera-length stockings without garters, and then back to the garters again as they roll around fighting on the floor.

In *The Quick and the Dead* (1995), Horace the Bartender (Pat Hingle) calls the marshal (Gene Hackman) Mr. Hasler when the character is first introduced, but the marshal is Herod for the rest of the movie. Examples of continuity errors are countless.

## Filming Outdoors

Once the script is finalized, filming begins. "Exteriors" are scenes filmed outside, shot either somewhere on location, on the back lot at the studio, or on a studio ranch. "Interiors" are scenes shot on a sound stage.

The first silent Westerns were typically filmed outdoors on location. Filmmakers soon realized, however, that filming was subject to the whims of the weather and the available sunlight. To compensate for this, movie companies built indoor stages where they could film interior shots, such as saloon scenes, and control the lighting. To maximize the light, these stages sometimes had no roof but were open to the sky, so that lighting could be supplied by the natural light of the sun. This saved on the cost of electrical lighting, which was expensive at the time, but had the disadvantage that filming was still subject to the vagaries of the weather.

Even today, for Westerns shot outdoors, scenes have to match from one moment to the next as the sun moves from sunup to sundown and shadows change. If the weather turns bad, the film crew may have to leave and move to a backup interior location. This can be a problem, as each extra day of shooting might cost as much as $150,000 to maintain the cast and crew.

## The Coming of Sound

The early Westerns were "silents," or movies filmed without sound, because the ability to record sound and synchronized speech had not yet been developed. Any explanatory material or "dialogue" was presented to the audience printed on intertitle cards sprinkled throughout the film.

The first system for playing sound with a movie involved synchronizing a phonograph recording with the action on the screen. The system had its limitations, however, and the first movie from Warner Bros. to include sound, *Don Juan* (1926), was a silent movie that used sound only for pre-recorded music and sound effects, without dialogue. The next year, in another technical leap forward, *The Jazz Singer* (1927) contained three songs and some dialogue that was synchronized with the actors' lips. Fox studios soon developed a method of putting a synchronized sound track onto the edge of the film itself—and the sound revolution was born.

When the ability to add recorded sound with dialogue arrived in 1927, most studios felt that sound was unsuitable for Westerns. They felt that the ability to incorporate sound meant that a movie should contain mostly talking, and also rightly assumed that audiences for Westerns wanted plenty of action instead of dialogue.

A further problem for introducing sound to Westerns was strictly logistical. Westerns were outdoor action movies, but the filming of early sound movies had to be carried out on special sound stages in order to control the pickup of unwanted noise. The cameras of the time were large and noisy, and had to be housed in soundproof enclosures to muffle these unwanted sounds. These massive stationary enclosures forced the camera to stay in one location, unable to follow action as it moved. In addition, the large microphones of the time had to be concealed close to the actors in order to pick up the dialogue clearly.

A totally unexpected problem was that many of the popular cowboy actors of the silent period couldn't make the transition to talkies because their voices were not what audiences expected.[14] But by the 1930s many of the technical problems of sound had been resolved, and Westerns were able to break away from interior sound stages and go back to the outdoors.

Outside shooting, however, can still be a problem because of extraneous noises created by the wind or planes flying overhead. Director Sergio Leone solved this problem by shooting his films without sound and then dubbing in voices and sound effects during post-production.

The coming of sound created other new problems for filmmakers. Sound recorded at the same time as filming often did not have the same sizzle as the action demanded. This spawned a whole technology of sound design and sound effects that are added to the sound track to make the action seem "more realistic." Directors go to great lengths to achieve what they feel is the correct "sound." In *Shane* (1953), for example, director George Stevens fired a howitzer into a can to get what he considered to be the right "sound" for gunshots.[15] There are also apocryphal stories of sound editors smacking objects like the head of a cabbage to get a "good" sound effect for a fist hitting a jaw during a saloon fight.

## The B-Westerns

During the 1930s the Poverty Row studios churned out hundreds of B-Westerns. B-Westerns were relatively inexpensive to produce, as they were often shot on the studio's back lot or at the studio's ranch. B-Westerns usually didn't have much supervision once the camera was rolling. Directors and producers of B-Westerns and serials needed to bring in a product on time for a cost at or under budget.[16] These oaters were filmed fast, with not much time for artistic composition and other cinematic niceties.

Often two or more directors filmed at the same time, one shooting dialogue scenes and a second-unit director filming action scenes and fights using doubles for the stars. The audience for serials expected as much action as possible, so directors tended to tone down romance and complex plotting.

The B-Westerns had a specific target audience and were constrained by a fixed running time. If the studio was cranking out serials, they also had to adhere to a fixed formula and standardized format. The average completed serial ran for twelve chapters (episodes), which translated into about five hours of running time.

Serials, whose production peaked in the early 1940s, ended each chapter with a cliffhanger, so that the audience would have to return the following week to see how the hero escaped. Serials were sometimes made so fast and haphazardly that the end of one chapter of a serial might leave no way out for the hero, but at the beginning of the next episode he had miraculously — even inexplicably — escaped. At the end of one chapter of *The Oregon Trail* (1939), for example, star Johnny Mack Brown disappears under a herd of stampeding horses. Yet at the beginning of the next episode he carries on as if nothing had happened.[17]

**Not all Western movie towns are what they seem to be. Often a substantial-looking building on the studio back lot is only a false front that is propped up by two-by-fours, with no substance behind it. Interiors were usually filmed indoors on a sound stage so that lighting and sound could be controlled, and the outside weather was not a factor.**

Scenes for B-Westerns were often shot so completely out of sequence and context that many times the actors did not know who or what they were reacting to. Retakes were minimal, and parts of the explanatory dialogue or scenes might be forgotten in the rush to finish shooting. By the time the film reached the editor, the cast and the director had moved on to another picture, so retakes weren't possible, even if the studio wanted them. As a result, the editor of the film often had to salvage mistakes or even figure out a way to cover up omissions in the plot or gaps in the dialogue.

The costs for both serials and B-Westerns were reduced by having permanent standing sets and by incorporating stock footage. Studios might use the same stock music in several serials to save costs. Directors had to use their ingenuity to make do and keep the camera cranking. A rather humorous, but clever, solution to a filming problem was described by Alan Barbour when he wrote, "A typical example is provided by a Universal serial of the mid-thirties, *Scouts to the Rescue* [1939], in which a lost tribe of Indians was given a most impressive and undecipherable guttural language.... The Indians spoke a perfectly normal dialogue — which was then printed in reverse."[18]

## Changes

By the late 1950s and early 1960s, filming was done mostly on real locations in the West rather than on a studio back lot. Although entries in other film genres often shot on sound stages, Westerns had always tended to be filmed outdoors. The outdoors was more suitable for action shots, such as the popular "running insert," which is fast-moving action filmed from alongside with the camera mounted on a car or truck. This is a specialized example of a "tracking shot," where the camera keeps pace with the action as it moves. One example is the camera keeping pace alongside a careening stagecoach or tracking actors as they ride horses and converse. The camera may be mounted on a moving truck for fast action, or on a dolly (a small, wheeled cart with rubber tires) or a cart that moves on miniature railroad tracks for slower action. Because of this cart, a tracking shot is also known as a "dolly shot."

Even though the trend was towards the outdoors, many exterior shots in Westerns in the 1950s were filmed on vast sound stages instead of in the real outdoors, so that the director could control the lighting and the sound. Many a fine outdoor shot has been ruined by the sound of an airplane overhead or a heavy truck passing by, thus running up the production cost with retakes. Cecil B. DeMille, for example, preferred to shoot most of his footage, even for Westerns, on sound stages in Hollywood in order to maximize efficiency. If the script called for an outdoor location, he usually sent a second unit director and crew to film it. Similarly, in *The Man Who Shot Liberty Valance* (1962), director John Ford chose to film many of the "exteriors," including the street sequence where Valance is shot, indoors on a sound stage.

Filming on a sound stage allowed better control of set lighting, sound, and weather, but typically did not look real. For example, in *Gunfight at the O.K. Corral* (1957), compare the scenes where Wyatt Earp and Doc Holliday are camping out and are attacked by three gunmen, which was filmed indoors on a sound stage, with the later scenes of the actual gunfight, which were filmed outdoors at Old Tucson Studios. The difference is obvious.

A return to outdoor filming on location in the 1960s brought reality back to these scenes, and, as audiences became more particular, it made better artistic sense to use the outdoors for outdoor locations. The town scenes in some television series, such as *The Rifleman* or *Wanted Dead or Alive*, which frequently filmed on interior sets, look very flat and sterile. Some critics felt that William Wellman's *The Ox-bow Incident* (1943), which was an "outdoor" type of movie, suffered from much of it being filmed indoors on a sound stage. Location filming also saved the cost of building complex sets, such as a town street, indoors on a sound stage.

During the 1950s another advance that furthered the trend towards using outdoor locations was the use of single-negative Eastmancolor film in place of the Technicolor process, which used three separate negatives to record the three primary colors necessary to later produce a single color print. This change removed the requirement for transporting a heavy Technicolor camera to a distant location, though filming was still not always easy. The Mitchell Panavision camera used in the 1970s weighed about 135 pounds.[19] The later handheld Mitchell Reflex 65mm camera AP-65 weighed only about twenty-seven pounds.

## Stunts and Stuntmen

From the earliest days of Westerns, including *The Great Train Robbery* (1903), plots have been filled with action, such as horse chases, fistfights, saloon free-for-alls, and runaway stagecoaches. These daring stunts added to the action and excitement of Western movies.

Westerns were driven by the principle that there should always be plenty of fights. Scripts called for saloon fights — preferably those that resulted in someone being thrown through a window into the street — and street fights, fights in stables around and under nervous horses, fights on top of speeding trains and runaway stagecoaches, on the edges of cliffs, in burning barns, or anywhere else that the scriptwriter or director could dream up. In the serials and singing Westerns of the 1930s and 1940s, fights were extended to airplanes, trucks, and modern machinery.

Fistfights have always been a mainstay of Westerns. Most of them were fights of epic proportions. The main character takes a punch from a villain that would fell an ox, then our hero jumps up, apparently unscathed, and returns a blow that would land a normal person in the hospital for weeks. Undaunted and unbloodied, the bad guy fights back, raining punches like a pile driver on the hero. And so the fight goes on.

Shootouts have also been a staple of the genre and include all sorts of variations, such as shooting from behind rocks, trees, water troughs (at one point in the final shootout in *Pale Rider* (1985), the Preacher (Clint Eastwood) actually shoots a bad guy from *inside* the water trough), hay bales, barns, and every other place conceivable. Another action element included chases of all types, such as posse chases, runaway horses, runaway stagecoaches, stampeding cattle, and runaway trains.

In the early days of moviemaking, Western stars and other players were expected to perform their own stunts. In the 1910s and 1920s, movies were laced with action, and stars might have to dangle from rooftops, hang from airplanes, and jump from fast-moving cars and trains. But as the movies and movie studios matured, these potentially dangerous feats of derring-do, such as falling off a horse or jumping off a cliff, were performed by stuntmen.

There were two reasons for this. The obvious is that though some movie stars were capable of performing dangerous stunts, many were not. So a stunt double who specialized in action would be used. A more important reason, however, was totally practical. If the star of a movie were to be injured during a stunt, filming might be shut down for weeks. The fixed costs of maintaining the rest of the cast and crew (which could cost up to $150,000 a day) would mount rapidly as the production idled while a star's broken arm or leg healed.

To be quite blunt about it, an injured stunt man could be replaced far more easily than an injured star. To compensate for this, stunt men were typically paid extra for individual stunts, such as specialized falls from a horse or building, or a body drag stunt where the stuntman falls from a horse and is dragged along the ground.

Early Westerns used dummies when performing some stunts. For example, a dummy was used during *The Great Train Robbery* (1903) to simulate the fireman being thrown off the train. In later Westerns, when directors and audiences demanded more realism in the action, stuntmen performed the falls and fistfights, and drove the runaway wagons.

Stunts were usually filmed in long shot, at a distance, or with the stunt double turning his face so that he would remain indistinguishable from the star. The action scenes with stuntmen were shot by the second unit director, while the first unit (with the main director) filmed the close-up and dialogue footage with the stars — often in a studio. The two sections of film were later edited together to form the complete narrative. This method had the advantage of speeding up production, as the second unit director could be filming doubles for the stars in long shots at the same time the stars were working on studio sets. It also carried the disadvantage of the two sections of film potentially failing to match well, with the stars acting awkwardly on a sound stage or in front of backgrounds that were rear-projected behind them.

In the cheaply-made B-Westerns, stunt men were sometimes dressed in the same clothes as the actor they were doubling, but the resemblance ended there. Other than the clothing, some of them looked quite different from the actor they were doing stunts for, sometimes even sporting a different hair color.

Popular stunts in B-Westerns often consisted of crashing or turning over a wagon during a chase, and horse falls, where the horse fell and the rider was thrown off into the dirt. Making the horse fall at the correct place and in the desired way was the responsibility of the stuntman. One of the early methods of achieving this was called the "Running W," in which wires connected to hobbles on the horse's legs were attached to a ring held by the rider. When the rider wanted to make the horse fall, he pulled on the ring (also called the "toe tapper") and tripped the horse. The rider was thrown off during the spectacular fall and hopefully made a relatively soft landing in a patch of dirt that had been dug up and prepared in the ground beforehand.[20]

Another technique to create spectacular horse falls was the "Stationary W," also known as the "Deadman's Fall." To perform this stunt, hobbles on the horse were attached to eighty or a hundred yards of piano wire that was connected to a buried post. When the running horse reached the limit of the wire, it tripped and fell head-first, catapulting the rider over its head as it fell.[21] This practice was outlawed in 1940 with pressure from the American Humane Society, because so many horses broke their necks or were otherwise injured during the fall and had to be destroyed. Now stuntmen create falls and other visually-exciting horse stunts with horses that have been specially trained to perform a particular trick. One horse by the name of Twister, in particular, could not do the tricks required of most movie horses, but at the tug of a rein could perform a spectacular twisting fall.[22]

Even though visually exciting, some stunts do not necessarily mirror reality. For example, when a stuntman is "shot" off a roof, he pitches forward off the front of the building in a slow fall for dramatic effect. In reality, the impact of a heavy-caliber rifle bullet would drive the body backwards — but that would push him out of sight of the camera. In the same line of dramatic effect, notice that when a stuntman is "shot" off a horse, often the horse falls, the rider pitches off, then the horse gets up and trots away unharmed.

### Yakima Canutt

One of the best-known stuntmen and second unit directors in the movie business was Yakima Canutt. Born Enos Edward Canutt in Colfax, Washington, near Yakima, he was a ranch hand, a Wild West show performer, and a championship rodeo rider of 1917 before becoming an actor in silent Westerns. He later became a premier stuntman. He received his film name of "Yakima" Canutt during his rodeo career after local newspapers labeled him "the Cowboy from Yakima."

Canutt started as an actor in silent films, often playing the villain, then went on to play similar villains in early sound pictures. His acting career failed to take off, so he concentrated on performing stunts. His acting experience helped him stage action scenes and film amazing stunts in a believable manner. As a result, he became the top stuntman and stunt coordinator at Mascot and Monogram, and later at Republic.[23] At Monogram, Canutt was a regular stuntman for John Wayne, and he helped Wayne learn both horsemanship and stunt brawling. Canutt also taught Gene Autry how to perform stunt fights. Canutt was an innovator in training horses to fall without being injured. Cliff Lyons, the stunt coordinator on many of John Ford's films, has also been credited with training horses to fall on cue instead of tripping them.[25]

*Stagecoach* (1939) contained several spectacular stunts orchestrated and performed by Canutt. One was when stagecoach driver Buck (Andy Devine) has been shot in the arm and loses two of the reins for the stage's three pairs of horses. Canutt, doubling for star John Wayne, leapt from the racing stage between the horses, jumped forward on the wagon tongue from each pair of horses to the next, and finally leapt onto one of the lead horses to retrieve the lost reins. In another daring stunt, Canutt, playing the part of an Indian, fell onto the stagecoach tongue, then slipped down between the horses, where he hung for a moment before he fell off and the stage passed over him.

A famous Yakima Canutt stunt was one he did on stagecoaches and wagons, typically during a fight on top of a careening, runaway vehicle.[26] To start the stunt, Canutt jumped or fell onto the horses pulling the galloping stagecoach. Then he dropped between the horses, hung onto the wooden tongue of the careening stage, released his hold, let the stage pass over him, grabbed a rope at the rear of the stage, pulled himself up, and clambered back onto the top of the stage. In one variation on this feat of daring (even for a stuntman) he went hand-over-hand underneath the stagecoach to the back, pulled himself up onto the back of the wagon or coach and resumed the fight.[27] Canutt developed this particular stunt for *Riders of the Dawn* (1937), during a chase across salt flats near Victorville, California. A similar stunt is seen in *Young Bill Hickok* (1940), where the stuntman takes a punch and falls onto the tongue of a racing wagon. He then falls off onto the ground, goes under the wagon, grabs a bar at the back, pulls himself up onto the wagon again, and gets the drop on one of the villains.

Canutt also developed the "pass system" of movie fighting. Before this method was introduced, the actors actually hit each other with their fists during a fight. The pass system uses camera angles, the positioning of the actors, and sound effects to create the illusion that a punch has connected, while the real blow actually sails through empty air, missing by a few inches.[28] In some of the low-budget B-Westerns these wide misses are obvious, as due to time constraints, scenes were rarely re-shot. In the climactic fight on the beach in *Apache Rose* (1946), for example, several swings visibly miss the victim, passing harmlessly — and obviously — in front of the intended recipient's face.

Canutt staged the action sequences in the film spectacles *Ben-Hur* (1959), *El Cid* (1961), and *The Fall of the Roman Empire* (1964). He won an Academy Award for staging the chariot race in *Ben-Hur* (1959).

## Special Effects and Process Photography

Through the use of movie magic, all is not always what it seems. Special effects are integral to making Western movies and are more commonly used than many moviegoers might suspect. The term "special effects" covers a wide range of illusions. Special effects and process photography can combine actors with a scene on a painting to produce a composite shot that creates the appearance of reality when it is not feasible to film the real setting. Special effects can also simulate the burning of an entire town, the derailing and crash of a railroad locomotive, or a group of men riding along a yawning chasm.

Process photography can be as complex as incorporating actors into impossible or dangerous locations or action, or can be as simple as combining actors speaking their lines on a sound stage with exterior background shots. Dialogue, for example, can often be recorded better on a sound stage than outdoors. The director might feel that it is easier to film the actors riding horses and conversing inside on a sound stage and later add a special-effects background that makes them appear to be out in the desert.

A painting is often combined with live action to create the illusion of the actors being somewhere else. Special effects in the early 1900s used what were called "glass shots" in which part of the desired scene, such as a ranch, mountains, or beautiful clouds, was painted on a piece of glass which was then placed in front of the camera. The painted glass was photographed at the same time as the action in the foreground to create the final image. This could, for example, be used to make an actor appear to be jumping his horse over a deep chasm. The chasm would be painted on the bottom of the glass placed in front of the camera lens, with the top of the glass left clear so that the actions of the actor could be photographed as he gallops across a flat meadow where, at the appropriate point, he makes his horse jump.

Matte paintings were an advance in filming that were used to achieve the same effect. The matte painting technique combined a painting of almost photographic quality in the background with live action by actors in the foreground. The "matte" was a mask that covered part of the camera field-of-view in order to leave part of the image black while the actors acted out their scene. Then, back at the studio, the film was rewound, the masked-off part of the lens was exposed, the area of the lens where the actors acted was masked off, and the film was re-exposed to a painting of the desired background. This double-exposure of the film combined the actors with the painted background.

An example of using a matte painting in a Western might be to show actors on horses traveling over a treacherous mountain pathway with a yawning drop-off beside them. This might be too dangerous or difficult to film on location, so a matte painting would be used. Of course, precise masking of the lens and registration of the film is required in order to achieve a believable and natural-looking result. This technique is called a stationary matte. In the film credits the artist who does this will be listed for "mattes" or "matte shots."

The process becomes more complicated when, rather than just adding a simple background, it is necessary to combine two or more separately photographed moving scenes into one final picture. This is done with a similar process called a traveling matte.

In essence, camera magic creates an image of each scene that contains a black, moving silhouette of the actors' motions. Several techniques can be used to create these black silhouettes for a traveling matte, but the most common today are the blue-screen or green-screen processes, which allow the creation of a corresponding traveling matte while the scene is being photographed. In this technique, the actors perform their scene in the studio in front of a blue screen. Blue was chosen because the color blue is rarely found on actors' faces or clothing. When re-photographed through an orange (the complementary color of blue) filter onto high-contrast film, the blue screen in the background turns to black but leaves the foreground action intact This image is then reversed to create a white background with a black silhouette of the desired action. When this is combined in an optical printer it is possible to place the images together. These silhouettes are used as moving mattes that allow each image to be combined without visually interfering with the other image or images when they are all placed on the final negative.

What made all this possible was the development of the optical printer. An optical printer is essentially a projector that projects an exposed piece of film into a camera, where it is re-photographed. In this way the optical printer allows several separately photographed images to be combined onto one piece of film by re-winding and re-exposing the master negative to each image separately before it is developed. The printer has to operate in a very accurate fashion to allow precise registration of all the images into one final composite negative. Optical printers are also used for other tasks, including various visual transitions, such as dissolves and fade-ins and fade-outs, and superimposing those blood-red titles and credits commonly used by Westerns in the 1950s. Readers wanting more than these brief descriptions can consult several good books on film technique.

Process photography is often used to avoid dangerous situations for the actors. This was the case in *The War Wagon* (1967) when Taw Jackson (John Wayne) and Billy Hyatt (Robert Walker) pack a bridge with nitroglycerine in order to blow it up and cut off a pursuing posse of stagecoach guards. Though they appeared to be dangling on beams over a deep gorge, through movie magic the two were only a few feet off the ground, with the image of the gorge added later through process photography. The same technique was used in *Mackenna's Gold* (1969) when Marshal Sam Mackenna (Gregory Peck) and the villainous gang led by Colorado (Omar Sharif) are crossing the swing bridge over a canyon on the way to find the lost gold. The deep chasm beneath them was added as a matte painting. In *Sergeants 3* (1962), the swinging bridge over the bottomless gorge that Sergeant Deal (Dean Martin) and Jonah (Sammy Davis, Jr.) cross to go to the "high country" was built about fifteen feet off the ground and was combined with a matte painting to create the illusion of the gorge.

Such scenes have to be carefully planned and photographed to make the painting and the live action blend together seamlessly. The correct perspective and lighting have to be carefully adjusted so that the final scene will not show any obvious defects, such as superimposing an actor on the wrong part of the screen. Most shots that use matte paintings are very brief in the final film so that the viewer does not detect the deception.

Two other systems were commonly used in the past to combine actors in a studio with an outdoor location: rear-screen projection and front projection. Rear-screen projection, which started to see extensive use in the 1930s, used a previously-filmed outside background scene (either static or moving) that was projected onto a translucent screen behind the actors as they acted out their scene in the foreground.

Rear projection fell into disfavor as improved film stock made the projected backgrounds look washed out and unreal. As a result, in the 1950s and 1960s, front projection

The two rocks at either side of this picture on Movie Flats in the Alabama Hills are notable because they were used as part of a scene over a deep gorge for the adventure movie *Gunga Din* (1939). The tops of the rocks are only about fifteen feet off the ground. A swing bridge was constructed between the two and then combined with special effects and clever camera angles to make it appear that the bridge was perched over a deep gorge.

started to be used. This system combines the actor's scene with a projected image that is reflected into the camera lens through a semi-reflective mirror placed in front of it, so that again the actors look like they are combined with the projected image. The camera and the projector for the background are synchronized in both the rear and front projection systems to ensure that there is no interfering flicker in the final image.

Some filmmakers feel that the front-projection system produces a sharper and more evenly lighted image than does rear projection.[29] Both techniques can be used to combine more than one image by using several projectors or by running the film several times through the camera or an optical printer to combine all the different images onto the final negative.

Today these types of scenes are shot using a fluorescent-green screen behind the actors, and the scenes are blended together with a computer.[30] Like the earlier blue, this color is rarely found on actors' faces and is easily recognized by the computer. The entire process is sometimes called "compositing," as the final result is a composite image. Film credits will be for "digital effects" or "digital compositing."

Although this all sounds complicated, the results are routinely found in almost all movies, whether they are Westerns or not. As one example in a Western, in *3:10 to Yuma* (2007) stagecoach guard Cyrus McElroy (Peter Fonda) shoots at a bundle of dynamite attached to one of the bandits' saddles. The resulting massive explosion, which eliminates the dynamite, rider, and horse, was produced by combining pieces of film containing the horse and the explosion to make it look like the rider was blown up. Similar optical techniques were used to intensify the explosion in the scene at the railroad tunnels when it looks as if the entire tunnel was blown up after the riders have raced through.

*Chapter Five*

# Location, Location, Location

Location shooting involves filming a picture in the outdoors, as opposed to on a sound stage or on a studio back lot. There is an old tongue-in-cheek saying in the real estate business that the three most important features for selling a house are location, location, and location. The locations where Western movies are filmed are of similar importance.

A major element of Western movies is the sweep and grandeur that can only be obtained by filming them at outdoor locations. The plains, the deserts, and the mountains of the West give these movies a majesty that emphasizes the American spirit of independence and pioneering. As film star John Wayne succinctly put it, "TV you can make on the back lot, but for the big screen, for the real outdoor dramas, you have to do it where God put the West."[1] The moviegoing public's perception of "the West," however, has been strongly shaped by the visual appearance of the locations used for filming each tale; and, interestingly, this perception has changed over the years as filmmakers sought out new locations to conform to their perception of how "the West" should look.

Audiences' tastes have always demanded spectacular outdoor scenery for Westerns. The promotional trailer for *Broken Arrow* (1950) trumpeted, "Photographed in the Last Primitive Western Locales," in large title lettering. The trailer for *Fury at Furnace Creek* (1948), which was filmed in the area around Kanab, Utah, advertised proudly that it was made on location instead of on a studio set — or "the artificial West of the motion picture studio," as the announcer disdainfully put it.

Since the beginning of Westerns and the movies of Broncho Billy Anderson, film companies have sought out what they considered to be better and better locations for filming. The California deserts and mountains were ideal for filming early Westerns; however, some of these locations were used so often that audiences grew to recognize them from film to film.

The western part of the United States, which is where the traditional "Western" is supposed to take place, consists of a wide variety of scenery, including such diverse landscapes as the flat, grassy plains of Kansas and Nebraska, the rolling, wooded foothills of the Black Hills of South Dakota, the prairies of eastern Montana, and the shimmering mountain peaks of Colorado, as well as the deserts of Utah, New Mexico, and Arizona. Colorado, for example, contains prairies in the eastern half of the state, lofty mountains in the center, and red-rock sandstone canyons on its western border. These elements are complemented by lakes, streams, rivers, forests, flower-strewn mountain meadows, and even an area with sand dunes that rise 750 feet. Utah contains a similar variety of scenery.

Yet, despite this variety of scenery in the West, Westerns have focused on the image of "the West" as the bleak and rugged canyon country of Utah and Arizona. In *My Darling Clemen-*

*tine* (1946), Wyatt Earp (Henry Fonda), seeing for the first time the country that in the movie was supposed to be around Tombstone, Arizona (though it was actually filmed in Monument Valley in Utah), comments to Ike Clanton (Walter Brennan), "Sure is rough-looking country!" What Earp was seeing and commenting on was not the western United States but "the West" as a mythic place that author John Hamilton has described as being "a timeless never-never land of great expectations and grand illusions."[2] This "movie West" is accepted as the red canyons and deserts of Utah and Arizona, and not the green mountains of Colorado.

The story of how moviegoers' perception of these lonely, bleak landscapes evolved to personify the West is reflected in the evolution of locations used in Western films. This phenomenon has shaped the image of "the West" in contemporary audiences' minds as barren and lonely deserts rather than the lush greenery of the East that appeared in the first Western movies. These rugged landscapes are what moviegoers feel "the West" should be like. When even the animated feature *Rango* (2011) wanted to depict the iconic West of the Westerns, the background setting was a cartoon version of Monument Valley.

To understand how this perception of "the West" changed over the years and arrived at this point, it is necessary to trace the history of early Western movies and the choices of location for filming them.

## The East as "The West"

The first Westerns, made in the early 1900s, were filmed in the East — because that is primarily where the studios making them were located. For obvious reasons, filmmakers used locations that were convenient to their places of business. As a result, the countrysides of New Jersey, New York, and Connecticut were popular locations. The location used to film *The Great Train Robbery* (1903), for example, was New Jersey. The scenery in the film featured landscapes characteristic of the East, such as trees, rivers, lakes, streams, lush woodlands, and grassy meadows. To audiences of the time, then, this was "the West."

In the winter of 1906, Harry Buckwalter and Max Aronson ("Broncho Billy" Anderson) of the Selig Polyscope Company filmed their first movie at an authentic Western location in the Rocky Mountains of Colorado and, in doing so, created the first "Western" movie.[3] Other established film companies, such as Biograph, soon followed to the West to shoot on authentic and scenic locations.[4] Though the biggest film manufacturers were located in the East, the big three moviemakers of the time, Vitagraph, Biograph, and Edison, made films in the West, with production performed by their Chicago film crews.[5] Selig also filmed in the area around Prescott, Arizona, producing gems with such odd titles as *The Policeman and the Baby* (1913) and *Cupid in the Cow Camp* (1913). Several Tom Mix Westerns were also filmed in the Prescott area.

"Bronco Billy" Anderson, who had meanwhile become a partner in Essanay Film Company in 1907, loved the West and filmed extensively in Golden, Colorado, and the surrounding Rocky Mountains.

## The Pacific Coast as "The West"

In 1908 Anderson relocated his Essanay film crew from Colorado to Niles, California, near San Francisco. Anderson liked to film in nearby Niles Canyon because of its wild and scenic look.[6] After 1910, Essanay Westerns were mostly produced around Niles, though Anderson also used locations all over the West as he searched for new scenery to film.

While filming "Westerns" outdoors in the East, and in the Rocky Mountains in the West, was easy in the summertime, one of the disadvantages was that filming could only take place for a limited number of months out of the year due to the weather. When winter and the snows arrived, outdoor filming in these locations essentially ground to a halt.

Movie companies quickly realized that the mild weather of southern California allowed movies to be filmed all year long. As a result, several film companies relocated crews to southern California to take advantage of the good weather. In the process they established Los Angeles as a center for moviemaking on the West Coast.

Another advantage of California was the almost constant sunshine. The photographic speed of movie film at the time was very slow and required high levels of lighting to produce the correct exposure. Artificial lighting for interior sets was expensive, so "interiors" were often filmed on sets that had no roof but were open to the bright sunshine above. The climate around Los Angeles was ideal for this.

When the weather in northern California turned cold in the fall, Anderson and his crew went to southern California to shoot. Like Anderson, Selig's film crews also looked for warm weather and bright sunshine so they could continue to film throughout the winter. In 1909 Selig converted a house into a studio in Edendale, an area northwest of downtown Los Angeles that was later known as Echo Park and Silver Lake.[7] The area around Edendale contained plenty of open space, along with woods, lakes, rivers, and buildings from California's Spanish past that were ideal for filming Westerns. The New York Motion Picture Company also opened a studio in Edendale, and the area became the center for filming Westerns, as well as the location of the first film processing lab in Los Angeles. Another important factor in the growth of the film industry in Edendale was that the town was easily reached from central Los Angeles by streetcar.

After 1911, most Westerns were filmed on the West Coast, so movies reflected a gradual change in background scenery from the lush woods of the East to the rocky deserts, grasslands, scrubby mountains, plains, and salt flats found around Los Angeles. The diversity and richness of the scenery was not lost on film crews, and made audiences aware of the narrowness of the scope of the "Wild West" of New Jersey. California scenery was here to stay.

By 1912, Selig Polyscope, New York Motion Picture, Kalem, Nestor, American, Pathé, and Essanay were all filming on the West Coast.[8] Up in Niles, Anderson built a full production facility in 1912 that consisted of an indoor studio with supporting carpentry shops, stables, and garages. When the studio was operating at maximum efficiency, Anderson could produce a film a day at a cost of around $700 to $800.

Meanwhile, Selig and Essanay continued to send production crews to other places in the West to find scenic and unphotographed locations for Westerns because they felt that original locations that had not been seen before on film made their movies seem more authentic. Filmmakers tended to seek locations in lush valleys, with lakes and rivers, such as would be found in the East and had been featured in the early Westerns.

Though Selig and Essanay were based in Chicago, they were two of the four most important companies making films in the West. The other two were the Biograph Company under D.W. Griffith, and the New York Motion Picture Company's Bison subsidiary under Thomas Ince. Selig was eventually absorbed by Vitagraph, which was in turn absorbed by Warner Bros. in 1925.

David Wark Griffith, who worked for the Biograph Company, went to California in 1910 to film because he liked the good weather and constant outdoor light that could be found there. He filmed in Los Angeles and also around Big Bear Lake in the San Bernadino Mountains northeast of Los Angeles, which was at the time a very remote location.[9] From January 1910 until he left Biograph in 1913 to work independently, D.W. Griffith wintered in southern California and returned to the company's home base in New York in April or May.[10] Between 1908 and 1913 Biograph made seventy-four Westerns. Biograph ceased production soon after Griffith left.

### New York Motion Picture Company and Inceville

New York Motion Picture Company was created when Adam Kessel and Charles Baumann, who ran their own film distribution and exhibition company, Empire Film Exchange, joined with Fred J. Balshofer to create a company to produce their own motion pictures.[11] After a period of modest success, they hired Thomas H. Ince, previously an actor, as manager to make films on the West Coast. There was a high demand at the time for cowboy movies, so the company started to produce Western films.

Ince leased several large tracts of land in the Santa Monica Mountains near Los Angeles from the Pacific Electric Railway, Santa Monica Mountain Parks, and Santa Monica Water and Power Company. In this way, New York Motion Picture Company eventually controlled eighteen thousand acres of scenic landscape for their exclusive use in filming Westerns. The area was characterized by small canyons and rolling grasslands that were ideal for portraying the contemporary perception of the West. At the mouth of Santa Ynez Canyon, just north of Santa Monica Bay at the edge of the Pacific Ocean, Ince built an elaborate outdoor studio, with several open air stages, a Western town set, a ranch set, and other buildings.[12] The complex had its own electric power plant and telephone system. The company even grew vegetables and raised cattle to feed the growing workforce of people employed there. The settlement later became known as Inceville. Ince eventually sold it to William S. Hart, who renamed the studio Hartsville.

In 1911, in another smart business move, Ince leased most of the *Miller Bros. 101 Ranch Wild West* show for $2,500 a week. The show was on tour in the West, but was wintering in Venice, California. The Miller Brothers show was created by Joseph, Zack, and George

The town of Inceville was created by Thomas Ince by the ocean at the mouth of Santa Ynez Canyon in the Santa Monica Mountains, west of Los Angeles. The town held elaborate sets and stages for filming Westerns, along with support buildings and services. Ince later sold the town to silent film star William S. Hart, who renamed it Hartsville. This view was taken in 1919 (Glenn Kinnaman Colorado and Western History Collection).

Miller, the sons of George W. Miller, the founder of a huge farming and ranching empire in Oklahoma, and Edward Arlington, a circus man. The show was one of several later rivals to *Buffalo Bill's Wild West* after Wild West shows became popular and others tried to copy Cody's popularity. Like Cody, the Millers wanted to keep a vision of the West alive, so they created a show built around their view of ranch life, featuring acts that consisted mostly of various types of riding and feats of horsemanship.[13]

So with one stroke of good business management Ince created instant access to seventy-five cowboys, twenty-five cowgirls, and thirty-five Indians, along with supporting oxen, buffalo, horses, stagecoaches, and wagons.[14] Ince produced a new series of Westerns under the trade name of "101 Bison," made with Miller Bros. riders and featuring stories created around the show's performers. Ince directed the first few films, then delegated the actual production to others while he retained creative control. Ince's plots were thin, but his movies were big on spectacle.

Out of all this came one of the giants of the motion picture industry. This was Universal, headed by Carl Laemmle. Laemmle opened his first nickelodeon in Chicago in 1906. He soon acquired a chain of movie houses and started his own exchange and film distribution company. He also founded the Independent Moving Pictures Company (IMP) in 1909 to make films to supply his own nickelodeons and distribution company. In 1912, New York Motion Picture Company, along with its Bison 101 subsidiary, merged into Universal Film Manufacturing Company, with Carl Laemmle as president.[15] Universal was the largest producer of Westerns in the 1920s.

Though the majority of filming for Westerns took place in southern California, other locations were also used. Ken Maynard's movies in the 1920s and 1930s, for example, were filmed on location in South Dakota, Arizona, Wyoming, and Montana, as well as in California. Tom Mix filmed extensively near Canon City in Colorado.

Multiple locations were usually used for most Westerns, depending on the director's and producer's tastes. *The Big Trail* (1930), starring John Wayne as Breck Coleman, for example, was filmed near Yuma, Arizona; St. George, Utah; Sequoia National Park; Moise National Buffalo Range in Montana; Grand Canyon National Park; Yellowstone National Park; Grand Teton National Park; Zion National Park; and Sacramento, as well as several other locations in California.

During the 1930s and 1940s most of the B-Westerns were filmed around Los Angeles, either on studio back lots or on their movie ranches. Other popular locations used were public outdoor locations around the Los Angeles area, such as Red Rocks Park and Griffith Park.

In the late 1950s and early 1960s, as well as the breakup of the studio system and smaller independent filmmakers going outside the studio system, audiences had discovered the beauty of locations outside California and clamored for more exotic Western outdoor locales. They were no longer content to watch phoney-looking rear projection, with actors mouthing their lines in front of a projection screen.

## Monument Valley

Of all the film locations for Westerns, arguably the one that is most often identified with "the West" by moviegoers is Monument Valley, a vast section of empty picturesque desert that lies on the Arizona-Utah border. Covering an area of about thirty thousand acres, the valley floor is dotted with spectacular rock formations. These are the hard rock layers that remained when softer sandstone and limestone eroded away and left a series of spectacular buttes, spires, and lofty pinnacles.[16] The brilliant red color of the rocks in the valley is due to the presence of iron oxides.

The greatest influence in creating the mindset that the deserts of Utah are "the West" was director John Ford. He made a series of popular Western movies in the valley, starting with *Stagecoach* (1939), that suggested the powerful images of scenic mesas and buttes that made up Monument Valley exemplified the iconic "West."[17]

*Stagecoach* (1939) was not Ford's first Western but his fiftieth. Over a fifty-three-year career, Ford made 220 films that included dramas, comedies, documentaries, and miscellaneous short subjects. In 1917 he directed a two-reel Western called *The Tornado* at Universal, and continued to direct Westerns for the rest of his career. He developed a cast of regular players that he liked to work with (often called the "John Ford stock company"), consisting of veteran actors such as Ward Bond, Ben Johnson, Victor McLaglen, Harry Carey, Jr., Grant Withers, and Hank Worden. Many of these ensemble actors also appeared in John Wayne's Batjac productions.

At the time that *Stagecoach* (1939) was made, Monument Valley was not an easy location for a film crew. It was about two hundred miles by road from the nearest rail connection, which was at Flagstaff, Arizona, and the existing roads, bridges, and telephone connections in the area were primitive at best. In 1955, at the time *The Searchers* (1956) was being made, the journey to Monument Valley involved a train ride from Los Angeles to Flagstaff, then a long ride on a bus to the filming location.

*Stagecoach* (1939) is always listed in popular movie histories as having been filmed in Monument Valley, but in reality only a few scenes of it appear in the released film. Though in lingering popular memory the scenery of Monument Valley seems to dominate *Stagecoach*, Ford filmed the few exterior scenes that were used in the movie in only four days in 1938, and they only last onscreen for about ninety seconds.[18] Other parts of the film were shot around Los Angeles and on the Goldwyn lot.[19] But this brief location shoot produced several stunning visual images, such as the stagecoach dashing across the floor of Monument Valley, with Merrick Butte and the Mittens in the background, that are still dramatic today.[20] Another spectacular outdoor location that appears in the film is Beale's Cut (Fremont Pass) in the San Fernando Valley north of Los Angeles. The sequence of the Indians chasing the stagecoach was shot on the bed of Lucerne Dry Lake near Victorville, California, with Yakima Canutt performing the daring stagecoach stunts.[21]

Ford went on to film six more Westerns in Monument Valley, which helped to confirm the image of this scenery as "the West." *Stagecoach* was followed by *My Darling Clementine* (1946), *Fort Apache* (1948), *She Wore a Yellow Ribbon* (1949), *The Searchers* (1956), *Sergeant Rutledge* (1960), and *Cheyenne Autumn* (1964).

The exteriors for *Fort Apache* (1948) were almost all filmed in Monument Valley and serve to enhance the story with dramatic images of rock formations and other scenery.[22] As a note of historical interest, Fort Apache was a real military fort in Arizona, originally known as Camp Ord.[23] The name was changed to Camp Apache as a gesture of friendship after a visit by Cochise. The post became Fort Apache in 1879 and was still in use in 1895.

Two of Ford's other Westerns, *Wagon Master* (1950) and *Rio Grande* (1950), are often thought to have been filmed in Monument Valley because of the similarity of the bluffs and other features in the two locations, but they were actually shot near Moab, Utah.

*The Searchers* (1956) is probably the most popular of Ford's Monument Valley films.

**Monument Valley in Utah represents the iconic "West" for generations of Western movie fans. This view shows Left Mitten on the left, Right Mitten in the center, and Merrick Butte on the right. "Hollywood Boulevard," seen in the foreground, was named because the dirt road was used in so many Westerns. This is the view from *Stagecoach* (1939) that showed the stagecoach and soldiers crossing the desert to Lordsburg, and brought fame to John Ford for using the valley as a film location.**

It was supposedly set in Texas in 1868, just after the end of the Civil War, but the exteriors were filmed almost entirely in Monument Valley. Shot in full color, *The Searchers* was one of the few films made using Paramount's VistaVision widescreen process. The interiors were shot at RKO-Pathé Studios in Culver City, and the final scenes of confrontation were filmed at Bronson Canyon in Hollywood.

Ford's Monument Valley films always contained a series of stunning images, such as Captain York (John Wayne) and Sergeant Beaufort (Pedro Armendariz) riding past Totem Pole Rock when looking for Cochise's camp in *Fort Apache* (1948). At the beginning of *The Searchers* (1956), as Martha Edwards (Dorothy Jordan) goes through the doorway of her cabin out into the sunlight, the camera tracks behind her out of the darkness and the viewer gradually sees the imposing formations of Mitchell Butte and Gray Whiskers out in the desert. Another stunning visual location used by Ford was Rock Door Canyon behind Goulding's Lodge, where the massacre of Colonel Thursday's (Henry Fonda) command by Indians was filmed for *Fort Apache* (1948).

One of the other iconic locations in Monument Valley is John Ford Point, a promontory of rock overlooking the valley. Towards the end of *The Searchers* (1956), Ethan Edwards

(John Wayne) and Captain Rev. Sam Clayton (Ward Bond) sneak up and view Scar's camp from John Ford Point. In the Western satire *The Villain* (1979), one of the opening shots in Monument Valley shows a lone rider going out to John Ford Point — before the action moves to Old Tucson Studios in Arizona.

One of the most spectacular sights in the valley is the view of the three rock formations — West (Left) Mitten, Merrick Butte, and East (Right) Mitten — that often appears in the background of movies, such as *Once Upon a Time in the West* (1968). The initial section of dusty, rutted dirt road that descends across the floor of the valley in front of the Mittens was used so much by Ford that it became known as "Hollywood Boulevard."

Though Ford is credited with discovering Monument Valley, he was not the first — or the only — director to film there. *The Vanishing American* (1925), made by George B. Seitz, was the first movie to use Monument Valley as a backdrop. Monument Valley was also used by Seitz for *Kit Carson* (1940), by King Vidor for *Billy the Kid* (1941), and by George Sidney for *The Harvey Girls* (1946). Monument Valley is seen in the final few moments of *How the West Was Won* (1962) after the climactic battle with bandits on the runaway train, when Zeb Rawlings (George Peppard) drives Lillith (Debbie Reynold) and his family to their new home in the West. The Mittens and some of the other iconic rock formations can be seen briefly in the background before the camera cuts to images of Lake Powell and the modern West.

It has been said that filmmakers didn't like to use what has been called "Ford's Valley" out of respect for Ford. Since Ford's death in 1973, however, Monument Valley has been used frequently for movies, television commercials, and advertising photographs.

The original promoter of Western movies in Monument Valley was a man named Harry Goulding, an ex-cowboy who raised sheep and traded with the Navajos living in the area. Goulding was a tall man, so the local Navajos called him *Dibé Nineez*, which loosely means "The long [tall] man with the sheep."[24]

Goulding was born in Durango, Colorado, in 1897. In 1923 Harry and his wife Leone (better known by her nickname of "Mike") moved to Monument Valley, to the base of Big Rock Door Mesa, to homestead 640 acres. They lived in a tent on the property until 1927 when they were able to build a two-story stone trading post that still stands today.

In an effort to promote the beauty of Monument Valley to the movie industry and bring some business to the area, Goulding went to Los Angeles in 1938 with a portfolio of twenty-four black-and-white photographs by noted Western landscape photographer Josef Muench. In Hollywood, Goulding made a pitch to independent producer Walter Wanger and John Ford, who were in pre-production for *Stagecoach* (1939). The result was that executives from United Artists, who were backing the film, approved filming backgrounds in Monument Valley for the picture.

The Gouldings eventually built a lodge to house the filmmakers who came to work in the area. Some scenes from Ford's films were shot right at or in front of Goulding's Lodge. In *She Wore a Yellow Ribbon* (1949), for example, the exterior of the real Goulding's trading post building was used as the post headquarters. The cabin with rock walls that was the home of Nathan Brittles (John Wayne) was a small building used by the Goulding's as a potato cellar, located right behind the Gouldings' trading post. As the camera moves back and forth between the post headquarters and the stone cabin in the movie, the view is just the same as it is today, except that now the parking lot has been paved. Scenes of the interior of the cabin were filmed on a Hollywood sound stage.

At the beginning of *Fort Apache* (1948), when Colonel Thursday (Henry Fonda) arrives to take over the fort, his stagecoach pulls up a dusty hill and stops in front of Goulding's

The exterior of this stone building that served as a potato cellar behind Goulding's Lodge in Monument Valley was pressed into service to portray the living quarters for Captain Nathan Brittles in *She Wore a Yellow Ribbon* (1949). The interior of the cellar was not filmed, and the inside scenes were shot in a Hollywood studio.

Lodge, which briefly played the part of the stagecoach station. The subsequent interior scenes inside the station were shot on a sound stage in Hollywood.

Goulding ran his trading post in Monument Valley with Mike from 1925 to 1963, when they retired and moved to Arizona. Harry died in 1981, Mike in 1992.

There are several other versions of how Monument Valley was "found" for Western movies. John Ford's nephew said that actor Harry Carey told Ford about it after Carey explored Navajo country in the 1920s. John Wayne claimed that he had found it and told Ford about it when Wayne was working on a George O'Brien film in 1929.[25] Ford claimed to have found Monument Valley on his own, either when driving across Arizona to Santa Fe, New Mexico, or when he discovered it on the location scout for *Stagecoach* (1939).[26]

## Other Popular Movie Locations in Utah

Western movies have also been filmed at several other locations in the area around Monument Valley, such as Kayenta, Arizona, to the southwest of the main valley. Ford himself filmed in other nearby areas in Utah. For instance, *The Searchers* (1956) and *Sergeant Rutledge* (1960) utilized locations on the San Juan River near Mexican Hat, about twenty miles to the northeast of Monument Valley.

### Moab

North and east of Monument Valley in east-central Utah is Moab, which contains scenery similar to that found in Monument Valley. Moab is a versatile area for filming West-

The scenes of the cavalry crossing the river for *Rio Grande* (1950) and *She Wore a Yellow Ribbon* (1949) and the river scene in *The Searchers* (1956) were filmed on the San Juan River near Mexican Hat, Utah, about twenty miles northwest of Monument Valley.

erns as it contains a variety of scenic locations, from spruce and aspen forests in nearby Manti-La Sal National Forest, to the red rocks of Arches National Park just to the north of town, and the dramatic canyons of nearby Canyonlands National Park. The town of Moab flourished as a support center for films crews by providing catering, lodging, extras, and stock, such as horses, cattle, oxen, and the wagons they pulled.

Among the many Westerns filmed near Moab are *Wagon Master* (1950), *Rio Grande* (1950), *The Battle at Apache Pass* (1952), *The Siege at Red River* (1953), *Taza, Son of Cochise* (1954), *Fort Dobbs* (1958), *Warlock* (1959), *Cheyenne Autumn* (1964), *Rio Conchos* (1964), *Wild Rovers* (1971), and *Geronimo: An American Legend* (1993). The river sequences for *The Searchers* (1956), *She Wore a Yellow Ribbon* (1949), and *Rio Grande* (1950) were shot at Mexican Hat. The winter scenes in *Cheyenne Autumn* (1964) were filmed around Gunnison, Colorado, to simulate the harsh conditions that the Cheyenne had to endure at Fort Robinson, Nebraska.

Ford's *Wagon Master* (1950) was filmed to the northeast of Moab in Castle Valley and Professor Valley, at scenic Fisher Towers, and at White's Ranch (now Red Cliffs Lodge) on Highway 128. *Rio Grande* (1950) was shot in Professor Valley. A movie fort built near Locomotive Rock in Professor Valley for *Rio Grande* (1950) was later used for *The Siege at Red River* (1954). The fort was built on a private ranch and has long since been demolished.

The Mexican village in *Rio Grande* (1950) was also built in Professor Valley. The Spanish Village seen in *The Comancheros* (1961) was built near Fisher Towers, then was burned down as part of the movie. Fort San Carlos, which was constructed for *Geronimo: An American Legend* (1993), was built on private property and dismantled after production was complete.

### Kanab

In 1949 the small town of Kanab, located in southwest Utah, was dubbed "Utah's Hollywood" by *Life* magazine because of the many Westerns that were filmed in the area. The town and surrounding Kane County were also known as "Little Hollywood" because more than a hundred movies were made in the area.

Moviemaking flourished in Kanab in the 1930s and 1940s after brothers Chauncey, Whit, and Gronway Parry persuaded Hollywood filmmakers to use the surrounding area to make Westerns. The brothers provided them with an integrated package of housing at their Parry Lodge, location scouting, transportation, and on-site catering for cast and crew, along with extras, livestock, stock wranglers, and Western props from the town. Kanab Canyon, just north of town, and Johnson Canyon, about ten miles east of town, were

Many outdoor movie sets fell into disrepair as the filming of Westerns decreased. This movie-set town in Johnson Canyon, near Kanab, Utah, was used for episodes of the television series *Gunsmoke, Have Gun Will Travel,* and others.

popular filming locations, and were used for many serials and television productions into the 1950s. *The Great Adventures of Wild Bill Hickok* (1938), the serial that gave star "Wild Bill" Elliott his nickname, was filmed in both canyons.

MGM built a studio outside Kanab in the 1940s. In 1943, 20th Century–Fox built a large, full-sized fort in upper Johnson Canyon on BLM land for the filming of *Buffalo Bill* (1944). The structure, nicknamed "Fort Wellman" after William Wellman, the director of the movie, was used for many years for other productions, such as *Sergeants 3* (1962), until it was finally demolished and removed.

Another fort was built on private land, just southwest of town, in 1953 for the filming of *Fort Bowie* (1954). This fort, too, was used for many movies until it was so damaged by a spectacular explosion in 1978 during the filming of *The Apple Dumpling Gang Rides Again* (1979) that it was never repaired.

A derelict movie set that still stands in Johnson Canyon was used for the exteriors for more than twenty episodes of the television Western *Gunsmoke*, which played from 1955 to 1976. North of town, in Kanab Canyon, is the barn built by Walt Disney Productions for *One Little Indian* (1973). The structure is still being used today to shelter horses.

Frontier Movie Town in downtown Kanab contains several buildings from movies shot in the area. The scenes in *The Outlaw Josey Wales* (1976) in which the motley group Wales (Clint Eastwood) has attracted homesteads by the river were filmed in Kanab Canyon, north of Kanab. After filming was completed, the adobe homestead building (actually made from sprayed fiberglass painted a tan color to look like weathered adobe) was moved to Frontier Movie Town as a tourist attraction.

Other scenes in *The Outlaw Josey Wales* (1976) were filmed in the 1,200 acres of Coral Pink Sand Dunes State Park, which is about ten miles west of Kanab. So were parts of the Civil War drama *A Time for Killing* (1967).

As an additional feature of interest to movie fans, locations for filming *Escape from Fort Bravo* (1953) were near Kanab and in Death Valley in California, along with some exterior scenes shot on a Hollywood set. In one sequence the cavalry is seen riding in the red rocks country of Utah, then gallops briefly across the floor of Death Valley, and then rides round the red-rock bluffs to appear near Kanab again.

### Paria

Paria Canyon, about thirty-five miles east of Kanab, north of U.S. Highway 89, is another location that has been frequently used for filming Westerns. Among others, the canyon and its later movie-set town appeared in parts of *Western Union* (1941), *Sergeants 3* (1962), *Mackenna's Gold* (1969), and *The Outlaw Josey Wales* (1976).

Early settlers founded the town of Pahreah in the canyon, looking for a reliable source of water, fertile land, and good grazing for their cattle. Overgrazing by sheep and cattle rapidly killed off the grass, and the town declined. By 1892 only eight families still lived there. By 1915 the post office had closed, and by the early 1930s the Pahreah Town Site had become a ghost town.

In the 1950s and 1960s Hollywood discovered the beauty of the canyon. A movie was set built in 1962 close to the historic ghost town for *Sergeants 3*. After the movie was completed, the set was abandoned and started to disintegrate. It was later restored and used for scenes in *The Outlaw Josey Wales* (1976), which was the last time that standing set was used for a movie. Another movie filmed near Paria was *Duel at Diablo* (1966). *Mackenna's Gold*

(1969) was partially shot in Paria and also in Kanab Canyon, as well as in Monument Valley and Bryce Canyon National Park. The canyon where the men finally find the gold was created by spray-painting part of the wall of Paria Canyon with gold paint.

Over the years, the buildings of the movie set at Paria were partially restored, torn down, threatened by flash flooding, rebuilt, and finally burned down completely by vandals on August 25, 2006. The picturesque rock formation behind the former location of the movie set, seen in the background of movies filmed there and which towers over the now-deserted area, is called the Cockscomb.

### Grafton

As well as Paria, some of the other Utah movie locations utilized by filmmakers have authentic historical backgrounds. One example is the small ghost town of Grafton, a few miles south of Zion National Park in southwest Utah. Grafton was originally settled by pioneers in 1861 and is an authentic town with a schoolhouse and several private homes that date from the 1860s, 1870s, and 1880s. The original settlers soon found out, though, that the sandy soil in the area was not suitable for growing crops. The last residents left in 1945.

The scenic quality of Grafton, complemented by the spectacular cliffs of Zion National Park in the background, attracted director Raoul Walsh from Fox Studios in 1929 to film *In Old Arizona*, a story of the adventures of the Cisco Kid. The success of the movie brought Walsh back to Grafton the next year to shoot *The Arizona Kid* (1930), which he filmed entirely on location. In 1947 director Andre de Toth partially shot *Ramrod* (1947) in Grafton because of the scenic background of Zion National Park. He used the little town's main street for the final shootout.

Several other movies were filmed around Grafton, often using Rockville Road, which runs between Grafton and the nearby town of Rockville. Probably the most well-known movie shot in Grafton was *Butch Cassidy and the Sundance Kid* (1969), which used the town as a major location.

## The Rocky Mountains

Colorado was popular for filming early Westerns, with Bronco Billy Anderson choosing it as a favorite location for many of his movies. Tom Mix made use of scenic locations around Canon City in central Colorado from 1911 until 1917, when Selig Polyscope went out of business. Mix filmed numerous movies in Colorado and the West. He particularly liked shooting in national parks, as he wanted to show off the natural wonders of the West to his audiences.

A few of the scenes from the Western comedy *The Duchess and the Dirtwater Fox* (1976) were filmed at Buckskin Joe, which was a combination tourist attraction and permanent Western film set built in 1957 about eight miles west of Canon City. The town has an interesting history because it is a manufactured historical town. The buildings are authentic, but they were moved to Buckskin Joe from other locations in Colorado to create the movie town. Over the years the town setting has appeared in various productions, including *The Cowboys* (1972). The entire town was sold to a private party in 2010 and is currently no longer open as a tourist attraction.

Scenes from the comedy Western *Cat Ballou* (1965) were filmed at Buckskin Joe. The ranch setting in *Cat Ballou* (1965) was in the Wet Mountain Valley near Westcliffe, Colorado,

Many Westerns required a town as one of their settings. This is the movie set town of Buckskin Joe in Colorado, a combination tourist attraction and filming location that was used for the background of many movies, including *The Cowboys* (1972) and *Cat Ballou* (1965). In 2010 the town was purchased by a private individual and closed to the public.

about thirty miles southwest of Canon City, with the rugged Sangre de Cristo Mountains prominently visible in the background. The railroad scenes used the Denver & Rio Grande railroad alongside the Arkansas River near Canon City.

In the same general area, *Saddle the Wind* (1958) was filmed at the ghost town of Rosita, also in the Wet Mountain Valley. Unlike Buckskin Joe, Rosita (whose name means "little rose" in Spanish) was an authentic historical Western town that was founded in 1861 as a result of silver mining in the area. The town, complete with a history of gunfighting and lynchings, was inhabited by about 1,200 people until 1881, when a disastrous fire burned most of the town. It was never fully rebuilt. For many years the town took on the authentic look of a ghost town — which it was — until Hollywood found it and made it look even *more* authentic than it was when people lived there. Metro-Goldwyn-Mayer rearranged the positions of some of the old buildings, built several new buildings (constructed to match the old ones), and added features such as signs and hitching rails to fit the set designer's conception of the town. Unfortunately, like the movie set at Paria in Utah, vandals set the remaining buildings on fire, and today basically nothing remains except the site.

*The Naked Spur* (1953) was filmed in the Rocky Mountains near Silverton, Colorado, with the green aspen forests of the mountains contrasting beautifully with the snow-covered peaks in the background.

Much of the original *True Grit* (1969) was filmed in Colorado. The scenes set in Fort Smith, Arkansas, were filmed in the little town of Ridgeway, Colorado, and used many of the authentic old buildings (with a few added movie trimmings). The final climactic shootout, in which Rooster Cogburn (John Wayne) thunders across the screen shooting at Ned Pepper (Robert Duvall) and the other baddies with rifle and revolver, was filmed in a meadow at an elevation of 10,000 feet near the summit of Owl Creek Pass, to the east of Ridgeway. Incidentally, though the plot is set in 1880, Pepper is shooting with a Colt double-action revolver that had not yet been invented.

A popular attraction for filmmakers in Colorado is the Durango & Silverton Narrow Gauge Railroad, which has appeared in numerous movies, including *A Ticket to Tomahawk* (1950), which was filmed at the Silverton end of the line; *Night Passage* (1957); *The Naked Spur* (1953); *Around the World in Eighty Days* (1956); and *Butch Cassidy and the Sundance Kid* (1969). The Durango and Silverton train is a narrow-gauge period steam railway which was built in 1881 by the Denver & Rio Grande Railway Company (D&RG) as a working railroad to transport passengers and freight around the area. The train runs today as a tourist attraction in the summer between Durango and Silverton, an authentic historical silver mining town in the mountains forty-five miles to the north. Depending on the amount of snowfall, it runs part of the way in the winter.

*Denver and Rio Grande* (1952) was based on fact and was filmed on location using the Durango & Silverton Narrow Gauge Railroad. The story of the film loosely combines several real-life incidents that occurred when survey crews from General Palmer's D&RG battled with the Atchison, Topeka & Santa Fe Railroad for the right of way across Raton Pass from Trinidad, Colorado, south to Raton, New Mexico, and on to El Paso. Mercenaries were hired by both sides to protect their rights-of-way and to prevent the other railway from grading a railbed through the canyon, and an armed confrontation actually took place between the rival railroads. The final fight, however, turned out to be bloodless and was eventually settled in the courts.

At the same time, the two railroads were also fighting for the right-of-way through the Royal Gorge, west of Canon City, Colorado, to the rich silver-mining town of Leadville. The resulting agreement was that each railroad won one battle. The D&RG agreed to stop building over Raton Pass, and the Atchison, Topeka & Santa Fe Railroad gave up their plans to build to Leadville.

The movie blurred the two incidents and put the armed confrontation in the Royal Gorge, but filmed it on the Durango & Silverton, north of Durango, where the production company built a small movie set alongside the existing railroad track. In the movie the competition for the D&RG was the fictional Cañon City and San Juan railroad. One of the most spectacular parts of the film comes when two locomotives collide. Two real, full-size railroad engines from the D&RG were used for the stunt and were crashed head-on on July 17, 1951. Both engines were totally wrecked in the collision and were eventually dismantled for scrap.

Uncredited stars of many Westerns are the historic railway engines and cars from the railroad museum at Jamestown, California. This was the location of the headquarters and maintenance shops for the Sierra Railroad Company from 1897 to 1955. The Sierra railway is also known as "the Movie Railroad" because its remaining rolling stock and stations have appeared in over two hundred film and television productions. The railroad is now maintained by the State of California as Railtown 1897 State Historic Park. The vintage engines and railroad cars, the remaining railroad line, and the old station at Jamestown have been a fixture of railroad movie scenes for many years. The engines and cars have replaceable shingles with the names of various real and fictional railroads on them so that the trains

**Vintage railroad engines and passenger cars are used in Westerns to add excitement to stories. The Denver & Silverton Narrow Gauge Railroad has appeared in many Westerns, including *Denver and Rio Grande* (1952) and *Butch Cassidy and the Sundance Kid* (1969). The railway also operates in the summer as a tourist ride from Durango to Silverton, Colorado.**

can appear to belong to many different railroads to meet script demands. Among other Westerns, the Sierra railway has appeared in *Dodge City* (1939), *3:10 to Yuma* (1957), *Man of the West* (1958), *The Rare Breed* (1966), *Pale Rider* (1985), *Unforgiven* (1992), and *Bad Girls* (1994). The railway continues to be used for filming today.

Many other parts of the Rocky Mountains have provided scenic backgrounds for Western stories. Location filming for *Shane* (1953), for example, took place in the Jackson Hole valley, north of Jackson, Wyoming, with the magnificent snow-capped peaks of the Teton Mountains in the background.

## The Rest of the West

Though Monument Valley is usually the location most often identified with "the West," many other places in the real West have been used for filming movies. The following are some of the common ones that will be easily recognized by Western film buffs. Some of them are the traditional desert-type locations, and some offered greener and more mountainous terrain.

National parks, national monuments, and national forests have been popular film locations. *Ride the High Country* (1962), for example, was filmed in Inyo National Forest in California. Uncompahgre National Forest in Colorado, Bryce Canyon National Park in Utah, and Black Canyon National Park are just a few more examples of popular filming locations in the West. *The Far Country* (1955), set against the Klondike gold rush of 1898 in Canada, was filmed in Jasper National Park in Alberta, Canada. *Open Range* (2004) was filmed near Calgary in Alberta, Canada.

Another desert location that has been used for Westerns is Valley of Fire State Park, fifty-five miles northeast of Las Vegas, Nevada. It was used as a filming location for *The Ballad of Cable Hogue* (1970), and for the scenes set in the red-rock canyons of *The Professionals* (1966). *The Shootist* (1976) was filmed in Carson City and on the back lot at Warner Bros.' Burbank studio.

The alkali waters of Mono Lake, just to the east of Yosemite National Park and Lee Vining, California, formed the scenic backdrop for the town of Lago seen in *High Plains Drifter* (1973). *Pale Rider* (1985) was filmed in the Sawtooth Mountain of Idaho.

*McCabe and Mrs. Miller* (1971) is set in the Northwest, in turn-of-the-century Washington. The story takes place in the town of Presbyterian Church, which is a cluttered town where "wretched people live out their wretched existences."[27] The depiction of the town is quite authentic for that sort of town in that type of location. The streets are covered with mud, snow, and water, are bordered by half-built structures with lumber lying around them on the ground, and are littered with trash and rubble. The location used for the film was actually in Canada in a town that was built as a movie set.

*Paint Your Wagon* (1969) was also filmed in the Northwest, near Baker, with the national forests of Oregon standing in for the Forty-Niner country of the Sierra Nevada Mountains of California. Director Joshua Logan and producer Alan Jay Lerner filmed it there because they couldn't find a suitable area in California that was untouched by signs of civilization. *The Virginian* (1929) was filmed in Sonora in the High Sierras in the original Forty-Niner country.

## New Mexico

During the 1930s, Gallup, New Mexico, was a popular center for Western productions, with the stars staying at the El Rancho Inn. *The Man from Laramie* (1955), *Cowboy* (1958), *Silverado* (1985), and *Wyatt Earp* (1994) were all filmed on private movie ranches in the Santa Fe area. The J.W. Eaves Movie Ranch, south of Santa Fe, is a cattle ranch that was later used for filming *The Cheyenne Social Club* (1970), *Silverado* (1985), and *Wyatt Earp* (1994). Some of the location filming for *Hang 'Em High* (1968) took place near Las Cruces and at White Sands National Monument. Some of the scenes from *My Name Is Nobody* (1973) were also filmed at White Sands National Monument, and on the old main street of the little ghost town of Mogollon, New Mexico.

*Young Guns* (1988), one of the many re-tellings of Billy the Kid and the Lincoln County War, was partially filmed in Cerillos. Some of the existing buildings in the town were painted to look like the 1878 town of Lincoln, including the Wortley Hotel and the L.G. Murphy store.

*Death Valley*

The barren wastes of Death Valley National Park on the California-Nevada border have always been a favorite dramatic filming location. Portions of *Escape from Fort Bravo* (1953), *The Bravados* (1958), *The Law and Jake Wade* (1958), and *The Professionals* (1966) were filmed there. Death Valley was the location for stories in the television series *Death Valley Days*, which ran for an amazing 452 episodes on television between 1952 and 1975.

*Lone Pine*

To the west of Death Valley is the little town of Lone Pine, California, and the Alabama Hills, which were named for a Civil War battleship. The Alabama Hills, marked by characteristic huge rounded boulders, will be immediately recognizable to fans of the movies as the background for many B-Westerns and serials. Almost four hundred movies, television shows, and commercials have been filmed in the area. Conservative estimates are that probably over three hundred Westerns have been filmed in the Alabama Hills. The area will also be instantly recognizable to Hopalong Cassidy fans for the stories filmed there, as well as many of the Westerns of Roy Rogers and Gene Autry. The flat floor of the valley, appropriately named Movie Flats, was ideal for filming running inserts from a camera car or truck. Some Westerns were shot so economically — with no time for retakes — that tire tracks from the camera car can be seen in the foreground — for example, in *Showdown* (1963) as riders race through the sagebrush.

The earliest Western filmed in the Alabama Hills was *The Round Up* (1920), starring comedian Fatty Arbuckle, in his first feature film, as Sheriff Slim Hoover. Another early Western filmed in the Alabama Hills was *Riders of the Purple Sage* (1925), starring the ubiquitous Tom Mix. Typical of the B-Westerns filmed in the area was *Wild Horse Mesa* (1947), which starred Tim Holt. Later Westerns, such as *The Law and Jake Wade* (1958) and *Joe Kidd* (1972), were partially filmed there as well. The terrain was so varied that it served as the village of Tantrapur in northern India for *Gunga Din* (1939) — with the Sierra Nevada mountains behind standing in for the Himalayas — and as Africa for two Tarzan movies.

One of the features that makes this such a dramatic location for filming is the spectacular east face of Mt. Whitney, located about fourteen miles away in the background and frequently filmed for best dramatic effect when snow covers the towering peak.[28]

*The Santa Monica Mountains*

The Santa Monica Mountains, which start just a few miles west of Los Angeles and north of Santa Monica Bay along the Pacific Coast, were a popular site for studio movie ranches, one of the earliest being Inceville in 1912.

In November 1927, Paramount purchased 2,700 acres of Rancho Las Virgenes, south of Agoura, California, to use as a location for filming Westerns. The property continued to be used as a movie ranch well into the television era. Among the many pictures shot there were *Under the Tonto Rim* (1928), *The Texas Rangers* (1936), and *Wells Fargo* (1937). The ranch also substituted for exotic locations in non–Westerns, such as *The Adventures of Marco Polo* (1938) and *Beau Geste* (1939). Paramount sold the ranch in 1943. The property subsequently went through several owners, being divided and sub-divided, until the remaining 750 acres was purchased by the National Park Service in 1980. Between 1992 and 1997 the Western town on the property was used as the location of the Colorado mining town where the lead character of *Dr. Quinn, Medicine Woman* lived. Incidentally, the television series was loosely based on the life of Susan Anderson, a real-life physician who lived for many years in Fraser, Colorado, in the early 1900s, caring for the local lumberjacks, miners, ranchers, and railroad workers.

## Los Angeles

Los Angeles and Hollywood were the primary locations for filming many Westerns because the major studios had back lots that contained standing Western towns. Many of the buildings were dressed so that it was possible to shoot interiors in them and save the expense of building a duplicate indoor set on a sound stage.

By the late 1930s, most studios had a ranch of at least twenty acres. Most were located in the Santa Monica Mountains west of Hollywood. The RKO ranch was in Reseda. Paramount's ranch was near Agoura. MGM was in Thousand Oaks. 20th Century–Fox's ranch was in the Santa Monica Mountains. The Disney Ranch was near Santa Clarita, though the studio also had a Western street on their back lot in Burbank. The Columbia Ranch was small but had a small town on it. Hadleyville, the town in *High Noon* (1952), was filmed on a Western street at the Columbia Ranch in Burbank. *High Noon* also used the real California towns of Columbia and Tuolumne for filming.

Melody Ranch at Newall was first used as a film location in 1915 for Monogram Studios. Later, portions of *Tumbling Tumbleweeds* (1935), *Stagecoach* (1939), and *High Noon* (1952) were filmed there.

Many of the studio lots were "recycled" over the years. For example, Mascot Studios was originally built by Mack Sennett in 1928. When Mascot and Republic merged, the lot was used by Republic, then was purchased by CBS television, who rented it out to independent production companies such as Four Star Television and MTM (Mary Tyler Moore) Enterprises. Among other productions, the lot saw service for the television series *Rawhide* and *The Wild Wild West*.

Some independent movie ranches, such as the Iverson Ranch and Corriganville in California, were not part of any studio and could be rented by anyone. Pioneertown was a Western movie set near Palm Springs, backed by Hollywood investors, including Roy Rogers, Russell Hayden, and Dick Curtis. Many Gene Autry films were shot there.

Other popular settings used by early filmmakers north of the Hollywood area were Red Rock Canyon State Recreation Area, Vasquez Rocks County Park, Placerita Canyon State and County Park, and Wildwood Park in Thousand Oaks. The canyons, streambeds, upturned red rocks, and bush-covered hills of these parks were ideal for Westerns involving horse chases, stagecoach robberies, and Indian attacks. A popular location even closer to Hollywood was Bronson Canyon Quarry, a steep-sided, rock-strewn canyon in Griffith Park that was used in filming many Westerns. The visual qualities of these locations helped to define the image of "the West" as portrayed in B-Westerns.

## Old Tucson Studios

Arizona, and in particular the movie-set town of Old Tucson Studios, has been used as a location for many films. Old Tucson, like Monument Valley, appears familiar from so many Western movies that its landscape also characterizes "the Old West." The town is

**Some popular movie locations are readily recognized by fans of Westerns. The movie-set town of Old Tucson Studios, west of Tucson, Arizona, is dwarfed by its identifying landmark of Golden Gate Peak towering behind it. The movie town and set is located in the Sonoran Desert and can also be easily recognized by the presence of the huge saguaro cactus (shown in the foreground), which only grows in very limited locations in the United States.**

located in the Sonoran Desert, west of Tucson, Arizona, in one of the few spots where the saguaro cactus grows naturally, thus helping to make the area instantly identifiable. Another readily identifiable landmark is Golden Gate Peak, the characteristic pointed mountain which is seen in the background of many Western movies filmed at Old Tucson Studios.

Old Tucson Studios was originally built in 1939 on a 320-acre plot of land leased from Pima County by Columbia Studios as the set for the movie *Arizona* (1940). The set was built as an exact replica of Tucson in the 1860s, which was the setting for the book the movie was based on. After filming was completed, the set was abandoned and the empty buildings sat deteriorating in the elements. In 1946 the Tucson Jaycees took over the property and started to repair it, leasing it out to movie companies to raise funds.

In 1959, Bob Shelton, a developer from Kansas, took over the property and turned it into a tourist attraction. He also built production facilities, including a large sound stage, in the town and leased it as a filming location to movie companies. Rooflines and porches on some buildings on the set could be changed to give buildings a different appearance for different movies. One building in Old Tucson was built so that it looked like four different structures, depending on which side was being photographed.[29]

Among the many productions that were at least partially filmed at Old Tucson Studios were *Winchester '73* (1950), *Gunfight at the O.K. Corral* (1957), *Rio Bravo* (1959), *McLintock!* (1963), *El Dorado* (1967), *Rio Lobo* (1970), *Wild Rovers* (1971), *The Villain* (1979), and *¡Three Amigos!* (1986). Television productions filmed at the studios include *Little House on the Prairie* and *The High Chaparral*.

### Mescal

Another filming location near Tucson is the town of Mescal. In 1969, Cinema Center Films, shooting *Monte Walsh* (1970) at Old Tucson Studios, needed a second location that looked like the Northern Plains. They built a movie-set town called Harmony about thirty miles east of Tucson. After filming was completed, the town was sold to Old Tucson Studios. Among other movies, the highly fictionalized *The Life and Times of Judge Roy Bean* (1972) and *The Quick and the Dead* (1995) were filmed there, and a replica of the town of Tombstone was built there for *Tombstone* (1993). Mescal is still used for filming and is currently not open to the public.

### Sedona

The area around the town of Sedona, off Interstate 17 twenty-five miles south of Flagstaff, Arizona, contains scenic red rock formations that draw tourists from around the world. They also drew Hollywood filmmakers, who shot there such movies as *Riders of the Purple Sage* (1931), *Billy the Kid* (1941), *Angel and the Badman* (1947), *Broken Arrow* (1950), *Flaming Feather* (1951), and *3:10 to Yuma* (1957).

## Mexico and Spain

Because the viewing public perceived the deserts of Utah and Arizona to be "the West," the similarly bleak and barren deserts of Mexico and Spain became popular as movie locations.

*The Magnificent Seven* (1960) was filmed in Cuernavaca, Mexico. *The Bravados* (1958) was shot in the gorges and mountains of Yucatan and Jalisco. John Wayne filmed a series of seven formula Westerns in Durango, Mexico, between 1964 and 1972. They were *The Sons of Katie Elder* (1965), *The War Wagon* (1967), *The Undefeated* (1969), *Chisum* (1970), *Big Jake* (1971), *The Train Robbers* (1973), and *Cahill — United States Marshal* (1973). He was John Wayne playing Duke Wayne, which was exactly what his audiences wanted to see. Durango made a fine background for these movies because, at the time, it was still primitive, unspoiled, and isolated, which made the location ideal for making Westerns.

*Two Mules for Sister Sara* (1970) was also filmed in Mexico. This movie contains a good example of the old Western movie cliché of a mountain lion making snarling noises. Mountain lions in the wild don't scream or snarl before they attack. As an animal who hunts by stealth and makes a fast, silent run at its prey to trap it before it escapes, it makes no sense for a mountain lion to scream out a warning. Instead it pounces in silence. The scream added to movie soundtracks is often that of an owl or a fox, both of which can make eerie screeching noises.

The popularity of Spain as "the West" started with the three movies, *A Fistful of Dollars* (1964), *For a Few Dollars More* (1965), and *The Good, the Bad and the Ugly* (1966). All three were filmed in Almeria by Italian director Sergio Leone and starred Clint Eastwood. This dry, sun-baked part of southern Spain contains deserts somewhat similar to the barren wastes of New Mexico, Utah, and Nevada, fulfilling Leone's vision of the West.

In the second film in the series, *For a Few Dollars More* (1965), the location for the town of El Paso was Tabernas in Almeria. Agua Caliente was Los Albaricoques in Andaliusia, Spain. The interiors were filmed at Rome's Cinecittà Studios and Santa Cruz was filmed on the back lot. In the third film in the series, *The Good, the Bad and the Ugly* (1966), Tabernas was used again for location filming and became Valverde, Santa Ana, and Santa Fe in various parts of the film. La Calahorra, outside Guardix, was used for the railroad station, and the battle between the Union and Confederate forces over control of the bridge was filmed north of Madrid, outside Bargos, at the River Arlanza.

The exteriors for Leone's *Once Upon a Time in the West* (1968) were filmed in the same locations. The opening sequence at the railroad station was shot at La Calahorra, with the town of Flagstone built behind it. The location for Sweetwater, which plays a major part in the film, was near Tabernas. When Jill McBain (Claudia Cardinale) arrives in Flagstone and rides out to Sweetwater in a wagon to meet her husband, the location used was Monument Valley. As she travels to Sweetwater, the road goes past a spectacular view of the Left Mitten and the Right Mitten. When she passes the railroad track-laying gang during the ride, Totem Pole Rock and the spires around it form the background to the scene. Sergio Leone used Monument Valley as a location for these particular scenes as a tribute to John Ford, whom he greatly admired.

*Chapter Six*

# Our "Cowboy" Heroes

Each Western story, whether it is in a book, a film, or a pulp novel, has to have a hero. As author Rita Parks succinctly summed it up, "The Western hero is a subject whose roots are in history, whose image has been transformed into myth, and whose chief function for the contemporary audience is to provide popular entertainment."[1] As a result, the depiction of real characters from history, particularly gunfighters and cowboys, in the movies does not always agree with the historical facts.

## Dime Novels

Before there were movies to tell lurid and fictionalized stories about real cowboys, gunfighters, and other Western heroes, there were the so-called "dime novels." These novels described the sensational — and often mostly fictional — exploits of real Westerners, such as Buffalo Bill Cody, Kit Carson, Billy the Kid, and Jesse James. Readers were treated to exaggerated tales of the dashing feats of rugged, virtuous heroes who rescued plucky heroines from dastardly villains in the mythic Wild West. The stories popularized the fame of their subjects and turned outlaw killers, such as Jesse James, into Robin Hood–like characters. The books also promoted the adventures of fictional characters, such as Deadwood Dick, Denver Dan, Arizona Joe, and Lariat Lil. Author Prentiss Ingraham wrote more than six hundred of these lurid novels, sometimes completing one in only a couple of days.

The development of the steam-powered rotary printing press in the mid–1840s allowed for the mass production of books and magazines at very economical prices, which meant that these books, also called "pulps" because of the cheap paper they were printed on, could be sold for a dime or even five cents. The first of this type of book was produced by publishers Irwin and Erastus Beadle in 1860. During the 1870s publishers such as Beadle and Adams cranked out over two thousand of these pulps, with imprints such as the *New York Dime Library*, *The Buffalo Stories*, *Brave and Bold*, *Wide Awake Library*, *Dime Western*, and *Beadle's Half-Dime Library*. The total for Beadle and Adams was somewhere close to 3,700 dime novels.

Indeed, one of the forces that helped create a glamorized perception of gunfighting among the general public in the latter half of the nineteenth century was the publication in these books of fictional stories about real-life gunfighters. This type of promotion is parodied in *Cat Ballou* (1965), in which gunman Kid Shelleen (Lee Marvin), made famous by dime novels, is really just a boozy, washed-up old man. As part of the plot in the movie, the gang decide to rob a train according to one of Kid Shelleen's plans from a dime novel.

The literary value of these pulp books was not particularly high, but the imagery of guns, cowboys, horses, and cattle drives, all set in the wide-open spaces of the Wild West, created a fascination among many readers. It was escapist literature at its finest. The stories were good-versus-evil at its best, with a white-hatted hero always emerging victorious in the end. These elements translated easily into movie plots.

## Movie and Television Heroes

No matter who the hero of a Western may be, he is usually referred to as "a cowboy." Few Western heroes of the silver screen, however, have been portrayed as actual cowboys in the sense of herding cattle. Most are shown as gunfighters and mythical law enforcers in frontier towns; however, their horses, style of dress, and other links to cowboys have caused them to be lumped into the same category. For example, Wyatt Earp was never a cowboy, though he did serve as a policeman in several of the cattle towns. In this sense, the title of this chapter is a bit misleading, but it follows the accepted terminology.

### Kit Carson (1809–1868)

One of the early Western heroes who was popularized and had his true history distorted by dime novelists was Christopher "Kit" Carson. In one pulp novel, *The Fighting Trapper*, Carson was credited with killing two Indians at the same time in a hand-to-hand fight. According to the author — and the drawing on the front cover — Carson stabbed them both at the same time with a knife in each hand. When questioned about this, the real-life Carson dryly said that he couldn't recall the incident.

Carson has been featured in several motion pictures, including *Kit Carson* (1940), and *Overland with Kit Carson* (1940) featuring Wild Bill Elliott. Carson was popularized on television in *The Adventures of Kit Carson*, an early black-and-white half-hour program that ran for 103 episodes between 1951 and 1955. Actor Bill Williams portrayed Carson as a frontier scout and Indian fighter in the same type of plots and adventures described in the earlier pulp novels and comic books. The television series co-starred supporting actor Don Diamond as Carson's Mexican sidekick El Toro, with the two roaming the American Wild West of the 1880s helping those in need. Nevermind that the real Kit Carson had died almost twenty years prior to this time frame.

The fact that in real life Kit Carson was never a cowboy or a sheriff, but was a mountain man, scout, guide, and trapper (and did not have a cohort named "The Bull") did not detract from his deeds of derring-do in the world of movie and television make-believe. A visit to the real Kit Carson's museum-home in Taos, New Mexico, immediately shows how far from the truth television and the pulp magazines strayed. Nonetheless, they provided tales of high adventure to the small boys who were the primary audience.

Christopher Carson was born near Richmond, Kentucky, in 1809 and grew up on a backwoods farm. At age sixteen he ran away and joined a wagon train headed for Santa Fe, New Mexico, by way of the Santa Fe Trail. Along the way he learned the ropes as a teamster. He was later lured by a sense of adventure to become a mountain man and fur trapper in what is now Colorado, Wyoming, Montana, and Idaho. In 1842, 1843, and 1845 he helped guide John Frémont's expeditions of exploration into the uncharted West.

Carson saw service with the Union army during the Civil War as a colonel of the First New Mexico Volunteers. In 1863, as Colonel Carson, he was sent by General James H. Carleton to carry out a winter campaign against the Navajo by destroying their crops and food. Afterwards, Carson continued to campaign against the Plains Indians. He was promoted to brevet brigadier general and later became the commandant at Fort Garland in southern Colorado.

After leaving the army, Carson took up ranching. He died after a brief illness at the army hospital at Fort Lyons, Colorado, on May 23, 1868, and was buried in the cemetery near his home in Taos, New Mexico.

### Wild Bill Hickok (1837–1876)

"Wild Bill" Hickok has appeared as a character in as many as thirty-five movies. William S. Hart played him in the silent film *Wild Bill Hickok* (1923). In the movie *Calamity Jane* (1953), Hickok was played by a singing Howard Keel sporting two low-slung Colt .45 Peacemakers (rather than the reversed Colt Navy cap-and-ball pistols that Hickok favored in real life). Another musical contribution to Hickok's pseudo-history was when Roy Rogers played a singing freight agent in *Young Bill Hickok* (1940) guarding a gold shipment against Southern

Mountain man and frontier scout Kit Carson from Taos, New Mexico, photographed here in the 1860s, was the subject of many dime novels, comic books, and Western movies. Like most of the overblown heroes of legend, Carson was an authentic product of the Old West and was the hero of many genuine adventures on the frontier, but never to the extent of those that were attributed to him (Library of Congress).

sympathizers with the aid of an equally vocalizing Calamity Jane. Gary Cooper played Wild Bill Hickok in *The Plainsman* (1936). William Elliott appeared in *The Great Adventures of Wild Bill Hickok* (1938), which gave him his permanent movie nickname of "Wild Bill" Elliott. In *Little Big Man* (1970), Hickok (Jeff Corey) appeared as a humorous minor character.

During the early days of television, *The Adventures of Wild Bill Hickok*, which ran from 1951 to 1958, was a popular Western series that ran for 113 episodes. Just as historically inaccurate as the other romanticized tales of famous gunfighters on television, this horse opera featured Guy Madison as a United States marshal. Along with Andy Devine as his fictional sidekick, Jingles Jones, Hickok hunted outlaws and worked his way through various adventures and shoot-outs in the Old West of the 1870s.

The real life of Hickok illustrates the difference between these fictionalized accounts and reality. James Butler Hickok was born in Homer (later renamed Troy Grove), Illinois, on May 27, 1837. At various times he was a scout for the Union Army during the Civil War, a deputy U.S. marshal, a scout for George Armstrong Custer, and an inveterate gambler.

In 1869, Hickok was elected sheriff of Ellis County (Hays City), Kansas, where he was involved in three killings. In April of 1871, Hickok was appointed city marshal of Abilene to keep the cowboys under control. He carried two Navy Colts in a sash around his waist, with the butts forward for a fast cross-draw. Hickok enforced the law and did what he had to to keep the peace. If he was threatened with a gun, he would draw without warning and shoot to kill. Hickok had a deadly aim, and legend had it that he could outdraw and outshoot anyone in the West. His reputation alone was often enough to discourage would-be challengers.

As with many of the other legendary gunmen of the Wild West, Hickok's number of kills has probably been exaggerated. Hickok himself, for example, boasted — presumably tongue-in-cheek — to an interviewer that he had killed at least a hundred men. The true number is probably closer to ten, and may be as few as seven.[2] Only two killings have been verified during the time that he spent in Kansas cattle towns, and one of them was his deputy whom he shot accidentally.

Hickok briefly joined Buffalo Bill Cody in the play *The Scouts of the Plains* in New York City in 1873. During the stage show Hickok traded yarns with Bill and gave an exhibition of trick revolver shooting. Hickok, however, was not comfortable on the stage and left the show in 1874.

The movie *Wild Bill* (1995) recreated a series of disconnected episodes in Hickok's (Jeff Bridges) life before his murder by Jack McCall (David Arquette) in Deadwood, South Dakota. Episodes include a fight with three soldiers in Hays City, how he shot his own deputy in Abilene in 1871, and how he joined Buffalo Bill for a short while. The film implied that he might have had glaucoma from consorting with loose women.[3] The film also suggested a fictional on-again-off-again relationship between an unmarried Hickok and Calamity Jane (Ellen Barkin), and Wild Bill is caught literally with his pants down with Jane by McCall in a saloon. The film did not mention the fact that in real life Hickok had recently married former circus owner Agnes Lake Thacher (also known as Agnes Lake) and was hoping to win enough money in Deadwood through gambling to settle down with her.

"Wild Bill" Hickok has always epitomized the popular image of a gunfighter in the Old West. Like many other gunmen on the frontier, in real life he was a part-time lawman and full-time gambler. He lived violently by the gun and died violently by the gun, as he was shot in the head while playing cards in Deadwood, South Dakota, in 1876. He was playing the so-called "Deadman's Hand," which consisted of black aces and eights (Glenn Kinnaman Colorado and Western History collection).

Wild Bill Hickok met his end when he was shot in the back of the head by a twenty-five-year-old itinerant named Jack McCall. The murder took place in Saloon No. 10 (also known as Nuttall &

Mann's) in Deadwood, South Dakota, on August 2, 1876, while Hickok was playing poker. Hickok was usually a very cautious man and always sat with his back to a wall so that he could see if anyone was approaching. On this particular day, one of the other players at the table refused to trade places with him, which left Hickok with his back to the open door. Unnoticed by the card players, McCall crept up behind Hickok and shot him with a Colt Navy revolver. Hickok's cards consisted of the aces and eights of spades and clubs. Ever since the shooting this combination has been known as the "Deadman's Hand." The fifth card has never been positively identified.

The Deadman's Hand has been used as a popular device in movies other than those about Hickok. In *Stagecoach* (1939), for example, the Deadman's Hand makes a symbolic appearance before the final gunfight between Luke Plummer (Tom Tyler) and the Ringo Kid (John Wayne). In *The Man Who Shot Liberty Valance* (1962), Valance's (Lee Marvin) poker hand sports aces and eights before he goes out on the street and is shot.

At the miners' trial that followed Hickok's murder, McCall claimed that Hickok had shot his brother, but there was no evidence presented to support the claim or that he even had a brother. A more likely reason was that McCall had lost money to Hickok during a card game the day before. In *Wild Bill* (1995) the motivation for McCall's revenge was supposedly that Hickok was in love with McCall's mother, which was not historically accurate. The real McCall was found not guilty by the miners' court, a verdict that was later determined to be invalid because Deadwood was officially on an Indian reservation and not part of the U.S. court system. McCall was eventually re-arrested for Hickok's murder by a deputy United States marshal, was re-tried, and was executed on March 1, 1877.

### Buffalo Bill Cody (1846–1917)

William F. "Buffalo Bill" Cody is an excellent example of a real-life frontiersman whose fame was exaggerated by dime novels and inflated by his own publicity to the point that his fictional exploits soared beyond reality. He has been the subject of over forty-seven Western movies. He was portrayed by Moroni Olsen in *Annie Oakley* (1935) and later by Louis Calhern in *Annie Get Your Gun* (1950), both of which were biographies of the famous female sharpshooter who starred in *Buffalo Bill's Wild West*. The later revisionist movies have not always been kind to Cody. *Buffalo Bill* (1944), with Joel McCrea, for example, suggested that he may have been a charlatan. *Buffalo Bill and the Indians* (1976) portrayed him as a heavy drinker and a bit of a con man.

None of these portraits is totally inaccurate. The real Buffalo Bill Cody was, however, a genuine product of the Old West. Before becoming famous and starring in a Wild West show of epic proportions, he had been a scout for the army, an Indian fighter, and a buffalo hunter for the railroad.

Cody's initial exaggerated fame was spread by the dime novels of Ned Buntline. Buntline, whose real name was Edward Carroll Zane Judson, was a pulp novelist who wrote over four hundred novels and stories, many of them under a pseudonym. Cody first met Buntline at Fort McPherson, Nebraska, on July 24, 1869, while Bill was scouting for the Fifth Cavalry. Buntline's first Cody story was *Buffalo Bill, the King of Border Men*. He penned tales about Cody in fourteen more lurid dime novels with titles such as *Buffalo Bill's Best Shot; or, the Heart of Spotted Tail*. Buntline wasn't the only pulp-novel writer who latched onto Buffalo Bill and helped propel him to the heights of fame. The Cody legend was also promoted by the prolific Colonel Prentiss Ingraham, who wrote over 120 sensational stories about Buffalo Bill.

The real Cody was born on February 26, 1846, as William Frederick Cody in Scott County, Iowa. His nickname of "Buffalo Bill" came from the time he spent as a buffalo hunter supplying meat for the Kansas Pacific Railroad in late 1867 and early 1868. From 1868 to 1876 he served as an army scout. He participated in the Battle of Summit Springs in eastern Colorado on July 11, 1869, and claimed that he killed Cheyenne chief Tall Bull during the fight. This has never been definitely confirmed.

In 1872 Buntline persuaded Cody to appear with him and scout "Texas Jack" Omohundro in a play called *The Scouts of the Prairie; or, Red Deviltry as It Is*. The principals played themselves, supported by a group of "Indians" recruited from locals in Chicago. In spite of inexperienced acting and an improbable plot, the play was a great success and pulled in packed crowds. Cody and his fellow actors toured for the next ten years in various interchangeable shows based on Indian lore and rescuing settlers from Indian attacks. Between acting seasons Cody continued to scout for the army and acted as a guide for hunting parties in the West.

In 1883 Cody organized *Buffalo Bill's Wild West*, which opened in May of 1884 in St. Louis. The spectacle consisted of exhibitions of riding and shooting, and reenactments of events such as an attack on the Deadwood Stage and an Indian attack on a settler's cabin. Part of the thrill of the outdoor spectacle was the characteristic smell that accompanied it, a gamy mixture of sweating horses, horse manure, and smoke from gunpowder. This was punctuated by the sounds of gunshots, the blood-curdling yells of the Indians, the pounding of horses' hooves, and the whoops of the cowboys. The cowboys in the show were all heavily armed, and shooting formed a noisy backdrop to many of the acts.

The playbill called the *Wild West* an "equestrian drama," as Cody didn't like the word "show." For Cody, the re-creation was authentic history, and he looked upon his presentation as a realistic portrayal of life on the Plains. Many of the Indians in his spectacle had fought against the U.S. cavalry in the Indian Wars and the cowboys were authentic cowboys from ranches in the West. Cody himself was an excellent shot with revolvers, rifles, and shotguns, and was a featured performer using all three weapons.

Buffalo Bill took the *Wild West* to Europe, visiting England, France, Italy, Germany, Austria, and Hungary. In 1908 Cody merged the show with *Pawnee Bill's Historic Far West and Great Far East*. Wild West shows, including Buffalo Bill's, struggled on for the next few years, but by the late 1910s the public had lost much of its interest in live cowboy performances and had turned to the new medium of motion pictures, which many felt depicted the West better.

Cody died in Colorado on January 10, 1917, and was buried on top of Lookout Mountain in Golden, just west of Denver.

## Jesse James (1847–1882)

The legend of Jesse James, as enhanced by romanticized stories in dime novels, presented him as America's version of Robin Hood. Supposedly he and his gang were avenging the wrongs and oppression of greedy bankers and railroads; however, it is more likely that the robbers were following their own natural instincts for violence gained during the Civil War. Glamorization of Jesse James started with the editor of the *Kansas City Times*, John N. Edwards, who created a "knight of the range" image for him. In real life Jesse James was a robber, an outlaw, and a cold-blooded killer.

The earliest Jesse James film was *The James Boys in Missouri* (1908), made by the Essanay Company while his brother Frank was still alive. The subsequent thirty-five or so movies about Jesse have ranged from the good to the bad. Probably the most well-known is *Jesse James* (1939), with Tyrone Power as Jesse and Henry Fonda as his brother Frank.[4] *The True Story of Jesse James* (1957) wasn't, nor was *Young Jesse James* (1960). One of the odder James films was *Jesse James Meets Frankinstein's Daughter* (1966). Many screen actors have portrayed Jesse James, including Roy Rogers, Robert Wagner, Audie Murphy, Robert Duvall, Dale Robertson, and Clayton Moore. More recently, *The Assassination of Jesse James by the Coward Robert Ford* (2007) was a very dark version of the shooting of Jesse James by Robert Ford, concluding with Ford's eventual real-life death in 1892 at the hands of Edward O. Kelly at Ford's Creede Exchange saloon in Creede, Colorado.

The real Jesse Woodson James was born near Kearney, Missouri, on September 5, 1847. During the Civil War, Jesse and his older brother Frank rode in a guerrilla band under William Quantrill's lieutenant, "Bloody Bill" Anderson, indiscriminately looting, pillaging, and killing Union troops and Northern supporters. After the Civil War, Jesse and Frank realized that they could use the same guerrilla tactics to carry out bank and train robberies. They hit swiftly, carried out a robbery, then disappeared and laid low until the chase died down. The brothers and their gang held up twelve banks, seven trains, and five stagecoaches in eleven states during a fifteen year period.

Various law enforcement agencies, including the famous Pinkerton Detective Agency, pursued the James brothers for many years, but Jesse remained at large. Like many other Western gunmen, James has been credited with a larger number of kills than he probably made. The number of men killed during his outlaw days after the Civil War may have been as few as one or two.[5]

One of the names Jesse used to disguise his identity was Thomas Howard, and under that name he was shot in the head from behind on April 3, 1882, by his cousin Bob Ford, who was trying to collect $10,000 in reward money put up by several railroads.

### Belle Starr (1848–1889)

Not as well know as Calamity Jane, but promoted to the public by a popular Western movie, was the female outlaw Belle Starr. The few real-life women bandits who used guns to further their careers weren't as glamorous looking as the Lady/Ellen (Sharon Stone) in *The Quick and the Dead* (1995) or Calamity Jane (Jean Arthur in leather pants) in *The Plainsman* (1936), but tended to be rather plain, like the real Calamity Jane and the real Belle Starr.

Like many of the other famous men and women idolized in dime novels and the movies, Starr's reputation as an outlaw far exceeded the reality, which consisted mostly of horse-stealing and consorting with a series of fellow outlaws. She is not known to have robbed any banks or killed anyone.

The movie *Belle Starr* (1941), with Gene Tierney in the title role, attempted to copy the success of the earlier *Jesse James* (1939), and at the same time glamorized women outlaws. Tierney plays the part as a passionate, willful Southern belle who marries a Confederate officer-turned-outlaw, Sam Starr (Randolph Scott). Sam is portrayed as another Robin Hood–like character who is trying to save Missouri from carpetbaggers. After Belle is killed, Starr heroically turns himself in when he realizes that lawlessness is not in the best interest of the people. Other Belle Starr–related movies are *Son of Belle Starr* (1953) and *Belle Starr's Daughter* (1948).

The real Belle Starr was born Myra Belle Shirley on February 5, 1848, in Carthage, Missouri. She became involved with bank robber Cole Younger when he hid out at the

Shirley's farm, and she bore his daughter Pearl in 1867. She gave the little girl Cole's surname of Younger, even though Myra and Cole never married. Over the next decade Starr drifted in and out of crime, stealing horses and rustling. She may not have actually stolen horses herself, but she was at least involved with the outlaws who did. At a time when women like Calamity Jane wore men's trousers and rode with legs astride their horse, Starr was unusual for a female outlaw in that she wore a skirt and rode side-saddle.

In 1880, Starr married a Cherokee Indian named Sam Starr, who was killed in 1886 by lawman Frank West (who also died during the fight) after an argument at a party in Whitfield, Arkansas. On February 3, 1889, Belle Starr was herself mysteriously killed by a shotgun blast from an unknown assailant while she was riding her horse near her house. The prime suspect was neighbor Edgar Watson, who had a running feud with Starr. Watson was arrested, but the charges were dropped at his trial. Another suspect was Belle's illegitimate son, Edwin "Eddie" Reed, but no case against him was ever proven.

### Wyatt Earp (1848–1929)

Wyatt Earp was one of the legendary gunfighters of the Old West. At various times he was also a farmer, a stagecoach driver, a buffalo hunter, a deputy town marshal, a saloon keeper, a gambler, a bounty hunter, and a bodyguard. Much of Earp's fame, however, stems from the notorious gunfight at the O.K. Corral in Tombstone and a popularized biography titled *Wyatt Earp: Frontier Marshal* published in 1931 by author and screenwriter Stuart Lake. Most historians have questioned the accuracy of many of the "facts" in the book. Historian John Mack Farragher put it in stronger terms when he said "the book was an imaginative hoax, a fabrication mixed with just enough fact to lend it credibility."[6] Nevertheless, Lake's book provided the source material for many of the major movies about Earp.

Earp has been portrayed by a variety of actors in over twenty-one movies, including Walter Huston in *Law and Order* (1932), George O'Brien in *Frontier Marshal* (1934), Randolph Scott in another *Frontier Marshal* (1939), Henry Fonda in *My Darling Clementine* (1946), Joel McCrea in *Wichita* (1955), and Burt Lancaster in *Gunfight at the O.K. Corral* (1957). Wyatt Earp has also appeared as a minor character in movies such as *Winchester '73* (1950), in which an aging and paunchy Earp (Will Geer) judges the shooting contest that leads to the loss of the titular gun. In the long-running television series *Gunsmoke*, Marshal Matt Dillon (James Arness) was a composite of Wyatt Earp and all the other lawmen who worked in Dodge City the 1870s.

A popular television series titled *The Life and Legend of Wyatt Earp* (starring Hugh O'Brien) ran for 229 30-minute episodes between 1955 and 1961. Part of the plot-line involved periodic clashes with the Clanton gang, and the finale of the series was a five-part dramatization of the shootout at the O.K. Corral. Wyatt Earp even appeared as a character in a 1968 episode of the science-fiction television series *Star Trek*, and in a 1966 episode of the British television fantasy series *Dr. Who*.

There have been many interpretations of Wyatt Earp. In *Frontier Marshal* (1934), the hero (George O'Brien) is named Michael Wyatt and his friend is Doc Warren. Despite being taken from Stuart Lake's *Wyatt Earp: Frontier Marshal*, which was a supposed historical account, director Allan Dwan later claimed that the character of Michael Wyatt was not meant to be Wyatt Earp but represented a "generic" frontier marshal.[7] Earp was also renamed in the 1939 *Frontier Marshal* when Earp's real-life long-time companion Josephine Marcus threatened to sue 20th Century–Fox for an "unauthorized portrayal."[8] The movie *Doc* (1971) went so far as to suggest an attraction that was more than friendship between the lead characters (Harris Yulin and Stacy Keach).

The real Wyatt Berry Stapp Earp was born in Monmouth, Illinois, on March 19, 1848. Over his lifetime he earned a highly exaggerated reputation for his exploits in the West. He had only one verified killing in Dodge City, which was the final outcome after he wounded a drunken cowboy named George Hoyt. Earp's total number of killings was probably five or six.

Earp served as a policeman in Wichita, Kansas, for brief periods in 1874 and 1875, but was removed from the force for assaulting William Smith, a fellow deputy who was running for the job of town marshal. Earp was appointed deputy city marshal of Dodge City, Kansas, in 1876, and again in 1878.

Wyatt first met Doc Holliday in Fort Griffin, Texas, in 1877, and the two formed a lasting friendship. Fort Griffin was where Earp also met Celia Ann "Mattie" Blaylock, who eventually became his mistress. In 1879, as the boom years of the drives to the Kansas cattle towns were fading, Wyatt, with Mattie and his brothers Virgil, Morgan, and James, moved to Tombstone, Arizona.[9] Virgil eventually became town marshal, and older brother James stayed with his profession of saloon keeper. Wyatt became a shotgun guard for Wells, Fargo & Co., then received a temporary appointment as deputy sheriff of Pima County (Tombstone) and operated a gambling concession at the Oriental Saloon.

During Wyatt's time in Tombstone he met Josephine Marcus, a minor actress in a theatrical troupe. She was the girlfriend of county sheriff Johnny Behan but switched her affections to Wyatt, thus helping to create animosity between the two men.[10]

After the fight at the O.K. Corral, Wyatt and Doc traveled to New Mexico, then to Colorado, waiting for the uproar and repercussions to subside. In 1883, Wyatt rejoined Josephine Marcus, and they went to San Francisco, to San Diego, and eventually to Los Angeles. They would be together for the next forty-six years. Over these ensuing years Wyatt was at various times a prospector, a saloon-keeper, a racehorse-owner, a boxing referee, a gambler, and a Wells Fargo guard. He operated a saloon during the gold rush to Nome, Alaska, in 1897, and in the gold mining districts of Nevada in 1901. Wyatt and Josephine finally settled permanently in southern California in 1906. He died in Los Angeles, California, on January 13, 1929, from complications brought on by chronic cystitis and prostate cancer.

### Doc Holliday (1851–1887)

Doc Holliday is a favorite character for Western movies, and has been portrayed by many actors. Some of the notable ones were Cesar Romero (though changed from dentist Holliday to an obstetrician named Halliday) in *Frontier Marshal* (1939), Walter Huston in *The Outlaw* (1943), Victor Mature in *My Darling Clementine* (1946), Kirk Douglas in *Gunfight at the O.K. Corral* (1957), and Val Kilmer in *Tombstone* (1993). Victor Mature did not portray Holliday as a dentist and a Southerner, as the real Doc was, but as an ex-surgeon from Boston. The "Clementine" of the title was Doc's supposed ex-nurse, Clementine Carter, from the East who came out to Tombstone looking for him. Victor Mature as Doc generally looks hale and hearty but occasionally coughs delicately into a handkerchief. Val Kilmer, on the other hand, played the part more accurately as a tubercular man from the South.

The real "Doc" Holliday was born John Henry Holliday in Spalding County, Georgia, on August 14, 1851. He attended dental school at the Pennsylvania College of Dental Surgery —

hence the nickname of "Doc"—but contracted consumption (a historical name for tuberculosis) in 1871, possibly from one of his dental patients.[11] The standard medical advice of the day was to move to the dry climate of the West, so Holliday moved to Dodge City, Kansas, where he hoped that the prairie air would improve his lungs and health.

He briefly practiced dentistry but found that he preferred gambling. At one time or another he appeared in the saloons and dance halls of almost every large gambling town in the West. To dull the pain of his disease, which was not cured by his move out West, he became a heavy drinker, often consuming a quart of whiskey a day. Doc had a poor disposition, which usually became worse after he had been drinking.

Holliday was a slight man who weighed only about 130 pounds. Like many other Western gamblers, he gained a reputation as a bad-tempered fighter and often tried to provoke gunplay, but it is unlikely that he killed as many men as he is credited for.

Though Doc was linked to various women in the movies, his girlfriend in real life was lady of the evening Kate Elder (her birth name was Kate Harony, Horony, or Haroney), who also used the last name Fisher or Fischer.[12] Unfortunately for her, history has more popularly recorded her as "Big Nose" Kate. She is thought to have met Doc for the first time in Fort Griffin, Texas, in 1875.

**Doc Holliday is buried in Glenwood Springs, Colorado, in Linwood Cemetery—somewhere. The marker at the foot of the grave reads, "This memorial is dedicated to Doc Holliday, who is buried someplace in this cemetery." His last resting place was lost when his wooden marker weathered away.**

One of Holliday's few friends was Wyatt Earp, and the two stood together at the shoot-out at the O.K. Corral. In spite of the ending of *The Outlaw* (1943), where a jealous Pat Garrett (Thomas Mitchell) pulls a gun on Doc (Walter Huston) and kills him, and the screen death of Holliday at the O.K. Corral in *My Darling Clementine* (1946), the real Doc Holliday received only a slight leg wound during the fight. He died in bed some years later from his tuberculosis at the Hotel Glenwood in Glenwood Springs, Colorado, on November 8, 1887, at the age of thirty-six. True to form, one of his last requests before he died was to ask for a drink of whiskey.

### Bat Masterson (1852–1921)

Most of Bat Masterson's present-day fame comes from the television series *Bat Masterson*, starring Gene Barry, which ran for 108 episodes from 1958 to 1961. His character has also appeared in supporting roles in movies, such as portrayed by Kenneth Tobey in *Gunfight at the O.K. Corral* (1957).

Bat Masterson was born on November 26, 1853, near Quebec, Canada. Masterson was christened Bartholomew, a name that his parents shortened to "Bat." The boy did not like his name, so he changed it to William Barclay Masterson.[13] In 1867, Bat moved to Wichita, Kansas, and was successively a railroad section hand, a buffalo hunter, and an Indian scout for the U.S. cavalry. In November of 1877 he was elected sheriff of Ford County, Kansas, which included the cattle town of Dodge City, where Bat's older brother Ed was town marshal.

As well as serving as a lawman, Masterson was a professional gambler, like many of the other gunmen who drifted in and out of law enforcement. Nevertheless he gained a reputation as a tough lawman and is reputed to have killed twenty-one men. This number, however, may be merely another part of his legend. He was involved in only three confirmed gunfights, during which he killed one man.[14] He did not kill anyone while he was sheriff in Dodge City. He was friends with most of the other gunfighters of the Old West, such as Wyatt Earp and Doc Holliday.

Bat Masterson is often shown with a cane and sometimes walking with a limp. In 1876 the real Masterson became involved with a dance hall girl named Mollie Brennan. A rival for her affections, Corporal Melvin King (real name Anthony Cook), came after them with a gun when he knew they were together. King's first shot killed Brennan. His second shot hit Masterson in the pelvis just before Bat was able to draw his gun and return fire, killing King. Masterson walked with a cane after the incident.[15]

In 1902, at age fifty, Masterson became a staff writer on the *New York Morning Telegraph* and wrote a sports column three times a week. His reminiscences of the old days in the West were particularly popular. He died of a heart attack at his desk on October 25, 1921, while working on his next column for the paper.

### Calamity Jane (1856–1903)

One of the legendary characters from the Old West was Calamity Jane. Her exploits in dime novels and on the screen have been based more on exaggerated fiction than fact. She has been played in Westerns with various degrees of authenticity by Jacqueline Wells, as the singing sidekick of Bill Hickok (Roy Rogers) in *Young Bill Hickok* (1940), Yvonne De Carlo, as a gun-slinging Calamity Jane in *Calamity Jane and Sam Bass* (1949) and Doris

The real Calamity Jane was not as glamorous as some of the Hollywood movie stars who have portrayed her on the screen. Her stories, and those written about her in dime novels, made her a larger-than-life legend. This studio portrait, taken in 1895, portrays her as a scout for General Crook. This story of her military service, however, has not been authenticated (Library of Congress).

Day, as a singing *Calamity Jane* (1953). In *The Paleface* (1948), a very glamorous Calamity Jane, played by Jane Russell, takes an undercover assignment to find out who is smuggling guns to the Indians in order to prevent an Indian war. Anjelica Huston played Calamity Jane in the television production of *Buffalo Girls* (1995). A much darker version of Calamity Jane was played in 2005 by Robin Weigert as a bad-tempered, foul-mouthed Jane in the television series *Deadwood* (a role that won her an Emmy nomination).

The real Calamity Jane was born Martha Canary near Princeton, Missouri, in May of 1856 and moved that same year to Virginia City, Montana, with her parents, two brothers, and three sisters.[16] Her popular middle name of "Jane" was not her given name. She claimed that she was originally named "Pretty Jane" and that her name was changed to "Calamity Jane" because of various calamities that seemed to take place when she was around. Another theory was that the name was given to her after she nursed the sick when an epidemic of smallpox struck Deadwood in 1878.

In the mid–1870s Jane became nationally famous after her real and fictional exploits were publicized in a series of dime novels. She never denied the stories and even invented some outlandish tales of her own to go with them. She was featured in a series of fanciful adventures in almost twenty of these pulp books in the early 1880s. She was characterized in the earlier novels as drinking, smoking, carousing, and swearing. The later novels in the series made her character more respectable.

In real life Jane was six feet tall, smoked cigars, and liked to carouse with the boys. She was a heavy drinker, and in her younger days she usually dressed in men's clothing. She worked for a while as an army teamster and was reported to swear like one. She had a reputation as an alcoholic at an early age and was not above occasional prostitution. She was one of the pioneers of Deadwood, South Dakota, and tended bar on the seamier side of town.

Doris Day in *Calamity Jane* (1953) presents a very different picture. She drinks sarsaparilla instead of whiskey, though she brags a lot and tells tall tales like the real Jane. At the beginning of the movie she wears greasy buckskin clothes. Then, after she tries to get a man in true movie fashion, she wears dresses. Then it's back to *clean* buckskins. There are a few other inconsistencies in the movie, not that they really matter. There is mention of the Cheyenne being on the warpath instead of the real-life Sioux who lived around Deadwood, and a dance is held at Fort Scully instead of the real Fort Meade, which was located on the northeastern edge of the Black Hills.

As the Western frontier was coming to a close, the real Calamity Jane lectured to the public on her life, appearing first at the Palace Museum in Minneapolis on January 20, 1896. As part of the tour she sold a pamphlet that she had supposedly written to describe her early life and adventures. It was probably not written by her, as she was poorly educated, but was put together as part of the publicity for the lecture tour. Canary increased her own reputation by recounting a series of exploits, both real and imagined, in which she claimed to have at various times been an army scout for General George Crook, a Pony Express rider, an Indian fighter, and the wife of Wild Bill Hickok.

Some of the exploits she recalled were legitimate. For example, she did indeed join an expedition with Colonel Dodge into the Black Hills in 1875; however, a different version than hers was related by Dr. Valentine McGillycuddy, the expedition's surgeon. He said that she was refused official permission to go but was so determined to be with her current lover, a Sergeant Shaw, that she put on an army uniform and rode unrecognized with the other troopers.

Much has been made of the rumor that Calamity Jane married Wild Bill Hickok, as happened in the film *Calamity Jane* (1953). In the movie version, Hickok (Howard Keel) runs after the singer who is pretending to be Adelaid Adams (Katie Brown) but ends up marrying Calamity Jane (Doris Day). In reality, Hickok married Agnes Lake, a widow and circus owner, on March 5, 1876, before he even moved to Deadwood. In real life, Calamity Jane married a Texan named Clinton E. "Charley" Burke (or Burk) on September 25, 1891, though the date is confused in her own memoirs.

Calamity Jane died in 1903 in Terry, South Dakota, but was buried in Deadwood. Her tombstone is next to Hickok's grave in Mount Moriah cemetery and has the name "Martha Jane Burke" carved below the inscription of "Calamity Jane."

## Billy the Kid (1859–1881)

Though Billy the Kid's gunfighting career was romanticized by dime novelists as a Robin Hood fighting for justice for the everyday man, in reality he was a killer. Various versions of Billy the Kid, portraying him from very good to very bad, have appeared in countless novels, songs, and movies. He has been variously treated as a champion of the little guy, as misunderstood, as persecuted, as a mental deficient, and as a defender of the common man against tyrannical bankers and businessmen. He has appeared in these various roles in King Vidor's *Billy the Kid* (1930), with Johnny Mack Brown; the remake *Billy the Kid* (1941), with Robert Taylor as Billy; *Billy the Kid Returns* (1938), with Roy Rogers; *The Outlaw* (1943), with Jack Buetel; *The Kid from Texas* (1949), with Audie Murphy; *The Law vs. Billy the Kid* (1954), with Scott Brady; *The Parson and the Outlaw* (1957); *The Left-Handed Gun* (1958), with Paul Newman; *Dirty Little Billy* (1972), with Michael J. Pollard; and *Pat Garret and Billy the Kid* (1973), with Kris Kristofferson as Billy and James Coburn as sheriff Pat Garrett. Over the years, Billy the Kid has featured in a total of forty-four movies. Typical of the films is *Billy the Kid* (1941), which presents a romantic story of how Billy (Robert Taylor) carries a grudge because his father was shot in the back, is later treated kindly by a peaceful rancher and becomes an upstanding citizen, then reverts back to type to avenge his benefactor's murder.

The real Billy the Kid was born Henry McCarty in 1859 on either September 17 or November 23, in either New York City or Indiana — accounts vary. He received the nickname of "Billy the Kid" after he moved to Silver City, New Mexico, with his mother, Catherine McCarty, in 1873. He has sometimes also been called William Antrim, after his stepfather, who married Billy's widowed mother after she moved to Silver City. Billy changed his name to William H. Bonney when he left Silver City, allegedly to shield his family from disgrace.[17]

The legend that grew up around Billy said that he had killed twenty-one men by the time he had reached twenty-one years of age, but the real number was probably between four and ten.[18] He killed his first man, a blacksmith named Frank Cahill, in 1877 after the man bullied him. Though Billy never led a gang, as is sometimes claimed, he increased his reputation as a killer when he participated in the Lincoln County cattle war between rival factions of ranchers and businessmen in New Mexico. *Young Guns* (1988) is a violent retelling of how Billy (Emilio Estevez) became involved with rancher John Tunstall and the Regulators during the war. To create additional drama, Billy wears two pistols, butts forward like Wild Bill Hickok, and pulls them out in a cross-draw.

The real Billy was brought to trial for murder in Lincoln in 1881 but escaped, killing two guards in the process. Pat Garrett, who was by then the new sheriff of Lincoln County, tracked Billy down and shot him on July 14, 1881, at Pete Maxwell's ranch near Fort Sumner, New Mexico. King Vidor's *Billy the Kid* (1930) ended happily, but falsely, with Billy escaping with his Mexican sweetheart across the border.

## Annie Oakley (1860–1926)

Arguably the most famous star who toured and performed with *Buffalo Bill's Wild West* was Annie Oakley. Oakley was born on August 13, 1860, in Woodland, Ohio, as Phoebe Ann Moses.[19] She started her famous shooting career at the age of twelve, supplying grouse, quail, and rabbits to a wholesale food supplier for hotels and restaurants in Dayton and Cincinnati to earn money for the family.

In 1875 she entered a competition against traveling exhibition sharpshooter Frank Butler and won by one shot. The two were married on June 20, 1876, and he became her manager and press agent, as well as her husband. The story of their romance and travel with Buffalo Bill has been fictionalized in Rogers and Hammerstein's Broadway musical, which was subsequently made into a singing movie as *Annie Get Your Gun* (1950) with Betty Hutton as Annie and Howard Keel as Frank Butler. Another lively Hollywood biography of her life was *Annie Oakley* (1935), with Barbara Stanwyck as Annie and Preston Foster as Frank Butler. The television series *Annie Oakley*, starring Gail Davis in the title role, ran for eighty-one episodes between 1953 and 1956, and was loosely based on her life. The setting was the fictional town of Diablo, Arizona, in the 1860s, which in reality would have made Oakley less than ten years old at the time. Actress Davis was also a good shot. During the years of her television show she toured with a promotional act that featured her riding and shooting skills.

In 1885 the real Annie and Frank joined *Buffalo Bill's Wild West*. Indian chief Sitting Bull dubbed her "Little Sure Shot" as a sign of his respect for her shooting ability. She had a flair for showmanship and a performing style that captivated audiences. She wore her hair long and full at a time when respectable women were only seen in public with their hair up, and she wore fancy costumes with calf-length skirts when women's legs were traditionally hidden under long dresses.

Annie's act consisted of shooting at targets while aiming over her shoulder in a mirror, from horseback and while riding a bicycle, and breaking multiple targets of glass balls. She could shoot the flame off a candle and a dime out of a man's hand without hitting his fingers. Annie's trick-shooting of glass balls was documented on film by the Edison Company in Edison's Black Maria Studio in West Orange, New Jersey, in 1894.

Annie was in a train wreck in North Carolina on October 29, 1901, and this is generally credited as the reason for her retirement from the *Wild West*. In reality she left the show later in 1901 after she suffered severe burns in a treatment bath at a hot springs resort in Arkansas.[20]

## Butch Cassidy (1866–1908)

One of the most engaging movie characters in Westerns of the 1960s was Paul Newman as the title character in *Butch Cassidy and the Sundance Kid* (1969). The movie depicted Cassidy's career as a train and bank robber as a series of light-hearted exploits. After the real gang pulled off bank and train robberies, they retreated to a hideout called Hole-in-the-Wall in a remote area fifteen miles southwest of the present town of Kaycee, Wyoming. This was

Annie Oakley — dubbed "Little Sure Shot" by Indian chief Sitting Bull — was an expert shooter who could shatter multiple glass balls thrown in the air and shoot a dime out of a man's hand without hitting his fingers. She was one of the stars of *Buffalo Bill's Wild West*, where she dazzled audiences with her shooting skills and lively personality when she performed. She is shown here in 1899 holding a shotgun and displaying a large number of her medals on the blouse of her dress. Among other awards, she was the holder of the *Police Gazette*'s championship medal (Library of Congress).

supposedly an impregnable outlaw hideout guarded by armed riflemen. In reality it was a few decrepit cabins where outlaws occasionally hid out. There were no reciprocal pursuit laws at the time, so bandits like Cassidy had only to cross a state line to escape pursuers. The gang's other hideout was Robbers' Roost in Utah's high desert country south of the town of Green River. This bleak country consists of several hundred square miles of narrow, twisting canyons with high, steep walls that suddenly stopped in abrupt dead-ends to perplex pursuers.

"Butch" Cassidy was born Robert LeRoy Parker on April 13, 1866, in Utah.[21] At various times Cassidy was a cowboy, a miner, and a rustler before he settled down to a serious career of bank and train robbery. In 1896 he formed the so-called Wild Bunch gang, whose members included Harvey Logan, Kid Curry, and Harry Longabaugh (the Sundance Kid).[22] Though the gang gained a fearsome reputation, Cassidy claimed that he never killed a man.

A typical exploit occurred on June 2, 1899, when Cassidy and the Wild Bunch stopped a Union Pacific train near Wilcox, Wyoming. When the express messenger refused to let them enter, the robbers placed a charge of dynamite outside the door of the car and blew most of the express car into the air, including $30,000 in bank notes and securities. The guard escaped with only minor injuries while the robbers chased down the paper money. On June 29, 1900, the Wild Bunch robbed a Union Pacific train near Tipton, Wyoming, and rode off with $55,000.

Cassidy's career as a train robber was parodied by Jane Fonda as *Cat Ballou* (1965), who gathers a gang consisting of a drunk, a would-be preacher, an Indian, and an old washed-up outlaw. At one of their train robberies the express agent refuses to open the safe until Kid Shelleen (Lee Marvin) fires a shot at him; then the man opens it rapidly in a situation not unlike that experienced by the real Cassidy. One of the humorous moments in the film, though tinged with pathos, occurs when Cat Ballou escapes with her "gang" to Hole-in-the-Wall where an aging Butch Cassidy (Arthur Hunnicutt) and a group of doddering has-beens are hiding out. As Kid Shelleen (Lee Marvin) is talking to the ancient proprietor of the bar, another old man comes up and says, "You remember me, old ... old..." then turns away, shaking his head and looking confused as he is so old that he can't even remember his own name. After Ballou's gang robs a train, Cassidy is horrified and says, "We don't bother them and they don't bother us." And later, when Cat Ballou exclaims in astonishment, "Hole-in-the-Wall's impregnable," Butch says, "No such a thing. Take more trouble than we've been worth to dig us out. Now you made it worthwhile."

In the movie *Butch Cassidy and the Sundance Kid* (1969), the two main characters are obliterated in a hail of off-screen bullets in South America. The end of the real Butch Cassidy remains a little more mysterious. In 1902, after the gang pulled off a string of robberies with varying degrees of success, Cassidy, Longabaugh, and Longabaugh's mistress, Etta Place, escaped just ahead of the law to South America. Whether or not Cassidy and Longabaugh died there has been the subject of debate among historians for many years. Some historians — and the movie — say that the two were killed by Bolivian soldiers on November 6, 1908, after robbing a mule train carrying silver from the Aramayo mine. There *was* such a robbery and shootout in San Vincente, Bolivia, but neither of the two bodies found afterwards has been definitely proven to be Butch or Sundance. Witnesses stated that both of the skeletons contained bullet holes in the skull, leading to the theory that Butch shot Sundance and then committed suicide rather than be captured.[23] Other historians claim that Cassidy escaped and returned to the United States, where he lived out his years under an assumed name. These theories have been the subject of scholarly controversy for some years, and neither has been definitely proven.

Etta Place was a real-life woman of the Old West whose name, but not much else, is known today among the general public because of her role in *Butch Cassidy and the Sundance Kid* (1969). Place's origins and subsequent disappearance have never been satisfactorily explained. One theory was that she was originally an inmate of Fannie Porter's bordello in Fort Worth, Texas, where the Wild Bunch sometime went to hide out after a robbery. Another theory was that she was Cassidy's girlfriend before becoming Longabaugh's mistress. Several historians have claimed to have found out who she really was by tracing some of her relatives, but definitive proof of her origins remain elusive.

Like Butch and Sundance, what finally happened to her is also shrouded in mystery. Place did travel with Cassidy and Longabaugh to Bolivia in 1901. She apparently returned to the United States without the others after the threesome's South America trip, but where she went is unknown. Conflicting accounts have her ending up either in Denver or back in Utah where the gang originated.

## Chapter Seven

# "I see by your outfit..."

The movie clothing worn in Westerns has evolved and changed over the years, along with the evolution and change in the movies themselves. From the dusty, grimy, somewhat worn clothing of film star William S. Hart to the duded-up singing cowboys of the 1930s in their fancy, tight, pinstriped trousers with the "smile" pockets, and then to the grubby anti-heroes of the spaghetti Westerns of the 1960s, movie cowboys have worn a wide array of clothing—from fancy to almost rags, from practical to purely dressy. In more modern movies, such as *True Grit* (2010), costume designers have made a conscientious effort to research clothing of the period and strive for authenticity, unlike the mythic movie world of the 1930s singing cowboys.

Hart tried for the authentic look of a cowboy, which was slightly worn and grimy, but the screen cowboys that followed him, particularly the singing cowboys, went for a flashy, highly-tailored look. The later clean-cut look of Wyatt Earp and Doc Holliday in *Gunfight at the O.K. Corral* (1957) eventually gave way to the grubby look of *McCabe and Mrs. Miller* (1971) and *The Assassination of Jesse James by the Coward Robert Ford* (2007). Grubby or clean, most stars had three or four sets of the same clothing for each picture in case costumes became torn or damaged, and had the same clothing in various conditions of wear to denote the passage of time. Even stunt doubles and stand-ins had to be outfitted with the same sets of clothing as the stars.

Real cowboys in the Old West worked long hard hours of riding, roping and branding cattle, digging post holes, and fixing fences. Loggers felled and stripped trees, hauling the trunks with oily drag cables through the dirt and brush onto greasy skid roads. Gold miners spent long, wet hours up to their knees in icy-cold streams panning for gold, or toiling in underground mine workings that ranged from cold and humid in the Rocky Mountains to hellishly hot and steamy in the deep mines of the Comstock district of Virginia City, Nevada.

All of these men needed clothing that was practical and would hold up under conditions of severe wear. Miners, prospectors, cowboys, and lumbermen wore simple, hard-wearing clothes, as did most workmen of the time. Tall work boots were essential for wet and rocky environments, wool pullover shirts supplied warmth, and leg protection was provided by heavy-duty wool or cotton pants with suspenders to hold them up. The basic outfit for farmers or men on a wagon train was denim or canvas overalls, a cotton work shirt, and a cap or a broad-brimmed hat. This outfit has almost become a parody of itself in movies about wagon trains.

## What the Cowboys Wore

The heroes of Western movies are typically cowboys. So, just as Monument Valley emerged as the iconic "West," the movie "cowboy" has emerged as the primary inhabitant of this mythic Western landscape. For a real cowboy, the essentials of his outfit were pants, shirt, large hat, and cowboy boots. Almost as important were his chaps, spurs, and saddle. Artist Charles Russell, who had been a working cowboy himself, illustrated many of his paintings with cowboys in wool shirts, California Pants, a flat-brimmed and low-crowned hat, and a plain bandana around the neck. The outfit was augmented by high-heeled boots, spurs, and a leather gunbelt. Russell's cowboys often had yellow rain-slickers tied to their saddles.

Real cowboys wore long-sleeved shirts, typically made from cotton or flannel, that they pulled on over their heads and buttoned up to the neck. The front of the shirt was typically fastened by three or four buttons, or by a rawhide lace. The popular fashion of the day favored pinstripes and a neck without a collar, and no necktie. By the 1880s and 1890s, shirts both with and without collars were commonly worn. Shirt colors might be solid, ranging from black or blue to red, or might consist of various mixed colors and patterns. Stripes were also popular. Blue shirts were in common use after the Civil War due to the ready availability of army surplus shirts.

Pants for Westerners were made from heavy wool, which was very durable and long-lasting, often with striped, checkered, or plaid designs. Solid tan or gray were also popular colors. The seat of the pants was often reinforced with a double layer of fabric or with buckskin for longer wear while riding. In *The Magnificent Seven* (1960), Calvera (Eli Wallach) wore striped pants with the seat reinforced with leather.

The pants worn by working cowboys were made with a tight waist and loose-fitting legs — a style called "California Pants" — which were patterned after those worn by the early California vaqueros. Most were made in Oregon City by the Oregon City Woolen Mills. Later pants were made from canvas or denim, but this material was not popular until the 1920s, so blue denim

This unidentified young cowboy is wearing what would be fancy clothes for someone who rode the range. His outfit includes a bright bandana, fringed gauntlets, chaps with fancy leather trimmings, and a revolver in a Mexican Loop holster worn for a crossdraw. But note that there are no bullets in his cartridge belt. His clothes and equipment look so clean and new that he may be wearing either a photographer's costume or his Sunday best. Note the suspenders to hold up his pants and the lack of a separate belt for that purpose (Glenn Kinnaman Colorado and Western History Collection).

jeans in the Old West are more typically seen on movie cowboys than on authentic cowmen. Red flannel drawers or combination suits were worn under the outer clothes all year round.

Contrary to the well-dressed image of the movies, lawmen of the Old West typically looked like anyone else. They wore wool pants, pullover shirts, vests, broad-brimmed hats, and dirty boots.

Early Western actors, such as William S. Hart, Ken Maynard, Hoot Gibson, Tom Mix, and Buck Jones, did not necessarily wear clothing that reflected reality. Movie cowboy clothing developed more from the desire of the stars to create a suitable entertainment image. The studios dressed their actors in screen costumes that they felt were appropriate for Western movies in order to individualize their characters and distinguish them as screen personalities.

Hart tried for accuracy in his screen image in order to reflect the reality of the Old West. Like the real cowboys, his costumes were not always neat, and he favored drab coats that were shiny from wear and dirty from travel. Though close to the real cowboy image, he was not totally accurate in costuming. He was realistic but still somewhat romanticized.

Authenticity wasn't always popular with audiences. Belts, for example, were not commonly worn for holding up men's trousers in the West until the late 1890s, and belt loops on trousers were not added until 1922. California Pants had a tight waist that held the pants up without the use of a belt. If support was needed, suspenders were attached to buttons on the trouser waistband. Suspenders were commonly worn by cowboys on a cattle drive because their use prevented chafing and soreness around the waist and hips from wearing a belt for long periods of time while riding and tending cattle. Suspenders were also commonly worn by miners, farmers, and loggers.

Showing this type of authenticity, however, wasn't always popular with movie fans. In *Stagecoach* (1939), the Ringo Kid (John Wayne) wore suspenders and a belt to hold up his pants. Though he was dressed authentically, audiences didn't like the image. On the other hand, at one point in *Gunfight at the O.K. Corral* (1957), Doc Holliday (Kirk Douglas) is seen correctly wearing no belt, as his pants are held up by their tight waist. The rest of the time the men wear conventional belts.

### Levi Strauss

The sturdy work pants that were a favorite of Westerners, and the jeans that later came to be identified with the movie cowboy, were descendants of the earlier practical trousers and overalls worn by sailors and European peasants. These trousers were made from wool, canvas, denim, or corduroy.

In 1853, Levi (birth name Loeb) Strauss moved from the East to San Francisco and opened a branch of the family wholesale dry-goods business. The pants he sold at first were not his creation. He was merely a reseller of corduroy and denim pants that were known simply as "trousers," "dungarees," or "waist overalls." Denim was a well-proven material for workwear.

In 1872 Strauss was supplying cloth to a tailor named Jacob Davis in Reno, Nevada, when Davis asked Strauss if he would be interested in paying for a patent application for an improved type of trouser. In exchange, Davis offered a half-interest in his business of making and selling them. What was different about these waist overalls was that Davis had added copper rivets to the corners of the pockets of the pants in order to give greater strength to points of stress. Strauss agreed to the deal, and in 1873 the two received a patent for "Improvement in Fastening Pocket Openings."[1]

Davis moved to San Francisco to supervise the manufacture of his new design. He purchased the denim from a company in New Hampshire and contracted with a series of seamstresses to manufacture the garment at home as piece goods. The popularity of these overalls grew so rapidly that Strauss and Davis decided to open a factory in San Francisco. The pants were made from denim material that was dyed the characteristic indigo blue color that it remains today. The brand of pants that Levis continued to call "waist overalls" into the 1950s eventually became known as denim jeans after "jean cloth," which is an old name for a heavy fabric used for working clothes that is made of a blend of cotton and wool or silk.

The original design of Levi's jeans had three pockets—two in front and one in the back. In 1890 a fourth was added to provide a little pocket for a watch. In 1905 a second back pocket was added to create the five-pocket Model 501, which became the standard of Levi's design and which is still popular today. On each of the back pockets the factory also added a trademarked wide "V" design, sewn with orange thread.

Other companies immediately saw the success of Levi's pants and within a few months entered into competition with him to supply miners who wanted sturdy clothing. In 1890, when Strauss's patent expired, many other competitors emerged. By 1920, jeans made with sturdy denim had taken over from wool and canvas pants.

The most successful competitors to Levi Strauss & Co. were H.D. Lee Mercantile, and the later Wrangler brand made by the Blue Bell company. In 1935 Lee introduced a series of denim pants called Lee Riders, which were aimed specifically at working cowboys and rodeo riders. In 1935 Levi's introduced Lady Levi's, aimed specifically at the women's market, and later produced a model with a side-zipper that was very popular in the 1950s. Wrangler introduced the first zip-up jeans for women in 1948.[2]

### Jeans in the Movies

In *She Wore a Yellow Ribbon* (1949), Nathan Brittles (John Wayne) said he was a lad in blue jeans when he joined the army. This would be incorrect, as he was of retirement age at the film's supposed setting of 1876, and modern blue jeans weren't created until 1873. In a similar anachronism, in *Rio Grande* (1950) Ben Johnson was a number of years ahead of his time, as he wore jeans in the style of the 1940s and 1950s, with rolled up trouser cuffs, while leading a Mormon wagon train. In *The Searchers* (1956), set in 1868, Ethan Edwards (John Wayne) is again wearing jeans, a belt, and suspenders in 1950s style. At one point Laurie Jorgensen (Vera Miles) is wearing her jeans also in 1950s style. The story of *Escape from Fort Bravo* (1953) is set in 1862, during the Civil War. During the escape from the fort, Carla Forester (Eleanor Parker) and Cabot Young (William Campbell) are shown wearing blue jeans. This style of jeans was not popular among real cowboys until the 1920s.

Even in the 1890s most real cowboys preferred wool trousers to denim Levis. Denim jeans didn't catch on quickly with cowboys and did not appear commonly in the West until the 1920s, despite turn-of-the-century advertising that showed paintings of cowboys wearing them. Part of the reason was that cowboys considered Levi's blue jeans to be the clothing of poor men and farmers, which made them unpopular for cowboy wear.

### Flamboyant or Garish?

As Western movies became more popular and individual stars began to emerge in the 1920s, their cowboy clothing became more striking. The first movie cowboy to dress in a really flamboyant style was Tom Mix. His flashy clothing earned him the nickname "Beau Brummell of the West."[3] Mix popularized the style of clothing that was later adopted and embellished by the singing cowboys, which included the characteristic pointed-yoke Western shirt with high button cuffs and "smile" pockets. Instead of the single button at the end of the sleeves that had characterized cowboys' earlier work shirts, Mix's fancy cowboy shirts sported cuffs with multiple buttons — as many as five on each sleeve in *The Texan* (1920). This was surpassed by Roy Rogers, who sported six buttons in *Son of Paleface* (1952) and other movies, and by silent Western star Jack Hoxie, who even had one shirt with eight buttons on each sleeve.

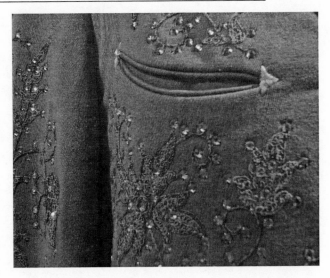

Close-up example of the characteristic "smile pocket" — so-called because it looks like a smile. This is also called an "arrow pocket" because of the pointed arrowheads at the corners of the pocket. Fancy embroidery and rhinestones also cover this jacket, a type once worn by B-Western singing stars.

Mix's (and Rogers') elaborate shirts had the openings of the breast pockets shaped into a crescent outlined with embroidered piping, which gave them the nickname "smile pockets." For further styling, the ends of the "smile" had embroidered arrowheads pointing outwards, which also gave them the name "arrow pockets."

Cowboy stars of the 1930s wore shirts with elaborate embroidery, boots with ornate designs stitched into the leather uppers, belts with decorative buckles, and gunbelts with ornate motifs tooled into the leather. Most noticeable were the five or more buttons on the cuffs of the shirts that the stars wore. These were not just plain shirt buttons, either, but dressy, metal-rimmed, mother-of-pearl snap buttons that had recently been invented.[4]

The fancy pants worn by movie cowboys of the 1930s and 1940s evolved even further away from the plain everyday wool trousers of the real cowboy to include more and more garish stripes. Movie stars usually wore their pants legs tucked inside the tops of their boots in order to show off the fancy stitching and designs that were inlaid into the upper leather of the boot.

Another article of clothing that was popular among Western stars of the 1930s was the bib-front or "fireman's" shirt, such as the one worn by John Wayne in *Stagecoach* (1939). This type of shirt was designed with a large flap of material over the chest that was attached to the rest of the shirt by a row of buttons down each side of the front. Though historically the bib-front shirt dated back to the days of the Civil War, this design was later commonly adopted by firemen in the Old West. For firemen, the additional material over the chest protected the upper body better than did a single layer of shirt cloth with a straight line of buttons down the front. To provide even more protection, the original fireman's shirt was made from heavy wool, typically in red for high visibility in smoky situations.[5] The movie stars upgraded the design of the basic bib shirt with ornate designs and used more fashionable material than wool, such as silk.

As movie stars sought to define their individual screen characters, their clothing became even more distinctive. The most outlandish mode of dress was adopted by the singing cowboy. Shirts, pants, and boots worn on the screen became even more elaborate as singing cowboys proliferated and tried to individualize their on screen personalities through their own styles of clothing. In *Young Bill Hickok* (1940), for example, an early Roy Rogers film, Rogers doesn't wear fancy clothing. Nor does he have an ornately-tooled, double-holster gunbelt. He wears two separate single gunbelts, one made for wear on the right hip and one for the left. By the time he made *Apache Rose* (1946), however, Rogers was wearing a fancy shirt with embroidered roses and six pearl snap-buttons on the cuff—and a fancy tooled double-holster gun rig.

This garish movie cowboy look became all the rage among the viewing public. In an interesting reverse twist on who was imitating who, working cowboys of the 1930s started to adopt the flashy clothing of the screen stars.

### Tailors to the Stars

Lynn Owsley, who played the steel guitar in Ernest Tubb's Texas Troubadours band, commented on the band's fancy stage clothing when he said, "A real cowboy would never allow clothes like these in his closet. But what our suits are supposed to do is draw attention and set us apart. And they do a good job of doing that."[6] As the outfits of the singing cowboys of the 1930s and 1940s became more and more outlandish, the stars turned to specialty tailors to help them create distinctive styles.

One of the famous tailors to the movie stars of the Westerns — and cowboy bands — was Nathan Turk, the owner of a stylish clothing shop on Ventura Boulevard in Van Nuys, California, from the 1930s to the 1950s. He provided custom Western clothing for Roy Rogers, Gene Autry, and many of the other cowboy stars.

Turk was born in 1895 in the village of Torshaw, near Minsk, Poland, then emigrated to the United States as a teenager. He eventually moved to California to Van Nuys, near Republic's studio and the ranches and other outdoor locations used for Western movies. After a period as a tailor's apprentice, in 1923 he started making elaborate costumes for movie stars and music recording artists. His trademark was Western shirts with distinctive piped collars, shaped cuffs with multiple snaps and buttons, and stitched arrowheads to reinforce the seams and pockets. Among his customers were Gene Autry, Roy Rogers, John Wayne, and Wild Bill Elliott, and recording stars such as Ernest Tubb, Hank Thompson, and Buck Owens.[7]

Another of the famous tailors to the cowboy stars was Rodeo Ben. Ben was born Bernard Lichenstein in 1893 in Stashowe, Poland. He emigrated to the United States and settled in Philadelphia in 1930, where he made costumes for circus and rodeo performers. Rodeo Ben was inspired by decorative motifs on Polish folk dresses and costumes from his native land. He combined these designs with cowboy styles to produce distinctive screen costumes that were covered with old-world embroidery. He designed pants with fancy belt loops and smile pockets, and his shirts were characterized by extensive piping and incorporated embroidered pictures of horses, flowers, and birds. Ben made clothing for Ken Maynard, Tim McCoy, and Tom Mix, among others, and later for Gene Autry and Roy Rogers.

Among Rodeo Ben's innovations was the use of snap closures on shirts instead of buttons. The concept grew out of the idea that a rodeo bull-rider might have part of his shirt hung up on a steer's horn if an accident should occur. Ben thought that if the shirts had snap closures instead of buttons, the snaps would safely pop back open, thus providing a measure of safety. Ben's idea of fancy snaps became popular and turned into a fashion design accessory. Eventually he used mother-of-pearl to dress up the snap design.

The third of the famous tailors to the Western stars was Nudie of Hollywood. Nudie was born in Kiev, Russia, in 1902 as Nutya (or Nudka) Kotlyrenko. After serving as a tailor's apprentice when he was young, he emigrated to the United States, where his last name became americanized to Cohn at his entry point of Ellis Island (as similarly happened to many other immigrants). His first name became Nudie when misspelled on his entrance papers. Cohn tried his hand at several different enterprises, then in 1934 he opened Nudie's for the Ladies in New York and sold skimpy costumes to burlesque dancers and strippers. One of his trademarks was the extensive use of spangles and rhinestones. In 1940 he moved to Los Angeles, where he opened a tailor shop specializing in alterations, before moving to North Hollywood and opening Nudie's Rodeo Tailors. He specialized in Western shirts and suits, and made clothes for Western studios and stars. From his earlier costume experience he added rhinestones to the suits for sparkle. Among his customers were Hoot Gibson, Roy Rogers, Dale Evans, Rex Allen, Audie Murphy, John Wayne, Glenn Ford, and Guy Madison.

## Vests

Vests made of wool or corduroy were popular among real cowboys. They provided extra protection against the weather without the encumbrance of a jacket, which restricted movement while working and could possibly become hung up on a tree branch or a cow's horn. Vests were also handy for storage, as they contained multiple pockets that could hold tobacco and cigarette paper, a watch, and a tally-book and pencil for counting cattle. As it was difficult to retrieve anything from pockets in pants while riding, a pocket in a vest was a more convenient place to stow all these small things.

Many real cowboys would not button their vests in the ill-founded fear that doing so would bring on colds and rheumatism. But then these were the same superstitious men who thought that changing their underwear on the trail would bring them bad luck. Movie cowboys, on the other hand, usually didn't wear a vest because they thought that a vest didn't provide a flamboyant enough image.

## Boots

Most working cowboys in the southwest wore tall leather boots to protect their feet and legs from cactus and brush, and to prevent chafing from their stirrups. Boots typically went seventeen inches up the leg to keep out dust and gravel, or water during a river crossing. The additional height also protected the lower legs from snakebite.

Early boots worn by cowboys typically featured leg-hugging tops, wide round toes, and flat heels of low or medium height. Before the introduction of specifically-designed "cowboy boots," many cowboys wore standard over-the-counter work boots, or, if they could not afford them, the surplus military boots that were commonly available in stores in the West. These boots had low, rounded heels, unlike the later cowboys boots, which sported higher heels that tapered in towards the foot.

The development of boots specific to cowboys has been attributed to Charles Hyer of Olathe, Kansas, at around 1875.[8] He patterned his boots after Civil War boots and the work boots of the time, making them with high tops and wide, rounded toes, but he also added other features that were attractive to working cowboys.

By the mid–1880s cowboy boots had achieved a distinctive style that was based on practical use. The entire boot was narrower, and the toe was pointed so that the boot would slip in and out of a stirrup easily. The sole of the boot was thin so that the wearer could feel the stirrup underneath it. The heel was raised so that the boot would fit the stirrup and hold securely. The back of the heel, however, was slanted so that the heel would not hang up in the stirrup and cause the cowboy to be dragged if he fell or was thrown from his horse. Leather loops (called "mule-ear straps" or "mule ears") were added to each side of the top of the boot to allow it to be pulled on easily. This combination of features made cowboy boots somewhat impractical for walking, but then no self-respecting cowboy ever walked if he could ride.

Early boots used by cowboys were the same work boots that miners, loggers, and other workmen wore. What are today considered to be "cowboy boots," shown here, were developed in the mid–1870s. They were tall to protect the legs from brush, thorns, snakebites, chafing from the stirrup, and bites from cranky cattle. Boot heels were slanted inwards so that the boot would not hang up in the stirrup if the cowboy fell from the saddle or was thrown off his horse. Most cowboys fastened on spurs with a leather strap across the boot, but blunted the rowels so that sharp points did not injure the horse. The U-shaped device in the foreground hooks onto the back of the boot to help make removing the boot from the foot easier.

Many later boot designs had fancy decorative patterns and stitching, as taken to excess by the singing cowboys of the 1930s. However, as garish as some of them seemed, the stitching served a practical purpose. The elaborate stitching stiffened the leather so that the boot would hold its original shape, and the tops would not wrinkle or pucker around the ankles and cause chafing.

Most cowboys added a pair of spurs, which were worn over the boots and carried the gruesome but self-explanatory nickname of "gut hooks" or "can openers." The rowels — the rotating disc-like part with the sharp points at the back — varied from small and functional to large and ornate. Some of the early Spanish rowel designs of the California vaqueros ranged up to six or seven inches in diameter.

The rowel of a spur could be sharp enough that it could be employed as a weapon, as used by Howard Kemp (James Stewart) in the finale of *The Naked Spur* (1953). Rowels, however, were usually filed down so that the points were blunted. A sharp rowel could cause serious injury to a horse's side, as well as making the horse nervous if it knew that the spurs caused pain. In this case, a jittery horse could throw its rider and cause him injury.

The leather straps that held the spurs to the boots were typically very ornate. They often had chains, silver inlays, and little pendants called "jingle-bobs" that chimed when the wearer walked. The rowels of some spurs became so large and ornate that it was difficult for the cowboy to walk when he dismounted.

## Hats

In the simplistic depiction of movie cowboys that emerged between the 1920s and the 1940s, black and white were used to differentiate between the hero and the villain. The good guy wore a white hat, and the bad guy wore a black hat. An exception in the 1930s was William Boyd as Hopalong Cassidy, who favored black (or dark blue) shirts, pants, and hats, which was contrary to the existing image that the good guys wore white. Robert Taylor dressed in the manner of a badman-turned-good in *The Law and Jake Wade* (1958), in which he wore a black hat, black pants, black shirt, and even a black leather holster.

Hats used by real cowboys were generally wide-brimmed in order to shade the eyes and protect the face and ears from the intense sun of the Southwest while spending hours in the saddle each day. Cowboy hats had a high crown to keep the head cool, and the hat might be oiled to make the felt waterproof. A hat with a large crown could be used to fan a campfire, carry water, or as a feedbag for the owner's horse. Large hats could be waved in the air to attract attention at a distance or used to steer cattle in a desired direction, such as when turning the herd. In very cold weather the brim could be pulled down and tied over the ears with a bandana to help prevent frostbite.

Interestingly, hat designs possessed a regional flavor that arose from their practical application. Southern cowboys typically wore hats with high crowns and wide brims to provide shade and protect the wearer from the intense sun of Texas and Arizona. This style was similar to the large-brimmed sombreros of the Mexican laborer. Northern cowboys, by contrast, typically wore hats with narrower brims and lower crowns. One reason was that the southern-style hats with their larger brims tended to be blown off more easily by the stronger winds of the northern ranges. By looking at the size and shape of a man's hat, therefore, a cowboy could guess fairly accurately which area of the country another cowboy hailed from.

By the 1890s most cowboys wore Stetson hats. John B. Stetson was a hatmaker who was originally from Philadelphia but moved to Colorado in 1865 after he contracted tuberculosis (then called "consumption"). The high dry air of the West was considered beneficial for tubercular patients, who were also known as "lungers." Stetson established a hat-making business and started to mass-produce hats.

Stetson's first model was called the "Boss of the Plains," or "the Boss" for short, with a four-inch flat brim and a four-inch rounded top. This was followed by designs such as the "Carlsbad," the "Buckeye," and the "Montana Peak." The latter had the crown pushed in on all four sides to create a high peak. In the television mini-series *Lonesome Dove* (1989), actor Robert Duvall wore what became known as a "Gus hat," otherwise known as a Montana Peak. This style remained popular into the 1920s.

Until about 1890 the crowns of cowboy hats tended to be about four to four-and-a-half inches tall. After 1900 the crown started to rise again. In 1925 movie star Tom Mix contracted with Stetson to endorse his signature hat, which had a five-inch brim and a seven-inch crown. The size of this huge hat popularized the nickname "ten-gallon hat, " even though the capacity wasn't anywhere near this amount. As the popularity of the Montana Peak waned, hats became smaller again, and the newer Stetsons tended to have a lower crown and smaller brim.

Cowboys were so attached to their hats that it was considered quite acceptable for men to wear their hats at the dinner table, while visiting friends, or at a dance.

## Other Accessories

Some of the accessories worn by cowboys tended to be confined more to the cowboy image than to real cowboys and gunfighters.

### Bandana

One useful accessory was the neckerchief or bandana, usually coming in red or blue. Black was also a common color as it tended not to show dirt. A bandana could be tied over the head to hold a cowboy's hat in place during a windstorm, pulled up over the nose and lower face to protect from a sandstorm (such as shown in *Hallelujah Trail* [1965]), or while riding in the dust raised by a herd of cattle. It could also be tied over the nose or ears for additional protection in cold or snowy weather. Other multipurpose uses included a blindfold for a horse, a sweat-rag, a towel, a potholder, a sling, a tourniquet to help treat snakebite, and a bandage. It could even be used to tie up a calf's feet or act as a pair of hobbles for a horse.

There was one unusual use for bandanas in the California gold fields. Due to the lack of available women, male miners often had to pair up to dance, and one had to play the female part. To distinguish who was who, one of the couple often wore a bright bandana tied around his left arm to identify that he was dancing the woman's part.

### Chaps

Some cowboys wore chaps for leg protection while riding through thorny brush, mesquite bushes, and tree branches. Chaps consisted of a pair of snug-fitting leather sheaths that were joined and buckled at the waist, had no seat, and pulled on over the pants. The name was a corruption of the Spanish word *chaparreras*. Chaps were typically made from cowhide or sheepskin; however, if the availability of this type of leather was limited, chaps might be made of horsehide or even doghide.

Cowhide chaps provided a cowboy's legs with some protection from rain, the snow and cold of winter, and bites from irritable horses or cows. For extra protection from the weather, chaps in California were sometimes made from bearskin, with the hair still attached. While warmer than plain leather in winter, these were hotter in summer and tended to smell unpleasant when wet.

On the northern cattle ranges, such as in Montana, chaps were also made from goatskin or sheepskin, with the wool still attached to the outside to make "woolies." These were used by real cowboys — rodeo and otherwise — into the 1910s and later. Over time, however, the appearance of huge, wooly sheepskin chaps in the movies was used to identify and caricature a dude.[9] This was done to good effect in *Son of Paleface* (1952), where Junior (Bob Hope)—as the ultimate travesty of an Eastern dude on the frontier—swaggers around with wooly white chaps and a hat that is taller than anything even Tom Mix ever wore.

In the late nineteenth century, cowboys typically wore "stovepipe" or "shotgun" chaps, which had narrow legs like a pair of pants and were sewn all the way down the leg. The name "stovepipe" came about because the legs looked like round pipes, similar to a stovepipe. "Shotgun" came from the two legs looking like the double barrels of a shotgun. These chaps were typically made from leather and had a pocket on the front of each leg, as exemplified by those worn by Charley Waite (Kevin Costner) in *Open Range* (2004). Shotgun chaps were either pulled on over the boots or the boots had to be taken off to put on the chaps.

The wide, flapping "batwing" type of chaps, as worn by the Ringo Kid (John Wayne) in

This well-worn pair of "shotgun" chaps was used by one of the cowboys who rode with Charlie Goodnight. The two pockets on the front could hold pencils, tobacco, cigarette paper, and other small personal items. Like most other cowboys, the owner of this pair of chaps was obviously a small man, as this set has a twenty-eight inch inseam.

*Stagecoach* (1939), were developed later than shotgun chaps and were not popularly worn until the 1920s, when shotgun and wooly chaps were on the way out. Batwing chaps—which eventually became wider and wider—were easier to put on than shotgun chaps because they fastened in place down the leg with straps and did not have to be pulled on over the boot like shotgun chaps. Batwing chaps became the trademark of the movie cowboy of the 1930s and later. For a real cowboy working with cattle, the narrower shotgun chaps were more practical because there was less likelihood of the wide, flapping legs catching on brush and branches, and possibly causing an accident.

### Wrist Cuffs

Leather wrist cuffs were originally part of a working cowboy's outfit. These cuffs, which extended to about eight inches above the wrist joint, originated in the 1880s among cowboys in Texas. After a cowboy had roped a cow, he would loop the rope around his arm to anchor it. Wearing a leather cuff protected his forearm and wrist from friction and any resulting rope burns. Leather wrist cuffs, however, were not particularly glamorous and were not often worn by screen cowboys, though early stars William S. Hart and Broncho Billy Anderson both wore them for authenticity.

Though wrist cuffs are not often seen in movies, purists can still occasionally spot them. In *Winchester '73* (1950), for example, Lin McAdam's (James Stewart) sidekick, High Spade (Millard Mitchell), wears leather wrist cuffs. In *The Paleface* (1948), one of the bad guys who tries to shoot Calamity Jane (Jane Russell) in the bath house wears leather cuffs, like a real cowboy would. At the beginning of *Wyatt Earp* (1994), when Earp (Kevin Costner) is working as a freighter, the shotgun guard riding beside him has leather cuffs.

## Oilskins

When the weather turned to rain or snow, cowboys needed protection from cold and wetness. In the winter, many cowboys used surplus wool army greatcoats or coats made from buffalo fur to protect against the bitter cold of the Northern Plains.

During the Civil War, soldiers carried a rubberized waterproof blanket with a slit in the middle to use as a poncho to protect against rain. Cowboys purchased these as war surplus for the same purpose. A later popular solution to protect against rain was Fish Brand slickers, a type of poncho first made in 1881 by Abner J. Tower. Fabricated from yellow oilskin (oiled linen), these slickers were called "fish skin" or "saddle coats." The slickers had a long slit up the back so that the material would drape down each side of a horse to fully protect the rider in the saddle. These rain slickers were also large enough that a cowboy could sleep under one in rainy weather. This style was very popular and was widely copied by other companies. Sometimes they were generically referred to simply as a "fish" or a "fishbrand."

The movies are not always accurate in their depiction of this clothing. The dusters seen in *Red River* (1948), for example, were not split up the back with extra material to accommodate the cantle at the back of the saddle for riding, and did not contain the extra fabric needed to cover the saddle pommel.[10] These garments were historically inaccurate and made strictly for the movies. Similar slickers showed up in *The Searchers* (1956), *The Wild Bunch* (1969), and *The Long Riders* (1980). In *Silverado* (1985), several of the characters wear slickers that are split for riding. Towards the end of *Wyatt Earp* (1994), Wyatt wears a duster that is correctly split up the back for riding.

Slickers have often been used in Westerns more for dramatic effect than for authenticity. For example, one of the sinister moments in *Pale Rider* (1985) occurs when the six deputies, led by Marshal Stockburn (John Russell), all dressed in identical tan dusters, line up in a row on the boardwalk before they shoot Spider Conway (Doug McGrath). For similar effect, the deputies surrounding town boss Marshal Herod (Gene Hackman) in *The Quick and the Dead* (1995) all wear long black slickers, whether it is raining or not. The Stranger (Clint Eastwood) wore a duster to create a suitable dramatic effect in *High Plains Drifter* (1973). This is parodied in *Rustlers' Rhapsody* (1985) when the Italian cowboys wear long slickers no matter how hot the weather is outside.

For a while Australian dusters were popularized by the movies and the fashion industry, but they were not a genuine American cowboy garment and were not styled for suitable use on a horse.

## Gloves

Leather gloves were a practical accessory for a real cowboy. They protected his hands from barbed wire while installing fencing, from rope burns while working with cattle, and from blisters while digging post holes or doing other heavy manual labor. Gloves also added a measure of protection for the hands and fingers in cold weather. Fringed gauntlets, such as those worn by showman Buffalo Bill Cody, were rarely worn by working cowboys, as most preferred wrist cuffs to protect their forearms.

Gloves worn by movie cowboys also had some practical aspects. Tom Mix started to wear gloves because he had soft hands and the leather protected them from injury. Other screen stars soon copied his look, and gloves became an important part of the screen cowboy's uniform.[11]

Gene Autry first wore gloves as part of his character's personality. During lulls in the action or conversation, he could pull them on slowly to make it look like he was doing something. They also kept his hands from being scraped and skinned during screen fights.[12]

In *Shane* (1953), Jack Wilson (Jack Palance) built plot tension by slowly pulling a glove onto his right hand. In real life, however, a gunfighter wouldn't wear a glove because it would interfere with his draw and firing his weapon. In *The War Wagon* (1967), Lomax (Kirk Douglas) wears a single black glove made from thin leather and occasionally pulls it on in sinister fashion—but not onto his gun hand.

### Eyeglasses

Though not strictly speaking a clothing accessory (as is today's fashion eyewear), eyeglasses were not commonly worn by cowboys. From a strictly practical standpoint eyeglasses were expensive, and the average cowboy who was making $30 or $40 a month could not afford them.

More than that, however, eyeglasses in the late 1800s had a stigma associated with them, because using glasses was considered to be a sign of old age and weakness. This is quite accurately portrayed by ex-marshal Steven Judd (Joel McCrea), when he is negotiating the contract with the bank in *Ride the High Country* (1962). Rather than put on his eyeglasses in front of his potential employers and thus admit weakness, he goes alone into the bathroom to bring out his glasses to read the fine print. In *She Wore a Yellow Ribbon* (1949), eyeglasses symbolize advancing age when Nathan Brittles (John Wayne) puts on his spectacles in order to read the inscription on the silver watch presented to him by the troop on his retirement. In *Big Jake* (1971), Jacob McCandles (John Wayne) uses glasses for reading. Eyeglasses were typically oval or round in shape, with wire rims.

## Women's Clothing

The clothing worn by male movie stars of the 1930s and 1940s bore little resemblance to those worn by authentic cowboys. The clothing worn by their female counterparts, however, is closer to reality.

Pioneer women headed west in wagon trains typically wore gingham or calico dresses, a sunbonnet, and a muslin apron. In fact, the 1858 National Wagon Road Guide recommended that women in wagon trains should dress plainly like this, avoiding fancy clothing and never drawing attention to themselves, because a gay dress or other finery would "lay woman open to severe misconstruction."[13] The bloomer costume developed by Amelia Jenks Bloomer to allow body freedom during exercise and bicycle riding were an Eastern fad and were not worn much in the West.

Respectable women in the movies typically wore what real Victorian women wore. Dresses had skirts that reached to the ground and necklines that went up to the neck. Real dance-hall girls wore skirts that were shockingly short for the time — but that meant that they were up to the ankle or mid-calf instead of brushing the ground. Actresses tended to wear scandalous costumes that consisted of short skirts, or skimpy circus-type costumes and tights.

Women such as Calamity Jane occasionally wore clothing of the same style as men, but that was unusual. Vintage photographs show three women identified as the Becker sisters branding cattle on their father's ranch in the San Luis Valley of Colorado in 1894. Even for roping and branding cows in a corral, two of them are shown wearing ground-length skirts, while the third has a shorter skirt that is nonetheless down to her ankles.

One consistent anachronism seen in Westerns is the zipper going up the back of women's dresses, even though the modern zipper wasn't developed until 1913. For example, Doc Holliday's girlfriend Kate Elder (Jo Van Fleet) has a zipper up the back of her dresses in *Gunfight at the O.K. Corral* (1957). Temperance crusader Cora Templeton Massingale (Lee Remick) and her convert Louise Gearhart (Pamela Tiffin) in *Hallelujah Trail* (1965) both have zippers up the backs of their dresses as well.

## Military Uniforms

Though the design of army uniforms changed over the years, the basics stayed the same. The standard enlisted man's uniform consisted of a gray or dark-blue flannel shirt underneath a navy-blue wool jacket, called a blouse. Trousers were light blue. Yellow trim on the uniform denoted the cavalry, with light blue or white for the infantry. Red trim was used for the artillery, though this color was not commonly seen on the frontier because artillery soldiers almost exclusively guarded the country's two sea coasts.

The basic uniform was completed with ill-fitting black leather boots or shoes, and a dark blue felt forage cap, or kepi, with a round, flat top and a leather visor. Enlisted men wore cap symbols made of stamped brass with crossed sabers for the cavalry, a bugle (later replaced by crossed rifles) for the infantry, and crossed cannon barrels for the artillery. The kepi was inadequate for protection against both sun and rain, so in 1873 a black, wide-brimmed felt hat was introduced for campaigning in the field.

Dress uniforms were specified for certain ceremonial occasions, such as formal dances and dress parades. When in the field, the soldiers' mode of dress was more casual, and many wore non-regulation items for comfort, including civilian hats, shirts, and trousers.

For the most part, the uniforms of Hollywood soldiers seem always to be the standard cavalry uniform of the 1870s, with the addition of yellow bandanas around the necks. The real cavalry did not wear these bandanas. This was a Hollywood addition to make the cavalry look more colorful, and this touch has become ensconced in the moviegoing public's view of how the cavalry dressed. Thinking about it, putting a bright yellow bandana on the neck would not be wise, as it makes a perfect target for Indians to shoot at.

### Gun Leather

Besides a gun, the other vital element of a movie cowboy's outfit and gunfighting rig was his gunbelt and holster. Holsters developed along with the revolvers they were intended to carry, so as to keep the weapon ready for immediate use.

The earliest of Colt's popular revolvers, the Dragoon, which was developed in 1847, weighed a whopping four pounds and nine ounces. This massive firearm was too heavy to be worn all day in a holster on a soldier's or gunfighter's belt, so it was typically carried in a holster that was draped over the pommel of the saddle. Typically, two holsters and two Dragoon revolvers were carried at the same time so that they balanced the weight across the horse's neck. These so-called "pommel holsters" had a flap that fastened over the butt of the gun to protect it from the elements and prevent it from bouncing out of the holster if the horse reared.

As handguns became lighter in weight, it became practical to wear them in a holster on a belt around the waist. The Colt Model 1851 Navy revolver weighed only two pounds and ten ounces, which allowed the firearm to be carried in a belt-supported holster. The military intended this holster to be worn so that the gun butt faced forward on the right hip. That way the revolver could be drawn in a crossdraw with the left hand, as a cavalry trooper's right hand was reserved for using his sword.

Military holsters used by the cavalry had a flap on the top to protect the gun from rain, snow, and sand, and to make sure that it remained firmly in the holster while on horseback, or while dismounting and mounting. Civilian holsters were commonly open at the top for faster and easier access to the revolver. Civilians who could not afford a new leather holster after the Civil War bought an army surplus military holster, which was commonly available on the civilian market, and cut the flap off the top to allow an easier draw. Holster-makers picked up on this open concept and eventually made their holsters without a flap.

The first true Western gunfighting holsters appeared in the California gold fields in the early 1850s. They had a slim, contoured fit for the long barrel of the popular Model 1851 Colt Navy percussion revolver. The design typically had an open top with deep sides to protect the cylinder and hammer of the gun. Because of their origin in the goldfields, these types of holsters became known as "California" pattern holsters. They also received the name "Slim Jim" holster, because the slim design fitted tightly to the long barrel of the Colt. These holsters were sometimes called "scabbards," as opposed to the word "scabbard" being more commonly applied today to the protective sheath for a sword.

Because a cowboy's trousers were usually not held up by a belt, a specific belt was used to carry and support the holster. Gun belts were typically made from several layers of leather that were doubled over for strength. This design created a thin compartment on the inside that was used to carry paper money, gold

Real gunfighters in the Old West wore holsters that were deep, fitted snugly around the cylinder of the revolver, and covered the hammer. This design was intended to protect the gun from damage. This example is the so-called Mexican Loop pattern of holster, where the gun pouch is passed through horizontal slits in the leather backing to form a large loop at the top, which rides high on the belt. This is contrasted to the later Buscadero holster, which rides much lower on the wearer's thigh.

coins, or small important papers. Cartridge loops, technically called "thimbles," were added to gun belts in the mid–1870s to carry additional ammunition. Some cartridge belts incorporated a double row of thimbles in order to increase their capacity.

After specifically-designed cartridge belts came into common use, holsters were adapted to fit over this type of thick, wide belt. When the holster was made, the leather was cut with an extended portion attached to the top that was about the same size as the back of the revolver pouch, but with horizontal slits in it. This piece was folded down behind the pouch, and the pouch was passed through the slits to create a large belt loop between the two pieces that would fit over the cartridges on the belt. This design became known as the "Mexican Loop" pattern.

Early holsters were not designed nor intended for the lightning-fast draws shown in the movies or on television. Instead the holsters were intentionally large and designed to protect the gun. The sides were high, and the gun fitted deeply into the holster to prevent it from falling out onto the ground. The outside leather portion of the pouch typically covered the trigger guard and trigger, as well as most of the hammer, so that the revolver would not accidentally discharge if the hammer were struck by mistake.

These holsters were also generally worn high on the waist rather than on the thigh in the low-slung style of the fast-draw holsters of Hollywood. Historical photographs show most revolvers being worn at about waist level and forward of the hip. Another option was to wear the holster lower, on the front of the thigh, instead of at the side. In *Lawman* (1971), Harvey Stenbaugh (Albert Salmi) wears his gun so far forward on the right that it is over his crotch.

Holsters for serious gunfighters had to be worn low enough that the gun could easily and quickly clear the top of the leather, and not catch on the holster. As a result, an alternate favored location was to wear the holster backwards on the opposite hip so that the gunman could perform a cross-draw.

Later holster designs incorporated a rounded notch on the top of the pouch that exposed the revolver's trigger guard and trigger. This created enough open space for the wearer to place his finger on the trigger while drawing the gun, before the barrel had cleared the holster. This could give a gunfighter a slight advantage in a competitive life-or-death fast-draw situation.

Some men who carried a gun did not use a holster. Instead, their revolver was carried in a leather-lined pants pocket. Small, specially-designed revolvers and derringers, specifically advertised as "pocket pistols," were intended to be carried in a man's hip pocket to make the gun easier to conceal and draw. Special leather holsters designed to be inserted in hip-pockets were fashioned to hold these small guns in a safe and easily-retrieved position. Without the internal leather support of a holster, a gun in a cloth pocket tended to sag at an angle and catch on the material when the shooter attempted a rapid draw.

Concealed holsters became common in the 1880s, as more and more towns banned the carrying of firearms. Thus, men who did not want to give up their weapons could conveniently carry a pistol in a pocket in a small holster. Legend has it that the hip pocket on men's trousers was invented in order to conveniently carry a gun. Holsters that clipped to the inside of a man's waistband or inside a jacket pocket were also available.

In *The Good, the Bad and the Ugly* (1966), set during the Civil War, Tuco (Eli Wallach) wears his gun in a leather-lined pants pocket, which was not unusual for the time, as holsters for civilian guns did not come into common use until after the Civil War. In another nice touch, Tuco wears a string around his neck that is attached to the butt of the gun, so that it will not be lost. Again, this method of wearing a gun was not uncommon, though typically this was a method used for securing the smaller pocket pistols, which were carried inside a shirt or jacket and attached to a lanyard around the neck.

## *The Cross-Draw and the Cavalry Draw*

Many gunfighters found it easier to cock the hammer of a revolver while the gun was coming out of the holster if the gun was carried with the butt foremost. The gun was drawn out of the belt or holster via a cross-draw, which meant that the hand opposite the holstered revolver came across the front of the body to pull the gun out. Colonel Mortimer (Lee Van Cleef), for example, wore his holster in a cross-draw fashion in *For a Few Dollars More* (1965).

Another method of drawing a revolver butt-forward was the inverted draw, also called the "cavalry draw" because army troopers wore their revolvers in this fashion. The revolver was worn in a holster on the right hip with the butt-forward, and was drawn with the hand on the same side as the gun. The left hand was used to hold the horse's reins. The draw was completed by twisting the hand inwards to grasp the butt of the gun, then pulling out the gun and rotating it at the same time. Some gunfighters claimed this was the fastest way to draw a revolver.

Wild Bill Hickok carried two Colt Model 1851 Navy revolvers tucked into a sash with the butts forward. Like his namesake, B-Western star Wild Bill Elliott wore his two guns with the butts forward, and pulled them out in a double cavalry draw.

## *The Buscadero Rig*

In the early 1920s a saddle-maker in El Paso, Texas, named Sam D. Myres joined with Texas Ranger John R. Hughes to develop what is called the "Buscadero" gun belt and holster.[14] With this type of rig a section of the leather cartridge belt on the holster side extends down lower than the main part of the gunbelt. Then, instead of the loop at the top of the holster passing over the entire cartridge belt, the holster attaches to a slot at the bottom of this downward extension. The back of the holster passes through the slot, is folded over, and is attached back onto itself for a secure fit. This arrangement places the gun much lower on the leg than previous designs. The butt of the revolver rides at the level of the gunman's wrist, which enables a faster draw. Because the holster rides so low on the leg, this rig is also called a "drop loop" holster.

The Buscadero style is the type of holster typically featured in Westerns from the 1920s onwards. Stars of the B-Westerns, such as Buck Jones, Tim McCoy, Gene Autry, Roy Rogers, and Hopalong Cassidy, took two-gun holster designs to extremes, with fancy tooling and border trims, ornate straps and buckles, and silver designs mounted onto the leather. Jewels were sometimes added to the inlaid silver designs, and floral motifs were common in the tooling of the holster and belt. Matching gloves and silver spurs often completed the outfit. Many of these rigs were made by craftsman Edward H. Bohlin of Hollywood between 1920 and 1945.

Because of the notoriety that these fancy Buscadero designs gained in B-Westerns, the outfit became an anachronism. It became mistakenly identified as the typical gunfighter's fast-draw holster from the 1870s and 1880s—a time period long before it was even invented.

After the 1940s holsters returned to simpler designs, as they were specifically developed for television and fast-draw competitions in the 1950s and 1960s. A plain-leather revolver pouch was attached to a simple Buscadero belt. In some cases the loop on the cartridge belt was dropped even lower so that the holster rode at mid-thigh and the butt of the revolver rode closer to the user's wrist. The gun pouch of the holster was simplified and streamlined until it looked more like a simple cylinder of leather. The top was also cut lower so that it did not cover the trigger guard or hammer at all. Some movie stars wore their guns with the butt forward to perform a cross-draw, but that was more difficult with a Buscadero rig.

Tying the holster down to the leg with a leather thong was another Hollywood invention. If the holster was worn high on the waist, like the real gunfighters of the West, it stayed put when the gun was drawn. When the holster was placed lower down on the thigh in Hollywood Buscadero style, it was necessary to tie the bottom of the pouch down to the leg or else the entire holster would be pulled up with the gun when an attempt was made to draw the firearm. Because the top of the gun was completely exposed, a leather thong that looped over the hammer spur was also added to hold the revolver securely in the holster when it was not in use.

### Arvo Ojala

Modern cowboy holsters have been designed specifically for fast-draw and allow for speeds that an old-time gunfighter would yearn for. The basic design of this type of fast-draw gun rig was developed around 1953 by Arvo Ojala, who arrived in Hollywood in 1950 from the Yakima Valley of Washington. Ojala was a stunt man and fast-draw expert who coached many of the Hollywood movie and television stars in fast-draw techniques, and doubled for many of them during fast-draw scenes. He was, for example, Marshal Dillon's opponent in the opening shoot-out scene of the television series *Gunsmoke*.

The holster that Ojala developed and patented was fabricated from two thin pieces of leather sewn together, with a thin piece of metal between the two. The purpose of this design was to stiffen the sides of the pouch and hold them open and away from the cylinder of the revolver. Thus the design allowed the cylinder to rotate and the hammer of the revolver to be cocked during the draw before the gun even cleared the holster. For safety reasons, shooters participating in fast-draw competitions were supposed to keep their forefinger alongside the trigger until after the barrel had cleared the holster and the gun was coming onto the target. The holster was tilted about fifteen degrees backwards on the cartridge belt to allow the barrel to clear the holster faster and provide some measure of safety in case the gun discharged before intended. A holster that pointed straight down the thigh would result in the bullet perforating the leg if a fast-draw expert using live ammunition was not as good as he thought he was. This type of fast-draw rig, with the distinctive backwards tilt and the butt of the gun tilted away from the body, is not often seen in the movies, though one example is the two-gun rig that gunfighter Jack Wilson (Jack Palance) wears in *Shane* (1953).

This type of holster design was useful for the type of quick-draw competition that was popular in the 1950s, using blank cartridges to stop a timer. The event started with the shooter's hand held about ten inches from his gun, with a finger on a control switch for the timer. When the shooter's hand left the switch, the timer started. The competitor drew his gun and fired a blank cartridge as fast as he could. The sound of the explosion then stopped the timer. Aim and accuracy were not important, only the speed of draw-and-shoot to stop the clock. Times of about two-tenths of a second could be achieved by a good shooter.[15]

*Chapter Eight*

# Firepower

In most Western movies a gunfighter is ready to draw his revolver at the drop of a hat and blast away with it at anybody giving the least provocation. In *The Train Robbers* (1973), Jesse (Ben Johnson) philosophizes around the camp fire as he says to his companions, "That's the trouble with young guns. Mighty tempting to cross over to the wild side."

A gun is an essential item of a movie cowboy's outfit and is crucial to the plot in order for him to resolve the conflicts that have been generated. While the brief description of firearms in this chapter is highly generalized and simplified, it will serve as a background for understanding the types of firearms used in the real West and in Western movies.

The major studios, such as MGM, RKO, and 20th Century–Fox, had their own armories to supply the guns needed for Westerns. Others could rent Peacemakers and Winchesters from specialized businesses, such as Stembridge Guns Rentals in Hollywood, which was founded by Cecil B. DeMille and James S. Stembridge in 1918 to supply guns to the movie industry.

Blank cartridges for use in the movies used various strengths of loads.[1] In addition, different loads were optimized for different uses. For example, flash powder might be added to special cartridges to give a more spectacular stream of flame from the barrel of the gun when shooting at night.

A typical movie blank cartridge was filled with a quarter-load, enough to make a satisfying bang but not enough to overwhelm the shooter with the recoil. An additional factor was protection of the shooter's ears. Over a lifetime of shooting blanks, even with reduced loads, most old Western movie stars suffered from some degree of hearing loss.

## Six-Shooters and More

Prior to the development of revolvers that reliably fired multiple shots, pistols generally fired only a single shot before they had to be reloaded. Revolvers of the Wild West, on the other hand, received their name because they contained a revolving cylinder with multiple chambers that could fire several bullets before the gun had to be reloaded. After the trigger was pulled and each shot fired, the cylinder revolved as the hammer was cocked for the next shot, and a fresh, unfired cartridge was lined up with the barrel.

Early revolvers had complicated and delicate mechanisms that were prone to breakage and failure during use. As a result, they were not particularly popular. It was not until Samuel Colt started to manufacture an improved type of revolver in the late 1830s that this type of gun became widespread. Contrary to popular opinion, Colt did not invent the single-action revolver, but he did make it simple, practical, and reliable.

Early handgun designs used five shots in a revolving cylinder. The capacity of the cylinder was later increased to six, leading to the common nicknames of "six-gun" and "six-shooter" for revolvers.

This apparently wasn't always known to Hollywood filmmakers, as bullets seem to multiply like rabbits in some six-shooters. At the end of *The Sons of Katie Elder* (1965), for example, during the climactic shoot-out that leads to the explosion in the villain's gunshop, John Elder (John Wayne) fires his trusty Peacemaker six times, then fires another eight times without reloading, making fourteen shots in all. In *The Sheepman* (1958), Chocktaw Neal (Pernell Roberts) fires his six-shooter seven times before he reloads and is gunned down by Jason Sweet (Glenn Ford) in their main-street shootout. William Blake (Johnny Depp) also fires seven times from a six-shooter in *Dead Man* (1996). In *The Villain* (1979), Handsome Stranger (Arnold Schwarzenegger) brags about having a seven-shot six-shooter.[2] In *The Train Robbers* (1973), the Pinkerton Man (Ricardo Montalban) fires an amazing nineteen shots in succession from a Winchester carbine without reloading.[3] In the final shootout with Jack McCall's confederates in *Wild Bill* (1995), Hickok (Jeff Bridges) fires a volley of twenty-five or twenty-six shots from his two six-shooters, one of the most impressive shooting records for a Colt revolver in a Western. But then such is the magic of Hollywood.

From a historical standpoint, the major technical improvements in guns and ammunition that led to the golden era of gunfighting were made during and after the Civil War. Revolvers became smaller, lighter, and easier to carry, which in turn led to their ease of use and an increased ability to shoot someone.

Three main types of handgun were used during the period from 1865 to 1890, when most Western movies were supposed to take place. In order of development, they were the single-action cap-and-ball revolver, the single-action revolver that used self-contained metallic cartridges, and the double-action revolver that used metallic cartridges.[4]

One of the most common anachronisms that appears in Westerns occurs in the use of these firearms, as the revolvers shown in many of these movies had not been developed at the time the story was set. A common mistake, for example, would be for the hero to use a .45 Peacemaker in a Civil War movie, when this particular model of gun wasn't manufactured until 1873. Even then it was in short supply as a military weapon and wasn't available to the general public until about 1875.

As a specific example, in *Abilene Town* (1946) Marshal Dan Brown (Randolph Scott) carries a Colt Peacemaker, which was first used by the army in 1873, but the movie set in 1870. Another typical example occurs in *The Paleface* (1948), where the villains are trying to ambush Calamity Jane (Jane Russell) in a bathhouse. One of them is carrying a Colt double-action revolver and appears to be fanning it, though he is actually pulling the trigger as he shoots. This action does not match the time period of the movie, as this type of revolver was not developed until at least 1888. *Dodge City* (1939), set in 1872, shows Wade Hatton (Errol Flynn) cleaning up the town. Unfortunately, he and his men do it with 1873 Colt Peacemakers. Earlier in the movie, Lee Irving (William Lundigan) draws his single-action revolver, then suddenly fires three shots in rapid succession from a double-action revolver. Again, these guns hadn't been invented by this time period.

Another common error is having the post–Civil War cavalry carry Winchester Model 1873 repeating rifles to fight off Indian attacks. In the first place, this rifle wasn't manufactured until 1873. Secondly, the Winchester repeater was never an official army weapon. In another classic case of anachronism, many Westerns use the Winchester Model 1894 in place of the Model 1873. In *Hallelujah Trail* (1965), when the Indians are issued surplus rifles from the Civil War — strictly for hunting, of course — the weapons look suspiciously like the Winchester Model 1894. The reasons for these types of errors will become clearer after considering the history of the development of these firearms.

In all fairness, though, these inconsistencies are not always matters of ignorance, and these particular guns may be used deliberately in movies for artistic reasons, because the Peacemaker and the Winchester repeater are the iconic symbols of the Old West and the classic Western movie.

## Ammunition

The development of revolvers before and just after the Civil War went hand-in-hand with improvements in ammunition. The handguns seen in Westerns fall into two very general categories based on the type of ammunition they used. The first is cap-and-ball ammunition, and the other is metallic cartridges.

All firearms contain three elements that allow the weapon to fire a bullet. The first component is gunpowder, which is ignited to push the bullet out of the gun barrel at a high rate of speed. Gunpowder burns very fast, and as it does so it generates a large volume of gas that rapidly creates a very high pressure inside the cartridge in the chamber of the gun. The only way that this gas can escape from the gun is to push the lead bullet out of the chamber, down the barrel, and thus towards the desired target.

The second important element is a method of igniting the gunpowder when the trigger is pulled. This is accomplished by a primer, which is a small explosive device. When hit by the hammer of the gun, the primer throws out a spark that is driven into the main charge of gunpowder and ignites it.

The third component is the bullet, which is a chunk of lead that is ejected from the barrel at a high rate of speed towards the target. The bullet kills by piercing and damaging a vital part of the body, such as the heart or lungs, or by sheer mechanical shock as the large amount of energy that propels the bullet is suddenly dissipated into the target. Early bullets for handguns were round balls of lead, often simply called a "ball." Later bullets were conical. This pointed design reduced resistance from the air as the bullet sped towards its target and helped it penetrate whatever it hit.

So, in essence, firing a gun involves pulling the trigger, which drops the hammer onto the primer. The force of the hammer hitting the primer causes the primer to explode and send a spark into the gunpowder. The powder ignites and burns very fast, and the subsequent large volume of gas that is created in the chamber of the gun drives the bullet down the barrel. Reduced to the basic elements of operation, all guns operate in this manner.

The historical difference in revolvers of interest in Western movies is the manner in which the ingredients were mechanically combined. In the earliest revolvers that appear in Western movies, loose gunpowder and lead bullets were loaded separately into the chambers of the gun. The explosive primer material was contained in a small, copper, cup-shaped device called a percussion cap, was placed on a projection at the back of the cylinder. Later guns used self-contained metallic cartridges in which all three components were combined into one metallic case.

*Cap-and-Ball Ammunition*

The earliest type of handgun that coincides with the era in which many Western movies are supposed to take place was the cap-and-ball revolver. The three components — powder, bullet, and primer — were separate. Named after the percussion cap, this type of weapon was often called a "percussion" revolver or a "cap-and-ball" revolver (short for "percussion cap" and "spherical ball bullet").

To prepare this type of gun for firing, a measured amount of gunpowder is poured into the front of each chamber and a bullet rammed down firmly on top of it with a plunger, seating the bullet solidly in the chamber. The primers are individually placed onto the back of each cylinder on a small metal projection called the "cone" or the "nipple." The nipple contains a small orifice that leads into the main powder charge in each chamber of the gun. This type of revolver is not common in Westerns but is occasionally seen. One example is in *The Quick and the Dead* (1995), where the Swede is seen laboriously loading his gun with round bullets and pushing them into the chambers with the loading lever. The Colt Dragoon revolver that Mattie Ross (Kim Darby) uses in *True Grit* (1969) is also a cap-and-ball percussion revolver.

The powder used in guns in the second half of the nineteenth century was black powder, also known by the generic name of "gunpowder." Gunpowder is made from a combination of saltpeter (potassium nitrate), sulfur, and charcoal. Using black powder in a revolver had several disadvantages. One was that the burning powder produced a spectacular cloud of flame and grayish smoke that exploded from the end of the barrel when the gun was fired. When shooting at a distance, this flame and smoke clearly marked the shooter's position for the opposition. Another disadvantage was that the smoke drifting around after several shots could obscure the shooter's view.

A third problem was that black powder was unstable and prone to degrade, and it could absorb moisture in a humid environment, both of which made the gun likely to misfire. An ironic example of misfires occurred with the death of the real Wild Bill Hickok. When Jack McCall's cap-and-ball revolver was examined after he shot Hickok, law officers in Deadwood discovered that he had fired the only chamber in the gun that was not defective.

Black powder burns slowly, as compared to modern smokeless powders. As a result, a residue of burned and unburned powder collected rapidly in the barrel of the revolver. After several shots, this could affect the accuracy of the gun. As a practical matter, if the range between shooters was only five or ten yards (or even closer, as in many gunfights), this was of no real consequence. When shooting at a greater distance, however, this fouling in the barrel of the gun might make the difference between a hit and a miss — and consequently between life and death.

Fouling could also occur in the nipple. The explosive fulminate of mercury used in the percussion cap was corrosive and could rapidly cause the nipple to become blocked. The nipple could also become blocked by debris from the exploding cap or from unburned powder that was forced backwards into the nipple and clogged the orifice. In either case, a blocked nipple would cause the gun to misfire.

Unburned powder forced out of the gun barrel might have other consequences. In *True Grit* (1969), Tom Cheney (Jeff Corey) has a black mark on his cheek from powder that got under his skin when a gun was supposedly pointed and fired in his face. This was not a figment of the screenwriter's imagination. This really happened to gunman Charles Bryant, who was too close to a gun that discharged during a fight. The shot peppered his cheek with a residue of black powder, embedding some of it in the flesh. As a result of this unintended tattoo, he became known as "Blackface Charlie" from then on.

### Metallic Cartridges

Loading or reloading a revolver that used loose powder and percussion caps was a time-consuming procedure. This could be a problem for a gunfighter during a firefight when every second and every shot counted. In addition, if the powder had inadvertently deteriorated, it might not even ignite and fire the gun.

A major development in ammunition to solve these problems was the self-contained metallic cartridge, which consisted of a cylindrical metal shell that housed the powder, the primer, and the bullet in one convenient sealed package. Self-contained metallic cartridges were easier to store, handle, and load, and were impervious to moisture. Instead of loading the components into the front of the cylinder, this new type of ammunition was loaded from the rear. The speed and ease of loading the gun, the lack of susceptibility to damp weather, and the added reliability of firing gave gunfighters more confidence that their weapons would fire reliably in a gunfight.

Percussion revolvers remained in use on the Western frontier through the 1860s and were the standard weapon of gunfighters well into the 1870s, partly because they performed well and partly because ball ammunition was more powerful than the first metallic cartridges. The introduction and improvement of metallic cartridges, however, eventually ended the use of loose gunpowder and percussion caps. Many of the old-time gunfighters, though, trusted and preferred their cap-and-ball revolvers, and felt that they were more accurate and reliable than weapons that used the newfangled metallic cartridges. Those who wanted to keep their old guns did not always have to stick with powder and ball ammunition, however. By re-boring the barrel and altering the loading mechanism, many percussion pistols and rifles were converted to use metallic cartridges and continued to function reliably for many years.

## Handguns

Improvements in ammunition generated improvements in handguns. The type of handguns typically seen in Westerns started to emerge when Samuel Colt received a patent on several design improvements for revolvers in 1835, thus ushering in the new era of rapid-fire killing technology that blossomed in the latter half of the nineteenth century. Because the change to newer models of guns was not immediate, a variety of older weapons remained in use in the West while the transition to newer designs was taking place. Thus, gunmen of the Old West carried weapons that were a mixed collection of pre–Civil War rifles and handguns, redesigned weapons developed for use during the war, converted percussion revolvers, and the improved revolvers that were continually being introduced.

### Cap-and-Ball Revolvers

The commonest type of early revolver seen in Westerns is the percussion revolver developed by Samuel Colt at the Colt Patents Arms Manufacturing Company in Hartford, Connecticut. In 1847 Colt developed the Dragoon Model.[5] This gun was known at the factory as the Old Model Holster Pistol. It was a massive .44 caliber percussion revolver with a 7½-inch barrel that weighed four pounds and two ounces.[6]

The weight of a Dragoon revolver made it impractical to carry on a belt, so it was usually carried in a pommel holster draped over a horse's neck in front of the saddle. This type of revolver is not commonly seen in Westerns but can occasionally be spotted. For example, there is a brief glimpse of a pommel holster slung across Rooster Cogburn's saddle horn in *True Grit* (2010). But for additional fire power, he also carries a cross-draw conventional .45 Colt. The massive revolvers that Josey Wales (Clint Eastwood) uses in *The Outlaw Josey Wales* (1976) are the Colt Walker Model revolvers, the immediate forerunner of the Dragoon model, with a 9-inch barrel and weight of four pounds and nine ounces.

### Single-Action Revolvers

Early revolvers, such as the Dragoon, were of the single-action (SA) type, which meant that the gun was prepared for firing by pulling back and cocking the hammer before each shot. Single-action revolvers typically contained six chambers, which was the amount of shots that could be fired by continuing to cock the hammer and pull the trigger before reloading was necessary. The mechanism of a double-action (DA) revolver, by contrast, is such that each time the shooter pulls the trigger the cylinder revolves, a fresh cartridge is lined up with the barrel, and the hammer is automatically raised and falls to strike the cartridge and fire the bullet.

To fire a single-action revolver, the hammer has to be cocked, or else the gun is not ready to fire. Sometimes in the movies the hero has not cocked his gun when pointing it at the bad guy, which means that the gun is not ready to fire. All the villain has to do is grab it before the hero can cock it and fire. At the beginning of *4 for Texas* (1963), for example, Joe Jarrett (Dean Martin) doesn't have his single-action gun cocked when he is covering Zach Thomas (Frank Sinatra). At one point in *The Villain* (1979) the Colt revolver that

The earliest historical type of revolver seen in Westerns is the percussion revolver. The Colt Navy cap-and-ball percussion revolver in .36 caliber was introduced in 1851. It was an important weapon for gunfighters in the Old West before 1873 and the introduction of the Peacemaker. Some old-time gunmen who preferred this revolver to the Peacemaker altered the loading mechanism to take the new metallic cartridges. As a result, this type of revolver was used on the frontier well into the 1870s. To load this percussion type of revolver, loose gunpowder is poured into the front of each chamber, and the lead bullet, or "ball," is forced into place on top of it with the hinged loading lever.

Cactus Jack (Kirk Douglas) is using is not fully cocked. Similarly, in some movies the person holding the gun has his thumb on the hammer, or is holding it with the web between his thumb and forefinger covering the spur of the hammer. By holding the gun in this fashion there is no way to make a fast shot.

One of Colt's revolvers that became extremely popular with gunfighters was the Model 1851 Navy Revolver.[7] This was a six-shot, .36 caliber, single-action percussion revolver with a 7½-inch octagonal barrel and varnished walnut grips. The 1851 Navy was much lighter than the Dragoon revolver. It weighed only two pounds and ten ounces, making it light enough to be carried in a holster attached to the wearer's belt. One option for the Model 1851 Navy was an attachable shoulder stock (called a "carbine breech") that converted it into a carbine.

Another extremely popular revolver among gunfighters was the Colt Model 1860 Army revolver. Also weighing two pounds and ten ounces, the Model 1860 Army was also considerably lighter than previous models, but fired a heavy .44 caliber bullet. The designations "Army" and "Navy" were used to distinguish between calibers rather than to designate a specific model of revolver for a specific branch of the military.

Though bullets could fly considerably farther, the maximum effective accurate range for both of these handguns was about fifty to seventy-five yards. At the beginning of *For a Few Dollar More* (1965), bounty hunter Colonel Mortimer (Lee Van Cleef) shoots it out with one of the low-life characters he is trying to capture. The man runs away, and when he shoots back from a distance, his bullets fall short and send up spurts of dust at Mortimer's feet, as the range is too great for his revolver. Mortimer attaches a carbine breech to his long-barreled pistol to effectively make it a rifle for better accuracy and range, and shoots the man down. Later in the same movie, during the hat-shooting contest on the main street between Manco/The Man with No Name (Clint Eastwood) and Mortimer, Mortimer walks down the street until Manco's bullets fall short, then turns and pulls out his long-barreled gun to return fire.

A similar situation occurs in *4 for Texas* (1963). Zach Thomas (Frank Sinatra) makes sure that Joe Jarrett (Dean Martin) is out of range with his handgun before Thomas uses his rifle at a longer distance and shoots Jarrett off his horse. When Jarrett shoots back with his standard Colt .45, his bullets fall short.

### The Peacemaker

The Model 1860 Army was Colt's most popular handgun until 1873, when the factory introduced the Model 1873 Single-Action Army (SAA) revolver, which fired a new, very reliable metallic cartridge. Officially known at the factory as the Model P, the .45 caliber version of this revolver received the unofficial but common nickname of the "Peacemaker." Less glamorous, but just as accurate, nicknames were "hogleg," "thumb-buster," and "equalizer." This is the most famous gun in American history and is the one seen in most Western movies.

The Model P was sturdy, accurate for the times, and delivered tremendous stopping power with a heavy bullet that was intended to be a man-killer. The velocity of the fired bullet was relatively low, but its size and weight made the impact appalling, and the results were devastating at close range.

The design of the Peacemaker allowed the gun to be aimed and fired by general feel, giving it excellent "pointability." This meant that, with sufficient practice and at very close

The second oldest type of revolver seen in Westerns — and the most common — is the Peacemaker, the iconic symbol of the cowboy and the gunfighter. The Colt Single-Action Army (SAA) revolver in .45 caliber was first introduced for the army in 1873 and was popularly used until after the turn of the century. This version sports the 4¾-inch barrel preferred by gunfighters over the army version, because the shorter barrel could clear the holster faster when drawn. The new, more reliable self-contained metallic cartridges are loaded into the rear of each chamber through a loading gate that snaps shut after loading.

range, the Peacemaker could be pointed at the target, and the shooter could expect to hit reasonably close without holding the gun up and sighting along the barrel. This was a feature appreciated by gunfighters who practiced close-in shooting. With other makes of revolvers this was not always true. Although most fights took place at close range, and guns were often fired point blank at a man's opponent, the Peacemaker was also considered to be very accurate at ranges of twenty-five to fifty yards.

One drawback to the earlier cap-and-ball revolvers was that there was a slight delay between the gun's hammer striking the primer and the bullet exiting the barrel. The gun had to therefore be held steady on the target until the firing action was complete. Fast, random, point-and-shoot firing was less accurate. The new metallic cartridges, by contrast, fired the bullet almost instantaneously when the primer was struck by the firing pin, thus allowing better accuracy in this type of shooting.

Some gunfighters had a better knack for using a gun's pointability than others. Lawman and gambler Bat Masterson is said to have been a good marksman, with the ability to accurately point and shoot from the hip. For serious shooting, however, he claimed that he always sighted carefully along the barrel before pulling the trigger.

One of the ultimate examples of pointability in the movies would have to be in *High Plains Drifter* (1973), when the Stranger (Clint Eastwood) shoots a thug square between the eyes while sitting in a barber's chair with his gun concealed from view under the barber's sheet.

The original Model P was manufactured for the cavalry with a barrel length of 7½ inches so that troopers could shoot accurately at long distances, which was the most common situation when they were under attack. The effective accurate range with this length of barrel was about sixty yards.

Another version, with a 4¾-inch barrel and listed in Colt catalogues as the Civilian Model, was manufactured starting in the late 1870s. This shorter barrel was more popular among the general public, as it was easier to carry and to draw. Because gunfighters typically used this version at a closer range than did the cavalry, the shorter barrel was not a problem for accuracy, but was faster and easier to draw clear of the holster. Some lawmen, however, preferred a longer barrel because it made a more effective club for subduing rowdy drunks.

In spite of the image of the B-Westerns, most Peacemakers came from the factory with a standard finish of "bluing"— actually a metallic black color — rather than the bright nickel plating or the fancy engraving sported by movie cowboys of the 1940s and 1950s. Likewise, most Peacemakers had plain wooden grips made of walnut or rosewood rather than the exotic carved ivory or mother-of-pearl grips of the B-Westerns. Later Peacemakers sported grips made of vulcanite (hardened black rubber).

As well as in .45 caliber, the Model P was also manufactured in .44–40 caliber, starting in 1878, in a model that was known as the "Colt Frontier Six-Shooter." This caliber was popular with many frontier men because it used the same cartridge as the Winchester Model 1873 lever-action rifle, thus eliminating the need to carry two different types of ammunition.

The Model P was manufactured continuously from 1873 to 1941, when production was halted because of World War II. Manufacture of the revolver was resumed in 1955 due to interest in gun collecting, cowboy movies, fast-draw competitions (against the clock, but with blank cartridges), and later cowboy action shooting (live ammunition but no fast draw; see Appendix B). Black powder cartridges were used from 1873 to 1898. The later production models fired cartridges that use smokeless powder, which results in greater firepower for an equivalent charge of powder.

### Variations on the Peacemaker

One variation of the Peacemaker that has received some notoriety was the Buntline Special, which had a barrel that ranged from ten to sixteen inches long. This model was first announced in 1876. An earlier experimental option for the 1851 Navy featured a 12-inch barrel, which, when combined with a carbine breech, made this variant close to a carbine for accuracy.

The Buntline Special was named for Ned Buntline, the prolific creator of Western dime novels. As the story goes, Buntline supposedly gave away a dozen or so of these special Peacemakers to his friends, including Bat Masterson and Wyatt Earp; however, there is no confirmation of this in Colt's shipping records.[8] It further appears that the origin of the story was Stuart Lake's highly suspect *Wyatt Earp: Frontier Marshal*, and Buntline probably had no part in naming these long-barreled revolvers.[9] Whatever the truth of the origin, Colt did manufacture Peacemakers with 16-inch barrels for special orders starting in 1876.

The Buntline Special received most of its fame from the television series *The Life and Legend of Wyatt Earp*, in which Earp (Hugh O'Brian) carried one of these unusual guns. In *Wichita* (1955), Wyatt Earp (Joel McCrea) uses a revolver with a standard cavalry 7½-inch barrel, while everyone else uses guns with 4¾-inch barrels. Perhaps it was chosen to make his Colt look longer than everyone else's, like a Buntline special. Note also that McCrea played the marshal of Wichita, which the real Earp never was.

Another unusual variation on the Peacemaker was called the Bridgeport Rig, manufactured by the Bridgeport Gun Implement Company of Bridgeport, Connecticut. In this 1882 design by Texas sheriff Louis S. Flatau, one of the screws on the side of the revolver had a large, extended, flat head that was fitted into a slot in a metal plate mounted on the user's gunbelt. This configuration allowed the gun to hang down at the wearer's side without a holster, so that it could be rapidly swiveled into a horizontal position and fired from the hip. Flatau thought that the gun could be brought into action faster because it did not have to be drawn from a holster before firing.

Real gunfighters soon discovered that the attachment screw was easily damaged and that the plate rusted. In addition, the lack of a holster meant that the gun had no protection from sand, dust, rain, and snow. As a result, this mechanism was manufactured for only a short period in the 1880s. The Bridgeport rig received very limited acceptance by real gunfighters and has remained mostly a curiosity of movies and Western novels. The Bridgeport rig was used by self-styled "shootist" Sergeant Clay Cantrell (Keith David) during his gunfight with Herod (Gene Hackman) in *The Quick and the Dead* (1995). It apparently didn't do Cantrell much good, as he lost his match.

## Other Revolvers

Another handgun that can be spotted occasionally in Westerns, such as in *Sergeants 3* (1962), is the Remington Model 1875, a .44 caliber revolver that used metallic cartridges.[10] This revolver looks very similar to the Colt Peacemaker but can be distinguished from it by a triangular metal web that runs underneath from the end of the barrel to the frame. In *Unforgiven* (1992), one of Little Bill Daggett's (Gene Hackman) deputies in the town of Big Whiskey uses a Remington single-action revolver.

In 1870 Smith & Wesson introduced its first large revolver, the Model 3 single-action "American." This was a .44 caliber "top-break" revolver, with a frame that hinged in the middle. This allowed the barrel to tip forward, ejecting all the spent shells at the same time from the cylinder, and gave easy access to the empty chambers for reloading. By contrast, the Colt Peacemaker was slower to reload because the empty shells had to be unloaded from the cylinder one at a time with an ejector rod before loading fresh shells.

Another Smith & Wesson handgun that earned a strong following among lawmen and outlaws on the Western frontier was the .45 caliber, single-action, six-shot Schofield revolver, named after its designer, Major George W. Schofield, an army officer in the Tenth Cavalry. Based on Smith & Wesson's Model 3 American, the Schofield was a favorite weapon of Jesse James, and, ironically, it was the make of weapon that Bob Ford used to murder him.[11] Both the Model 3 and the Schofield are occasionally seen in Westerns. In *3:10 to Yuma* (2007), for example, Charlie Prince (Ben Foster) uses two Schofield revolvers. In *Unforgiven* (1992), William Munny (Clint Eastwood) and Ned Logan (Morgan Freeman) join forces with the Schofield Kid (Jaimz Woolvett), who calls himself that because he uses a Smith & Wesson Schofield model of revolver.

## Double Action Revolvers

Unlike the single-action (SA) revolver, which had to have the hammer cocked each time before firing, the double-action (DA) revolver cocked automatically so that a shot was fired each time the trigger was pulled. For this reason the double-action revolver was also known as a "self-cocking" revolver. The Colt company started to make double-action (DA) revolvers in 1877 with their Lightning model in .38 caliber. This was used by some gunmen, notably John Wesley Hardin and Doc Holliday. A major advance in double-action revolvers occurred when a design with a swing-out cylinder that pivoted out of the side of the frame was developed in 1889 to increase the speed of loading.

Although faster to fire, the new double-action revolvers were often less accurate than the single-action type because a greater trigger pressure was required to both pull back the hammer and work the action. This additional finger pressure tended to pull the aim off-target at the wrong moment unless the shooter was very steady. To allow greater accuracy in critical shooting, most double-action revolvers could also be fired in a single-action manner, where the hammer was pulled back manually and cocked each time a shot was fired, thus requiring less trigger pressure for each shot and increasing the accuracy.

Though double-action revolvers were popular with lawmen and outlaws because they were faster-firing, not everybody liked them. Compared to single-action models, double-action revolvers had very complex internal mechanisms that were susceptible to breakage, and many gunfighters considered them to be too delicate for reliable use. Interestingly, Samuel Colt had experimented with self-cocking revolvers early in his career but had abandoned the idea when he concluded that double-action mechanisms were too unreliable. The design of the mainspring on some early models, for example, made them prone to misfires and accidental discharges.

Lawman Matt Warner said, "A real cowboy wouldn't look at a double-action revolver. The machinery is too complicated and uncertain. He can shoot straighter and faster with a single-action six-shooter."[12] Others, however, disagreed. Double-action revolvers were among the favorite weapons of gunmen Doc Holliday, John Wesley Hardin, notorious saloon-owner "Rowdy Joe" Lowe, and Billy the Kid.

In an attempt to modernize its sidearms, the army started to phase out the Model P during the 1890s and equipped troops with the double-action Colt Model 1889 and Model 1892 New Army and Navy revolvers in .38 caliber. Though Colt's first double-action revolvers dated back to the Lightning model in 1877, the 1889 and 1892 models were the first to be widely adopted by the government.

Unlike the earlier .44 and .45 caliber bullets, which were man-killers, the new .38 caliber handguns turned out to possess inadequate stopping power. In the early 1900s the army went back to a .45 caliber cartridge, culminating in the design of the Colt Model 1911 automatic pistol (actually developed in 1905), which was the standard army sidearm until modern 9 mm handguns were adopted by NATO nations. *The Professionals* (1966), set mostly in Mexico after the Pancho Villa revolution, includes the whole range of these guns — single-

The third type of revolver, and newest from a movie standpoint, is the double-action (DA) revolver. This is the Colt double-action Model 1892 New Navy revolver, which was issued from late the 1880s onward during a military weapons upgrade. The lightweight .38 caliber bullet was found to have inadequate stopping power, however, leading the military to later return to the more powerful .45 cartridge. The cylinder of this type of revolver swings out of the side of the frame to allow a bullet to be loaded into each chamber.

action revolvers, double-action revolvers, the Colt 1911 automatic, and the newly-invented machine gun. In *Big Jake* (1971), set in 1909, Jake's son Michael (Chris Mitchum) uses an eight-shot automatic pistol.

Double-action revolvers in Westerns are occasionally randomly substituted for the Peacemaker. In one scene in *The Villain* (1979), Cactus Jack (Kirk Douglas) switches from a Colt Peacemaker to a double-action revolver when he fires three shots in rapid succession, then three more. In *5 Card Stud* (1968), which takes place in 1880, several of the characters switch back and forth between Colt Peacemakers and what looks like the Colt Model 1914 double-action revolver. This even occurs between shots in the same sequence, such as when Jonathan Rudd (Robert Mitchum) and Van Morgan (Dean Martin) are practicing shooting bottles and cans. In *Sergeants 3* (1962), Sergeant Deal (Dean Martin) carries a double-action revolver. Perhaps they were all just ahead of their time.

A classic case of anachronism occurs at the end of *Winchester '73* (1950), during the climactic shootout that takes place outside the saloon at Old Tucson Studios. Waco Johnny Dean (Dan Duryea) grabs a single-action Peacemaker from a nearby cowboy's holster to shoot at Lin McAdam (James Stewart), but in the next shot, when he fires several times into the ground, he is using a double-action revolver. The shooting takes place very fast and is hard to see, but it would still be considered anachronistic, as the movie is set in 1876 and this type of revolver wasn't manufactured until at least 1889.

## Rifles

The Colt Peacemaker with the 4¾-inch barrel is the primary weapon of the movie cowboy. In real life, rifles were useful for long-range fighting but not for close-up shooting. They were also not useful for shooting from horses, as the movie cowboys liked to do during their many chases.

Though there were many makes and models of rifles manufactured and used during the "cowboy era," three of them are commonly seen in the movies. These were the Spencer carbine, the Sharps carbine, and the Winchester repeating rifle. The Spencer and the Sharps were originally military rifles and are seen primarily in cavalry movies, such as *She Wore a Yellow Ribbon* (1949) and *Fort Apache*. Curiously, in *Fort Apache* (1948), the Indians are all armed with Winchester repeaters (Model 1894s!), but the soldiers left at the wagons are armed with single-shot carbines. The group trapped with Colonel Thursday seems to be armed only with Colt Peacemaker handguns.

The Winchester is sometimes seen as armament for the cavalry, but this is historically inaccurate, as the Winchester was a civilian rifle and was not officially adopted for army use. Some cavalry movies use the Henry repeating rifle, but this was the direct predecessor of the Winchester.

### Improvements in Rifles

Before the Civil War, the insides of rifle barrels were smooth; hence the name "smooth-bore" when applied to muskets. Bullets were round balls of lead. This combination gave the smooth-bore musket an effective range of about one hundred yards.

An improvement introduced at the beginning of the Civil War was the rifling of barrels. Rifling consisted of cutting a series of spiral grooves down the inside of the barrel. This imparted a spin to the bullet as it traveled through the air, which stabilized its trajectory after it was fired and thus caused it to travel further in a straight line. The addition of rifling increased the accuracy of a rifle with a round bullet to about four hundred yards. The change from a round ball to a bullet with a pointed cone at the leading end extended the accurate range of a rifled barrel to over a thousand yards.

These improvements in rifles brought about a change in fighting tactics. Before and during the Civil War, waves of soldiers often charged each other's lines or charged a fixed defensive position. This is shown at the beginning of *Dances with Wolves* (1990) and during the scene that ends the siege at the bridge over the Arlanza River in *The Good, the Bad, and the Ugly* (1966). The limited range of smooth-bore muskets meant that such a charge could be made over long distances with relative safety, because the accurate range of the defensive fire was only about a hundred yards. The addition of rifling and conical bullets meant that charging against armed soldiers who were in a fixed defensive position was suicidal. Indians found this out to their disadvantage when charging and attacking well-armed soldiers and military forts.

Muskets and early rifles were single-shot shoulder arms that used loose gunpowder, a round lead ball, and a percussion cap — just like the early percussion revolvers. The introduction of metallic self-contained cartridges enabled the design of rifles that fired multiple shots before reloading. For obvious reasons these were called "repeating rifles" or "repeaters," but were also known as "magazine rifles" because the cartridges were loaded into a magazine on the rifle. Repeating rifles like the Winchester had a tubular spring-loaded magazine that held from seven to fifteen metallic cartridges, which made these rifles extremely fast to fire and reload. As a result, lever-action rifles and carbines became very popular. The lever-action reloading mechanism worked by pushing down then pulling up on an oval, ring-like lever, with the three smallest fingers of the hand holding the butt of the rifle. This ejected the empty case, slid a new cartridge into the chamber from the magazine, cocked the hammer, and realigned the index finger on the trigger for the next shot, all in one smooth action.

### Sharps Rifles

The military rifle that was most widespread during and after the Civil War was the Sharps Model 1859, a single-shot carbine developed by Christian Sharps of the Sharps Rifle Manufacturing Company of Hartford, Connecticut. By 1861 the Sharps breech-loading carbine was the standard shoulder arm of the cavalry. The original Sharps used a cartridge that had a cylindrical paper or linen casing, with the bullet attached to the front. Using this cartridge the Sharps could be loaded and fired approximately five times in a minute, which was a vast improvement over the conventional muzzle-loaders of the time. In 1867 the army contracted for refurbishment of these rifles and their conversion to metallic cartridges. A new military model was produced in 1869 to use the heavier .50–70 cartridge.

Single-shot rifles, such as the Sharps, were still common on the frontier until about 1880. They enjoyed continued popularity because they used more powerful cartridges than contemporary repeating rifles.

### Spencer Rifles

One of the most popular firearms used by the Union Army during the Civil War was the Spencer repeating carbine, designed by Christopher Miner Spencer and produced by his Spencer Repeating Rifle Company of Boston, Massachusetts. After the Civil War the Spencer essentially became the standard long arm that was issued to the regular army. It was subsequently adopted by the cavalry and was widespread on the frontier during the Indian wars.

The army found the Spencer to be cheap, reliable, and long-lasting, thus making it a clear favorite for many years. The carbine used lever-action to load the cartridges from a seven-shot, spring-fed, tubular magazine contained in the buttstock. A skilled trooper could fire the entire magazine in ten to twelve seconds. Perversely, the Spencer was initially rejected by the military because officers were concerned that the repeating action would allow soldiers to shoot rapidly and carelessly, thus consuming too much ammunition. Slight redesign of the Spencer resulted in the Model 1865, which could be used as a single-shot breechloader as well as a seven-shot repeater. Contemporary military tactics favored using the carbine as a single-shot weapon while holding the full magazine as a ready reserve in case of an overwhelming attack that did not allow time for reloading.

Military interest in the Spencer carbine as a standard weapon started to decline in the late 1860s in favor of the more powerful converted Sharps carbines. The Spencer's popularity with the military eventually led to the company's downfall. So many Spencer rifles and carbines were sold to the Union army during the Civil War that surplus arms flooded the postwar market and were extremely common on the Western frontier. In spite of the Spencer's popularity, the market for new carbines was very small and the company eventually went out of business.

### Winchester Repeating Rifles

The Winchester lever-action rifle is the rifle solidly identified with the Old West. The weapon had its origin in a multi-shot, lever-action pistol produced by the Volcanic Repeating Arms Company in the 1850s. The Volcanic Company was failing financially when a shirt manufacturer from New Haven, Connecticut, named Oliver Fisher Winchester invested enough money to salvage the company. Winchester did not know much about guns but was an accomplished financier and entrepreneur, and was a good salesman. In spite of this, finances continued to fail, and in 1857 the Volcanic Repeating Arms Company was still struggling. At this point Winchester acquired all the assets of the company, re-formed it as the New Haven Arms Company, and installed Benjamin Tyler Henry as manager. Henry was an experienced gunsmith who had previously worked at the government's Springfield Armory.

In 1858 Henry designed a self-contained metallic cartridge and re-designed the Volcanic rifle to use this new cartridge. This innovative rifle, first marketed in 1862, was nicknamed "the Henry" by satisfied users. It had a 24-inch octagonal barrel with a tubular magazine underneath it. Tests showed that the entire magazine of fifteen cartridges could be fired in as little as fifteen seconds. This was appealing to men under attack, as they were interested in firing as many bullets as possible as fast as possible at their opponents. Sales of the Henry were good because the capacity of the magazine and the speed of firing were much better than anything else then available.

Henry retired after the end of the Civil War, and in 1866 an improved version of his rifle was designed by Nelson King, Winchester's plant superintendent. This new model was designated the Winchester Model 1866. The Winchester kept the bright brass frame of the earlier Henry rifle, a characteristic that soon earned it the nickname of "the Yellow Boy." The brass frame was later changed to iron, then to blued steel.

The new Winchester rifle could be fully loaded with eighteen cartridges. The magazine of the rifle held seventeen cartridges, with one more loaded into the chamber, making a total of eighteen. In the hands of a skilled shooter the entire rifle magazine could be fired in about fifteen seconds. A carbine version, with a shorter 20-inch barrel, could hold fourteen cartridges. Further design improvements led to the Winchester Model 1873 lever-action rifle (first manufactured, naturally, in 1873), which was probably the most famous rifle in the West. This Winchester rifle's popularity and fame are reflected in the fact that 720,000 of them were produced.

Though the entire magazine of the Winchester could be fired rapidly, the .44 caliber cartridge did not have the stopping power of the Springfield and its cartridge, so the military rejected the Model 1873 because they wanted a more powerful rifle. Continued requests from the field for a military rifle that reloaded rapidly led to a review of repeating rifles. Testing by the Springfield Armory in 1876, and again in 1879, showed that the Sharp's rifle and the Model 1873 Winchester did not perform as well at one hundred yards in accuracy or penetration as the standard military Springfield carbine, which was reported to be accurate at up to seven hundred yards.

The Model 1873 Winchester was the star of its own movie. *Winchester '73* (1950) opens in Dodge City in 1876 at a shooting contest where Lin McAdam (James Stewart) wins a one-of-one-thousand Winchester Model 1873 rifle. The gist of the plot is that the gun is stolen, then passes through the hands of a succession of miscellaneous shady characters, including a bandit, a gunrunner, the savage Indian chief Young Bull (Rock Hudson), and McAdam's murderous brother, Dutch Henry Brown (Steven McNally), until it ends up back in McAdam's hands at the conclusion of the movie.

The one-of-one-thousand rifle was indeed a legitimate factory option. When each rifle barrel was made at Winchester, the manufacturing process included firing proof shots. Rifles with the most extreme accuracy were singled out for additional finishing and sold as prestige items. Only 133 Model 1873 rifles reached this state of perfection.[13] In a remarkable display of shooting skills, even for one of these guns, McAdam shoots through the hole in the middle of a piece of jewelry that is shaped like a round washer. Though such a gun is historically accurate, this plot device stretches the limits of credibility for any kind of shooting accuracy.

Though rifles played a major role as a weapon in the development of the west, early single-shot rifles and carbines were not a weapon of choice for gunfighters, except perhaps for ambushing an adversary from a long distance and counting on one shot to do the job. Rifles designed before 1860 were cumbersome to use at short range, were often inaccurate at long range, and were slow to reload. Thus, these rifles were not easy to use during a confrontation between gunfighters that required instant action. The later repeating rifles were far more appealing to gunfighters because they could be fired multiple times before reloading was necessary. As a result, lever-action rifles and carbines eventually became very popular with bandits, gunmen, lawmen, and stagecoach guards.

In terms of accuracy and distance, serious gunfighters preferred repeating rifles to handguns. Real-life lawman Matt Warner explained, "In close-in fighting the six-shooter is the best weapon, but in long-range fighting the rifle can't be beat. In close-in fighting you throw the rifle down on your man like you do the pistol, and often shoot from the hip, but in long-range fighting you sight the rifle."[14] Sheriff John T. Chance in *Rio Bravo* (1959) preferred a rifle for short-range work. Just before one of the film's shootouts, Colorado (Ricky Nelson) asks Chance (John Wayne) why he carries his carbine always cocked. Chance replies, "I found some were faster than me with a short gun." Perhaps he was right. Ramon (Gian Maria Volonté) in *A Fistful of Dollars* (1964), quotes a supposed old Mexican proverb when he says, "When a man with a .45 meets a man with a rifle, the man with the pistol will be a dead man." Actually, in the movie he was proven wrong at the final shoot-out.

Readers who have seen *El Dorado* (1967) may wonder what the rifle is that Bull (Arthur Hunnicutt) is using. This is a Colt rifle with a revolving cylinder mechanism, a type that the factory made for a short while in the late 1850s.[15] These rifles did not rate high in popularity with users, as they produced a spray of smoke, powder, and lead shavings from the front side of the cylinder that could burn the hand and cheek of the shooter, and pepper anyone else standing close.

As a side-note of historical interest, for a short period between 1883 and 1885, in an attempt to break into the repeating rifle market, Colt produced a lever-action repeating rifle named the Colt-Burgess rifle (after its designer, Andrew Burgess) that looked somewhat like the Winchester 1873. The Winchester Company, which dominated the lever-action rifle market at the time, saw this as a threat to their sales and in retaliation threatened to produce a revolver that would have gone into direct competition with the Peacemaker. The apocryphal part of the story is that the two companies suddenly realized that such direct competition of their major product lines could backfire and be a financial disaster for both of them. According to manufacturers' legend, the top officials at each company came to a gentleman's agreement that Colt would discontinue manufacture of rifles and stick to revolvers, and Winchester would stay with rifles and not manufacture revolvers.[16]

### Shotguns

Contrary to the legend of fast-drawn six-shooters, many lawmen — in particular, Texas Rangers, U.S. marshals, and Wells Fargo stagecoach guards — preferred shotguns. At short range they were superior to rifles and revolvers. Two barrels of buckshot made a most effective weapon for short-range shooting, either at road agents, robbers, or would-be hold-up men. Many bartenders kept a loaded shotgun at the ready underneath the bar to discourage troublemakers or crooked gamblers.

Shotguns did not need to be particularly accurate because the lead shot spread out after leaving the barrel, thus allowing the shooter to merely aim in the general direction of his target, with the likelihood of hitting it being good. In *Big Jake* (1971), Indian tracker Sam Sharpnose (Bruce Cabot) says that he prefers a double-barreled shotgun with short barrels because his eyes aren't as good as they used to be.

Some of the favorite shotguns in the Old West were those made by Winchester, Parker, Colt, Springfield, and American Arms. Common shotgun calibers ranged from 10 gauge to 20 gauge. Serious gunmen who were aiming to kill a man might use double-ought buckshot.[17] For a more devastating effect, some gunmen loaded their shotguns with old nails and small pieces of scrap metal.

A barrel length of twenty-four inches was popular, though some barrels were cut as short as twelve inches. When the barrel of a shotgun was shortened, the pattern of shot grew wider, though the effective range was much shorter. This was, however, desirable for short-range shooting. A very short barrel was the best for a barroom fight or for use by a stagecoach guard. In this situation the shooters didn't need good range but wanted good covering power for close-in shooting. Wells Fargo guards, for example, wanted a wide dispersal of shot at a very short range, so they carried 10-gauge shotguns with very short barrels.

The wide pattern of shot sprayed out by a sawed-off barrel led to shotguns being named "scatter guns."

## Other Weapons

In addition to basic revolvers, gunfighters in the Old West used a variety of other weapons. Rifles, shotguns, and knives all had their places as tools to kill, maim, and wound other gunfighters and whoever else the owner chose as a target. Knives were popular in fights. Most men already carried some type of knife because knives were also commonly used as tools to assist in performing many everyday tasks, such as cutting rope or opening tin cans.

### Derringers

Small guns that could be easily concealed in clothing were popular with gamblers and women, and with cowboys and outlaws who wanted to carry a hidden gun. They were also carried as concealed weapons in towns such as Dodge City and Tombstone, where carrying firearms was against the law. An example of this in a Western movie is where Ed Bailey (Lee Van Cleef) has a small gun hidden in his boot when he confronts Doc Holliday (Kirk Douglas) in *Gunfight at the O.K. Corral* (1957), because carrying guns in town was not allowed. In this movie Holliday knew that he wasn't supposed to carry a gun, so he won the fight with a concealed knife.

One name for a small handgun that could be easily concealed was a "derringer."[18] The essential feature of a derringer was its small size. The barrels of most models were from one to three inches in length; thus a gambler might carry a derringer that was easily concealed in his vest or jacket pocket for quick use. Some gunmen didn't even bother to draw their derringers but fired a shot straight through the cloth of their pockets.

A man could carry a derringer in the top of his boot, up his shirt sleeve, clipped inside his hat, or fastened alongside his wrist with spring clips that attached to leather bands around his arm. One ingenious device attached to the arm slid a derringer into the wearer's hand when he flexed the muscles of his forearm.

A woman could carry a loaded derringer in her purse, in the pocket of her dress, or down her cleavage. She could also carry the firearm tucked into one of her garters or in a holster strapped to her thigh. Concealed under her skirts, a derringer might not be instantly available for a fast draw, but it was certainly close at hand if the need for protection arose.

Though many companies manufactured derringers, a favorite in the Old West that also shows up frequently in the movies was the Remington over-and-under version made in .41 caliber. This palm-sized gun had two three-inch barrels mounted one on top of the other, firing alternately as the hammer was cocked and the trigger pulled. Even though this was a very small gun, its large bullet made it extremely destructive at close range. Given their small size and relatively large caliber, these particular derringers were sometimes called "pocket cannons." The common use of derringers by women, particularly ladies of the evening, led them to be nicknamed "boudoir cannons."

One drawback to these small weapons was that they were wildly inaccurate in a gunfight, except at very close range, because their barrels were only a couple of inches in length. The shooter assumed that his target would be sitting or standing only a few feet away, so one quick shot aimed across the card table or into the man drinking next to him at the bar would be adequate to put his opponent out of action.

## *Dynamite*

To maximize mayhem, characters both good and bad in Westerns often employ dynamite.

The first useful explosive, which was used for blasting in mines as well as in contemporary revolver and rifle cartridges, was black powder. In 1867 chemist Alfred Nobel in Sweden developed a far more powerful explosive named dynamite. Dynamite was made from stabilized nitroglycerin, an explosive substance that was so unstable that it was not suitable for use in its pure form. In spite of its instability in real life, Taw Jackson (John Wayne) and Billy Hyatt (Robert Walker) use liquid nitroglycerine to blow up a the bridge in *The War Wagon* (1967).

To make nitroglycerin more stable for general use, it was combined with wood-flour, sawdust, or chalk to become dynamite. This mixture was formed into round sticks about eight inches long and an inch or so in diameter, then wrapped in paper coated with paraffin.

A stick of dynamite was very stable and had to be ignited by a sharp blow, which was provided by a percussion cap, a short cylindrical device about two inches long and a half-inch in diameter filled with fulminate of mercury. Sparks from a burning fuse ignited the percussion cap, which then exploded and, in turn, caused the stick of dynamite to explode.

The use of dynamite in Westerns is too ubiquitous to detail here. One example of many occurs in *Rio Bravo* (1959) when John T. Chance (John Wayne) and Dude (Dean Martin) throw sticks of dynamite and then shoot at them to blow up the barn where the bad guys are holed up.

*Chapter Nine*

# Itchy Trigger Fingers

A Hollywood Western has to contain a heroic confrontation that culminates in a dramatic gunfight between good and bad. It is also typical to have various episodes of shooting and gunplay spaced throughout the movie. As part of this, Western movies promote the concept that a gun was a vital tool for any man who was a real man in the West.

When the hero finds himself in a situation where has to use his gun, however, he plays by a strange set of rules. As succinctly summarized by author Jenni Calder:

> We learn to distinguish the good man with a gun from the bad man with a gun, and this distinction is crucial to our enjoyment of the Western. According to the mythic code the bad man will crouch behind a rock ... and shoot a man in the back. The good man will face his enemy and make sure his enemy is facing him. He will call out to warn him before he draws and fires. These are the rules of the game.[1]

The result is a type of face-to-face confrontation that never took place.

In spite of its seeming authenticity, this type of shoot-out between hero and villain in the Westerns is primarily a product of the imaginations of movie scriptwriters. Only a few real gunfights were conducted in the classic movie manner. One occurred on July 21, 1865, when Wild Bill Hickok and Davis Tutt squared off in the town square of Springfield, Missouri, after competing for the affections of Susanna Moore. The two men faced each other at a distance of about fifty to seventy-five yards, then both pulled their revolvers and fired. Hickok was the better shot, and Davis was killed.

The result of a real face-to-face showdown was risky and was not always what was desired. On November 8, 1878, U.S. Marshal Bill Anderson finally caught up with train robber William Collins after a long chase. The two men started shooting and walking towards each other. The result was that they both died from their wounds.[2]

Though shootings and gunplay certainly occurred in Western towns, particularly in cattle towns when cowboys were around, the frequent gunfights shown in the movies between sheriffs and the bad guys are also historically inaccurate. Besides, the gunmen and outlaws who robbed and killed made up only a small minority of the men who lived in the West. Many men carried a gun for protection or for the sake of appearance, but few were gunfighters. A real gunfight was more likely to be part of an impromptu brawl than a melodramatic, staged, face-to-face showdown.

Gunfights were rare in the 1850s because the rapid-fire killing technology of reliable revolvers was not widely available. The occurrence of Western gunfights was also low in the early 1860s because most of the impetuous young men were off killing each other during the Civil War. However, fighting with guns as a way of life rose sharply after the Civil War due to the common availability of revolvers. In addition, some of the men who emigrated to the West took with them the fighting and killing skills they had developed during the war. Then there were those who could not function in the structured society of the post-war East and were looking for the freedom to continue to shoot, kill, and loot after the war was over.

Most gunfighters during the height of the gunfighting era of the 1870s and 1880s were in their twenties or thirties. Many only made it to their early forties before they died — usually violently.

Being a professional gunman required a keen mind, skill with a gun, and a willingness to kill another person. But marksmanship alone was not enough. After the Schofield Kid (Jaimz Woolvett) kills his first man in *Unforgiven* (1992), he realizes that gunfighting is not the glamorous profession he thought it was and quits.

The number of shootouts in the Old West was highest in the 1870s and 1880s, with a peak of thirty-six recorded gunfights taking place in 1878. The number leveled off and then declined in the 1890s as law and order became more prevalent on the Western frontier.[3] But even with all the gunfights that occurred in the Old West, there were not as many deaths from shooting as might be supposed. Wyatt Earp, for example, is thought to have killed only one man while he was a Dodge City lawman. He used his gun barrel more frequently as a club to knock lawbreakers senseless.

According to Western movies, the cowboy was the premier gunfighter of the Old West. In reality, cowboys were not professional gunmen but were common laborers who tended and herded cattle for a living. In spite of their movie image, cowboys who tried to be gunmen were amateurs. Cowboys were not gunfighters, and professional gunfighters were not cowboys. Each stuck to their own trade. Cowboys did get into shooting situations and sometimes shot each other, but they did not make their livings with guns.

The real gunfighters of the Old West were the men who made their livelihood with their guns. These men appeared on both sides of the law. Some were legitimate lawmen and used their guns to keep the peace, but most were outlaws, stage robbers, cattle rustlers, hired guns, gamblers, horse thieves, bank robbers, or others who used their guns as tools to accumulate goods and money. This kind of man was often hired as a lawman because a cold-blooded attitude was required to stand up to other bandits, outlaws, and lawbreakers. The distinction between the two was not always clear-cut, as lawmen were sometimes gunmen who had previously been lawbreakers but who had turned to enforcing the law because this offered a steady job. Others who ended up as killers were trapped in circumstances beyond their control, such as Billy the Kid during the Lincoln County Range War, or those who became embroiled in senseless drunken arguments and confrontations in cattle towns.

The appellation "gunfighter," which is today's common name for men who participated in gun battles, was not commonly used before the turn of the twentieth century. The term "gunslinger" was invented by imaginative writers of pulp novels. Instead, various other names were used including "shootist." Real-life gunman Clay Allison called himself a shootist, and this was the title applied to gunman J.B. Books (John Wayne) in *The Shootist* (1976). This designation, however, eventually fell out of favor with real gunfighters because it also came to apply to exhibition shooters and marksmen.

Other terms that were in common use for gunmen were "man-killer" or "pistoleer," which were simple, but accurate, appellations. Wild Bill Hickok was sometimes called "the Prince of Pistoleers." Another contemporary description for a gunfighter was the generic term "badman," such as was used for the mythical generic "Badman from Bodie," who was supposed to be worse than other "badmen."

## Reality — Hollywood-Style

When movie gunmen prepare to draw, they are shown in the "gunman's crouch," where they sag at the knees, hunch their shoulders, and adopt a squinty-eyed expression. Shane (Alan Ladd), for example, in *Shane* (1953) goes into this characteristic crouch and grabs for the butt of his revolver when he hears a rifle being cocked behind him. This sinister crouch actually does nothing to improve drawing a gun and has no advantage for shooting, but it does make a dramatic image for the movies. Real gunmen who were involved in a dangerous confrontation stood upright and did not telegraph their intentions to their opponent via their body position. When a real gunman made the decision to fight, he simply drew his gun and fired. The first shot was the most important one and tough gunmen made it count in order to end the fight as quickly as possible.

Professional gunfighters typically did not touch their holstered weapon or let their hand stray close to their gun butt unless they were serious about using it. If one of them showed any appearance that his hand was coming close to his revolver, his opponent might take that as a signal to draw his own gun. This threat is illustrated in *Open Range* (2004) when Charley Waite (Kevin Costner) confronts the marshal in the saloon. Waite places his hand on the butt of his gun, grasps it without drawing it, and stands there ready for a quick draw. The marshal realizes by this action that Waite is ready to draw and wisely makes no move towards his own gun.

In real life, an event like this happened on January 7, 1874, when notorious gunman Clay Allison ate dinner with fellow gunman Chunk Colbert at a restaurant called the Clifton House in northern New Mexico. Allison and Colbert had a history of previous disagreements and were in the middle of an uneasy truce after a disagreement over which one of them had won a horse race. Colbert had apparently decided to kill Allison, and as the two finished their meal, Colbert started fondling

What's wrong with this picture? What isn't? This Hollywood wannabe gunman certainly isn't authentic. (1) The unnatural movie gunman's crouch is a product of Hollywood. (2) This type of gunbelt and low-slung Buscadero holster wasn't introduced until the 1920s. (3) The hammer thong at the front of the holster pouch to prevent the gun from falling out of the holster wasn't used in the Old West. (4) The tie-down thong on the leg is a Hollywood invention. (5) Blue jeans weren't popular with cowboys until the 1920s. (6) Rolled-up cuffs on jeans were a 1940s/1950s fashion trend. (7) Fancy tooled belt holding up pants. (8) Pearl snap-buttons on cowboy shirts weren't introduced until the 1930s. The only authentic part of this picture is the dust on the boots.

his holstered gun. Allison, suspecting what might be coming, took no chances but suddenly drew his own gun and shot Colbert through the head. He then cold-bloodedly finished his dinner.

### The Hollywood Way

For those with a keen eye, various errors on the part of Hollywood gunmen can be spotted in Westerns. One obvious shortcoming is that looking from the front into the chambers of the hero's handgun, the cylinder is sometimes seen to be empty, containing no bullets. This is often seen in publicity stills where the actor is dramatically posed with a drawn gun.

Another significant error that real gunmen would not make is that revolvers are sometimes held in a manner that would be unsuitable for immediate firing. For example, the hammer of the gun is held by the web of flesh between the thumb and forefinger of the hand. When Howard Kemp (James Stewart) is pointing his Colt at old prospector Jesse Tate (Millard Mitchell) at the beginning of *The Naked Spur* (1953), he is holding the web of his thumb over the spur of the hammer of the gun. He couldn't have fired it if he wanted to. Incidentally, the movie is set 1868, but characters carry Peacemakers and Winchester Model 1873s, both of which weren't developed until five years later.

Even worse in terms of immediate action is a single-action revolver held without the hammer cocked. In this circumstance the gun could be knocked off-target long before the person holding it could realign his hand to cock the gun and fire it. At the beginning of *4 for Texas* (1963), for example, Joe Jarrett (Dean Martin) doesn't have his single-action revolver cocked when he is pointing it at Zach Thomas (Frank Sinatra).

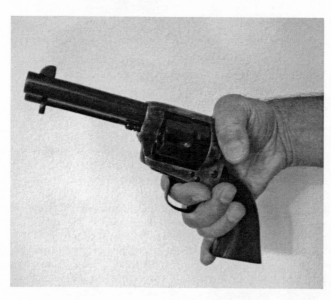

This would not be the correct way to hold a gun on another man, though this type of grip is seen frequently in Westerns. The hammer is not cocked, so this revolver is not ready for immediate action. In addition, holding the hand over the hammer like this blocks the revolver from being cocked in a hurry.

Another common error made by a movie gunman is cocking his single-action revolver for dramatic effect *after* getting the drop on a bad guy, or someone re-cocking a lever-action rifle at the vital moment. If a revolver or rifle has to be cocked, it is obviously not ready for immediate use, and the shooter would lose vital seconds cocking the revolver or jacking a shell into the chamber of a rifle while he is being shot at. Pumping the lever-action of a rifle works well for dramatic effect and makes a sinister mechanical noise, but if this has to be performed, either the gun does not have a shell in the chamber and is not ready to fire, or this additional action would eject an unfired cartridge from the chamber, which would limit the number of shots that could be subsequently fired. In reality, in a dangerous situation that might involve shooting, a shell would be in the chamber, the hammer cocked, and the finger on the trigger, ready for immediate use.

The B-Westerns inadvertently got it right when they show endless chase scenes with the heroes and villains shooting at each other from wildly galloping horses. They never seem to hit anyone or anything, which is what would really happen, as it is virtually impossible to accurately fire a revolver or a rifle from a fast-moving horse on rough terrain. In the movie *Tom Horn* (1980), even Horn (Steve McQueen), who preferred to use a rifle both in the movie and in real life, couldn't hit anything from a galloping horse with his rifle until he dismounted and took careful aim.

In the older Westerns, particularly the B-Westerns, the camera never records a bullet striking a body. The good guy fires his gun, then a quick edit cuts to the bad guy clutching his chest or shoulder and falling off his horse. This gives the illusion of the bullet hitting the villain. More demanding audiences during the 1960s wanted more realism. Moviemakers complied and simulated bullets hitting bodies, with clothing exploding outwards and blood squirting all over the place. This was achieved by placing a small explosive device, called a "squib," which was detonated electrically, under the actor's clothing over a metal backing plate to protect him or her. At the appropriate time the squib was exploded outwards through a plastic or rubber capsule of synthetic movie blood, which then blows out through the actors clothing (often weakened to allow the "blood" to explode through the cloth) to appear as if the actor has been shot. In a real shooting the bullet goes inward and does not cause a fountain of blood. Entry wounds are typically small puncture wounds, though exit wounds can be quite large.

Among other inconsistencies in the movies, characters fall to the ground when shot, but their white shirts have no bloodstains or holes as they fall. In *The Sheepman* (1958), when Jason Sweet (Glenn Ford) is shot in the shoulder, he clutches his hand to his jacketed shoulder, but there is no blood or other evidence of a wound. In the following sequence he has his arm in a sling, but there is no visible hole in the material of his jacket. One can't blame the moviemakers — it was a nice jacket, no point in ruining it. However, if this movie had been made ten years later, in the more violent period of Westerns, there would have been a close-up of a blood-capsule exploding outwards from his shoulder, tearing a large red-spattered hole in the jacket and ruining the material.

## Real Gunfighting

Real gunfights were not like Hollywood shootouts; they were messy. On December 7, 1870, in El Paso, Texas, a lawyer named Williams entered into an altercation with District Judge Gaylord Clarke and a man named Albert Fountain. The result was that Williams shot Fountain in the arm, scalp, and chest. The wounded Fountain staggered home and got his rifle. When he returned, Williams was firing at Clarke with a shotgun, finally blasting him in the chest. Fountain, in retribution, shot Williams. Williams was preparing to shoot back at Fountain when a policeman ran over and shot him in the head.

Many other gunfights were equally unpleasant. Chet Van Meter was shot to death in Caldwell, Kansas, on November 21, 1883, by two law officers who tried to arrest him. After the shooting was over, the body was found to have five chest wounds, a large wound in the right side, a gunshot in the belly, and wounds on both hands.[4] Definitely a messy ending.

The movies, on the other hand, show nice, clean gunfights. The hero downs the villain with one clean gunshot. In *Lawman* (1971), Marshal Jered Maddox (Burt Lancaster) claims that he never drew his gun first on a man, as that was the right way to participate in a gunfight. However, that was not the way it worked in reality. Real gunfighters did not hold to the movie cowboy's code of honor that the other man had to draw first. One of the few exceptions was gunfighter Ben Thompson. His theory was that if he let the other man draw first, then he would always be able to claim self-defense afterwards. Thompson felt that the other man would hurry to shoot first and miss, whereas he never did. He felt that accuracy, rather than speed, was crucial. But then Thompson had the steady nerves of a professional gunman who could stand up and shoot with precision at someone who was shooting back.

Real gunmen did not mess around. They did what they felt they had to. After Juan Bideno killed cowboy William Cohron, several of his friends, including noted gunfighter John Wesley Hardin, obtained a warrant and sought to arrest him. When they caught up with him in Bluff City, Kansas, on July 7, 1871, Hardin ordered him to surrender. When Bideno resisted, Hardin simply pulled out a gun and shot him in the head.[5]

The difficulties in shooting effectively at another man in a gunfight, though, were compounded by the fact that many shoot-outs took place in crowded saloons where precise aim could be easily jostled by bystanders, the lighting was often only a dim glow from an oil lamp, and the shooter's aim was made inaccurate by too much drink. To compound the combatants' problems, many contemporary handguns were not accurate, the black powder used to propel the bullet was highly unstable and likely to degrade, and cartridge primers were quite apt to misfire at the crucial moment. A cattleman named George Littlefield and his neighbor found this out in a rather exciting way. During a heated argument, both pulled their guns and aimed at each other. Both guns misfired.[6]

As in many detective stories, the villain in the movies often has to talk ... and talk ... and talk to explain to the hero what is going on as he is getting ready to shoot him. Any gunman wanting to survive knew that he had to shoot quickly and first in order to avoid being shot. This philosophy is admirably summed up in *The Good, the Bad and the Ugly* (1966) when Tuco (Eli Wallach), without warning, shoots a man gunning for him and says to the corpse, "When you have to shoot, shoot. Don't talk."

## All's Fair

The winner of a gun battle in the Old West was usually the one who started with his gun in his hand, kept a cool head, took his time, and aimed carefully. The objective in a real gunfight was to shoot the other man in such a way that he would be knocked out of the fight by the first shot. Though practice helped Wild Bill Hickok to be fast on the draw, he did not shoot from the hip or use other fancy shots. Instead, he took the time to level the gun at the end of his arm to ensure a deliberate aim down the sights as he fired.

A man intent on killing another, or defending himself from being killed, would rarely wait for his opponent to draw first; in fact, it would be suicide to let the other man draw first and then try to outdraw him. An example of this occurred on July 18, 1884, when assistant marshal Tom Nixon of Dodge City, Kansas, argued with Dave Mather, who had previously held the job. Nixon fired a shot at Mather but missed. On July 21 Mather sneaked up behind Nixon and softly called out his name. When Nixon turned around, Mather shot him four times without warning. Mather was later acquitted, as it was felt that Nixon had provoked the original fight.

The gunfighter who wanted to win a shootout went into the fight with his revolver drawn, probably also with it cocked, and with his trigger finger at the ready. Each of the participants in a gunfight knew that the one who had a gun in his hand first and shot first would almost certainly win the gunfight. When John McCabe (Warren Beatty) is being chased by one of the killers in *McCabe & Mrs. Miller* (1971), he shoots the man without warning when he sees him through the glass pane in a door. In *One-Eyed Jacks* (1961), Rio (Marlon Brando) is cunning and vicious, and finally shoots the sheriff in the back. The messages here reflect rough justice, revenge, and no morals.

Many real-life cowboys, sheriffs, and badmen were notoriously bad shots and were slow on the trigger. Lawmen going after someone often liked to better the odds by carrying a cocked shotgun. Wild Bill Hickok was an excellent marksman, but when he received death threats from Texas cowboys in Abilene, he obtained a shotgun, shortened the barrel to twelve inches and kept it on his night table ready for immediate use. When John McCabe knows he is going to have to fight the three hired killers from the syndicate, he gets out a double-barreled shotgun as well as his pistol.

Real gunmen went for a solid body shot, not a head shot or a fancy shoot-the-gun-out-of-the-hand shot. They aimed for the largest, lowest target they could—usually the belly—so that they could get their gun out fast and make a quick shot, yet still make it count. Wild Bill Hickok once told a friend, "I hope you never have to shoot any man, but if you do shoot him in the Guts near the Navel. *You* may not make a fatal shot, but *he* will get a shock that will paralyze his brain and arm so much that the fight is all over."[7]

This was the gruesome finale to a real gunfight. Gunman and train robber John Sontag lies wounded against a hay bale on September 13, 1892, after a marathon eight-hour shoot-out with this posse at Sampson's Flats, California. Two deputies were killed during the gun battle, and Sontag died later that night (National Archives).

Most shootings took place at a distance of about five to fifteen feet. Professional gunmen did not like to shoot it out at a longer range because of the inaccuracy of contemporary handguns and ammunition. In line with this thinking, expert marksman Walter Winans commented, "When a revolver is used ... the shooting is generally done at a few yards' distance, and at a rapidly moving object. Further, it often happens that a succession of shots has to be fired in a few seconds."[8]

Some successful gunfighters even tried to crowd very close to their opponent so that their intended target was unable to draw his gun. This was a favorite technique of gambler and gunman Luke Short. This ploy sometimes backfired, however, like when Short shot it out with fellow gunman Timothy "Longhaired Jim" Courtright in Fort Worth, Texas, on February 8, 1887. Short crowded so close that he couldn't even pull his own gun, and Courtright's gun caught on Short's watch chain. It took a brief struggle before Short could free his gun and win the fight.

One of the advantages of crowding close was that, as well as improving the chances of making a direct hit, the unfortunate victim also got the full blast from the muzzle of the gun. Even better for the shooter, the flames that shot out of the barrel when the black powder in the cartridge ignited could even set the victim's clothes on fire. This happened when Ed Masterson (Bat Masterson's brother) was acting as the town marshal of Dodge City and was killed when he tried to arrest a drunken Jack Wagner. Wagner shot Masterson in the side at such a close range that the marshal's clothes caught on fire.[9] This incident is accurately portrayed in *Wyatt Earp* (1994).

Some gunfighters, including Bat Masterson and Wild Bill Hickok, practiced their aim by shooting at targets to try to gain a competitive edge that might help them in a gunfight. Practicing by shooting at a target, however, cannot compare to shooting at a man who is shooting back. Walter Winans also noted, "In my opinion revolver shooting is essentially a matter of firing rapidly at short ranges. Deliberate shooting at stationary targets, especially at long ranges, is all wrong. To begin with, the revolver is not accurate enough for such work."[10]

When it came to life and death, not all gunfights were fair. In 1902, in Lewis County, Washington, Harry Tracy challenged his brother-in-law Dave Merrill to a gunfight after an argument. In the best dueling tradition they agreed to walk ten paces, then turn and fire. Tracy didn't play by the rules they had agreed on but turned after a few paces and shot the other man in the back.[11] Mirroring reality, this kind of fighting was also not always fair in the movies. In *Pat Garrett and Billy the Kid* (1973), Alamosa (Jack Elam) and Billy the Kid (Kris Kristofferson) both cheat during the shoot-out between them. They agree to count to ten. Alamosa turns and shoots at the count of eight, but Billy turns and shoots when the count is only up to three. Likewise, *The Man Who Shot Liberty Valance* (1962) does not involve a fair gunfight at the end of the movie. Tom Doniphan (John Wayne) shoots Liberty Valance (Lee Marvin) from the sidelines with a rifle just as Valance is about to shoot Ransom Stoddard (James Stewart). After a ferocious, bloody fist-fight in *The Cowboys* (1972) in which Long Hair (Bruce Dern) loses, he pulls a gun and shoots Wil Andersen (John Wayne) several times in the back. And then he walks unconcernedly away.

The climactic gunfight in *Open Range* (2004), with its unexpected beginning is closer to the reality of a serious gunfight in the Old West than most Hollywood movies. At the start of the gun battle, Charley Waite (Kevin Costner), one of the "good" guys, suddenly pulls his gun and shoots one of the bad guys in the head without any warning. The fighting then degenerates into bloody mayhem as a dozen or so participants blaze away relentlessly at each other with shotguns, rifles, and revolvers, killing some and wounding others amidst streaming splatters of gore. The *un*realistic aspect of the fight is that it lasts for so long, as this type of extended battle was uncommon in the West. Like the real fight at the O.K. Corral, the gunplay between Waite and Boss Spearman (Robert Duvall), and Denton Baxter (Michael Gambon) and his henchmen is essentially over in less than a minute of intense shooting. But the rest of the fighting and shooting continue sporadically for another eighteen minutes until Boss' and Charley's revenge is complete.

Full-scale shootouts that lasted for more than a few minutes happened only rarely in the Old West. Hollywood typically extends the final shootout in a movie in order to make a dramatic story. In *The Cowboys* (1972), the final violence lasts for fifteen minutes as the boys avenge the death of Wil Andersen and kill off Long Hair's (Bruce Dern) gang. The climactic gunfight in *Pale Rider* (1985), where the Preacher cleans up the town, lasts for 9½ minutes on the screen.

The use of every trick in a gunfight was fair game. In *A Fistful of Dollars* (1964), the Man with No Name (Clint Eastwood) fashions an iron breastplate from a piece of old boiler. When he enters the final shootout, villainous Ramon (Gian Maria Volonté) shoots at his chest. The Stranger is knocked down, but each time he rises up like a phoenix and advances nearer until he shoots Ramon at close range. This seems like incredible fiction, but it actually happened in Pecos, Texas, when "Bud" Frazer got into a gunfight with Jim Miller on December 26, 1894. Even after Frazer shot Miller point-blank in the chest the man would not fall down and die, because he had a steel breastplate hidden under his clothes.[12]

Fights, such as a saloon brawl or a confrontation out on the range, typically involved guns. Other weapons used to try to win a fight consisted of knives, fists, and clubs. Brawling methods included wrestling, kicking, chewing, and biting. Biting and chewing were accepted fighting tactics, and more than one unlucky fighter was missing part or all of an ear, or sported scars from bites on his hands, arms, or even his nose. Mike McGowan from Bodie, California, was known as the "man-eater" because of his habit of chewing on the noses and ears of his opponents in a fight.

## Quick on the Draw

Strictly speaking, in the Old West the term for someone who could draw their gun in a hurry was "quick," as in "quick on the draw." The designation "fast" was more commonly used at that time to describe a woman with loose morals, or a lawless establishment or town. It was not until much later that the term "fast" was applied by common usage to drawing a gun, as in the 1950s "fast-draw" competitions. Because the term "fast-draw" has entered modern terminology, the terms "quick" and "fast" should be understood to be interchangeable here.

Part of the reason for having a gun in the hand and being ready to shoot immediately in a threatening situation was that many of the old-time gunfighters were not particularly quick on the draw. Holsters were deep by design and, rather than designed for fast action, were intended to protect the hammer and trigger of a revolver to prevent accidental discharge of the gun into the wearer's leg. Instead of these holsters facilitating lightning-fast draws, guns were more likely to become stuck in these cumbersome devices. During a confrontation that occurred in Texas on June 10, 1877, between rancher John Good and a man named Robinson over a stolen horse, Robinson reached for his gun. The gun caught in his clothing, and Good shot him four times before Robinson could fire back.

Contemporary photographs show that most men in the Old West wore their holsters high on the waist, as this was a more practical and convenient location than hanging low on their hip. But revolvers might not be carried in a holster at all. A gun might simply be stuck into a belt or carried in a leather-lined pants pocket, both of which did not allow for the lightning-fast draw of the Hollywood movie cowboy.

There are differing opinions on how best to perform a fast draw. Shane, in *Shane* (1953), says that a revolver should be worn so that it falls between the wrist and the elbow, but never at arm's length. He wore his gun at his waist, like the old-time gunfighters, at the level of the belt on his pants. The fast-draw Hollywood type of rig developed by Arvo Ojala and used by later Hollywood gunfighters, however, dropped the gun down low on the thigh so that the butt lay close to the wrist.

Gun expert John Bianchi has estimated that old-time gunfighters could draw and fire a first shot in approximately half a second.[13] In *The Plainsman* (1936), Gary Cooper as Wild Bill Hickok, reportedly drew his guns and fired at the target in less than one-third of a second.[14] In reality, once a serious gunfighter had started to draw, it was not possible for his opponent to draw faster and still get in the first shot. Reaction time of the human nervous system is on the order of two-tenths to three-tenths of a second. Therefore it would take that long for the gunman to observe the other man drawing his gun and react to draw his own gun, in addition to the time required for him to clear the holster.

In *The Magnificent Seven* (1960), one scene shows Chris (Yul Brynner) testing Chico's (Horst Buchholtz) draw by clapping his hands and telling Chico to draw his gun and put it between Chris' hands before they slap together. He then successfully demonstrates the technique. Somewhat the same is done in *Cat Ballou* (1965), where Kid Shelleen, as part of his recuperation training, does the same routine of clapping his hands over a gun — and surprisingly, for a boozy old has-been, succeeds.

The ability to draw this fast and beat a hand-clap would seem to be simply a staged trick of the camera, but it is actually possible. The subject came up during the filming of a scene in *The Man Who Shot Liberty Valance* (1962), where a villain (Lee Van Cleef) was supposed to draw a gun on Tom Doniphan (John Wayne) and Doniphan would knock it out of the way. On the set during filming, Wayne asked Van Cleef how fast he could draw his gun. Van Cleef replied, "I can draw this gun so fast you won't be able to clap your hands before I put it between your hands." Wayne said he wanted to see that. Fellow actor Lee Marvin agreed to count to three and see what happened. As Van Cleef told the rest of the story, "[Wayne] clapped his hands and I drew my gun, and I had the gun between his hands before he could bring them together."[15]

There is also the standard Western movie plot of the fast gun and the young men trying to prove that they are faster. This type of story is told in *The Gunfighter* (1950). Gunfighter Jimmy Ringo (Gregory Peck) tries to avoid trouble as he visits his estranged wife and son. In spite of this, he is shot by punk Hunt Bromley (Skip Homeier), who is trying to make a reputation for himself by shooting a famous fast gunman. The dying Ringo allows his killer to live so that he will in turn be hounded and hunted down, and, like him, have to face his own final gunfight with someone who is faster.

## The Road Agent's Spin

One gun trick occasionally used by gunmen was "the spin," also known as "the road agent's spin," "the border roll," or "the gun spin." This was most commonly used by a gunman who had his revolver still in his holster while a lawman held a gun on him. If the lawman told the gunman to give him his gun, the gunman might figure he could escape by using the spin. To perform this maneuver, the gunman slowly pulled out his gun with his forefinger through the trigger guard and held the gun out to the other man with the butt forward. By holding it like this, if he wished, he could rotate the gun around his finger with a jerk of the wrist and bring the barrel forward ready to shoot.

The border roll was probably used on November 6, 1880, when Town Marshal Fred White tried to arrest "Curly Bill" Brocius (real name William Graham) in Tombstone, Arizona. When White ordered Brocius to hand over his gun butt-first, Brocius did so, with the gun positioned to perform the spin. What Brocius intended to do is unclear; but when White suddenly grabbed for the gun, it fired, inflicting a fatal wound on White. This event is reenacted in *Wyatt Earp* (1994) when Marshal White (Harry Carey, Jr.) is shot in this manner on the street. In *The Outlaw Josey Wales* (1976), Wales (Clint Eastwod) does the border spin and outshoots the bad guys when he is threatened by two men in a saloon.

### Accuracy

Another misconception from the movies is the incredible shooting accuracy of the good guys. In reality, shooting accuracy was often not very good. In *Young Guns* (1988), when Doc Spurlock (Kiefer Sutherland) reads an account of their fire-fight in a newspaper, he finds that one parts of the account says "including a miraculous shot at fifty yards." Given the frenzy and confusion of a real gunfight, the participants involved were doing well if they even hit their opponent at all, let alone performing such fancy skills as shooting a gun out of their hand with pinpoint accuracy, or even hitting him in a fatal spot.

In spite of the clever shooting skills of the movie cowboy and lawman, accuracy by real gunfighters with revolvers was dubious at best. It was not unusual for innocent bystanders to be killed or wounded along with the participants of a fight. When rival saloon-owners "Rowdy Joe" Lowe and "Red" Beard shot it out in Delano, Kansas, on October 27, 1873, an innocent bystander named Bill Anderson was shot in the face, and dancehall girl Annie Franklin was seriously wounded in the stomach.[16] Similar stray shots that sprayed a saloon in Dodge City caused havoc when Dave Mather shot it out with Dave Barnes after an argument over a card game. Barnes was shot dead, innocent bystander James Wall was shot in the leg, bystander C.P. Camp was shot through both legs, and Mather received a bullet wound to the head.[17]

An incident like this, which was intended to be humorous, takes place in the Western comedy *The Duchess and the Dirtwater Fox* (1976). The Dirtwater Fox (George Segal) is caught cheating at cards, and the player opposite him at the gambling table pulls a gun and prepares to shoot. Just as the man fires, the Dirtwater Fox bends over to pick up a card that has fallen out of his sleeve, and the bullet misses him and hits an innocent man lounging against the saloon wall watching the game.

Guns had reasonable accuracy. It was the shooters who often did not. The Colt .45 Peacemaker was considered to be very accurate at a range of between twenty-five and fifty yards, though its bullets could carry with reasonable accuracy for up to about four hundred yards.[18] Army tests showed that the gun could produce a grouping of shots that was a little over three inches across at fifty yards. Viewers of Westerns have to consider this range and accuracy as one villain shoots another off a horse at the end of the street with apparent ease and nonchalance. The effective range of a Sharps carbine, on the other hand, was considered to be about one hundred to two hundred yards.

One of the favorite tricks of the movie cowboy (or in some cases the movie cowgirl) was to shoot the gun out of the hand of a bad guy — preferably without drawing blood. Examples of this are numerous. One is in *The Paleface* (1948), where Calamity Jane (Jane Russell) shoots across a room to knock the revolver out of the hand of a man who pulls out a gun to shoot her. In *El Dorado* (1967), Cole Thornton (John Wayne) shoots a gun out of the hand of one of the badmen in the cantina. Similarly, in *Rio Bravo* (1959), Duke (Dean Martin) shoots a gun out of a cowboy's hand in a saloon.[19]

In an even more incredible display of accuracy, in *The Outlaw* (1943), Billy the Kid (Jack Buetel) shoots a hole through a piece of wood lengthwise to make a whistle for a kid (while the young boy is holding it!). Even more miraculously, Billy draws and shoots the hole with a double-action revolver, then slips it back into his apparently-magic holster where it is transformed back into a single-action.

Other fancy shooting tricks are common in the Westerns. In *The Sheepman* (1958), Jason Sweet (Glenn Ford) balances a shot glass with a poker chip on top on the back of his hand. He tosses the glass into the air, draws with the same hand, shoots the glass, holsters his gun, and catches the chip on the back of his hand again. In *Winchester '73* (1950), Lin McAdam (James Stewart) shoots a rifle bullet *through* the hole in the middle of a piece of jewelry shaped like a metal washer, without damaging the jewelry. Anyone who has made a snap shot with a .45 caliber Peacemaker without really aiming will realize that these improbable direct hits would be due more to good luck than to skill.

A popular exhibition trick in Wild West shows was to shoot and break glass balls thrown into the air. The way that sharpshooters achieved this consistently was to use smooth-bore revolvers and rifles loaded with cartridges containing lead shot instead of solid bullets. This gave the shooter a better chance of hitting and breaking a greater number of balls than he or she would have with a single bullet. The pattern of the shot at twenty yards, which was a typical distance for this shooting trick, was about three inches across. In all fairness, an additional important factor was safety, as lead shot carried only over a very short distance and would not travel out into the audience and injure a spectator.

### One Gun or Two?

Some gunmen in the Old West favored carrying more than one revolver. If a second handgun was carried, however, it was typically *not* intended to be shot simultaneously with the first, as is often shown in the movies. Jack Wilson (Jack Palance) in *Shane* (1953), for example, plays the classic two-gun villain when he shoots down Stonewall Torrey (Elisha Cook, Jr.). In real life, the second gun was carried to provide additional firepower and backup in the case of an extended fight. Gunfighters like Wild Bill Hickok, who used cap-and-ball revolvers, wore two Colts so that the second one could be used if the first ran out of bullets or if it failed to fire. Cap-and-ball revolvers were slow to reload, so in a gunfight where many shots were fired, the second gun added extra shooting capability.

Most people shoot best with one particular hand, though Herod (Gene Hackman) in *The Quick and the Dead* (1995) claimed to be equally good with both. Real gunfighters, however, usually brought the second gun into play with the dominant hand by using the "border shift." For a right-handed shooter using this technique, the empty gun was tossed and caught in the left hand, while at the same time "shifting" the loaded gun from the left into the right hand.

Though rare, some shooters did use their two guns simultaneously. In Frio County, Texas, a deputy sheriff named Rhodes started to argue with fellow deputy Alfred Allee about who had the faster draw. To settle their dispute, both men drew and fired at each other. Allee must have been the better shooter because he drew both of his guns at the same time and shot Rhodes eight times, hitting the man in the heart with four of his shots. Allee was acquitted at the subsequent trial on the grounds that Rhodes had drawn first.[20]

In *The Outlaw* (1943), Billy (Jack Buetel) wears two guns, unlike the real Billy the Kid, who wore one revolver on his right side and favored a Colt. Tim Holt, in *Wild Horse Mesa* (1947), carried two guns. The right one was worn in conventional fashion with the butt backwards. The left one was carried with the butt forwards for a cavalry or cross-draw.

Usually one gun was adequate, as most gunfighters were only able to squeeze off one or two shots before a fight was over. Usually, even six shots were not needed. During a shooting lesson, J.B. Books (John Wayne) in *The Shootist* (1976) tells Gillom Rogers (Ron Howard) to put five shots into a tree with his six-shooter. When Gillom ask why only five, Books replies, "You keep your hammer on an empty chamber for safety." This was a common practice in the Old West for carrying a six-shooter. In *True Grit* (1969), Mattie Ross (Kim Darby) asks Rooster Cogburn (John Wayne) why he carries his gun with one chamber empty. Rooster replies it is so that he won't shoot off his own foot.

Though single-action revolvers had a safety notch when the hammer was pulled partially back so that the gun would not accidentally discharge, if the gun fell out of a holster and landed on the hammer, the impact could cause the gun to fire anyway. This happened on January 9, 1876, when Wyatt Earp was involved in a card game in Wichita, Kansas. At one point he leaned back too far in his chair and his revolver fell out of its holster. The gun landed on the hammer and discharged; luckily it only shot a hole in Earp's coat.[21] As a result of such mishaps, experienced gunmen only loaded five of the six chambers and kept the hammer resting on the empty chamber for safety.

A myth from the dime novels is the modification of revolvers to make them faster and easier to fire in an attempt to gain a slight edge in a gunfight. Though a few gunfighters did perform modifications, the factory really did know best and altering these features lowered the safety of the weapon. Simple modifications included filing the main spring to reduce the pressure required to pull back the hammer, and filing or polishing the internal mechanism to produce a "hair trigger." If too much metal was removed, however, the revolver became unstable and fired the cartridge as soon as the hammer was pulled back.

Another modification was to tie the trigger back with a leather thong or to remove the trigger completely so that the revolver was fired by rapidly pulling back on the hammer and releasing it. The trigger guard was sometimes removed from the frame of a revolver for additional speed in firing, but this left the trigger unprotected and the gun liable to discharge if it became entangled in clothing.

### Fanning a Gun

A common technique for rapid-fire shooting that is commonly seen in Westerns is "fanning" a revolver. To do this the gun is held in one hand, with the trigger held back by the trigger finger (or a string or leather thong, or was removed completely), and the hammer is repeatedly slapped back with the heel of the other hand to fire the bullets. Though flashy, this technique was not used in serious gunfights because of the potential inaccuracy that occurred when repeatedly hitting the gun with the hand.

Fanning was inaccurate for two reasons. One was that the revolver had to be held low in front of the body in order to be able to slap the hammer with the palm of the other hand.

This meant that the user's aim depended solely on the "pointability" of the gun. The main reason, though, was because each impact of the hand on the spur of the hammer was liable to jerk the barrel away from the direction of the intended target. This spastic motion often sent the bullet wild and meant that the barrel had to be lined up on the target again between each shot. At very close range (for example, only a few feet), this technique could work and send a random barrage of bullets into a man-sized target. At a range of more than a few feet, however, the wavering motion of the barrel would send shots spraying all over the place.

Though popular in the movies, such as in *The Magnificent Seven* (1960) when Chris (Yul Brynner) disarms and wounds two men by fanning his gun in the scene where he drives the hearse up to the cemetery, fanning a gun was not commonly used in real life. Wyatt Earp commented, "In all my life as a frontier peace officer, I did not know a really proficient gun-fighter who had anything but contempt for the gun-fanner or the man who literally shot from the hip.... What could happen to him in a gunfight was pretty close to murder."[22]

One real-life example that illustrates why fanning a gun is not successful was a shooting spree between "Cockeyed Frank" Loving and buffalo hunter Levi Richardson at the Long Branch Saloon in Dodge City on April 5, 1879. Both pulled their guns at the same time. Richardson fanned his revolver and fired five times before Loving had even fired his first shot, but Richardson missed with all his shots. Loving took his time, aimed carefully, and shot and killed Richardson.

### That Large Number of Kills

Another of the legends of the Old West is the large number of kills attributed to some gunfighters. The number of victims claimed for famous gunmen often grew to legendary proportions. In many cases the number of men killed was inflated by the gunfighter himself. Gunfighter John Wesley Hardin claimed to have killed forty men, and he possibly did, though the true number was more likely closer to a dozen. Hardin has been credited with killing twelve men by the age of eighteen, which is unlikely. Gunman Clay Allison reportedly killed forty men but, again, this number seems high.

Lawman Bat Masterson is reputed to have killed twenty-one individuals; however, he was involved in only three confirmed gunfights, during which he killed only one man. He did not kill anyone while he was sheriff in Dodge City. Wyatt Earp had only one verified killing, though his total was probably higher, perhaps five or six. The total for Jesse James during his outlaw days after the Civil War may have been as few as one or two men. Billy the Kid was popularly credited with twenty-one killings before he was twenty-one years of age, but the reality may have been between four and ten.[23]

### Notches on the Old Shooting Iron

Another enduring legend from the B-Westerns and dime novels is the practice of putting notches on the butt of a gun to record the number of kills. In *The Fastest Gun Alive* (1956), for example, peace-loving storekeeper George Temple (Glenn Ford) has notches on his gun put there by the previous owner. In reality, gunfighters didn't notch their guns. Noted gun expert R.L. Wilson wrote, "The writer has yet to see a historically associated handgun of a prominent lawman, gunfighter, or outlaw—known to have been a man-killer—boasting notches."[24] Other historians and gun experts have said the same.

There is an apocryphal story about a gun owned by General George Smith Patton, Jr., the commander of the U.S. Third Army in Europe during World War II. Patton's favorite handgun was an ivory-handled Colt single-action .45 caliber revolver. Earlier in his career he used it to shoot two of Pancho Villa's lieutenants on the border between Texas and Mexico when he was involved in the Punitive Expedition of 1916 into Mexico. To commemorate this incident, Patton supposedly made two small cuts at the top of the underside of the grip. This would apparently be a very rare example of notches being added to a gun.

Another example may or may not be true, but it makes a good story. After Bat Masterson became a newspaper columnist in New York, he was supposedly pestered by an admiring fan who wanted one of Masterson's guns from a famous gunfight. Finally, in an effort to get rid of the man, Masterson bought an old gun from a pawnshop, cut twenty-two notches into the butt and gave it to him.

One possibly authentic instance of notching is five grooves cut across the butt of a .36 caliber percussion Colt revolver once owned by lawman Dave Mather, now in a museum in Kansas. However, it is not known whether these "notches" were placed there as a record of kills or were added later for effect.

### Dance to the Tune

Westerns occasionally show a gunman shooting at someone's feet to make him dance. One example appears in *The Great Train Robbery* (1903) when the "boys" in a dancehall make a bowler-hatted dude join in the dance by shooting at his feet. The same occurs in a

The image of shooting at someone's feet as a bullying tactic to make him dance, which did indeed happen in the Old West from time to time, is parodied in this satirical political cartoon presented as a centerfold for *Puck* magazine in 1906. Six large cowboys make a small man perform to their tune, titled "Dance, yer little runt! Dance!" (Library of Congress).

more malevolent way in *Pale Rider* (1985), when Marshal Stockburn's (John Russell) thugs make Spider Conway (Doug McGrath) dance by shooting at the ground in front of his feet before aiming higher and filling him full of lead. In *Tom Horn* (1980), bullies make John Coble (Richard Farnsworth) dance by shooting at his feet.

These sorts of high-jinks had a basis in reality. When gunfighter Clay Allison went on a drunken spree in 1874 with the local sheriff, Mason "Mace" Bowman, at a saloon near Cimarron, New Mexico, the two stripped to their underwear and shot at each other's feet to see who was the better dancer. Their aim was either very good or very bad, because neither dancer suffered any injury. Another instance occurred in 1888 when a train conductor named Clark on the Northern Pacific railway was forced to dance on the platform of a train station when several of the local cowboys, in a playful mood, fired bullets at his feet.[25] Butch Cassidy's Wild Bunch reportedly made strangers dance a jig at the Bull Dog Saloon in Baggs, Wyoming.[26] In Frisco, New Mexico, on November 30, 1884, a drunken cowboy named McCarty amused himself by shooting at the feet of some local Mexicans to make them "dance."[27]

## Bullet Wounds

Real gunfighting was a messy business, unlike the gunfights of the B-Westerns where the bad guy claps a hand to an unseen wound in his shoulder and drops his gun. Even though characters in B-Westerns jump, twitch, clutch their chests, and are thrown backwards and fall to the ground with high drama when shot, their shirts do not show bloodstains or holes as they fall. *Rough Night in Jericho* (1967) is a gory film, but in a way it is more realistic than the B-Westerns as it shows packets of movie blood exploding outwards, leaving large holes in shirts and a red stain all over the cloth. But even this is not totally accurate. In reality, a bullet goes inwards and leaves only a small hole in the cloth and skin underneath. The real damage is inside. Genuine blood blows out of the exit wound or may leak out of the entry hole later.

Real wounds in the Old West were serious occurrences and could cause devastating damage. Bullets produced a hugely destructive result upon impact at close range, as the lead bullet fragmented, flattened, or mushroomed when it hit, creating a dreadful wound. The bullet also carried with it bacteria, lubricating grease, particles of dirt, and fragments of clothing that became embedded in the flesh. If the victim did not die immediately from the effects of the wound, foreign matter carried deep into the body by the bullet often led to infection and a subsequent horrible, lingering death.

Suitable measures to effectively combat infection, such as antibiotics, were not available at the time, and the result was usually gangrene. If this occurred in an arm or leg, the only possible course of medical action was amputation of the limb. This removed the infected flesh and possibly saved the man's life. At the beginning of *Dances with Wolves* (1990), Lt. John Dunbar (Kevin Costner) is about to undergo a leg amputation for this very reason after he suffers a foot injury in the Civil War. Wounds in the torso were particularly nasty. If infection occurred in the belly or chest, nothing could save the poor victim.

As another example of gruesome wounds, in *The Man from Laramie* (1955), Will Lockhart (James Stewart) is shot in the hand at close range. He suffers but is later able to use the hand. In real life such an injury would have broken the tendons and severed the nerves. The hand would have been rendered useless, even when healed, because the surgical techniques to repair such extensive damage had not yet been developed. Being shot at such close range, the blast of gunpowder would have also permanently tattooed his hand.

In the second version of *3:10 to Yuma* (2007), bounty hunter and stagecoach guard Byron McElroy (Peter Fonda) is shot squarely in the gut with a .45 bullet by outlaw Charlie Prince (Ben Foster). A veterinarian operates to remove the bullet, which McElroy suffers stoically as the "Doc" probes for the projectile. In reality, he would have been screaming in agony. Even more unbelievable was that after this major surgery McElroy is up walking around and riding his horse within a half-hour of being operated on. In reality, he would have required a couple of months of nursing and recuperation. He also would have probably contracted serious infection because of the wound, with only a 10 percent chance of survival, particularly as he was operated on by a veterinarian. A more realistic outcome might be what occurred in *El Dorado* (1967) when Luke MacDonald (Johnny Crawford) shoots himself rather than face a painful, lingering death from a wound in the belly.

A similar improbability occurs when Chocktaw Neal (Pernell Roberts) loses his final fight with Jason Sweet (Glenn Ford) in *The Sheepman* (1958). When Chocktaw is shot squarely in the middle, he clutches his belly, then falls sideways and lands on his back, unmoving, on the ground. In reality, such a shot would probably not have killed him immediately; he would have survived in agony for several days while bacteria did its insidious work and he died from internal infection.

In one television episode of the television series *Have Gun Will Travel*, both Paladin (Richard Boone) and the bad guy receive a gunshot wound in the shoulder. A few minutes later Paladin lights a cigarette with his bad hand. If he had really been shot in the shoulder, the bullet would probably have destroyed the rotator cuff and bone, and he would never have been able to use the arm again. In a similar fashion, in *The Professionals* (1966), Ehrengard (Robert Ryan) seems to recover and carry on rather quickly after being shot in the chest.

In *The Stalking Moon* (1969), Sam Varner (Gregory Peck), the ex-army scout who protects Sarah Carver (Eva Marie Saint), receives a wound in the shoulder from a buffalo rifle but recovers well enough in a day or so to participate in the final violent fist and gun fight. He even receives a serious knife wound in the leg during the fight and can hardly hobble around, but he valiantly overcomes his opponent. A solid hit from the large-caliber bullet fired by the buffalo rifle alone would probably have killed him from the shock of the impact.

After the gunfight at the O.K. Corral, the real Virgil Earp was badly wounded in the back and left elbow. The result was that he lost the use of his arm and was crippled for life.

Arrow wounds were similar to bullet wounds. In the movie *Red River* (1948), Tess (Joanne Dru) is hit in the shoulder by an arrow, apparently square in the shoulder bone, but Matthew Garth (Montgomery Clift) cuts it out quite easily. A scene or two later, sporting a light sling, her wound does not seem to bother her a bit. In reality, metal Indian arrowheads made from iron often bent and stuck in a wound like a fish-hook, becoming firmly embedded and very hard to pull out. Flint arrowhead created horrible jagged wounds that usually became infected. In addition, arrowheads were usually bound to the shaft of the arrow with animal sinew which softened and caused the arrowhead to come off the shaft, making the head very difficult to extract.

### Buffaloing

Blows to the head or jaw are commonly used in the movies to render someone unconscious. If the blow that outlaw Clint Hollister (Richard Widmark) landed on the back of the deputy's head as he escaped from jail in *The Law and Jake Wade* (1958) had been a real one, it would have probably crushed the man's skull like an eggshell. Similarly, in *Shane* (1953), if the blows during the fight sequences in the saloon and in the yard at Joe Starrett's ranch had landed as depicted, they would have dislocated jaws, split lips, broken noses, bruised eyes, and cracked skulls. As it is, the participants pick themselves up and go back for more.

In *Open Range* (2004), Marshal Poole (James Russo) hits Mose Harrison (Abraham Benrubi) over the head to break up a fight. In reality, a severe blow to the head like this causes a concussion, as the brain is slammed against the inside of the skull with sufficient force to induce temporary unconsciousness.

A favorite technique for subduing someone in Westerns is to hit them on the head and knock them out. Heroes who are "knocked out," particularly in the B-Westerns, just open their eyes, shake their heads, and continue on as if nothing has happened. In real life a blow severe enough to make a man lose consciousness would cause some degree of brain damage each time it happened. The result of such a series of brain injuries would be headaches, vertigo, memory loss, and other symptoms. This type of neurological damage is seen in "punch-drunk" boxers who have been repeatedly knocked unconscious and are suffering from mental impairment. The damage and its symptoms may be temporary or permanent, and can last for up to a year.[28] Any silver-screen hero who was knocked out as many times as is shown would be at best permanently impaired mentally or at worst like a vegetable.

The favorite weapon for knocking someone out in the movies is the butt of a revolver, reversed and held by the barrel as a club. In real life this method has two shortcomings. One is that reversing the gun and holding it by the barrel results in the barrel pointing at the man performing the clubbing. Given the instability of black powder weapons, it would not be unlikely for the gun to discharge accidentally, shooting the man holding it in the chest or stomach. This would not be the desired result.

Another problem in using this technique is knowing how hard to hit the victim. In real life it would be easy to misjudge the strength of the blow and either fail to render the victim unconscious or hit too hard and crack his skull. In real life this happened in the Old West. There were several instances of cowboys who were clubbed over the head with a revolver and reportedly suffered brain damage as a result. Even more serious was what happened in November of 1872 in Newton, Kansas, when a man named Sullivan hit a cowboy over the head with his revolver after a gambling dispute. The spur of the hammer on Sullivan's revolver went through the Texan's skull and killed him.[29]

A different technique was favored by some real law officers, such as Wyatt Earp, who would occasionally club cowboys with his Colt in order to arrest them. Earp would hold the gun in the regular fashion with the barrel pointing at the cowboy, so that the man was covered in case he tried to shoot back. Earp would then approach the man and, without warning, club him alongside the head with the barrel. This technique, called "buffaloing," was also favored by Texas Ranger Jack Hays.

*Chapter Ten*

# Enforcers of the Law

Contrary to the image portrayed by many Westerns, most frontier towns were not wide-open, lawless places filled with constant shootings and gunfights. Towns had laws on the books and law officers to enforce them. The lawlessness that did occur came when individuals chose to break the regulations. The types of crimes most commonly committed in frontier towns were murders, assaults, various types of robberies, and a large category of minor crimes that involved public drunkenness. There were few instances of other crimes against persons, such as domestic violence, rape, child abuse, and attacks upon women.

The Westerns show a variety of law enforcers who oppose crime and criminals, and the distinction between them is often confusing. The primary law officers whose job it was to uphold the law and keep the peace were United States marshals, county sheriffs, and town marshals. Other men involved with various aspects of law enforcement were Texas Rangers, Pinkerton operatives, vigilantes, bounty hunters, and guards who worked for railroads and stage lines.

## U.S. Marshals

United States marshals were officers of the U.S. District Courts. The position of marshal was a political appointment by the president of the United States, with confirmation by the Senate. Because the job of a U.S. marshal was essentially a political one, it was not essential for the candidate to have had law enforcement experience.

The U.S. marshals and their deputies enforced federal laws and pursued those accused of federal crimes, such as mail robbery or desertion from the army. Because the mission of U.S. marshals was to police federal crimes, they and their deputies did not usually interfere in cases that involved local crimes, unless they were specifically ordered to by superiors or their help was requested by local authorities. Local robberies, shootings, and murders were the jurisdiction of the town marshal or the county sheriff.

After a U.S. marshal was appointed, he in turn appointed his own deputies — usually experienced gunfighters — to perform the routine tasks of federal law enforcement, such as tracking down and capturing bank robbers and similar criminals. One reason that so many grim photographs exist of dead criminals propped up on backboards was that deputy marshals often required proof that they had done their duty in order to receive payment. These photographs served as proof that a criminal was dead.

Deputy U.S. marshals were also often commissioned as deputy sheriffs or town marshals so that they could help support local law enforcement when necessary.

Real lawmen were not as glamorous as their flashy movie counterparts. This is a group of deputy U.S. marshals and their clerical support staff at Perry, in the Oklahoma Territory, in 1893. Only a few of the lawmen are displaying their guns (National Archives)

## County Sheriffs

The local sheriff was an elected official who was in overall charge of a particular county in his political jurisdiction. Like the U.S. marshal, the sheriff did not necessarily have law-enforcement experience, as the job was an elected post.

The county sheriff was assisted by several deputies. In an emergency, the sheriff could deputize ordinary citizens to assist him in protecting the town or to form a posse to capture fugitives. The sheriff's duties included maintaining the county jail, serving court orders, and collecting taxes and fines. As an incentive for getting the job done, sheriffs often received a percentage of the taxes they collected.

## Town Marshals

The third layer of law enforcement was the town marshal or city marshal, who was appointed by the mayor or the city council of a town to be the chief of police. Similar to the county sheriff, the town marshal did not operate alone but was usually supported by several deputies who were sometimes called town constables or simply "policemen." A municipal police force might consist of four or five men.

Western movies typically show the law being enforced by a single marshal or sheriff who backs up his demands with a gun. The idea of the town marshal as a lone pillar of justice, single-handedly protecting a town from oncoming villains, as in *High Noon* (1952), is incorrect. A lawman didn't keep the peace alone. He had deputies to assist him. The town marshal could also call on the local sheriff and his deputies for assistance, and he could rally and deputize local townspeople to form a posse. In an emergency, the town marshal could call on the entire citizenry for support if a situation warranted.

In *High Noon* (1952), Marshal Will Kane (Gary Cooper) is left alone to defend Hadleyville against a criminal just released from prison because the cowardly townspeople will not stand behind him. Kane responds to the threat to the community he has sworn to protect, even though it means his possible death. Director Howard Hawks disliked *High Noon* (1952)

All together at one time, some of the toughest gunmen of the West pose for the photographer in 1890. From left to right, standing at the back, are W.H. Harris, Luke Short, and Bat Masterson. Seated at the front are Charlie Bassett, Wyatt Earp, Frank McLane (or McLean), and Neal Brown. These men made up the Dodge City Peace Commission, all friends of gunman and saloon owner Luke Short, with no legal standing. They convened when Short needed to display some extra muscle during a dispute with the city fathers of Dodge City — one of whom happened to own a rival saloon (National Archives).

because it was against what he believed. Hawks said, "I didn't think a good sheriff was going to go running around town like a chicken with his head cut off, asking for help, and finally his Quaker wife had to save him. That isn't my idea of a good western sheriff."[1]

Hawks supposedly made *Rio Bravo* (1959) as a rebuttal to this concept. In *Rio Bravo* (1959), Sheriff John T. Chance (John Wayne) deliberately turns down the offers of assistance from the townspeople who are willing to help because he feels that the situation should be handled by professionals. When friend and wagon-boss Pat Wheeler (Ward Bond) offers his wagon drivers as help, Chance calls them "well-meaning amateurs." In reality, though, both Kane and Chance were wrong. The sheriff or marshal could, and did, call upon and deputize as many of the townspeople as he needed to help him maintain the law.

Actor Gary Cooper had first-hand experience with this. Cooper referred to his father when he said, "As a trial lawyer and later a judge in the Montana Supreme Court, Dad knew sheriffs all over the West, and he knew what they were up against. Law enforcement, as he taught it to me, was everybody's job. The sheriff was not a lone figure, but the representative of the people's desire for law and order, and unless he had the people behind him, he was in poor shape."[2]

The duties of the town marshal included serving civil and criminal warrants, maintaining the town jail, locking up drunks, recording arrests, and collecting taxes and fines. He might also be the town dog-catcher and be responsible for street maintenance and clean-up. The town marshal might be called on to shoot ownerless dogs to prevent rabies. When Wild Bill Hickok was marshal of Abilene he earned fifty cents for each stray dog he shot.

Though Western movies are full of gunfights, the reality of all three types of law enforcement was more mundane most of the time. Many lawmen did not fire a single shot at another man during their entire appointment. Most of the arrests made by town marshals were for drunk-and-disorderly conduct, disturbing the peace, fighting, and carrying a concealed weapon where prohibited by local ordinances.

On the other hand, sheriffs could be as tough as they had to be. In June of 1881, five cowboys rode into Tascosa, Texas, and started drinking in Jack Ryan's saloon. Sheriff Cape Willingham came in and told them in a friendly manner that it was against the law to carry guns in town. Four of the five handed over their guns to the barkeeper, but Fred Leigh continued to drink in defiance of the request. When the sheriff brought a shotgun to arrest him, Leigh went for his revolver. Willingham simply pulled the trigger and resolved the situation.


## Those Who Went Bad

Because law enforcement required a tough attitude and skill with a gun, lawmen were often former gunfighters, outlaws, or killers. They turned to enforcing the law because being a town marshal offered a steady job with a reasonable income. Some of these lawmen, however, occasionally forgot which side of the law they were on and reverted to their old ways. Billy Brooks, for example, who was town marshal of Newton, Kansas, in 1872, was hanged as a horse thief in 1874.

Another example was Henry Brown, who was appointed town marshal of Caldwell, Kansas, in July of 1882. On April 30, 1884, Brown, his deputy Ben Wheeler, and two others tried to rob a bank in Medicine Lodge, Kansas. They failed. Brown and the other would-be robbers were immediately captured, arrested, and jailed. Brown was shot dead by a lynch mob, and the other three were hung later that night.

# The Texas Rangers

The idea for the Lone Ranger came from the real-life Texas Rangers. This legendary character had his origins on the radio, moved on to movie serials, appeared on television from 1949 to 1965 (for 221 episodes), and was the subject of a feature film *The Legend of the Lone Ranger* (1981). In the original Lone Ranger story, six Texas Rangers, led by Captain Dan Reid, were ambushed at Bryant's Gap by the Cavendish Gang. All of the rangers were killed except one, John Reid, who was found barely alive but was nursed back to health by a Mohawk Indian named Tonto.[3] After Reid regains his health, he takes a piece of black cloth from his brother's vest to make a mask to conceal his identity ("who was that masked man?") as he seeks to avenge the deaths of his comrades and his brother. He calls himself the Lone Ranger as he pursues outlaws and continues to fight injustice. The Lone Ranger used silver bullets and was remarkably good at shooting guns out of people's hands. His horse was even named Silver.

The real Texas Rangers were part of a quasi-military force of lawmen originally appointed by Stephen Austin to protect American settlers against Indian attacks in Texas in the early 1820s. These groups of militia men became known as "ranging companies," a name which was later formalized into "Texas Rangers." Their mobility and fierce fighting abilities were used to successfully track and capture outlaws, horse thieves, and other law-breakers.

The formal organization that became the Texas Rangers was officially sanctioned on November 24, 1835. Their mission included hunting down cattle rustlers, bandits, bank robbers, and any other outlaws who threatened the safety and well-being of Texas citizens. Traveling in groups of two or three, the Rangers soon earned a reputation for being a tough, no-nonsense band of hard-riding men who had considerable latitude in enforcing the law.

As well as continuing to protect Texas citizens against Indian attacks, one of the primary tasks of the Rangers after the Civil War was tracking down and controlling rustling and robbery by lawless gangs of ex-soldiers who preyed on Texas ranchers and settlers. This was accomplished by sending these tough, hard-riding, fast-shooting lawmen to chase down cattle thieves operating along the border between Texas and Mexico. Legend had it that one crime rated the services of one ranger, no matter how complex the problem or how many outlaws were involved. The reality was that the more serious incidents might require fifteen or twenty Rangers riding together.

The Rangers were always well-armed with the most modern weaponry. By the mid–1870s the Rangers were mostly armed with Colt single-action .45 caliber Peacemakers and Model 1873 Winchester carbines.

Though not as well-known as the Texas Rangers, both Arizona and New Mexico had similar armed gunmen who operated against rustlers and enforced territorial laws. The Arizona Rangers were formed in 1901, followed by the New Mexico Rangers in 1905.

# Vigilantes

Vigilante crowds often show up in Westerns, usually with rope in hand, intent on carrying out their own type of justice. Vigilante groups in the early West were not authorized lawmen, but were ordinary citizens who did not want to wait for the slow progress of regular justice and took the law into their own hands to deal with outlaws, bandits, and cattle thieves. Individual vigilantes were usually anonymous, and outsiders never learned their names. Usually they were responding to extreme crimes, such as constant cattle rustling, incessant robberies, or the flagrant murder of a prominent citizen.

The justice of the vigilantes was swift and violent. After a few lynchings from the nearest tree, lawbreakers usually got the message and left town. The vigilantes, their work done for the time being, faded back into their regular lives until their form of justice might be needed again.

Typical of the conditions that prompted vigilante law were those in Bannack, Montana, late in 1863. The local sheriff, Henry Plummer, was the leader of a gang of fifty killers and bandits who called themselves "the Innocents." These gunmen, many of whom were Plummer's deputies, terrorized Bannack, robbing, looting and murdering. When the truth about Plummer began to leak out, the local people organized a vigilante group. The vigilantes captured and lynched twenty-one of The Innocents, including Plummer, solving the problem with their own rough brand of justice.

Another Montana vigilante group was named the "Stranglers," which was organized in 1884 in response to widespread cattle rustling. To try and clean out the rustlers, the group tracked down and lynched every horse bandit and cattle thief they could find. The vigilantes hung at least thirty-five men, which finally stopped the rustlers and the rustling.

Cattlemen sometimes employed "range detectives," or other tough men with some such vague title, in a form of vigilante justice to track down cattle rustlers. These men were professional gunfighters who used violent methods to protect the cattle barons' stock and other property from thieves and outlaws. The general method employed by these men was to shoot, hang, or run outlaws out of town in whatever manner they could. As shown in some Western movies, these "cattle inspectors" or "range detectives" sometimes went beyond simple stock protection. They were used by powerful ranchers to control local cattle ranges and scare away settlers, sheepmen, and any competitive small ranchers. In reality, of course, they had no legal authority.

One such "enforcer" was Tom Horn, whose activities served as the basis for the movie *Tom Horn* (1980). Horn had been an army scout, a cowboy, a teamster, a stagecoach driver, and a Pinkerton operative before being hired as a "range detective." He worked for the Wyoming Stock Growers Association in 1892, then for the Swan Land and Cattle Company in 1894. His job was to track down cattle rustlers, and he quite honestly called himself a "cattle rustler exterminator."[4] Horn's specialty was shooting suspected rustlers from cover with a high-powered rifle.[5] On July 18, 1901, Horn mistakenly shot a fourteen-year-old boy, thinking that he was ambushing the boy's father instead. After drinking a little too much, Horn inadvertently confessed the crime to Deputy U.S. Marshal Joe LeFors, who arrested him. Horn later retracted his "confession," but he was nonetheless convicted of murder and hung on November 20, 1903.

## Pinkerton's Detectives

Another type of law-enforcer was employed by Pinkerton's detective agency, whose origins were in the Civil War. Allan Pinkerton, the founder of the agency, was born in Scotland, joined the Chicago police force as its first detective, then went on to form his own detective agency. Pinkerton's National Detective Agency consisted of the most famous group of detectives that worked in the West hunting down outlaws. Pinkerton preferred the name "operative" rather than "detective." Pinkerton's major business was protecting railroads and express companies, both of which routinely transported large sums of money and other valuables, and operatives were often hired to solve train and bank robberies.

Pinkerton's stopped at nothing to get their man, and criminals were usually worried if they knew that Pinkerton operatives were on their trail. One of the agency's favorite techniques was to have operatives go under cover and infiltrate the gangs they were pursuing. This was dangerous work, and men who were identified as operatives by the gang they were infiltrating often mysteriously disappeared.

Pinkerton operatives had no legal standing and didn't directly arrest outlaws and thieves. Instead, they gathered information and evidence that could be used by local law enforcement officials to make the actual arrest.

The agency symbol was a picture of an open eye with the motto "We Never Sleep" underneath it. Another version of the motto was "The Eye That Never Sleeps." This symbol eventually led to the name "private eye" being applied for a private detective.

In *The Train Robbers* (1973), the Pinkerton Man (Ricardo Montalban) says that he is a Wells Fargo agent. In the next shot, Lane (John Wayne) calls him a Pinkerton man. The two agencies were totally different, of course, though Pinkerton's did occasionally guard trains.

## Judges

Judges appear in Westerns as major or minor characters who enforce the law. Judge Isaac Charles Parker, for example, also known as the "Hanging Judge," was the inspiration for Judge Fenton (Pat Hingle) in *Hang 'Em High* (1968). Like the real Parker, the fictional Fenton determinedly pursues the legal hanging of assorted murderers, rapists, and cattle thieves in Fort Grant. In *True Grit* (1969), Rooster Cogburn (John Wayne) is one of the marshals working for Judge Parker out of Ft. Smith, Arkansas.[6]

Parker was appointed as a district judge in 1875. His territory was the 70,000-square-mile Western District of Arkansas, which included the Indian Territory known as the "Cherokee Strip." The notorious Cherokee Strip was so full of horse thieves, cattle rustlers, crooked gamblers, whiskey peddlers, and outlaw gangs that even lawmen were reluctant to travel into it. For safety, deputy marshals would only travel there in groups of at least four or five men. During Parker's tenure as a judge, sixty-five deputy U.S. marshals were killed while trying to arrest various criminals.

From 1875 until his death in 1896, Parker presided over almost fourteen thousand civil and criminal trials, and sentenced 160 criminals to be hanged. Of these, seventy-nine were actually executed. The rest had their sentences commuted, were pardoned, or were killed while trying to escape. There was no higher court than Parker's, and his sentences could only be commuted by the President of the United States.

*True Grit* (2010) starts with a triple hanging at Fort Smith. This was relatively mild for Parker. Some of Parker's notoriety came from his multiple hangings, which were carried out by his chief executioner, George Maledon. Maledon erected a twelve-man gallows to carry out multiple executions, but when he hung six convicted men at the same time on September 3, 1875, he and Parker were roundly condemned, and further executions were closed to the public.

Another real judge who served as the inspiration for characters in several movies was Judge Roy Bean, the self-styled "Law West of the Pecos." In *The Westerner* (1940), Bean

Judge Roy Bean (seated, with the white beard and the hat) presides over his court at Langtry, Texas, while trying a horsethief. Bean called his combination saloon and courthouse "the Jersey Lilly" to commemorate his obsession with famous British actress Lillie Langtry. One of Bean's unusual claims to fame was that he had once been lynched, though luckily he was cut down in the nick of time (National Archives).

(Walter Brennan) dies of a gunshot wound in a theater, whereas the real Judge Bean was removed from office in 1892 when the number of votes he received was greater than the number of eligible voters. The judge starred in a television series, *Judge Roy Bean*, which ran in the 1955 television season for thirty-nine episodes, with Edgar Buchanan playing the judge. In a self-reflexive explanation of the fictions in Western movies that were foisted on the public by Hollywood, the prologue to the later *The Life and Times of Judge Roy Bean* (1972), with Paul Newman as the judge, states, "Maybe this isn't the way it was, but this is the way it should have been."

The real Roy Bean was a saloon owner who became a self-appointed justice of the peace at age fifty-six. Bean enjoyed being a judge and set up his official courtroom in his saloon, where he often interrupted the court proceedings to sell a few drinks of whiskey to the principals and jury. Bean's entire law library consisted of a copy of the 1879 *Revised Statutes of Texas*, so he often used his personal sense of justice to justify some of the sentences he handed down. In one of Bean's more unusual rulings, he found a revolver and $40 on a man who was killed when he fell off a high bridge. Bean would have only earned a $5 fee as coroner for burying the man, so in a stroke of inspiration he fined the dead man $40 for carrying a concealed weapon before burying him and collecting the other $5.

## The Gunfight at the O.K. Corral

Arguably the most-quoted example of lawmen versus "the bad guys" is the gunfight that occurred at the O.K. Corral in Tombstone, Arizona. This shootout, which has been called the most famous gun battle of the Old West, has appeared, with varying degrees of accuracy, in numerous movies, so it is important to briefly present the central facts surrounding the fight and how they relate to the versions presented by Hollywood. It should be noted that this gunfight was in itself unusual even for the Wild West, as it was a pitched battle between multiple participants that took place in broad daylight and in front of many witnesses.

## The Reality

The deadly gunfight took place in the silver-mining town of Tombstone in southern Arizona on October 26, 1881. The participants on one side were the Earp brothers, Wyatt, Virgil, and Morgan, backed up by Doc Holliday. Facing them on the other were Ike and Phin Clanton, and Frank and Tom McLaury (also sometimes spelled McLowery).

The Earp-Clanton conflict that led to the fight at the O.K. Corral had its origins in the cattle rustling that formed part of the criminal activities around remote, lawless Tombstone in the late 1870s. Even some of the respectable ranchers surreptitiously bought and sold stolen cattle so that they could adequately fill government contracts to supply beef to local Indian reservations, as well as to the hungry miners in Tombstone and the surrounding mining towns.

The original usage of the word "rustler" was actually an innocent one, and the name was initially applied to men who rounded up wild cattle for sale. Only later was it applied to those who stole cattle.[7] Before the term "cowboy" came to denote men who herded cattle, it was used as a generic name for Texas bandits who rustled cattle. As a result, the Tombstone rustlers liked to call themselves "cowboys," often spelled in the 1870s either as two words — "cow boy"— or hyphenated as "cow-boy" (the hyphen was not dropped until about 1900).

One of the ringleaders of the rustlers was Newman Haynes Clanton, known locally as "Old Man" Clanton. Clanton was a rancher who rustled cattle in Mexico in order to build his herds at his ranch near Charleston, which was about seven miles southwest of Tombstone. He had three sons: Joseph Isaac (Ike), Phineas (Phin), and William (Billy). He also employed two gunmen, Johnny Ringo and William "Curly Bill" Brocius.

In December of 1879, brothers Wyatt, Virgil, and James Earp traveled to Tombstone, along with Wyatt's mistress Mattie, Virgil's wife Allie, and James' wife Bessie. Wyatt found work as a Wells Fargo shotgun guard and later became a deputy sheriff for surrounding Pima County. He also worked as a gambler at the Oriental Saloon and the Eagle Brewery. Older brother Virgil had previously been appointed deputy U.S. marshal for southeast Arizona Territory, which included the town of Tombstone. James Earp was not a lawman like the others. He ran a saloon, while his wife Bessie ran a bawdy house — occasionally as an active participant from time to time, an arrangement that was not unusual in saloons that offered prostitution along with drinking. Younger brother Morgan joined the brothers in Tombstone later the next year, along with Doc Holliday and his mistress, Kate Elder.

Virgil Earp expanded his lawman activities and became assistant city marshal under Marshal Fred White. On October 28, 1880, White and Virgil went out into the streets of Tombstone to arrest gunman "Curly Bill" Brocius and several other cow-boys who were shooting up the town. White demanded Curly Bill's gun. Curly Bill handed it to him and then performed the road agent's spin. In the resulting struggle with Virgil, the gun went off and White fell to the ground with a mortal wound. After Fred White's death, Virgil was appointed acting town marshal. He was occasionally assisted by Wyatt as his deputy.

During the first part of 1881, various inflammatory incidents and accusations created tension between the Earps, the Clantons, and the other cow-boys. Among the bones of contention were a disagreement over the ownership of a horse, the disposition of some stolen army mules, and heated accusations from both sides concerning a recent stagecoach robbery.

As well as horses and cattle, a variety of other goods, such as coins, bullion, and liquor, continued to be smuggled across the border via the San Pedro River valley, west of Tombstone, in order to avoid customs duties. Violence was rampant on both sides of the border, and some of the local cow-boys even went into business for themselves by robbing the smugglers. In July of 1881, "Old Man" Clanton and a group of cow-boys ambushed and killed a group of Mexican smugglers in Skeleton Canyon. In retribution, Mexican soldiers killed Clanton and four other men in Guadalupe Canyon on August 13 while they were driving a herd of stolen cattle to Tombstone.

By late 1881, all of this border smuggling and rustling activity had created a state of tension in Tombstone, where Wyatt Earp and Johnny Behan were in competition for the position of sheriff of the newly-created Cochise County. This was a lucrative post which carried with it a percentage of the local taxes and fines collected. Silver mining in Tombstone was so successful that the tax collected by the sheriff was estimated to be worth more than $30,000 a year — more than enough to provide a good income. As it turned out, Governor John Fremont appointed Behan to the job, and Behan followed his own personal policy of turning a blind eye to the rustling.[8] Further conflict had developed between Behan and Wyatt Earp because Earp had taken up with Josephine Sarah Marcus, an actress who had been Behan's mistress.

The escalating situation between the Clantons, Behan, and the Earps finally led to the showdown that has been immortalized as the gunfight at the O.K. Corral. Though the feud simmered for some time, it didn't come to a head until October 26, 1881. Altercations early in the day included Virgil Earp clubbing and arresting a drunken Ike Clanton, and hauling him to court for carrying firearms (which was against a city ordinance); and Wyatt buffaloing Tom McLaury after trading insults and threats. Later in the day, Virgil received word that the Clantons and the McLaurys were in town carrying guns in violation of the law. The cow-boys had gathered at the O.K. Corral, which was located on Fremont Street, between Third and Fourth Streets. Wyatt and Morgan, who had been deputized by Virgil, were joined by Doc Holliday, and the four of them went to disarm — or, failing that, to arrest — the Clantons and the McLaurys. The result was gunfire.

The actual fight took place not in the O.K. Corral itself but just off Fremont Street in a vacant lot behind the corral, between the Harwood house and C.S. Fly's boarding house and photographic gallery. There are still arguments and disagreements over who fired the first shot and what happened in the thirty seconds that followed. After the shooting was over, the general opinion was that Frank McLaury went for his gun first, followed almost simultaneously by Billy Clanton and Wyatt Earp. General shooting continued from there. It is known that seventeen shots were fired in a space of time later estimated to have been approximately thirty seconds, with a distance of about six to eight feet between the two factions. When the gunsmoke cleared, Frank and Tom McLaury, and Billy Clanton, were fatally wounded, Virgil was shot in the right leg, Morgan was wounded in the neck, and Doc Holliday had received a minor wound on the hip. Only Wyatt was not wounded. Ike Clanton ran away.

After the deadly gunfight the feelings of some of the townspeople ran high against the Earps. Several witnesses at the subsequent hearing stated that the Earps had provoked the

The graves of the McLaury brothers, Frank and Tom, and Billy Clanton are located in Boot Hill in Tombstone, Arizona, where they were buried after the famous thirty-second shootout at the O.K. Corral in 1881. As Clanton's marker shows, angry supporters of the cowboys termed the deaths "murdered on the streets of Tombstone." The coroner and the presiding judge at the subsequent hearing ruled otherwise.

fight, then killed Clanton and the McLaurys under the pretense of enforcing the law. In defense of his actions, Wyatt Earp testified, "When Billy Clanton and Frank McLowry drew their pistols, I knew it was a fight for life and I drew and fired in defense of my own life and the lives of my brothers and Doc Holliday."[9]

After several witnesses gave conflicting testimony, and nothing was found to contradict the facts given by independent witnesses, neither the coroner's inquest nor the hearing presided over by Judge Wells Spicer found enough evidence to put the Earps on trial for any criminal action. The brothers had obviously killed the three cow-boys, but had done so in the commission of their prescribed official law-enforcement duties. Spicer did, however, comment that in his opinion they had committed "an injudicious and censurable act."

The gunfight was by no means the end of the conflict, and the killings continued. A few days later Wyatt left Tombstone with Doc and several members of a posse to search for other members of the cow-boys' gang. The posse went on what has been called the Vendetta Ride, tracking down the killers and exacting vigilante retribution.

On December 28, 1881, Virgil Earp was ambushed on a street in Tombstone and hit by two loads of buckshot from a shotgun. He was badly wounded in the back and left elbow. Doctors operated and took five inches of bone from his arm (a procedure called resection that was common at the time for shattered bone, but it left the arm useless). It saved his life, but he never fully recovered.

Morgan recovered from the wound he received at the gunfight but was killed on March 18, 1882, by a shotgun blast through a window that hit him in the spine while he was playing billiards in Campbell and Hatch's Saloon. The coroner's jury concluded that the killers were Frank Stilwell, Pete Spence, and "Indian Charlie" Cruz. Stilwell, previously Behan's deputy, was subsequently mysteriously found dead, full of bullets and buckshot, near the tracks in the railroad yards at Tucson on March 20, 1882.

"Curly Bill" Brocius disappeared, probably murdered. On July 13, 1882, Johnny Ringo was found shot in the head, leaning up against a tree in Turkey Creek Canyon in the nearby mountains. The coroner called it suicide, but Brocius had no boots either on his feet or nearby; there were no powder burns around the wound; and, inexplicably, a small part of his scalp appeared to have been cut away with a knife. His death was generally thought to be the result of the Earp feud. Ike Clanton was later killed while rustling cattle in Apache County on June 1, 1887.

The violence that continued in the aftermath of the gunfight was so bad that President Chester Arthur telegraphed a presidential proclamation on May 3, 1882, threatening to invoke martial law if local law enforcement officials could not stop the lawlessness. By early 1884 the outraged citizen of Tombstone decided that they could no longer stand by and allow cow-boys, gunmen, and outlaws to disrupt their town. After one or two were summarily hung as examples of vigilante justice, Tombstone's violent years came to an end.

In 1886, local rancher and former Texas Ranger John Slaughter was elected sheriff of Cochise County. He arrested some of the remaining undesirables, ran the others out of town, and finally brought law and order to the town that still calls itself "The Town Too Tough to Die."

Those are the essential facts.[10]

## The Movie Versions

Because of its subsequent notoriety, the gun battle at the O.K. Corral has played a prominent part in popular movies, such as *My Darling Clementine* (1946), *Gunfight at the O.K. Corral* (1957), *Tombstone* (1993), and *Wyatt Earp* (1994), but the screen versions haven't always been accurate. A fictionalized story of Tombstone also appeared in *Tombstone Territory*, a television series between 1957 and 1959, starring Pat Conway as Sheriff Clay Hollister.

The real Wyatt Earp was only thirty-three in 1881 at the time of the famous gunfight, but he has traditionally been played in motion pictures by older actors, such as Walter Huston, aged forty-eight, in *Law and Order* (1932) (which placed the final shootout at the O.K. Barn!); by Joel McCrea, aged fifty, in *Wichita* (1955) and Burt Lancaster, aged forty-three, in *Gunfight at the O.K. Corral* (1957).

### MY DARLING CLEMENTINE (1946)

*My Darling Clementine* is one of the movies that played fast and loose with the facts. Stuart Lake's book *Frontier Marshal* is credited as the source, but director John Ford changed even that into his vision of a romantic fantasy. Ford also moved the film's location from southern Arizona to a special movie set for the town of Tombstone that was built in Monument Valley on the Arizona-Utah border.

The movie starts with the Earp brothers driving cattle to Tombstone. In reality, the Earps were not cattlemen or cowboys, and did not drive a herd of cattle to Tombstone. In *My Darling Clementine* the Earps are unmarried, and Doc is a physician from Boston. The

Though not quite as rugged as its depiction in *My Darling Clementine*, Tombstone, the town that still boasts that it is "The Town Too Tough to Die," today retains much of the flavor of the early 1880s. Allen Street is still covered with dirt, verandas shade board sidewalks, and adjoining Fremont Street still rings out with gunshots from periodic reenactments of the famous gun battle at the O.K. Corral.

fictional Clementine is the object of romantic rivalry between Doc Holliday and Wyatt. In reality the Earps were married, or at least had liasons with women, when they reached Tombstone. Wyatt was accompanied by Mattie Blaylock, his common-law wife, and Virgil was married to Allie.

Wyatt Earp (Henry Fonda) goes into Tombstone, subdues a troublemaker, and is offered a job as the town marshal. The Earp brothers thus become the only law officers in Tombstone, with no mention of a county sheriff. James Earp, who is a younger brother in this movie, is left guarding the cattle while Virgil and Wyatt go into town. When they return they find that James has been murdered and the cattle stolen, presumable by Old Man Clanton. When "James" is buried, his grave marker reads "James Earp 1862." This is an interesting reference, as James Earp was the oldest of the Earp brothers and had no part in the lawman activities of the others. Warren Earp was the youngest, and was killed in 1900 in Willcox, Arizona, as the result of a drunken fight in a saloon.

In this movie Wyatt does not meet Doc (Victor Mature) until after he arrives in Tombstone, where Doc basically runs the town. In reality, Wyatt and Doc had known each other for years, dating back to their time at Fort Griffin, Texas, and the cattle towns of Abilene and Dodge. The real Doc did not arrive in Tombstone until about six months after Wyatt.

In *My Darling Clementine*, Doc has a girlfriend named Chihuahua (Linda Darnell), a fictional sultry dancehall girl who is shot by Billy Clanton. The Clementine (Cathy Downs) of the title is Doc's former nurse who took care of him during his tuberculosis illness in the East. In reality, Doc's long-time girlfriend was Kate Fisher, also known as "Big Nose" Kate.

The final climactic confrontation and gunfight pits Wyatt Earp and Doc Holliday against the Clantons, led by Old Man Clanton (who in real life would not have even been there, as he had been killed the previous August in the Guadalupe Canyon Massacre). There is no sheriff Johnny Behan, and gunfighters Johnny Ringo and Curly Bill Brocius are missing from the plot.

Doc is killed at the end of the gunfight, and Wyatt rides off after saying goodbye to Clementine, who remains in town to be the local schoolmarm. In reality, Wyatt stayed on in Tombstone for the hearing and then took part in the vengeance ride. The real Doc survived his wound in the leg for six more years after the gunfight and died at a sanitarium in Glenwood Springs, Colorado, in November 1887.

John Ford liked to "edit" his films in his mind's eye while he was filming and did not shoot much additional material. In this way he felt that his movies could not be altered later. However, when producer Darryl Zanuck saw the movie, he didn't like it. Zanuck re-edited *My Darling Clementine*, in the process cutting thirty minutes and thus altering Ford's version and vision.[11]

### *GUNFIGHT AT THE O.K. CORRAL* (1957)

In this version of the gunfight, real-life sheriff Johnny Behan is replaced by sheriff Cotton Wilson, a fictional sheriff from earlier scenes in Fort Griffin, who is at odds with town marshal Wyatt Earp (Burt Lancaster) over the Clantons' rustling. As town marshal, Earp is correctly responsible for keeping the peace in the town of Tombstone. Wilson, on the other hand, is sheriff of Cochise County. In reality, Virgil Earp was the town marshal, not Wyatt.

The Clanton gang in this movie includes Johnny Ringo (John Ireland) as a hired gun but leaves out Curly Bill Brocius, who killed the real Marshal Fred White. *Gunfight at the O.K. Corral* ends after a ferocious version of the gunfight but doesn't continue on to show the aftermath and vendetta ride. In this movie Johnny Ringo is shot by Doc Holliday (Kirk Douglas) during the gunfight, whereas the real Ringo met a mysterious death later, though possibly as part of the feud.

Wyatt has a fictional romance in Dodge City with equally fictional lady gambler Laura Denbow (Rhonda Fleming). She declines to follow him to Tombstone, but Wyatt hopes to meet up with her in California after the gunfight. There is no mention of Mattie or Josephine Marcus, who was the real Wyatt's companion for the rest of his life.

A bowler-hatted Bat Masterson (Kenneth Tobey) appears briefly as the local sheriff in Dodge City (Ford County), who has come to Wyatt to borrow deputies to form a posse — contrary to the premise of both *High Noon* (1952) and *Rio Bravo* (1959), where the sheriff stands alone. While still in Dodge City, Earp shows off a Buntline Special fitted with a carbine stock to his deputy, but there is no further mention of it. The early part of the movie correctly shows Mayor Kelly at the Long Branch Saloon, as he was indeed the mayor of Dodge City and was owner of the real saloon. Johnny Ringo (John Ireland) appears as a major character, though in real life he was only a minor gunfighter who participated in shooting scrapes around Tombstone (though he is thought to have been involved in Virgil Earp's ambush after the main gunfight). For a short while he was one of Behan's deputies. Jimmy Earp appears as a nineteen-year-old little brother and deputy sheriff who is ambushed and killed in the movie, though he was actually the oldest brother and a saloon owner.

At the end of the movie, after the shooting of Billy Clanton in Fly's photographic shop by Doc Holliday, Wyatt dramatically drops his gun and badge to the ground and retires from being a lawman, then heads to California to meet Laura Denbow. In reality, he went on to avenge his brothers.

The final shootout in *Gunfight at the O.K. Corral* (1957) lasts for seven minutes and ten seconds on the screen, from the first gunshots to the shooting of Billy Clanton in Fly's photo studio. The real gunfight, of course, lasted for only thirty seconds.

Old Tucson Studios stood in for Fort Griffin at the beginning of the movie, then, with different camera angles, for Tombstone and the site of the final gunfight at the end. The rest of the town of "Tombstone" was shot on Paramount's back lot in Hollywood, as were the earlier Dodge City sequences.

*Hour of the Gun* (1967), also directed by John Sturges, starts where *Gunfight at the O.K. Corral* (1957) leaves off, with Wyatt Earp (James Garner) and Doc Holliday (Jason Robards) on the vengeance ride.

## TOMBSTONE (1993)

The movie opens with a violent massacre at a wedding, including the killing of a priest, as the cow-boys strut their stuff while wearing red sashes. One critic dismissed *Tombstone* (1993) with the comment that "the historicity of Tombstone, however, is merely skin deep. Its heart belongs to the pop culture of today.... Tombstone's cowboys wear gang colors."[12] In actual fact, yes, the cow-boys did wear a type of "gang" color, and the depiction was historically accurate. The cow-boys wore red sashes as a badge of membership, a fashion that was derived from the earlier California vaqueros.

*Tombstone* (1993) is probably the most accurate cinematic version of the gunfight in its portrayal of the facts. Many small details in the movie are correct. Wyatt (Kurt Russell) arrives in Tombstone with his (common-law) wife Mattie. Doc Holliday (Val Kilmer) is called a "lunger," which was a common nickname at the time for someone with tuberculosis. Curly Bill Brocius (Powers Boothe) shoots Fred White (Harry Carey, Jr.) out on the street after performing a road agent's spin. Virgil Earp (Sam Elliott) is a marshal, is wounded in the leg at the gunfight, and then is later ambushed and wounded in the arm. Morgan Earp (Bill Paxton) is shot and killed at the pool hall. Johnny Ringo (Michael Biehn) plays a part in the story. Actress Josephine Marcus comes to town and is in a show at the Bird Cage theater (in reality she appeared in Gilbert and Sullivan's *Pirates of Penzance* at Schieffelin Hall, a more sedate theater on the north side of town, but this was close), and she eventually steals Wyatt away from Mattie. And Doc dies correctly at a sanitorium in Glenwood Springs, Colorado, from his tuberculosis.

In a humorous nod, the camera pans past the famous Les Moore sign in Boot Hill when the Earps arrive in Tombstone. The often-quoted grave marker reads:

> *Here lies*
> *Lester Moore,*
> *Four slugs from a .44,*
> *No Les, no more.*

The real Les Moore was a freight agent at nearby Naco, Arizona, who became embroiled in an argument over a damaged package with customer Harry Dunstan. Apparently unable to resolve the dispute, both men drew their guns and started firing. Both died.

The depiction of the state of booming Tombstone in 1881 as being under construction was so accurate that a film critic for *Entertainment Weekly* complained that it looked as though the town hadn't been completed before filming — but then that was the point.

## WYATT EARP (1994)

*Wyatt Earp* (1994), another re-telling of the famous gunfight, also contains many accurate details. The saloon in Fort Griffin is a tent with walls coming part way up the sides, typical of the times. As Wyatt (Kevin Costner) passes through the saloon, the audience sees a barber at work inside. Real barbers often worked in the back of saloons. The death of Ed Masterson at the hands of a drunk correctly shows him with his clothes on fire. The movie also correctly shows the road agent's spin that was involved in the killing of Marshal Fred White of Tombstone. Doc uses a Colt Lightning, which was reputed to be a favorite of the real Holliday.

## Chapter Eleven

# From Lacy to Racy —
# Wine, Wimmen and Song

Women in movies during the golden age of Westerns, often derisively referred to by the hero's sidekick as "wimmen," occupy a place that had no particular historical precedent. Traditional Westerns emphasized male roles and macho behavior, and women were typically given only secondary roles. As Magers and Fitzgerald have aptly summed it up, "Usually, a woman was relegated to background dressing — a pretty young thing who is the rancher's daughter, the banker's daughter, or the kind-hearted tart who has employment in the local saloon."[1] This thought was echoed by Republic leading lady Vivian Austin who said, "Frankly, fifty years ago, women in Westerns didn't do much."[2]

Women's clothing in Westerns has often been used to categorize and emphasize the stereotypes. One category was the hard-working pioneer wife in a sunbonnet and an old-fashioned, frumpy cotton dress who toiled to make a home out of the wilderness. This type is seen in movies such as *Wagon Master* (1950) and *Abilene Town* (1946) as nondescript women usually married to equally nondescript farmers or sod busters. Another group included the heroine or "nice girl," who doesn't wear a sunbonnet, but wears long modest dresses with high necklines. A third category offered the dancehall girl and the prostitute-with-a-heart-of-gold, who wear silk dresses with short skirts and ruffled petticoats, have bare shoulders, and act the part of a tough floozy.

In the later singing cowboy era, heroines and cowgirls were stereotyped by elaborate fringed skirts and fancy boots. Only in more modern movies have women been shown wearing semi-masculine, practical clothing such as pants and boots, like the four women in *Bad Girls* (1994), and appeared in tougher roles, such as the Lady (Sharon Stone) in *The Quick and the Dead* (1995).

In early Westerns women were often put in relatively passive supporting roles for men. Women were subservient to the male heroes and were often relegated to performing tasks such as cooking and tending the wounded. They followed the traditional role of the Victorian view that the weaker sex had to be protected and defended by a strong male. In many movies, particularly during the 1930s, Western heroines were portrayed as helpless maidens and often treated as window dressing. In William S. Hart's *Tumbleweeds* (1925), in one of the intertitle dialogue cards, his character says, "Women ain't reliable, cows are."[3] In *Son of Paleface* (1952), the song "Four Legged Friend" extols the virtues of a horse and the unreliability of women. This sexist attitude pervades many Westerns, and a similar attitude still existed years later when Sam McCord (John Wayne) in *North to Alaska* (1960) said, "Ah, women! I never met one yet that was half as reliable as a horse."

If women were occasionally included in Westerns as major characters, their roles were influenced by the male attitudes of those who made the movies, and were scripted and directed from a masculine perspective according to male expectations of women's behavior.[4] Even movies about women, such as *Bad Girls* (1994) and the television production of *Buffalo Girls* (1995), were made by men and reflected male attitudes more than women's.

## Victorian Attitudes Towards Women

The time period in which the classic Westerns are set, from roughly 1865 to 1900, corresponds to the Victorian era.[5] As part of the double morality that was a characteristic of the Victorian era, women in Western movies were divided into two distinct categories. One category included the "nice" women, who were wives, daughters, heroines, and sweethearts, all of whom were to be honored, protected, respected — and married. These chaste women provided social and moral stability for society through the characteristics of "goodness" and "purity." In Victorian times, one measure of a woman's morality was her ability to keep a neat, clean house. A dirty house was considered to be the sign of a fallen woman.

The other Victorian category of women featured "naughty" girls, such as dancehall and saloon girls. This classification included prostitutes, though they were rarely called by that name in older Westerns. Newer Westerns, such as *Unforgiven* (1992), *McCabe and Mrs. Miller* (1971), *The Ballad of Cable Hogue* (1970), and *Bad Girls* (1994), are more explicit about their profession. These "bad" women were outwardly the opposite of the "pure" heroine. In Victorian terms, the "nice" women were for marrying and the "naughty" ones were for young men to sow their wild oats with.

The contrast between the two types is seen in many Westerns. For example, Rita (Ann Dvorak) in *Abilene Town* (1946) is the "bad girl" saloon entertainer in abbreviated singing costumes. Her character contrasts with Sherry Balder (Rhonda Fleming), the "nice" storekeeper's daughter in long dresses who marries one of the farmers who has arrived to tame the West with barbed wire.

In some cases in the Old West the difference between "respectable" and "naughty" ladies was visible as well as moral. The inmates of bordellos in Western communities often used heavy make-up that included liberal applications of rouge and lipstick. At one time it was fashionable for these ladies of easy virtue to have chalk-white faces with scarlet lips and cheeks, as seen on the saloon girls in *Breakheart Pass* (1976). Some prostitutes went so far as to use sour milk or buttermilk as a facial cream at night to assist in bleaching their skin. White wax was used as a make-up base, along with flour or cornstarch for powder. As genuine rouge was expensive, beet juice might be used to redden the cheeks. This startling appearance gave them the nickname "painted ladies" or "painted cats." As a result, respectable women in the West avoided the use of heavy facial make-up in order to avoid being mistaken for members of the world's oldest profession.

"Nice" girls, on the other hand, were supposed to produce their healthy-looking glow by pinching or lightly slapping their cheeks in order to make the blood rush to them. Another reason for using natural enhancement rather than "warpaint" was the misguided idea that the use of cosmetics could lead to paralysis and premature death.[6]

## Women's Screen Costumes

Westerns of the mid–twentieth century contradicted two Victorian principles. One was that respectable women were not seen in public with their hair down. Their long hair was always pinned up. The other was that this was a time when women wore long dresses, down to the ground, and showed no hint of ankle or leg underneath. Skirts that showed any leg below the calf were considered scandalous and the sign of a fallen woman.

By contrast, leading women in Westerns of the 1940s, 1950s, and 1960s wore their hair down and were often dressed in tight pants to characterize their tomboy attitudes — but mostly to emphasize their figures. Joey (Michele Carey), the tomboy daughter of the Mac-Donald clan in *El Dorado* (1967), who rides and shoots like a young man, wears her hair down and wild, and wears form-fitting pants while riding a horse. In *5 Card Stud* (1968), love interest Nora Evers (Katherine Justice) wears tight pants and has her hair down as she chases around after Van Morgan (Dean Martin). In *The Train Robbers* (1973), Mrs. Lowe (Ann-Margret) has her hair down, wears tight pants, and rides astride her horse. In *The Desperadoes* (1943), heroine Allison McLeod (Evelyn Keyes) wears tight-fitting leather pants when she works in the stable or rides hard. Abby Nixon (Virginia Mayo) in *Devil's Canyon* (1953) wears tight jeans that show off her figure to advantage. Movie critic Jon Tuska once recalled that leading lady "Peggy Stewart, under contract at Republic Pictures, once confided in me that she resented making Westerns because her backside was to the camera more than her face."[7]

As appealing as tight pants were to the men in movie audiences, in reality this type of clothing was not considered appealing to men of the Victorian era. Ramon Adams, an authority on old-time cowboys, commented that "[the cowboy] wanted her feminine with frills and fluffs all over. He had no use for those he-women who wore pants and tried to dress like a man."[8] This wisdom was not totally lost on scriptwriters, because when these movie women try to get their man, they typically resort to dresses and frilly feminine outfits. When Cheyenne Rogers (Glenn Ford) and the heroine fall in love in *The Desperadoes* (1943), she reverts back to wearing a dress. At the beginning of *Calamity Jane* (1953), Calamity (Doris Day) wears dirty buckskin pants, but when Jane tries to get her cavalryman's attention, she switches to wearing dresses. In *The Paleface* (1948), Calamity Jane (Jane Russell) switches from gingham dresses and fancy bonnets when she is playing the respectable wife to fringed buckskins and a cowboy hat perched jauntily on the back of her black curls when she plays the undercover agent. Elsa Knudsen (Mariette Hartley), in *Ride the High Country* (1962), wears pants, a dirty shirt, and an old farmer's hat when forking horse manure out of the barn, but immediately changes into a dress when the men appear at her family farm. In true Victorian fashion, however, her religious-zealot father makes her put on a dress that is not quite so low-cut.

## Those Girls of the Night

Another stereotyped character in Westerns is the shady saloon girl with a heart of gold. This sort of woman has appeared in *Stagecoach* (1939), *The Cheyenne Social Club* (1970), *The Ballad of Cable Hogue* (1970), and *McCabe and Mrs. Miller* (1971). Most Westerns portray prostitutes as beautiful, happy in their chosen profession, and proud of it. The reality was closer to the women portrayed in *Unforgiven* (1992).

**These two small clapboard houses in Virginia City, Montana, make up the Green Front Boarding House, a notorious bordello owned by Myrtle Butler and Pearl McGinnis. This type of establishment was more typical of the Western bawdy house than the movie opulence and beautiful girls of *The Cheyenne Social Club* (1970).**

The Old West was primarily a male world. As the banner over the main street at the entrance to the mining camp in *Paint Your Wagon* (1969) succinctly put it: "NO NAME CITY, population: MALE." The 1850 census in California showed that less than eight percent of the white population was female. In the remote mining camps the figures were even more unbalanced, and men might outnumber women by a hundred to one. In 1860 in Virginia City, Nevada, there were 2,857 men but only 159 women. The population of the mining camp of Alder Gulch, Montana, in the 1850s consisted of 604 men and 65 women. In Oro City, Colorado, the 1860 census recorded 2,000 males and only 36 females. Many of the early mining camps had no women at all.

Women were such a rare sight in the early West that men would flock to a mining camp where a woman was reported just to look at her and listen to her voice. There are accounts of men traveling forty miles to a neighboring camp just to stare at a woman. This is poignantly illustrated by the scene in *Paint Your Wagon* (1969) when the Mormon family comes to No Name City and the burly miners pay a small fortune in gold dust just to hold their baby.

As a result of the lack of suitable women to become wives, many of these lonely men turned to saloon girls for companionship. So, right behind the hopeful prospectors flocking west to make their fortunes came a tide of ladies of the night, drawn by the lure of young single male customers and a chance to make their fortunes from the gold-seekers.

Historian Robert Brown, discussing a town called Bugtown in the Colorado mountains, with great understatement commented that "no work was permitted on the Sabbath and no drinking or gambling establishments were allowed to dissipate the men's morals. Abstinence and celibacy weighed heavily on the minds of the bachelors of Bugtown."[9] The nearby gold mining area of Poverty Flats—a seemingly depressing name for a mining town where the residents expected to strike it rich—was apparently a wide-open town that was more popular with off-duty miners seeking the more earthy types of recreation.

The two primary conditions that fuel prostitution are a population of young single men and a shortage of female partners. This was the situation that existed in much of the early West. So bar-girls congregated in the towns and other population centers of the Old West, which offered the major concentrations of men without women. As a result, most towns in the Old West had a red light district that contained saloons, dancehalls, gambling dens, and bawdy houses. This was usually designated as a specific area of town, and respectable people were reluctant to visit there.

In the Victorian era the outlook and opportunities for a young woman on her own in the West were limited. Upper-class women were expected to either have enough money to live independently or to be married. Among the few possible jobs for a working-class Victorian woman was sewing clothes, working as a domestic servant, becoming an unskilled worker, or being a housewife. Those with more education might be a teacher or a governess, which was one of the few respectable job opportunities open for women, but these were limited and paid extremely low wages. For women without an education on their own in the West, working in a saloon and entertaining men might be the only job available to them.

Two other services for which women were prized were cooking and doing laundry. Women who ran restaurants or boarding houses with home-cooked meals made almost as much money as some of the prostitutes. Washing clothes was another chore that few of the early miners wanted to do, and they were willing to pay handsomely for someone else to do it.

## Meanwhile, Back at the Saloon

One of the enduring institutions in movies set in the Wild West is the saloon, which appears to be the hub around which the town revolves. And in one sense it did. Saloons in the Old West were used as meeting halls, churches for itinerant preachers, trading posts, employment agencies, temporary mortuaries, post offices, and hotels. A man could have a drink in a saloon, relax among friends, play a friendly game of cards, and conduct his business. Saloons were a place where a man could get a bath, a cigar, a meal, and a haircut. *Rio Bravo* (1959), *Paint Your Wagon* (1969), and *Wyatt Earp* (1994) accurately show barbers working in the back of a saloon as various characters walk through.

Some saloons offered mail boxes where customers could receive letters, along with a bulletin board where notices could be posted. A card or billiard table might also double as an impromptu operating table to treat a bullet wound or a broken bone. This was shown in *Tombstone* (1993) after Morgan Earp (Bill Paxton) is ambushed while playing billiards.

The larger and fancier saloons might provide music from a small orchestra to attract and entertain patrons, but not on the lavish scale shown in *Destry Rides Again* (1939) or *Calamity Jane* (1953). This was not the reality of most saloons on the frontier, though such a sumptuous atmosphere might be found in large cities such as Seattle or San Francisco. An "orchestra" in the Old West more likely ranged in size from an accordion and banjo to a small group that might include a cornet, drums, fiddle, and piano. To someone expecting the extravagance of the Golden Garter in *Calamity Jane* (1953), or the Hen House in Seattle in *North to Alaska* (1960), with can-can girls and a full orchestra, the real-life saloons found in most early frontier towns would be a big disappointment.

An example of a real Western saloon where a young man could go for relaxation was Wyman's Place in Leadville, Colorado, which was a combination saloon, dancehall, and variety theater. The waitresses were pretty and were allowed to sit on a miner's lap between shows to try and entice him to buy champagne. Another wild and raucous place on the frontier was the Bird Cage Theater in Tombstone, Arizona. The Bird Cage grandly called itself an "opera house," but in reality it was a combination bar, gambling hall, dancehall, and variety theater. The audience sat around tables on the main floor and drank beer and whiskey while watching women entertain in shows on the small stage. As shown in many Westerns, the shows at the Bird Cage primarily featured scantily-clad young women dancing and singing. The can-can, with its high kicks, was very popular. When the show was over, dancing and drinking continued on the main floor until dawn.

The Westerns have given us elaborate visions of ornate woodwork, fancy furniture, huge plate glass mirrors, crystal chandeliers, and rows of long-legged, pretty girls dancing the can-can. The gaming tables are crowded and busy all the time with roulette and faro. Countless barflies are hanging out at the tables, apparently with nothing better to do than drink and gamble no matter what the time of day or night, then move hastily out of the way when the principals clash for a gunfight.

In some ways this image had some basis in fact. Men who lived in tents, boarding houses, or rough pine shacks eagerly sought out the companionship that could be found in saloons and gambling halls. The saloon offered a drink and temporary relief from herding cattle or working underground in a mine. Thus the noise, drinking, and friendly atmosphere served to drive away the loneliness felt by many of the single men.

Typical of the raucous saloons shown in the movies are those that appear in *Destry Rides Again* (1939) and *Dodge City* (1939). As in most Western movies, in *Dodge City* (1939) the saloon is crowded in the middle of the day with men gambling and drinking, with Ruby Gilman (Ann Sheridan) and six singing girls in abbreviated costumes dancing on the stage. *Abilene Town* (1946) contains a classic movie version of the saloon theater, with the lead singer in a revealing costume and six dancing chorus girls in similar costumes backing her up. Other movie saloons are featured in *Barbary Coast* (1935), showing San Francisco in the 1849 gold rush, and *Call of the Wild* (1935), set in the Yukon.

The reality, however, was usually not quite so exotic. A saloon in a newly-founded town might be only a canvas tent, hurriedly brought in and erected while thirsty customers waited impatiently in line. The "bar" might be the back of a wagon or a rough-sawn board thrown across two whiskey barrels or beer kegs. A tent was the cheapest way to start a saloon and was the best way for a saloon-keeper in a booming gold-mining area to protect his investment. If a new settlement prospered and grew into a permanent town, the saloon could be easily moved from a tent to a more substantial wooden building. If a mining camp did not last, the saloon-keeper could pack the tent back into his wagon and move on to the next strike, as the townspeople do at the end of *Paint Your Wagon* (1969).

One of these temporary saloons might consist only of a wooden platform for the floor, board walls three or four feet high around the sides, and heavy canvas supported by a rough wooden framework for the roof and upper walls. This type of "building" is seen in the railroad town in *Breakheart Pass* (1976), where the train stops to take on water and wood. In *Paint Your Wagon* (1969) the first gambling "hall" is a tent.

As a town became more permanent, early tent saloons became permanent wooden structures built from logs or boards. Eventually better tables and chairs were added, along with pictures and mirrors on the walls, and fancy glassware. If business was good, the saloon evolved further into an ornate frame building of finished clapboard with a false front to give a substantial and imposing air. The bar evolved from the rough boards of the early saloon into a counter made with ornately-carved wooden fittings. The saloon in White Rock, where Manco (Clint Eastwood) has his introductory shootout in *For a Few Dollars More* (1965) is quite accurate in this regard.

A typical saloon was a narrow, deep room in a building made from logs or sawn lumber, with a long wooden bar that stretched from front to back along one of the longer sides. Windows were small or non-existent. The inside of the saloon consisted of one large, open, low-roofed room that ranged in size from twenty feet wide by thirty feet deep to perhaps thirty feet wide and eighty feet deep. The floor might be hard-packed dirt and the walls made of unfinished logs. The swinging batwing doors popularized in the movies were not in general use in most saloons. Regular doors were more common, particularly in the colder climates of the northern Plains or the mountains. At night the interior of the saloon was lit by candles or oil lamps. Saloons often had a characteristic aroma of unwashed customers, stale beer, fumes from the oil lamp, and the smell of strong tobacco.

**A typical saloon in a small town in the Old West might be a simple wooden building with a few tables for socializing and playing cards. Illumination was provided by candles or oil lamps. This was not exactly the fancy setting of some movie saloons that offered a stage, an orchestra, and glamorous dancing girls in tights.**

Running along the front of the bar would be a brass foot-rail for the patron to hook his boot heel onto. Placed at intervals along the rail were brass cuspidors; however, photographs of early saloons show that the aim of tobacco-chewing patrons was poor. The floor was often sprinkled with sawdust to soak up drips and spills from beer glasses, as well as food, whatever missed the cuspidor, and anything else that might end up on the floor. Even when dirt floors were later replaced by plank construction, sawdust was still spread on the boards to soak up beer, tobacco juice, and other falling debris. In gold-mining towns this debris often included spilled gold dust, and saloon owners might lease the rights to "mine" the sawdust for a price. In *Paint Your Wagon* (1969), Partner and his pals dig tunnels under the saloons to collect the gold dust that inadvertently spills onto the floors.

### Saloon Women

While a saloon offered a relaxed masculine social atmosphere where a man could drink, gamble, and socialize with his male friends, men also knew that this was a meeting point for female companionship. These women had various tasks, all of which were aimed at parting men from their money. Women would dance with them, entice them to buy more drinks than they needed, and bargain with them to go upstairs or into one of the back rooms for private entertainment.

Dancehalls and dancehall girls were common in early Western towns. Not all of these women, however, were prostitutes. Some were legitimately there to dance and try to earn a living. They were a partner for a man for a quick dance, then tried to sell him as many drinks as they could, because high profits were to be made with alcohol. Drinks cost from

This was Hovey's Dance Hall in Clifton, Arizona, in 1884. Dance halls were popular places for young men to socialize with a woman and hold one for a few minutes during a dance. Here, patrons, their dance partners, and a few small boys line up for the camera. Two bartenders in long white aprons stand at the left with belligerent looks (National Archives).

twenty-five cents to a dollar, and the women typically received a percentage of from 25 percent to 75 percent of the price of the drinks they sold.

The young single men in a mining camp usually had no women of their own for marriage or social companionship, so many of them had to rely on dancehall girls to fulfill their needs and on the saloon to replace the social environment of the home. In the movies these women are often referred to simply as "dancehall girls" or "saloon girls." The real place of these women in the early social structure can be judged by considering that among the many names for prostitutes were "single men's wives" and "brides of the multitude."

Though many of the contemporary written descriptions describe saloon girls as pretty, young, and vivacious, some of these descriptions were probably colored by the lack of females and a longing for feminine companionship. Contemporary photographs show that the girls of the saloons and dancehalls looked just the same as women of any era. In the smaller towns, the "girls" were just as likely to be overweight, coarse, older women who could not compete with the younger prostitutes coming in from the larger towns.

Willing women could also be found in parlor houses, such as the one shown in *The Cheyenne Social Club* (1970), though the typical frontier bawdy house was not as fancy and did not have women who were as good-looking. As a side note, the movie was vaguely based on the Cheyenne Club, which was a luxurious but very sedate gentlemen's club for rich ranch owners in Wyoming. It was founded by the elite of the cattlemen and the local business community, and became one of the richest and most exclusive clubs in the West. The real Cheyenne Club was not a bordello or the scene of the improper goings-on in the movie. It was, however, where the cattlemen hatched the nefarious plot to invade Johnson County during the Johnson County Cattle War. The building used for *The Cheyenne Social Club* (1970) looked just like the historical club in Cheyenne, Wyoming, but was built for the film as a set on a movie ranch in New Mexico.

A typical parlor house in the Old West offered the services of four or five women, though the number might range from only two or three up to a dozen or so. A madam, who was a combination of house mother, employer, and business manager, was in charge of the house and the girls. Among the madam's duties were hiring the girls, attracting the customers, making any necessary arrangements with the local law or other authorities, welcoming the clients, collecting the money, encouraging the flow of liquor, and keeping whatever business records were necessary.

The madam occasionally ended up being the referee and mediator when fights broke out between the women. Fights between bar-girls, such as the knock-down drag-out fight in *Destry Rides Again* (1939) between Frenchy (Marlene Dietrich) and Lily Belle (Una Merkel), were not uncommon. These fights could be face-clawing, eye-scratching, hair-pulling, shin-kicking disputes between the girls.

One such fight took place in Dodge City on August 7, 1884. The disagreement started when two dancehall girls, named Bertha Lockwood and Sadie Hudson, entered into a violent argument over a mutual boyfriend. When Sadie slapped Bertha, Bertha pulled out a knife and stabbed Sadie in the back, side, and chest. Luckily the wounds were not life-threatening and Sadie recovered. Bertha was arrested, but as the event was not considered to have been a serious crime, she was soon out on bail. Another occurred in 1899 in Cripple Creek, Colorado, when Julia Belmont attacked Maggie Walsh with a knife because Walsh was dancing with a favorite customer.[10]

In September 1880 the *News and Courier* of Boulder, Colorado, reported on a fight that "resulted in the complete destruction of one of the ladies, whose head came in contact with an empty beer bottle." A well-known fight occurred in Tombstone, Arizona, when Gold Dollar (Little Gertie) from a local bordello found her live-in boyfriend Billy Milgreen, a local gambler, with another woman named Margarita. Gold Dollar grabbed Margarita's hair, then stabbed and killed her with a knife. Gold Dollar was not charged for the murder.

*McCabe & Mrs. Miller* (1971) shows a fairly realistic representation of the link between a bordello and town development as it really happened. In this movie an enterprising gambler named John McCabe (Warren Beatty) arrives in the town of Presbyterian Church, a mining enclave in the Northwest (actually filmed in British Columbia), and opens a saloon. The town has fifteen hundred men, so he imports three women to "entertain" the men. McCabe eventually goes into partnership with Mrs. Constance Miller (Julie Christie), who builds his faltering enterprise into a full-blown bordello with five more women that she brings up from Seattle. Mrs. Miller works in the house and acts as the madam. This type of arrangement, where a businessman or saloon owner put up the money and went into partnership with a madam to run the house, was not unusual. A running theme throughout the movie is the building of the town church. The movie set for the town was built at the same time the movie was being filmed, which gives the impression of the development of a mining town as it really happened.

## Drinking

Everybody drinks in the Westerns. Like Taw Jackson in *The War Wagon* (1967), cowboys stepped up to the bar and demanded "whiskey." Occasionally "whiskey" referred to rye whiskey; Doc Boone (Thomas Mitchell) in *Stagecoach* (1939) drinks rye whiskey, though rye was more commonly a drink of the Midwest. "Drinking" in the Old West usually referred to guzzling down bourbon whiskey. Scotch whiskey was not introduced to the frontier until after the turn of the century. Though not as commonly shown in the movies, wine was also a popular alcoholic drink in the Old West.

The selection of drinks in the early tent saloons was usually limited. Often the only choice was whiskey ladled out of a barrel into unwashed tin cups. Beer was a popular beverage but was slower to arrive in most towns because of the difficulty and expense of freighting beer across the prairies. Beer was too bulky, fragile, and inexpensive to be shipped for great distances until the arrival of the railroads provided cheap freight rates.

Drinking and drunkenness were a primary cause of fights, though sometimes not for the reasons one might think. In October, 1881, in Tombstone, William Claiborne finally pulled out a gun and shot James Hickey — because Hickey was pestering him to take a drink.[11] Ironically, Claiborne himself became a belligerent drunk a year later and was shot by Buckskin Frank Leslie in Tombstone. In a similar turn of events in Safford, Arizona, in 1879, gunman Johnny Ringo tried to get Louis Hancock to have a drink. When Hancock refused, Ringo took out his gun and hit him over the head.[12]

## Temperance

One aspect of drinking that does not show up much in Westerns is the temperance movement, though one such meeting *is* shown as it was being held in the building right next door to a wild saloon in *Dodge City* (1939). While drinking was a major form of entertainment in the Old West, not everyone was in favor of alcohol. Because of the tendency of men to routinely overindulge in alcohol, the temperance movement grew in the West in the 1870s and 1880s. The movement considered alcohol and prostitution to be two interrelated evils, so their main target was the saloon. Worked up into a frenzy by fiery speakers and anti-liquor songs, a group would march to the nearest saloon carrying temperance banners and singing hymns. This aspect of the temperance movement is shown with humor via the antics of crusader Cora Templeton Massengale (Lee Remick) in *Hallelujah Trail* (1965), as she tries to enlist the inhabitants of Fort Russell in her cause.

One of the leading groups that crusaded against saloons in the real West was the Woman's Christian Temperance Union (WCTU), which was formally founded in 1874. By 1890 the organization had about 160,000 members, some of them quite zealous. The more militant supporters marched into saloons and smashed the fixtures and furnishings.

This anti-saloon fever was characterized by the turn-of-the-century ax-wielding crusades of Carry Nation (sometimes spelled Carrie by newspapers). Born Carry Amelia Moore in 1846, she became fanatically anti-liquor after her husband, David Nation, was beaten up

Not everyone agreed with the quaint notion that drinking was a healthy and suitable pastime for men who were men in the Old West. Crusading temperance women would kneel and pray on the boardwalk outside a saloon to block the entrance. Others would sing hymns and temperance songs outside the door. In this woodcut that appeared in *Harper's Weekly* in 1874, several curious onlookers are attracted by the spectacle. The temperance movement was a powerful force that was influential in passing the Nineteenth Amendment to the United States Constitution in 1919 to introduce Prohibition. The singing of temperance songs and the almost religious fervor of the participants was satirized in *Hallelujah Trail* (1965) (Library of Congress).

by drunks at the Red Hot Bar in Richmond, Texas, in 1889. Almost six feet tall, weighing 175 pounds, and with a formidable appearance, she campaigned vigorously against "Demon Rum" across the plains of Kansas. She would stride into a saloon with fellow crusaders and destroy bottles, windows, mirrors, and pictures of barroom nudes with a hatchet. She soon became a famous figure for her destructive axe-swinging, which she called "hatchetation." She was so popular that she engaged an agent and accepted lecture bookings across the United States.

In the end, the temperance movement forced the National Prohibition Act (also called the Volstead Act after the Minnesota congressman who sponsored it) and the passage of the Eighteenth Amendment to the U.S. Constitution in 1918.

## Gambling

Following the first saloon-keeper, some of the earliest arrivals in a mining camp or cattle town were gamblers. As the early towns matured, saloons added gambling tables to attract patrons and provide diversion between drinks. Gambling was a popular saloon activity and was one that increased the profits for the house. Professional gamblers often rented a table in a saloon or split the winnings with the saloon owner, as was shown in *Tombstone* (1993).

Like much of Western movie lore, the excesses of gambling have been exaggerated. Games in which thousands of dollars were piled on the table, and ranches and mines were won or lost by the turn of a single card (as in 1939 *Destry Rides Again*), were rare. The typical cowboy didn't have that kind of money. More common was a twenty-five or fifty cent bet with a $25 table limit. Games with high stakes were reserved for the rich cattlemen, railroad owners, or mine owners who had enough money that they could afford to lose. Rich games were typically restricted to the large cities, such as San Francisco or Denver.

In a time when women's liberation was not encouraged, some women were card dealers, such as Laura Denbow (Rhonda Fleming) in *Gunfight at the O.K. Corral* (1957). If the gambling hall owner could find a woman with good skills at cards, it may have been a clever business tactic because players may not have been as resentful when handing over their money to a woman dealer instead of to a man. Female dealers were not usually as glamorous as Laura Denbow in her yellow silk dress, but were more on the order of the real Poker Alice Ivers, who would not be considered a beauty. In her later years Poker Alice's typical gambling outfit consisted of a man's shirt, a khaki skirt, and a floppy hat. Her grey hair was usually pulled back in a bun, and she nearly always had a cigar stuck in the corner of her mouth. It was far from the glamorous picture of Miss Denbow.

Cheating during gambling was common, and so were rigged games. Deceit was not hard to accomplish, as some companies were in the business of making and selling dishonest gambling supplies. The potential for violence if the cheater was discovered led many gamblers to carry concealed weapons, such as a knife, a dagger, brass knuckles, or a derringer. Other gamblers were less aggressive but did what they had to if caught. One gambler in Dodge City, when he realized that he was suspected of being a cheat, quickly ordered some food, slipped the card from up his sleeve under a piece of bread, and calmly ate it as a sandwich.[13]

Some methods of cheating were simple, such as placing reflecting objects on the table that could be used to identify cards that were dealt face-down. Other methods were more complicated, such as cards that were marked, trimmed, or pricked in various ways to mark their value.

# Vice, Censorship, and Hollywood

Drinking, gambling, loose women, and other vices that became prevalent in the movies eventually led to the imposition of a set of rules of behavior that affected Westerns. The censorship that was finally imposed on Hollywood was not a new issue but started with the advent of motion pictures. Cries for censorship had arisen among shocked Victorian viewers as early as the mid–1890s with the showing of a silent film titled *The Kiss* (1896), made by the Edison Company. This short film showed a twenty-second close-up of a snuggle and kiss between a middle-aged couple played by actors May Irwin and John Rice, who had done the same thing in a farcical play called *The Widow Jones*. Victorian viewers were similarly appalled by *Fatima* (1897), which recorded the gyrations of a belly dancer at Coney Island. The movie *The Gay Shoe Clerk* (1903) shows a salesman fitting a pair of shoes on a woman customer. As he ties the shoelaces, the camera shows a close-up of the woman's ankle, which was a daring and forbidden subject at the time when women's dresses swept the ground to hide any hint of leg. As he puts the shoe on, the camera shows her gradually lifting her skirt to reveal her calf, striped stockings, and lacy petticoat. When the humorous vignette ends, the shoe salesman is so overcome by the sight of her leg that he gives her a big smooch while her mother beats him over the head with her umbrella.

By the early 1920s, two issues had brought Hollywood under attack. One was that the morals depicted in many movies had declined. By 1921, movies were perceived as being such a bad influence on the general public that thirty-seven state legislatures had between them introduced a hundred or so censorship bills.[14] The second problem for Hollywood was that real-life scandals that involved popular major movie stars of the time were being featured prominently in the press. As a result, Hollywood suddenly woke up to the fact that it needed to censor itself before the government stepped in and did it for them.

To forestall any such repercussions, in 1922 the heads of the major Hollywood studios formed an organization named the Motion Picture Producers and Distributors of America (MPPDA) to clean up the movie industry. As president they installed Will H. Hays, who had previously been the Postmaster General under President Warren Harding.[15] The MPPDA's self-regulating body, the Studio Relation Committee (SRC), was later renamed the Production Code Administration (PCA).

Hays started his clean-up by demanding that a morals clauses be put into actors' studio contracts in an attempt to ensure that movie stars would conduct their daily lives in an upright manner that would not reflect badly on their studios. To further weed out actors with poor morals, Hays established the Central Casting Agency as a clearing house for the employment for extras, and more importantly, to investigate their morals before employment.

In 1924 Hays introduced a series of recommendations, called "the Formula," that were intended to guide film studios in the do's and don'ts of morals. Mostly these turned out to be "absolutely don't" and "be careful." Hays also requested plot outlines of proposed movies so that he could review them for improprieties that did not conform to the Formula. Hays tried to have moviemakers adhere to the guidelines, but he was widely ignored because he had no enforcement authority.

To combat this overt flaunting of racy or violent content, a new, stricter list of prohibited screen behavior was drawn up in 1930. It was called the "Cardinal's Code," as it was written primarily by Cardinal Mundelein of Chicago, assisted by Father Daniel A. Lord (a Jesuit priest), Fitzgeorge Dinneen, Martin Quigley (a Catholic layman who was also the publisher of a movie trade journal), and Joseph I. Breen (a Catholic newspaperman).[16]

This censorship code was more commonly called the Production Code, or the "Hays Code" after its enforcer. In part, the code stated that movies could not show two people who were not married living together, and that they could not display nudity or depict lustful behavior. Part of the code specified that the sympathies of the audience were not to be with a criminal, and a film should not encourage criminal behavior. One movie about Billy the Kid, for example, violated the code because it glorified a criminal and depicted murderous revenge. The end (or beginning) scene in *The Great Train Robbery* (1903), where the bandit fires a gun directly at the audience, was considered inappropriate by the censor in New York and was usually removed.

Other taboo subjects covered by the code were organized crime, gambling, and drunkenness. Sex, crime, and booze in movies were subjects that were not tolerated by Hays, which became a difficult situation for the motion picture studios as sex and violence were sure draws for audiences and led to greater profits.

Filmmakers skirted the intent of the Code by continuing to show bad behavior, often blatantly flaunting the Code. Other movies showcased "bad" behavior but ended on a note of righteous disapproval by including some form of just retribution (capture, imprisonment, or death) by the end of the last reel. The reality was that moviemakers made a criminal as bad as they could, yet at the end "redeemed" him or her by having him punished or killed off. The unstated Hollywood formula at the time was "six reels of sin, one of condemnation."[17] In *Destry Rides Again* (1939), for example, the saloon girl Frenchy (Marlene Dietrich) has to be shot and die at the end in order to gain redemption for her behavior. Violence like this gradually became acceptable, but any hint of sexuality was still prohibited.

To help enforce the new code, Joseph Breen was added to the Hays office in 1934. Some of his demands were viewed by Hollywood as extreme, such as reducing the length of a kiss from four seconds to one-and-a-half seconds.[18] Other odd prohibitions included showing a cow being milked or even a cow's udders.[19] This last taboo could make it somewhat difficult for the producer of a Western that included cattle. Hayes Office rules also didn't allow Western heroes to draw until they were drawn upon, a taboo later incorporated into the Cowboy Code.

In the early 1930s, during the Great Depression, declining audiences in the theaters made Hollywood reluctant to accept these new restrictions. In an attempt to win back slumping audiences, mainstream Hollywood gradually included more violence, brutal gangsters, love-making, bathing and lingerie scenes, and racier dialogue. Breen, however, was backed by the authority to impose a $25,000 fine on producers who did not comply with his demands.[20]

Suggestive scenes also crept into Westerns, and background action involving chorus girls in skimpy costumes were commonplace in saloon settings. As a specific example, in *Destry Rides Again* (1939), Frenchy (Marlene Dietrich) is a high class dancehall queen in the town of Bottleneck. At one point in the movie as filmed, Frenchy slipped money down the front of her dress and uttered the line, "Thar's gold in them thar hills." The PCA demanded that the studio eliminate the line, so it was removed from release prints.[21]

One of the significant censorship battles of the time involved MGM's appeal of the Hays Office rejection of a scene in *Tarzan and His Mate* (1934) in which a double for Maureen O'Sullivan swam totally naked in a jungle pool. For obvious reasons the Hays Office refused to accept the film. Then, for the first time, a jury panel for the Hays Office upheld the ban against a major studio, MGM, showing that the Production Code was a force to be reckoned with. There is, however, also the theory that the studio intended to concede the scene all along as a bargaining tool in the hopes of being able to keep other, slightly-less-erotic scenes in the movie.[22]

The first movie to openly defy the code was a Western, *The Outlaw* (1943), a story about a fictional three-way triangle between Billy the Kid (Jack Buetel), Doc Holliday (Walter Huston), and a girl named Rio MacDonald (Jane Russell).[23] The film was directed and produced by aircraft tycoon Howard Hughes. Production was completed in 1941, but the film did not receive a seal of approval from the PCA because of the ensuing controversy over the emphasis on Russell's bosom. Hughes refused to make the ordered cuts and released the film without a seal of approval to any exhibitors who were willing to take it. It received a limited release in 1943. The film went into general release in 1946 after Hughes cut about thirty seconds of footage that accentuated Russell's bosom. In another nod to appease the censors, Rio appears suddenly and inexplicably married to Billy to make it acceptable that they are in the same bedroom together.

Violence had always been a part of Westerns by the very nature of their basic premise. Shootings, brawls, and miscellaneous fights were simply a part of the genre. Most B-Westerns didn't have significant problems with code violations because they were geared towards horse chases and fist-fights. Some problems did, however, arise in the wake of the more adult themes found in the A-Westerns of the 1950s, which sometimes included story elements that were not found in B-Westerns. Their plots might include drinking, gambling, hints of sex, rape, prostitution, and excessive violence.

**Excessive drinking and other saloon activities were frowned on, but not necessarily forbidden, by the Hays Code. This example of a saloon in Cripple Creek, Colorado, shows the patrons having a social drink at the bar, though the inclusion of "our pet" on the right seems somewhat unsanitary (Glenn Kinnaman Colorado and Western History Collection).**

Prostitutes and saloon girls were a reality in the Old West, but their role as such was usually played down in the movies. Hundreds of Westerns used polite euphemisms for the free-loving girls with the heart of gold that were found in movie dancehalls.

A minor erotic element that was periodically added to quite a few Westerns was a spanking scene. Sometimes, for no good reason, the hero takes the heroine across his knee and gives her a few good whacks on the bottom. Marvin Hayden (Tim Holt), for example, spanked Ellie Jorth (Martha Hyer) in *Thunder Mountain* (1947), though after he chastises her they kiss and make up. Frank Hewitt (Audie Murphy) similarly spanked Anne Martin (Kathryn Grant) in *The Guns of Fort Petticoat* (1957). In the final scene of *Frontier Gal* (1945), Johnny Hart (Rod Cameron) puts wife Lorena Dumont (Yvonne de Carlo) over his knee and spanks her, which perversely makes her realize that he loves her. Though this type of behavior would not be considered politically correct today, when asked about the scene, De Carlo is reported to have said, "I think a spanking is cute." Perhaps with some unsubtle significance, the film was retitled for distribution in England as *The Bride Wasn't Willing*.

Heroines were also spanked in several B-Westerns — for example, *Gold Mine in the Sky* (1938), starring Gene Autry and Carol Hughes as Cody Langham, and *Outlaws of the Desert* (1941) with William Boyd. Though no doubt this sort of behavior may have taken place occasionally in the Old West, this type of situation has been emphasized in the movies more as a type of erotic, voyeuristic behavior. At one point in *True Grit* (1969), Texas Ranger La Boeuf (Glen Campbell) is whacking Mattie Ross (Kim Darby) on the bottom with a switch, and Rooster Cogburn (John Wayne), who is watching, tells him to stop because he's enjoying it too much.

Maureen O'Hara was spanked by John Wayne in several of their movies together. The most blatant was the chase around the set and ensuing spanking in *McClintock!* (1963), as G.W. McLintock (Wayne) determinedly followed his wife (O'Hara), dressed in her frilly white movie underwear, through the local town. At the climactic end of the movie, McLintock puts his rebellious wife over his knee and spanks her with a small coal shovel. Earlier in the movie McLintock's feisty daughter is spanked in a similar fashion by her fiancé. At the end of the film it is presumed that this makes both couples settle down to wedded bliss.

The production code gradually eroded away, starting in the early 1960s, and was essentially abandoned by 1966. As a result, nudity, coarse language, and sexual situations became more common. In 1968 the MPPDA abandoned the Code and substituted a series of voluntary rating classifications, such as G for "general audiences" and R for "restricted."[24]

As a result of this loosening of censorship, sex and violence crept back into all genres of movies, including Westerns. *Two Mules for Sister Sara* (1970) contains sexual innuendo in the conversations between nun Sara (Shirley MacLaine) and cowboy Hogan (Clint Eastwood). Saloon girl Billie Ellis (Julie London) is forced to strip in order to save the life of Link Jones (Gary Cooper) in *Man of the West* (1958).

Also, lengthy scenes of gratuitous nudity occurred more frequently in Westerns. Examples are *The Ballad of Cable Hogue* (1970), as prostitute Hildy (Stella Stevens) runs around the desert with nothing on, and *Mackenna's Gold* (1969), where Hesh-Ke (Julie Newmar) swims naked in a desert pool (actually filmed at a fish hatchery in Panguitch, Utah). The beginning of *Unforgiven* (1992) contains a very explicit sex scene in the bedroom of a bordello, followed by a brutal knife-slashing and beating scene. However, this again demonstrates that sex and violence are popular with audiences, as the picture won four Academy Awards, including Best Picture, Best Director (Clint Eastwood), Best Supporting Actor (Gene Hackman), and Best Film Editing.

*Chapter Twelve*

# The Boys in Blue

Because warfare between the whites and various Indian tribes was constant during the development of the West, the story of the cavalry versus the Indians, often inaccurately dubbed "cowboys and Indians," often plays a large role in Western movies. Like with other aspects of Westerns, some elements are accurate, some are not.

Estimates have placed the number of Indians in the West in the last half of the nineteenth century at approximately 270,000, with about 100,000 of them considered to be hostile. Between the end of the Civil War and 1890, when peace generally prevailed on the frontier, approximately 950 fights took place between the two sides. Army records show that 932 soldiers were killed in action between 1865 and 1890, and 1,060 were wounded.[1]

## The Indian Wars

To place the role of the Hollywood movie cavalry on the frontier in perspective, it will be helpful to look at the real history of the Indian wars that were the major mission of the army in the West after the Civil War.

Prior to the Civil War, military presence on the Western frontier was small. The army was charged with protecting emigrants traveling on the Oregon and California Trails, and with protecting settlers, miners, ranchers, surveyors, and railroad construction crews from hostile Indians. In addition, the army was supposed to act as a general force to police against rustlers, bandits, and thieves.

In 1860 there were sixty-five forts and about ten thousand soldiers to guard and protect approximately 2½ million square miles of the West. The army's task was monumental. Frontier forts were small and poorly manned. As a result, the small number of soldiers that were widely scattered in the West in these isolated garrisons were basically inadequate to perform the overwhelming task of trying to respond to settlers' demands for protection. It was only because the small number of whites who were living permanently in the West were also sparsely scattered among the Indians that relatively few hostile encounters took place.

As a further difficulty for the army, the tactics of warfare that had to be used against the Indians were different than the strategy of pitched battles that the army was trained for and which it employed against Southern troops and fortifications during the Civil War. The enemy in the West that the army was supposed to subdue consisted of nomadic or semi-nomadic tribes of Indians. This elusive foe was rarely found twice in the same location, and the Indians waged war in guerrilla fashion, primarily in the form of lightning raids, which were followed by rapid retreats into desolate country.

During the Civil War, most of the army troops were withdrawn from the West to fight in the conflict in the East. After the Civil War ended, about five thousand soldiers were sent back to the West to guard the expanding frontier, a number that was wholly inadequate. At some frontier forts the entire garrison of soldiers consisted of only one or two companies, each of which might contain as few as thirty to forty men, instead of the one hundred soldiers authorized by army regulations in 1867.

Though there were many different Indian tribes involved in the Indian Wars, Western movies have been characterized and stereotyped by the Indian of the Great Plains and those of the Southwest, so only these two groups will be detailed here.

### The Indians of the Great Plains

The Great Plains were dominated by the Sioux, the Cheyenne, the Arapaho, the Comanche, and the Kiowa. Before 1850, the Plains Indians generally did not harass the few settlers and occasional gold prospectors who roamed the West because there were not enough of these white men to make any impact on the land or the Indians' way of life. However, the gradually increasing influx of buffalo hunters, trappers, settlers, and gold-seekers after mid-century, along with the establishment of army forts and the arrival of the overland stage (and later the transcontinental railroad), eventually led to increasing tensions and conflicts between white settlers and the Plains Indians. Among the Indians' legitimate concerns was that all the game would be scattered or killed, thus leaving them with no source of food.

To try and drive away the unwanted invaders from the East who were swarming all over the land, the Indians started raiding settlements and killing any whites they encountered. During the 1850s, Comanches and Kiowas started to raid settlements in Texas, and by the 1860s had extended their raids into Kansas. Also during the 1860s, Cheyenne and Arapaho warriors carried out fierce raids on isolated settlers in eastern Colorado. This series of clashes culminated in the Sand Creek Massacre, carried out by volunteer soldiers in southeast Colorado on November 29, 1864, that left between 130 and 175 Indians dead. The subsequent history of the Great Plains was marked by a succession of Indian battles and skirmishes, finally culminating in the complete subjugation of the Plains tribes and their removal to reservations.

The Indian Wars on the Great Plains started when Lt. John Grattan and thirty soldiers under his command were wiped out in the Grattan Massacre of August 19, 1854, after they confronted a Sioux village over a butchered stolen cow. War with the Sioux escalated steadily and reached a climax with the savage fighting of 1866–1868 along the Bozeman Trail that ran from Fort Laramie to the gold fields around Virginia City, Montana. More fierce fighting continued in 1874–1876 after gold was confirmed in the Black Hills of South Dakota, the result being Custer's defeat at the Battle of the Little Bighorn in 1876. The Indian Wars on the Plains ended with the disastrous battle at Wounded Knee in South Dakota in 1890.

### The Indians of the Southwest

Some of the fiercest fighting in the West involved the Navajo. The Navajo had been fighting with anyone they perceived to be invaders of the lands where they had raised their crops and livestock since 1598, when Spanish and Mexican settlers first arrived in the Southwest. Finally the scout and Indian fighter Colonel Christopher "Kit" Carson was sent by

General James H. Carleton to deal with the situation. Carson carried out a winter campaign of destruction of crops and food supplies that ultimately bullied the Navajo into submission. The climax occurred when Carson invaded the supposedly impregnable sacred Navajo stronghold of Canyon de Chelly in northeast Arizona on January 12, 1864, and destroyed hogans, sheep, and fruit trees. After this final insult, the majority of the Navajos surrendered, and by early 1865 a total of nine thousand Navajo and Apache men, women, and children had been relocated to the remote Bosque Redondo Reservation in eastern New Mexico. An estimated three hundred Navajos died on the "Long Walk," which was the tribal name for the forced relocation march from eastern Arizona to the reservation at Fort Sumner. After the Navajo's arrival, crop failures, floods, plagues of grasshoppers, and a lack of local game left them unable to feed themselves. Over two thousand Navajos died between 1864 and 1868, when they were finally allowed to return to their homelands. Though the Bosque Redondo experiment was a disaster, General Carleton had accomplished his goal and completely crushed all Navajo resistance.

Indian warfare in the Southwest was dominated by the Apache, and involved some of the most ferocious and ruthless fighting of all the Indian encounters. Two of the prominent leaders of the Apaches were Mangas Coloradas (Spanish for "Red Sleeves") of the Mimbres Apaches in southern New Mexico, and Cochise of the Chiricahua Apache in southeast Arizona. The Apaches under Cochise, and later Geronimo, his son-in-law, were responsible for some of the fiercest and bloodiest conflicts between whites and Indians.

In the 1850s the southwestern tribes were generally ambivalent towards the whites and allowed them to travel unmolested through their territories. This changed abruptly in 1860 when warfare erupted between the Mimbres Apaches and the whites. The discovery of gold in southwestern New Mexico in May of 1860 had brought two thousand or so hopeful prospectors to a mining camp called Pinos Altos. An unfortunate incident occurred in which Mangas Coloradas was seized by some miners, tied to a tree, and severely beaten. After this humiliation, Mangas Coloradas swore revenge and attacked all white settlers and soldiers on sight. After several years of attacks and skirmishes, Mangas Coloradas was captured by soldiers in January of 1863. He was subsequently killed, reportedly while trying to escape, though the circumstances surrounding his death were questionable.

The Chiricahua Apaches, led by Cochise and later by Geronimo, attacked pioneers and settlers in Arizona for more than twenty-five years. Cochise organized highly effective guerrilla tactics, waging war on horseback on other tribes and whites to protect his homeland in the Chiricahua Mountains and Dragoon Mountains of southeast Arizona. Cochise was generally not hostile towards Americans passing through his territory until what has been called the Bascom Affair took place near Apache Pass.

In October of 1860 a band of Apaches attacked the ranch of John Ward, stole some of his stock and kidnapped the 12-year-old son of Ward's mistress. In January of 1861 the army sent Lt. George Bascom with fifty-four soldiers to confront Cochise. Cochise, who was not responsible for either the theft or kidnapping, was confused and then insulted by Bascom's accusations, and fought his way out of the camp where they met. As a result, Bascom held some of Cochise's family hostage and demanded the return of the boy. Seeking revenge, Cochise went on a rampage and killed several whites from a nearby wagon train. In retaliation, Bascom was ordered by the army to hang Cochise's brother and two nephews. After this, the conflict escalated into full-scale warfare. The Apaches terrorized white settlers, miners, and ranchers, pillaging and killing all they could find. Cochise is estimated to have killed 150 whites over the next two months.

Cochise finally agreed to stop fighting and surrendered in 1872. As part of the peace agreement, the Apaches were given a reservation that included their homelands in the Chiricahua Mountains of Arizona. Cochise died of natural causes on June 8, 1874. His son Taza assumed leadership of the Chiricahua Apache, but he was not the charismatic chief that his father was and was ultimately rejected as a leader by his people.

Jeff Chandler portrayed Cochise in *Broken Arrow* (1950), a story in which he tries to work with an ex-soldier to seek peace between settlers and the Apache. Chandler reprised the Cochise role in *The Battle at Apache Pass* (1952), where the chief similarly tries to prevent warfare between the Apache and the whites.

Geronimo was born to an Apache tribe in 1829 with the birth name of Goyathlay, which means "one who yawns." Geronimo was generally friendly towards the whites until Mexican soldiers killed his wife and three children in 1858. He then started a quest for vengeance against all whites. He received his name of Geronimo during a battle with Mexican troops at the town of Arizpe. One of the soldiers unaccountably yelled "Geronimo" (which was Spanish for Jerome) at him, and he took that as his new war name.

Geronimo and a band of Chiricahua Apaches continued to fight the whites during the 1860s, using the Sierra Madre Mountains of Mexico as a base and raiding on both sides of the border. Geronimo was captured in 1877 and placed on the San Carlos Reservation in Arizona. In 1881 Geronimo left the reservation with seventy-four Chiricahua Apaches and returned to Mexico, where he continued his raids against the whites.

In 1882, General George Crook was assigned to Arizona to solve the Apache problem. In 1883, with the cooperation of the Mexican government, Crook led an expedition into the Sierra Madre Mountains and accepted the surrender of many of the rebels. In March of 1884, Geronimo surrendered and returned to the reservation, but fled to Mexico again in May of 1885 with thirty-two warriors, accompanied by a hundred women and children. From there he continued to attack white settlers and soldiers, while the army's efforts to capture him proved fruitless. Geronimo finally agreed to yield to the reservation but soon changed his mind and returned to Mexico.

On-again, off-again peace talks resulted, but nothing definite was accomplished, so General Crook was replaced by General Nelson Miles, who moved swiftly to try to defeat the Indians. Geronimo's final attempt at freedom started on May 17, 1885, and lasted for the next fifteen months. Miles took to the field with five thousand troops (which, at that time, made up about one-quarter of the U.S. army) to try to round up Geronimo's small band of Apache men, women, and children. Amazingly, the Indians were able to remain at large while living off a desolate, savage land, with no permanent camp and virtually no sources of water, in temperatures that rose as high as 120 degrees.

Geronimo and his band of sixty warriors killed seventy-five people in New Mexico and Arizona, along with an estimated several hundred Mexicans. True to movie depictions, some of the victims were tortured before being killed, suffering such horrors as being roasted alive, being forced to walk on hot sand with the soles of their feet cut off, and being staked on anthills after being covered with honey.

Miles was relentless in his pursuit but finally extended an offer of peace. Geronimo surrendered on September 4, 1886, at Skeleton Canyon, a location about seventy miles southwest of Fort Bowie, Arizona, that was strewn with the skeletons of victims of Apache massacres. Geronimo and most of his men were shipped off to Fort Marion in Florida, where many died. In 1894 the surviving Apaches were moved to Fort Sill, Oklahoma, where Geronimo died in 1909 without ever returning to his beloved mountains in Arizona.

Ferocious Apache Indian chief Geronimo, with a small band of men, women, and children, led one-fourth of the U.S. army on a frantic chase for fifteen months in 1885 and 1886. Geronimo is pictured here before his surrender to General Crook on March 27, 1886 (Library of Congress).

The Apache Indian leader Geronimo has been featured in several Westerns, such as *Geronimo* (1939), with Preston Foster, and *Geronimo* (1962), with Chuck Conners as the Indian chief. The later *Geronimo: An American Legend* (1993), with Wes Studi in the title role and Gene Hackman as General Crook, was an authentic retelling of the last months of Geronimo's fight against the U.S. army in 1885–1886.

Another of those who escaped from the San Carlos Reservation with Geronimo was Victorio, sometimes called Vittorio. Known also as the Apache Wolf, Victorio was a cunning leader who specialized in employing hit-and-run tactics. He was arguably one of the best Apache strategists and managed to elude the pursuing cavalry for over three years.

Victorio escaped in September of 1877 with three hundred of his fellow Apaches. However, with winter coming, Victorio decided to surrender, after which he and his followers were relocated to the Mescalero Reservation. This did not last, and he soon fled back to the mountains of Mexico, vowing to make war on the soldiers forever.

Victorio was like a ghost. He came out of nowhere and attacked the soldiers, then vanished back into the mountains of Mexico just as mysteriously. In August of 1880 the Tenth Cavalry killed and wounded some of Victorio's men, and chased the rest back into Mexico. On October 15 the Mexican army surrounded the Apaches and killed Victorio and most of his remaining men.

Vittorio has also appeared in Westerns. In *Hondo* (1953), for example, Vittorio (Michael Pate) claims Angie Lowe's (Geraldine Page) son, Johnny (Lee Aaker), as a blood brother.

## Who Were Those Hollywood Indians?

In most Hollywood movies the Indians are shown as stereotypes, as an anonymous danger, and as a convenient enemy that can be shot to pieces *en masse*. Indians have generally not been portrayed from an Indian viewpoint. Even *Dances with Wolves* (1990), which was sympathetic to the Indian way of life, was presented from the white man's perspective.

The trend in Western productions was for Hollywood actors to portray Indian characters. Don Ameche played an Indian chief in *Ramona* (1936). Victor Mature played an Indian in *Chief Crazy Horse* (1955), and Suzan Ball played his wife, Black Shawl. Jeff Chandler played Apache leader Cochise in *Broken Arrow* (1950) and again in *The Battle at Apache Pass* (1952). Rock Hudson played his son in *Taza, Son of Cochise* (1954). Charlton Heston played the Sioux leader Warbonnet in *The Savage* (1952). Robert Taylor played a Shoshone Indian in *Devil's Doorway* (1950). In *Apache* (1954), Burt Lancaster played Masai, an Apache warrior who escapes while being transported to a reservation in Florida and tries to return home, a story supposedly based on a true incident. The cast of *Winchester '73* (1950) included Rock Hudson in a very early role as an Indian chief. In *McLintock!* (1963), Michael Pate played Chief Puma. Henry Silva played an Indian in *Sergeants 3* (1962) and a Mexican in *The Bravados* (1958). In *Cheyenne Autumn* (1964), Director John Ford cast Ricardo Montalban as Cheyenne chief Little Wolf, Gilbert Roland as Dull Knife, and Sal Mineo as Red Shirt. Singer Howard Keel appeared as an Indian in *The War Wagon* (1967). Anthony Quinn played Crazy Horse in *They Died with Their Boots On* (1941). Bruce Cabot played Indian tracker Sam Sharpnose in *Big Jake* (1971). Even comic Indians were played by whites. Robert Wilke played Chief Five Barrels in *Hallelujah Trail* (1965). Joey Bishop played a comic Indian with deadpan humor in *Texas Across the River* (1966), with Tina Marquand as a young squaw. Comedian Paul Lynde played the not-so-subtle Indian Chief Nervous Elk in

*The Villain* (1979). Even English actors were not exempt. British movie star Trevor Howard played an old, blue-eyed Cheyenne in *Windwalker* (1980). The list of white actors who portrayed Indians is almost endless.

Some actors had frequent roles as Indians. Director John Ford cast Henry Brandon, a white character actor born in Berlin, Germany, as Scar in *The Searchers* (1956). Ford cast him again as Quanah Parker in *Two Rode Together* (1961), along with Woody Strode, who also played an Indian.

Debra Paget played an Indian woman in *White Feather* (1955). In *Broken Arrow* (1950), Paget played the Indian maiden Morning Star, who marries white man Tom Jeffords (James Stewart) during peace negotiations with Cochise (Jeff Chandler). As an interesting side note to the Indian wars, *Broken Arrow* (1950) was based on a true incident. The real-life Tom Jeffords was superintendent of the mail route between Fort Bowie, near the Arizona–New Mexico border, and Tucson in central Arizona. During one sixteen-month period he lost fourteen mail drivers to marauding Apaches. Showing great courage, Jeffords went alone to Cochise's mountain camp, laid down his weapons, and said he wanted to talk to Cochise. Surprisingly, the Apaches did not kill him. Cochise, who was also a man of great courage, recognized a similar spirit in Jeffords and the two became friends. As a result, the Apaches stopped their attacks on Jeffords' drivers. Jeffords was eventually appointed Indian agent for the Chiricahua Apaches. He was instrumental in stopping the Apache wars and moving Cochise and his band onto the reservation.

In *A Man Called Horse* (1970), British actor Richard Harris played Lord John Morgan, who was captured by the Sioux and underwent the "Sun Vow ceremony" to prove his courage and endurance. A certain amount of artistic license by the makers altered facts into drama. For example, the movie changed the tribe into Sioux from the Crows in the book, and the ceremony into the Sioux Sun Dance Ceremony. In one of the most dramatic scenes in the movie, Morgan was suspended in the air by ropes tied to skewers through his flesh. In reality, the Sioux did not practice suspension in the air like this. The ceremony in the movie was actually patterned after one from the Mandan Indians, though it was not an initiation ceremony.[2] Despite praise by critics for the movie's realism, the ritual was never as extreme as that shown in the movie.[3]

Later film productions employed authentic Indians; however, in some cases moviemakers assumed that the audience could not tell one tribe of Indians from another. For example, director John Ford used local Navajos from Monument Valley to play the parts of Apaches and Cheyenne in *She Wore a Yellow Ribbon* (1949), as Comanches in *The Searchers* (1956), and as Cheyenne in *Cheyenne Autumn* (1964).[4] In *The Searchers* (1956), the Navajos playing the parts of Comanches spoke in their native Navajo language in the film, and some of them can even be seen wearing traditional Navajo jewelry.[5] This type of incorrect casting of ethnic groups was not an unusual practice for Hollywood at the time. When director Dick Powell made *The Conqueror* (1956) — one of John Wayne's few non–Westerns — near St. George, Utah, the studio hired three hundred Indians from a nearby reservation to play the parts of Mongol warriors.[6]

*The Paleface* (1948) was not typical in its depiction of Indians for films of the time period in that two authentic Indians acted in major roles. Chief Yowlachie played Chief Yellow Feather, and Iron Eyes Cody, who appeared in many Hollywood productions, played Chief Iron Eyes. Henry Brandon was again cast in an Indian role, playing Wapato, the Indian medicine man.

## The Cavalry

Western movies focus on the cavalry as they present a dashing picture of men riding off into the sunset to patrol for hostiles. The inaccurate impression portrayed is that forts in the West were manned solely by the cavalry. In reality, army forts on the Western frontier were garrisoned by both infantry and cavalry companies who worked together.

The infantry generally did not pursue Indians in the field because infantry soldiers on foot were not particularly effective against highly-mobile Indians on horseback. The cavalry, being a mounted force, had the primary responsibility for searching out, pursuing, and subduing the Indians. The infantry supported the cavalry by maintaining and guarding military establishments, and carrying out the day-to-day activities necessary to support the fort. Many of the infantry's duties were not glamorous, such as constructing roads, chopping wood, and maintaining telegraph lines, but these tasks were essential to keep the army in the field.

After seeing action in battle during the Civil War, life at a frontier fort was comparatively dull and routine for many of the men. Scouting and patrols relieved some of the boredom of daily life, but soldiering in the field was mostly confined by weather to a period between about April and October each year. Particularly on the Great Plains during winter, where the weather was often severe, most of the soldiers' time was spent at the post. Even during the summer there was often very little real action or Indian fighting, though patrols scouted or sometimes served as escorts for wagon trains or stagecoaches.

### Daily Life at the Fort

The definition of a "post" is a place where troops are garrisoned. A "fort" is an enclosed place that is fortified for military defense. Fort is also the name applied to a permanent army post, as opposed to a temporary training camp. On the Western frontier, "fort" was a catchall name for anything that provided a base of operations for the army. The function of forts in the West was to house soldiers, to guard transportation routes, wagon trails, and railroads, and to keep watch over the Indians.

Few frontier forts had a stockade, such as that shown in most cavalry movies like *Buffalo Bill* (1944) and *Sergeants 3* (1962) (actually the same set!), which is a defensive barrier around an army post, made of stakes driven side-by-side vertically into the ground. An exception were the three forts along the Bozeman Trail, where the forts were enclosed by a stockade. Soldiers at Fort Reno, Fort Phil Kearny, and Fort C.F. Smith, who protected travelers on their way to the mines in Montana, were under constant threat of attack and soon realized the danger of leaving the protection of the enclosure.

Army recruits after the Civil War were volunteers, and the ranks were filled with a variety of men. The commonest nationalities were Irish, German, and English. The men enlisted for a basic term of five years at a base pay of $13 a month. Civilian scouts were employed by the army to serve as trackers, guides, interpreters, and general experts on local Indian lore and warfare. Scouts dressed as they pleased and used their own choice of weapons. Among others, Buffalo Bill Cody, Wild Bill Hickok, and Kit Carson served as army scouts from time to time.

Most of a soldier's time was spent marching, drilling, and standing guard duty. Other time-consuming tasks included constant fatigue details (non-military tasks of manual labor), such as logging and quarrying. At the more peaceful forts, many of the enlisted men's hours were spent in post maintenance, doing the jobs of common laborers (such as constructing

Most forts in the Old West were open all around, without any of the surrounding stockades seen in popular cavalry movies. Most military posts consisted of rows of buildings surrounding each side of a central parade ground, such as this example at Fort Larned in Kansas. Note the ceremonial howitzer in the center of the parade ground. This artillery was seldom used in the field but was usually left behind at the fort for ceremonial functions.

buildings, digging ditches, and chopping firewood). Soldiers spent most of their days performing these boring, repetitive duties. There was very little shooting practice because ammunition was in short supply. Consequently, most of the men never developed any worthwhile shooting skills to prepare them for battle. Luckily, though, most soldiers never saw a hostile Indian, and disease, accidents, and the harsh weather of the Plains in winter took more soldiers' lives than fighting the Indians did.

Army duty was hard and discipline was harsh. Minor infractions of the rules resulted in severe penalties, and the men typically didn't experience the glamorous life of a soldier that they had expected upon enlistment. In addition, many of the towns located near military installations did not treat soldiers well. Soldiers were often the only police presence on the early frontier, and there was resentment of soldiers interfering in what settlers considered to be local affairs. A combination of boredom, hard work, and low pay resulted in a high level of desertion among enlisted personnel, and a high rate of alcoholism for those who stuck it out. Between 1865 and 1890 approximately one-third of the enlisted men deserted, one of the most serious military crimes.

Though soldiers spent much of their time drilling and working around their home fort, a major part of their responsibility was to conduct campaigns in the field. Patrols into

The army sometimes depended on the firepower of artillery to overcome their opponents, as happened at the Battle of Wounded Knee. This group of Indian scouts and uniformed soldiers from Battery E of the 1st Artillery are practicing in 1891 with a light-weight Hotchkiss mountain cannon (also called a Hotchkiss mountain rifle), probably near Wounded Knee, South Dakota. Several unfired artillery shells are shown on the ground at the left (Library of Congress).

Indian country varied from short trips of a few days to long scouting expeditions and campaigns. Major field expeditions could involve several thousand soldiers and last as long as five or six months.

The usual small scouting detachment consisted of ten men, an officer, and a scout. During their normal thirty-day patrols, cavalry units routinely covered five hundred to six hundred miles. Typical travel for the cavalry was about forty miles a day. Indians might be encountered within a few hours of leaving the fort, or the men might travel for weeks without seeing any signs of hostiles at all.

## Soldiers as Gunfighters

Soldiers were a contradiction in the world of gunfighters in the Old West. They had access to weapons, and they were trained to shoot and kill. Soldiers, however, were rarely gunfighters. Most of the time, off-duty enlisted soldiers were not even armed with guns. When the men were not on active duty or in the field patrolling or chasing Indians, their carbines and revolvers were locked in racks in their barracks.

Soldiers' fights tended to be saloon brawls in which one or several of the participants had too much to drink, resulting in a fist fight rather than a gunfight. Soldiers generally socialized with other soldiers, and if they fought, they fought among themselves rather than with outsiders. Of course this didn't always happen. On July 17, 1870, for example, five drunken soldiers grabbed Wild Bill Hickok in a saloon in Hays City, Kansas. Hickok freed himself and pulled his revolvers, then shot and wounded two of the troopers. The other three retreated

If an off-duty soldier did carry a gun and became involved in a shoot-out, it was not generally a fast-draw type of fight. But soldiers still managed to get into trouble. On June 3, 1873, in Delano, Kansas, a group of soldiers were drinking in Edward "Red" Beard's saloon when one drunken soldier got into a dispute with prostitute Emma Stanley over her price. Being in an argumentative mood, he pulled out a gun and shot her in the thigh. Infuriated by that, proprietor Beard also pulled out a revolver and opened fire on the soldiers. He wounded two of them and ran them all off into the night. [7]

### Women and Drink

Most army posts were isolated on the far frontier, and the only women present were some officers' wives and their servants, a few enlisted men's wives, and the camp laundresses. Laundresses who were not married often did more than laundry, supplementing their income through prostitution, and it was common for laundresses to have illegitimate children living with them. If there were a nearby town, the soldiers could also find partners among local women.

One of the few off-duty pastimes for soldiers was drinking, and heavy drinking was an accepted practice in the army. Boredom resulted in many of the soldiers becoming alcoholics, and it was not uncommon for enlisted men and officers to be drunk on duty. In the 1880s, four percent of the army's soldiers were hospitalized for alcoholism. Alcoholism became such a problem for the army that the sale of liquor was banned on military reservations in 1881. This action, however, did not reduce the level of drinking as anticipated, but merely moved it off the post to a nearby location.

One place from which soldiers could usually obtain drink and other pleasures was the small community that sprang up near most forts. These settlements usually included a saloon or other establishment where whiskey and beer were sold, and where there was a thriving business in prostitution and gambling. One example was the town of Loma Parda, which was located about five miles from Fort Union in northern New Mexico. A wagon shuttle service ran between the fort and the town, and a well-worn connecting footpath was available for those who could not afford the fare. The town offered dance-hall women, along with all the other diversions and amusements soldiers might want. Drinking, fighting, and whoring in Loma Parda eventually became such a problem that the commandant at the fort finally made the town off-limits for soldiers.

### The Camel Corps

One short-lived, off-beat military experiment that seems too strange to be true was the army's use of camels. One movie in which this featured is *One Little Indian* (1973), which is the story of AWOL cavalry trooper Keyes (James Garner), who escapes across the desert on a camel named Rosie. Incredible as this premise sounds, the concept was indeed factual. [8]

In the early 1850s, Secretary of War Jefferson Davis realized that some form of mounted troops were necessary to police the Southwest. Looking at the similarity between the deserts of North Africa and the arid deserts of the American Southwest, Davis reasoned that troops mounted on camels might be effective and could operate successfully with limited water sources. In 1855, Navy ships transported thirty-four camels from Tunisia to Texas to form the nucleus of the United States Army Camel Corps. Initial experiments were promising. Camels could travel for days without water and could survive successfully on sagebrush, thistles, and shrubbery. Each one could carry three or four times the load of an army mule. Despite this limited success, the use of camels was short-lived. Camels could not exist on the corn that was used to feed army horses, and their soft padded feet did not hold up well in the rocky Southwest. So the army returned to using mules.

Racing a camel against horses for money comprised a sequence in *Ride the High Country* (1962).

### Military Weapons

The category of "small arms" includes long arms and handguns. Firearms that are larger than small arms are called artillery.

The designation "long arms" (also called "long guns" or "shoulder arms") includes rifles, carbines, and muskets. Carbines have the shortest barrel length, typically twenty to twenty-two inches. Rifle barrels are longer, on the order of twenty-four to thirty-two inches. Muskets have the longest barrels. Single-shot rifles and muskets were typically issued to the infantry because they provided improved accuracy at long distances due to their long barrel length. Foot-soldiers carried their rifles in a sling over the shoulder, with the barrel pointing downward, like a sword. Carbines, which had a shorter barrel length, were issued to the cavalry to allow improved ability to shoot while maneuvering on horseback.

Many movies show the cavalry firing Winchester repeating rifles. The army of the 1870s and 1880s did not use Winchesters but were issued instead with the Springfield single-shot rifle. Though repeating rifles, such as the Spencer, *were* issued to soldiers, the army preferred single-shot rifles, such as the Springfield or Sharps, because they felt that repeating rifles would use too much ammunition.

Immediately following the Civil War, the primary military weapons were the Spencer seven-shot .50 caliber rifle (used in the single-shot mode) and the .44 caliber Colt or Remington percussion revolver. Cavalry firearms were standardized after 1873 with the adoption of the .45 caliber Springfield Model 1873 single-shot breech-loading carbine and the six-shot .45 caliber Colt Model P single-action revolver. The carbine had an effective accurate range of up to three hundred yards, though the bullet could carry up to a thousand yards. In the rifle version, the Springfield had an effective accurate range of up to six hundred yards.

Though swords and sabers were commonly used during the Civil War, they were not considered effective weapons on the Western frontier. Sabers were mostly for ceremonial functions and used as ritual symbols of authority by non-commissioned officers. Cavalry sabers were heavy, awkward to wield, and rattled so much that they could give away the troops' position to the enemy. They were also not much use against a mounted Indian attack because the Indians seldom came close enough for such hand-to-hand combat. So they were often left behind in the barracks.

Cavalry troopers carried their revolvers on their right hip in holsters that placed the weapon with the butt forward and the barrel pointed behind the wearer. This configuration originated when mounted troopers carried sabers. Because most men were right-handed, they used their saber with their right hand. Their revolver, then, was carried on the right side so that it could be drawn in a cross-draw with their left hand, leaving them able to fight with both at once. The troopers could also draw their guns with their right hand by turning the wrist and hand inwards, grasping the butt of the gun, and pulling it clear of the leather with a reverse twist, known as the "cavalry draw."

Several rapid-fire military weapons were developed during the late 1800s, but the one known best to Western movie fans is the Gatling gun.[9] This early type of machine gun was invented in 1862 by Dr. Richard Jordan Gatling from Maney's Neck, North Carolina. Ironically, Dr. Gatling designed the gun because he believed that a rapid-fire weapon would reduce the need for large armies and hence diminish the horrors of warfare. The gun was officially adopted by the U.S. army in 1866. The first order for one hundred guns was filled by Samuel Colt's company.

The original Gatling gun was designed with four revolving barrels of .58 caliber, each with a separate firing system. Later models featured six to ten barrels mounted in a circle. The gun was fired by turning a hand crank on the right side of the breech housing that

The Gatling gun, developed by Dr. Richard Gatling, made a lot of noise and scared the Indians but wasn't commonly used in the field. The weapon was too cumbersome and difficult to transport, and to set up against a foe that was constantly moving during rapid skirmishes. This model has eight barrels mounted in a circle and a magazine that feeds shells into the breech from the top. A good operator with a strong arm could fire three hundred or more rounds a minute.

caused the individual barrels to revolve and fire. Cartridges were loaded into a vertical (later round) magazine, which fed them by gravity into the barrels. The gun was mounted on a wooden tripod, with the entire mechanism sometimes carried on a two-wheeled carriage for portability. Depending on the strength and stamina of the operator's arm, the gun could fire three hundred or more rounds per minute, with an effective range of about a thousand yards.

In spite of what is shown in the movies, Gatling guns were not often used in the field because they were heavy to transport and cumbersome to use. Some commanders did not consider it worth the trouble it took to transport the gun and set it up for a fight. Besides being cumbersome and heavy, the accuracy was poor, as the barrels tended to foul rapidly, and after a short period of use, the barrels heated up so much that the gun tended to jam. Instead, Gatling guns were used primarily for the defense of fixed positions, such as army forts. The gun was useful as a psychological weapon because its rapid rate of fire terrified the Indians who saw and heard it in action.

The Gatling gun has shown up in Westerns such as *The War Wagon* (1967), where the armor-plated wagon for transporting gold has one mounted on top for protection. Similarly, in *3:10 to Yuma* (2007) the Pinkerton operatives guarding the money that is stolen by Ben Wade (Russell Crowe) protected the stage with sawn-off shotguns and a Gatling gun. The gun also featured prominently in *The Gatling Gun* (1972), where the cavalry, a group of renegade soldiers, and the Apache all fight for possession of a Gatling gun.

Cavalry movies, such as *Hallelujah Trail* (1965), sometimes feature the use of light artillery. Fixed, heavy artillery, such as the huge siege guns and mortars used in the East during the Civil War, were not much use on the frontier. These massive weapons operated from fixed, reinforced emplacements, and were cumbersome and ineffective against an Indian adversary who was elusive and nomadic. In addition, Indians were always moving during battle and seldom massed together long enough to present a fixed target to warrant the preparation required for heavy field artillery.

Instead, the Western frontier army sported light artillery that was mobile enough to be used in the field. The primary weapon was the howitzer, which was originally intended for defense of open forts on the frontier.[10] Army field artillery of the 1850s and 1860s consisted primarily of the 12-pounder mountain howitzer, named for the weight of the ammunition it fired. The Indians called these large-wheeled, muzzle-loading light cannons "shooting wagons," "wagon guns," or "big medicine guns." The howitzer used various types of deadly missiles that exploded on contact and sprayed hot metal in all directions. The exploding shell made the Indians think that the guns were firing twice.[11]

Even though lighter than heavy artillery, these guns were hard to transport in the mountains or over the rocky, uneven terrain of the Southwest desert where there were no roads. They were also difficult to set up and prepare, so a battle was often over by the time the howitzers were ready for use. As a result, artillery was not often used in the field. Its primary use was at a post for ceremonial functions, though Gatling guns and light artillery might be included as part of a wagon convoy on major campaigns. When Kit Carson and his troops unexpectedly encountered a massed force of more than a thousand Comanche and Kiowa warriors at the Battle of Adobe Walls in 1864, what saved them was the fact that they had brought two 12-pounder mountain howitzers with them and were able to use them to cover their withdrawal from the field of battle.

In 1877 the army started to convert field artillery to a new two-pounder Hotchkiss mountain cannon. This light cannon had a rapid rate of fire with two-inch self-contained metallic cartridges, and an effective range of about four thousand yards. Its lighter weight and increased mobility made the Hotchkiss more effective against the Indians.

## Warfare — Indian-Style

When aggravated by the encroachment of white settlers, Indians attacked the nearest whites. In retaliation, the whites often attacked the nearest Indians, whether or not they were friendly and whether or not they were responsible for the latest attacks.

The Indian method of warfare was different than that for which soldiers were trained. The Indians existed in individual tribes and bands with shifting goals and allegiances and, as such, they formed groups of small, highly-mobile fighting forces. In most Westerns, Hollywood Indians attack without much common sense, and as a result are killed off in large anonymous numbers. For example, in *Stagecoach* (1939), even director John Ford pointed out that the Indians should have shot and killed the horses to stop the stagecoach instead of chasing it.[12]

Army soldiers fought as a cohesive unit under the direction of trained officers. Experience showed that a force of soldiers who were trained and well-equipped could usually win a battle, even if outnumbered by as many as ten to one. The Plains Indians, however, did not join together into a single enemy that could be forced into a fixed engagement, and one of the hardest parts of Indian warfare for the soldiers was to find and engage them in battle. Soldiers were trained to fight in fixed battles and felt frustrated by the hit-and-run tactics of the Indians.

Most of the fighting consisted of lightning raids by Indians and brief skirmishes with individuals or small bands of hostiles, rather than a definite fight against any organized Indian resistance. Few battles lasted longer than a day, and the Indians rarely fought unless they thought they had the advantage and could win. If the Indians were not winning during a battle, they would almost always flee if given the opportunity, particularly if their women and children were threatened. This was not considered dishonorable.

Indians approached the conflict with the soldiers as they did fights with other bands of Indians. Lengthy battles and sustained fighting were rare. Instead, Indian warfare consisted of a series of brief fights because raiding and harassment were viewed by the Indians as a form of sport. During a typical skirmish, hundreds of shots might be fired, but because marksmen were poor on both sides, the likely outcome was few casualties and no pitched battle. Furthermore, each warrior could fight or not as he felt suited the occasion. Indians were free to follow different chiefs or leaders at different times. If a leader was not successful, the rest would follow a different one who offered better accomplishments.

In spite of various Hollywood portrayals, Indians rarely attacked a fort directly, particularly those with defensive fortifications, because a frontal attack would be suicidal in the face of army weapons and marksmanship, and would provoke a level of retaliation that they were not prepared to face. Indians were more likely to ambush soldiers riding or marching in and out of the fort.

Because of their method of fighting, Indians avoided injuries whenever possible and casualties were usually light. Indians were reluctant to engage in fights if they thought there would be heavy casualties because the loss of warriors from a small band was serious. The army could easily recruit more soldiers, but the Indians required a generation to replace warriors lost in battle. The loss of even a few warriors from a small band led to a significant reduction in hunting and fighting power. Because of this, Indians rarely made open frontal assaults. For example, Fort Phil Kearny in Wyoming, with its stockade and firing loopholes, was too formidable for the Indians to attack directly, so instead they tried to draw the soldiers out of the fort in order to ambush them. Just as the Indians lured unsuspecting game into traps during the hunt, they lured unsuspecting soldiers into ambushes, often with success.

By the same token, Hollywood settlers were not very sensible. In *The Searchers* (1956), the Jorgensen homestead and the Edwards cabin are both in poor locations, as the buildings are totally exposed to attack from all sides. It is also unlikely that these homesteaders would have settled in this area, as it is unsuitable for cattle grazing. The film was supposedly set in Texas, which was grazing country, but showcased the outstanding cinematic quality of Monument Valley for visual effect.

A common movie image is Indians attacking a wagon train, with the wagons pulled into a circle and Indians riding round and round, constantly being shot off their horses. At one point in *Red River* (1948) the cowboys happen upon a wagon train that's under attack. The wagons are pulled into a circle, with Indians galloping around them firing their guns into the massed grouping. This is the classic movie confrontation of Indians versus settlers. In real life, this type of confrontation happened only very rarely. It makes no sense strategically, as Indians riding around without cover would be easily picked off by the protected settlers. Shooting across a circle like this also leaves Indians on the other side vulnerable to their own crossfire.

When the cowboys in *Red River* (1948) arrive, they ride into the ring of wagons through the circling Indians. Again this makes no sense, as the Indians would easily pick them off. It would have been a better strategy for the cowboys to stay on the outside and catch the Indians in a crossfire. The purpose of the Hollywood Indian charge towards the fortified wagons is to show them being cut down in large numbers. This makes good cinematic drama but was not realistic.

There is a perversely humorous sequence in *Hallelujah Trail* (1965) in which the Indians are grouped inside a circle of wagons for a change, while the cavalry rides round and round them shooting and whooping. The Indians look confused by this reverse turn of events.

A non-humorous situation occurs in *Winchester '73* (1950) when the Indians attack the wagon train and ride straight at the defenders, who are protected behind fallen trees. The Indians attacking the wagon train didn't know the defenders had two Winchester repeaters and a Henry repeating rifle, which are used to good advantage to drive off the attackers. This type of situation happened in real life in several fights soon after repeating rifles were introduced. One of these battles was the so-called Hayfield Fight that took place in Montana on August 1, 1867. Chief Crazy Horse, with between five hundred and eight hundred Sioux warriors, attacked nineteen soldiers and six civilians who were cutting hay near Fort C.F. Smith. Most of the soldiers were armed with newly-issued .50 caliber breech-loading, single-shot Springfield rifles. The Indians knew from experience that reloading single-shot rifles would take a few moments, so they assumed that they could attack after the first volley without much resistance while the men were engaged in reloading. What the Indians didn't know was that the civilians were armed with Spencer and Henry repeating rifles. What happened was that the besieged unexpectedly continued firing while the Indians were confidently making their charge. The firing was so rapid and fierce that rifle barrels overheated and burned the men's hands.

### Save the Last Bullet

A popular tradition from pulp fiction, stage plays, and cavalry movies is that of saving the last bullet for the woman, in order to prevent capture and "a fate worse than death." In *Winchester '73* (1950), Lin McAdam (James Stewart) hands shady dance-hall girl Lola Manners (Shelley Winters) a revolver before the Indian attack. He does not say anything but implies that she should shoot herself rather than be captured. She looks at him and says, "I understand about the last one." In *Stagecoach* (1939) the gambler Hatfield (John Carradine), ever the southern gentleman, saves his last bullet for Lucy Malloy (Louise Platt), the cavalry officer's wife, during an Indian attack. Luckily, the cavalry arrives just in time, and he is shot just as he is about to shoot her.

In reality, capture by savage Indians was indeed something that preyed on women's minds, and this threat was their worst dread. A captured white woman might be forced to be the slave of one or several warriors, and might be married against her will to an Indian husband. "Besieged by Sioux and Crows on the Plains in 1867, an army wife wrote in her diary that the women had 'decided that if the Ft [fort] could not be held then we preferred to be shot by our own officers rather than to be taken captive.'"[13]

When Indians stole a herd of mules from Fort Abraham Lincoln in North Dakota, almost the entire regiment went after them. The fearful wives, who were left virtually unguarded at the fort, decided that they would kill themselves rather than be captured by Indians. Luckily, the men returned before that happened.[14]

The attitude promoted among the whites was grim, even if it was melodramatic. Colonel Richard Dodge assumed that all white women would be captured and raped when he said, "I believe I am perfectly safe in the assertion that there is not a single wild tribe of Indians in all the wide territory of the United States which does not regard the person of the female captive as the inherent right of the captor, and I venture to assert further that in the last twenty-five years no woman has been taken prisoner by any plains Indians who did not as soon after as practicable become a victim to the lust of every one of her captors."[15]

There were, however, instances of some captured white women—especially if taken as a young child—who were integrated into a tribe, married Indian husbands, and when "rescued" were reluctant to leave their Indian family and children. One of the best-known cases was Cynthia Ann Parker, who was taken captive in 1836 at age nine by Comanche raiders. She grew up in captivity, eventually married a young chief, and had his children. When she and her two-year-old daughter were "rescued" twenty-four years later, she made several attempts to return to her Indian family and finally starved herself to death in grief after her daughter died. In *The Stalking Moon* (1969), Sarah Carver (Eva Marie Saint) is a white woman who has been captured by the Indians and has a half-breed son as a result. In the same movie, Nick Tana (Robert Forster) is a half-breed scout.

## The Battle of the Little Bighorn

Like the gunfight at the O.K. Corral, the Battle of the Little Bighorn in southern Montana, on June 22, 1876, has gone down as one of the most famous battles in Western lore, with George Armstrong Custer as its legendary hero. The story of Custer has appeared in over thirty-four movie versions. The movies, however, have not always treated Custer well. In *Little Big Man* (1970), for instance, Custer is portrayed as pompous and patronizing, with a peculiar turn of mind.

Though Custer graduated last in his class at West Point military academy, he was a bright star in the Civil War, rising to the brevet rank of major-general and commanding a cavalry division.[16] After the war he returned to his regular army rank of lieutenant-colonel and took command of the Seventh Cavalry.

In 1876 the public demanded that the Black Hills of South Dakota be opened for gold prospecting. The eventual solution proposed by the government was a military one. On May 17, Custer and the Seventh Cavalry marched out of Fort Abraham Lincoln, accompanied by 110 wagons and three Gatling Guns. His mission was to find and engage the Indians. He expected an easy victory.

Custer was leading six hundred soldiers on June 25, 1876, as he approached an Indian village of Sioux and Northern Cheyenne near the Little Bighorn River, which the Indians called the Greasy Grass River. He split his force into three groups, intending to surround the village. Custer took command of the largest detachment. Another group under the command of Major Marcus Reno, consisted of 140 officers and enlisted men. A third group, under the command of Captain Frederick Benteen, consisted of 125 men assigned to scout the Little Bighorn Valley. Unknown to Custer, the great annual summer gathering of all the Sioux was under way, and the village he was approaching contained an estimated eight thousand Indians, about three thousand of whom were fighting men.

While Custer rode forward, Reno started to attack but encountered heavy resistance. Fierce fighting forced Reno and his men to retreat to a nearby hilltop and form a defensive position. He was joined shortly afterwards by Benteen and the men under his command. Both Reno and Benteen and their men found themselves pinned down by enemy fire. As a result, Custer found himself trapped in a difficult position, surrounded by an overwhelming force of Indians, with Reno and Benteen unable to come to his assistance. Custer's final stand took place on the north end of Battle Ridge.

The fight was over in about two hours. Custer and the 210 officers and enlisted men with him were all killed. The Indian dead were estimated at between sixty and a hundred.

The only survivor of Custer's Last Stand was an army horse named Comanche, owned by Captain Miles W. Keogh, who was killed during the battle. The horse received his name after being struck by an arrow during a skirmish with Comanche Indians in 1868. The story of Comanche was filmed as *Tonka* (1958), and was also presented on television as *A Horse Called Comanche*.

The massacre of Custer's entire command horrified and enraged the American public. People could not believe that the seemingly invincible Indian fighter had been killed. The horror was intensified by the fact that the bodies had been mutilated.

Analysis of the defeat started soon after the battle, and most of the principals, including Benteen, Reno, and Custer himself, were blamed for what happened. It is certainly easy with hindsight to assign reasons for what went wrong, but Custer's orders were to find the Indians and attack them, and he did. One valid criticism, however, is that Custer may have attacked prematurely before fully assessing the enemy's strength. The reality of the defeat was that Custer stumbled onto a far greater force than he anticipated; consequently, he and his men were vastly outnumbered and were overcome.

With Custer's resounding defeat at the Little Bighorn, public sentiment forced a campaign of retribution against the Sioux and Cheyenne. Military threats and reprisals forced the Sioux to agree to a treaty, and most settled on various reservations.

The Battle of the Little Bighorn has appeared on the silver screen starting with a Selig production called *On the Little Big Horn; or, Custer's Last Stand* (1909), in which Tom Mix

The last stand of Custer and the Seventh Cavalry at the Little Bighorn in Montana has been immortalized in paintings, books, and movies until the legend became the myth. This version by Henry Steinhegger is titled *General Custer's Death Struggle*, published by the Pacific Art Company of San Francisco in 1878. The reality of the battle was that Custer unexpectedly came up against an overwhelmingly large force of Indians and was defeated (Library of Congress).

played a part. *Custer's Last Fight* (1925) was typical of early Westerns in its portrayal of the military as very positive, while also presenting a negative image of the Indians. Other versions of the Custer saga include *Custer's Last Fight* (1912), *The Flaming Frontier* (1925), *Santa Fe Trail* (1940), and the Cinerama epic *Custer of the West* (1968).

The most widespread version of the fight is *They Died with Their Boots On* (1941), in which the rousing climax is the battle itself. One critic has called it a whitewashed account of Custer (Errol Flynn) from his days as a cadet at West Point to his final battle.[17] Historian Alvin M. Josephy, Jr. offered a stronger opinion when he said, "The screenwriters and director Raoul Walsh based much of the production on known historical facts, though they embellished, refashioned, twisted, and distorted most of these facts into their own hodge-podge of truth and melodramatic fairy tale."[18] Perhaps it is fairer to say that the screenwriters took some literary license with the facts to make a rousing adventure film. Even director Raoul Walsh admitted that it was "a romanticized biography." The strangest line in the movie comes when General Sheridan says to Custer's wife, Libbie, after the battle, "Your soldier won his last fight after all."

The exteriors for *They Died with Their Boots On* (1941) were filmed about forty miles north of Los Angeles in a wide valley that resembled the plains of Montana. Director Walsh couldn't find enough Indians to play the Sioux warriors, so he filled out the Indian ranks with Filipinos.

## The End of the Indian Wars

The Indian wars on the Plains drew to a close in 1890 with a disaster of epic proportions. Throughout the 1880s the Indians who had submitted to the reservation were treated harshly. They suffered as their allotments of food, clothing, and other supplies were reduced. The seeds for the final disaster were sown in 1889 when a new religion called the Ghost Dance originated in Nevada with a Paiute shaman (medicine man) named Wovoka (known to the whites as Jack Wilson). This shaman taught that if the Indians performed a ceremony of non-violent chanting and communal dancing, the buffalo would return, dead relatives would be reunited with their families for eternal life, and the whites would be driven from Indian lands. This real-life event formed the background of the plot of *Sergeants 3* (1962), where a leader named Wanaka directs his followers in the Ghost Dance against the white soldiers.

A shortage of food in 1889 and 1890 made these new beliefs very attractive. The popularity of the new religion spread, and it was quickly embraced by the Sioux on the Great Plains, but they added a new militant feature to the dance. They felt that if the dancers wore special shirts painted with magical symbols they would be immune to bullets. Local whites, and in particular Indian agents and army officials, started to become nervous about this new religion. Part of their concern was why the participants required "bulletproof" shirts if the teachings of this new religion were as peaceful as the Indians claimed.

In the wake of this, about 350 Sioux Indians under Chief Big Foot left the Pine Ridge Reservation in South Dakota on December 23, 1890. Army troops pursued them, caught up with them, and started them back to the reservation. On December 28, Big Foot's people, surrounded by soldiers and four Hotchkiss howitzers, camped at Wounded Knee Creek, about twenty miles east of the reservation.

Colonel James Forsyth arrived at the scene and decided that the Indians should surrender their weapons. When they refused, Forsyth ordered his men to forcibly disarm them. A scuffle ensued and a weapon discharged — whether accidentally or deliberately was never established. The tragic result was that the soldiers surrounding the camp opened fire with small arms and the howitzers, killing about 250 Indians (estimates of the number of dead vary). After the firing stopped, the soldiers realized that they had killed thirty-one of their own and wounded thirty-nine, probably in their own cross-fire. The Indian dead were thrown into a mass grave and buried. The bloody carnage at Wounded Knee was the last major Indian confrontation after twenty-five savage years of warfare on the Plains.

# Postscript

What I have done in this book is to present some of the history of the Old West and relate this to Western films and how they were made. Hopefully integrating the two subjects has increased the reader's understanding and enjoyment of Western films as an art form.

How well has Hollywood portrayed the West and its history? As we have seen over the course of this book, the history shown in most Westerns is usually less than accurate. Western movies are not history lessons. They present the same type of drama and conflicts as most novels and other movie genres, except that they are set in the early American West. They merely use the history and setting of the West as a background for conflicts and their resolution. The question then becomes: how well does Hollywood portray this background against which the drama and conflict between characters is played out?

Westerns do not necessarily portray reality but are oriented more towards presenting a rousing story. Like Western movies, even the earlier Wild West shows of Buffalo Bill Cody and others were not an accurate portrayal of the West, but presented only a narrow view of history that was laced with action and adventure in order to provide rousing entertainment.

The Western movie has its roots in the lurid dime novels of the late 1800s, and it has retained many of the conventions of that type of literature. The hero is often a loner who comes to town and becomes the impetus for the conflict that drives the plot. Classic examples of this structure stretch throughout the genre from *Hell's Hinges* (1916), through *Shane* (1953), *High Plains Drifter* (1973) and *Pale Rider* (1985). The hero rides in out of nowhere, creates a conflict or finds himself in the middle of it, solves the problem, then rides out of town back to nowhere. The mythic world of the Western movie will always culminate in the grand shoot-out at the end.

The Old West of reality was not a constant succession of these lawmen and gunfighters who are always embroiled in fights and shootings on the main street, or cowboys "hurrahing" every town in the West. The hero-cowboy-sheriff-gunfighter of the Western — whoever he really is — is not a real cowboy but a mythic Robin Hood. He does not herd cattle, and he is not the same as the historical cowboys of the great cattle drives. Even the term "cowboys-and-Indians" is a misnomer, as the Indians of the movies fought the cavalry and not the cowboys.

We have seen that there is not just one "Western." Western movies gradually evolved over a period of about seventy years from the first vignettes into action movies that tell a complete story. The plots and construction of Western movies have changed over time to cater to changing audience tastes. Many early Westerns were dominated by the "good bad-man" type of character portrayed by Broncho Billy Anderson and William S. Hart. When audiences tired of this formula, Westerns evolved into action programmers with an occasional epic, such as *The Big Trail* (1930) and *Stagecoach* (1939), breaking out of the mold. The Westerns of the late 1930s were mostly defined by several standardized plot devices, such as the singing cowboy, the comic sidekick, the heavy in the black hat, and the sexy saloon girl whose profession remains nameless. These devices helped change and define the genre of the Western at that particular time, and audiences came to expect them. This type of plotting, which started in the B-Westerns, carried over to the A-Westerns. Like other genres of movies, the later Westerns contain more adult themes and encompass more violence.

As Westerns changed and matured, the audience's vision of where and what the landscape of "the West" looks like has also changed, heavily influenced by the personal vision of various filmmakers. The forests and streams of the early Westerns filmed in the East shifted to the West Coast around Los Angeles for practical reasons, and then moved to the deserts of the southwestern United States, and to Mexico and Spain.

The lore and legend of the Wild West lives on in Western movies, but it is not the reality of the nineteenth century cowboy or gunfighter. It is a blend of a small amount of history and fact, and a healthy dose of imagination. It is the legend of the movie cowboy and the mythic Wild West that is set somewhere in the desert of red spires that is Monument Valley. It is John Wayne and Roy Rogers riding off into the sunset. It is pure entertainment.

Thanks to the silver screen, the legendary character of the cowboy-gunfighter lives on in the Western. Long may he last.

# Who Does What? A Brief Tour Behind the Camera

For readers unfamiliar with the process of making movies, this appendix will be helpful in understanding the function behind the names that appear at the beginning of older movies or at the end of newer films. There are, of course, many more people who are involved in making a Western than those listed here, and there are many variations of these titles, but this list will outline the key players behind the camera.

While these descriptions are couched generally in male terms for simplicity and because Hollywood filmmaking was dominated by men during the peak production years of the Western, it should be noted that women can and do fill many of these roles. For example, early stunts involving female characters were performed by stuntmen wearing dresses, but now women play just as important a part as men in ensuring that dangerous stunts are transformed successfully to the screen.

## ADR Editor

The ADR editor is responsible for performing Additional Dialogue Replacement (also called "sound dubbing") after filming, if the sound recorded when the film was shot is not suitable. This may be necessary if a background noise or wind noise was captured on the recorded soundtrack, or if PG-rated dialogue needs to be substituted for R-rated dialogue for different markets.

## Art Director

The art director turns the director's mental images into reality. The art director is responsible for designing all the sets and locations, and may oversee design of the costumes. He may be referred to as the production designer or the set designer.

## Bit-players

Supporting actors who have very small speaking parts, perhaps only one line, in a film.

## Casting Director

The one who finds the appropriate actors to recommend to the director and/or producer to fill various roles in the movie. The major stars for a particular movie are often cast by the studio, the director, or the producer. The casting director draws from a pool of actors he knows or knows about to conduct auditions to fill the smaller roles.

## Costume Designer

The person responsible for designing and making the many costumes required for a production. Also see "wardrobe."

## Director

The one with the responsibility for putting the story and script on film. He literally directs the action as the scenes are being filmed. He is like the captain of a ship or the conductor of an orchestra. He tells the actors what to do and how to do it; thus he exerts the most creative control over the visual aspects of a film. He interacts directly with the director of photography, the editor, and others, to make the story coherent. He is assisted by a first assistant director and a second assistant director (and perhaps more), who perform much of the detailed work of organizing the cast and crew under the director's supervision. While the producer usually has the final word on business decisions, overall movie structure, and cast, the director has the final say on the creative and artistic aspects of the film, usually including locations.

## Director of Photography

The one responsible for the lighting on the sets to create the appropriate mood and artistic setting for each scene, and for putting the scene on film. This position has also been called the cameraman, lighting cameraman, or cinematographer. In the early days of Westerns the cameraman actually operated the camera and looked through the camera eyepiece during filming. Now he is assisted in the routine tasks of filming by a camera operator, a focus-puller, a film-loader, and other subordinate helpers who actually set up and operate the camera.

## Editor or Film Editor

The one who cuts the raw film that has been shot and assembles it into the correct sequence, while pacing and timing the various scenes in the film for coherence and dramatic effect. This function is often performed in close cooperation with the director. The editor assembles the "dailies," or the results of the previous day's shooting, which are reviewed to ensure that the film is progressing as planned. He also assembles the "rough cut," so that the director and producer can see in rough terms what the final film will look like. An editor is sometimes called the "cutter" because he cuts the film. With rapidly advancing digital video technology, much of the work is now accomplished with computers.

## Extras

Actors who appear in crowd scenes or in other very minor non-speaking roles. They provide background crowds for army columns, Indian attacks, posses, dances, and other large group or crowd scenes. Often they are faceless and unrecognizable in the background of a scene.

## Foley Editor

The Foley editor adds in sound effects that were not practical or necessary during filming, after the original scene is shot. He also dubs in sound effects, such as footsteps, hoofbeats, or train noises, if the scene was shot without sound.

## Gaffer, Grips and Best Boy

These curious names are included here because they puzzle many who see them in the titles. The gaffer is the historic name for the chief electrician (also know as the "boss electrician," or the "chief juicer" because he provides the "juice" or electricity), who is responsible for providing the correct lighting for each scene. He is assisted by other electricians who provide power for various functions required on the set. In moviemaking, this odd name came from references to the man who moved the overhead lights with a gaff, which is a long pole with a hook on the end.

The "best boy" is the first assistant to the gaffer. The "grips" are the manual laborers who move, dig, build, push, assemble, lift, and provide the other practical physical skills required on the set for a film production. The key grip moves the camera around on the set. Grips push and pull the camera for dolly and tracking shots.

## Make-up

Provides the make-up that is necessary to make the actors look realistic onscreen and improve their looks. Also responsible for special make-up needs, such as wounds and scars.

## Producer

The one who is responsible for the financial and business end of the production on all aspects of the film. He reports either to the studio for a studio-financed film or to the investors for an independent production. He develops the budget, chooses the script or oversees script-writing, assists the director, and has the final say in anything related to the budget. The producer is assisted by associate producers, supervising producers, production executives, and people with similar titles. The producer typically chooses the scriptwriter, the director, and the major actors, though in the heyday of the Hollywood studio system, when most actors were under contract to a particular studio, they would be assigned to any picture that the studio wanted.

Independent producers are those outside the studio system who perform all these tasks as well as arranging for financing through banks, or from private or corporate investors. Independent producers typically retain more control over a production than the studio producers, who are responsible to the studio heads for business and financial aspects of the production.

## Property Master or Mistress

Responsible for the acquisition, creation, and maintenance of the many small miscellaneous, non-fixed objects, known as "properties" or "props," that are used on the set. He may also be responsible for weapons, though in larger productions there may also be a separate armorer who is specifically responsible for guns and other weapons, along with their use and safety on the set.

## Scriptwriter

The one who writes the script for the story being filmed. There may be several other writers involved before a final screenplay is approved, such as a writer who writes the story, one who adapts it for the screen, one who polishes the final script, and one who performs rewrites. Also called scenarist or scenario writer.

## Second Unit Director

The primary (or first unit) director typically directs action and dialogue on the sets for the principal actors. The second unit director takes a second photographic unit to distant locations and films action that will later be edited into the movie at the appropriate places. This may or may not involve the principal actors, but may be comprised of a series of long shots filmed so far away that the director can use doubles for the principals. The second unit director is typically responsible for stunts and action scenes.

## Stand-In

A stand-in is someone who physically resembles a star, and stands or sits in costume in the actor's place while all the preparations, such as lighting and camera position, are worked out before shooting a scene on film. A stand-in who closely resembles an actor may perform this function for the same actor on many pictures but never actually appear in a final film.

## Stunt Coordinator

Creates and supervises the physical action and other stunts that are too dangerous for the main actors to perform. Plans and coordinates the stunts so that they can be performed in the safest possible manner. Stunt men often specialize in different type of stunts, such as falling off buildings, crashing wagons, or falling from horses.

## Wardrobe

The person responsible for designing, finding, fitting, repairing, and cleaning the costumes, and performing all the other tasks required to keep the costumes available and intact through a production. Each lead actor, for example, may require up to eight identical costumes, or ones in various states of wear, so that the costumes produce continuity throughout the production.

*Appendix B*

# Cowboy Action Shooting

Guns have always appealed to small boys of all ages. The make-believe world of the gun-filled Western movies still continues today on a smaller scale with Cowboy Action Shooting, a sport in which competitors in authentic dress of the Western frontier participate in shooting competitions. Cowboy Action Shooting is a relatively recent sport, dating from the founding of the Single Action Shooting Society in California in 1981. Today affiliate clubs are found around the world, and over forty thousand shooters compete in various club events.

The participants compete with period revolvers, rifles, and shotguns, using live ammunition on a shooting range. The competitors dress in period costumes or those of a favorite Hollywood character from the Westerns, and adopt the mannerisms and identities of real or fictional gunmen from the Old West.

Competition on the shooting range is a three-gun event. Each participant requires one (or two) single-action revolvers, a lever-action or pump-action rifle, and a period shotgun, either double-barreled or a pump-action with an exposed hammer. Some participants use original models of firearms, but because of the scarcity and costs involved in purchasing authentic antique weapons, competitors have turned increasingly to modern replicas. Though weapons constructed in modern times may be used, their predecessors had to be in production before 1900.

There are several different competitive shooting events. The main event is a timed run through a Western town street that looks like a movie set while shooting at steel targets with all three types of weapon at specified stops. Movie-like props and various scenarios are used to provide added authenticity. The lowest time, or times, to complete the event determines the winner. Some shooters are so good that fractions of a second can make the difference between winning top place and losing — somewhat like a real gunfight in the Old West. Because live ammunition is used, a strong emphasis is placed on gun training and range safety, and all events are constantly monitored by range-safety officers.

To retain the authenticity of the gunfighting era, black powder is often used. This provides the sight and sound of the jets of flame of authentic historical gunfights, along with the smell of burnt gunpowder and the accompanying dense clouds of swirling gray smoke. Because of the difficulty of obtaining real black powder and the danger of dealing with such an unstable substance, a modern powder equivalent is often substituted.

Favorite revolvers for these modern gunfighters are the .45 caliber Colt single-action Peacemaker with the 4¾-inch barrel, the favorite of the movie cowboy and of gunfighters of the late 1870s and 1880s. The Peacemaker with the 7½-inch barrel offers better accuracy at long range, but because most of the targets are at between eight and ten yards distance for Cowboy Action Shooting events, the longer barrel does not provide any significant advantage. The .38 Special cartridge is also commonly used because it provides a lighter recoil than the heavier .45 round.

Now, as then, .44–40 caliber is very popular because of its authenticity and because only one type of cartridge is required if competing with both a single-action Colt revolver and a Winchester Model '73 rifle. Some participants, in a further quest for authenticity, use cap-and-ball revolvers, usually replicas of the Colt Model 1851 Navy or the Colt Model 1860 Army. Like the real gunfighters, the cap-and-ball shooters are fewer in number than those who use metallic cartridges because of the logistics and time involved in reloading while competing.

# Filmography

This listing is intended to be a representative, rather than comprehensive, listing of Western films chosen from among the thousands that were made during the "golden era" of the Western. Most of them were made from the 1930s through the 1970s. This list should be viewed as a convenient reference for readers who are not familiar with some of the films that are discussed in the text as examples. Each entry includes the title, year of release, director, three of the major stars (space precludes listing them all), and a very brief synopsis of the plot.

*Abilene Town* (1946). D: Edwin Marin. Randolph Scott, Ann Dvorak, Edgar Buchanan. The town marshal tries to keep the peace as settlers arrive and come into conflict with cattlemen driving herds to the end of the trail at the rip-roaring cattle town of Abilene.

*Annie Get Your Gun* (1950). D: George Sidney. Betty Hutton, Howard Keel, Louis Calhern. Musical biography of real-life sharpshooter Annie Oakley and her romance and eventual marriage to fellow sharpshooter Frank Butler, set against the background of *Buffalo Bill's Wild West*.

*Apache Rose* (1946). D: William Witney. Roy Rogers, Dale Evans, Olin Howlin. Oil wildcatter Roy and his sidekick Alkali stumble on a rich oil deposit and are up against crooks who will stop at nothing to take it from its rightful owners.

*The Assassination of Jesse James by the Coward Robert Ford* (2007). D: Andrew Dominik. Casey Affleck, Brad Pitt, Sam Shepard. The story of Robert Ford, leading up to his cold-blooded shooting of his cousin, outlaw Jesse James, in the back.

*Bad Girls* (1994). D: Jonathan Kaplan. Madeleine Stowe, Mary Stuart Masterson, Andie Mac-Dowell. The troubles of four girls from a bordello who hightail it out of town after a justifiable shooting, and the problems that ensue when they meet up with the former-boyfriend-turned-outlaw of one of them.

*Bells of Coronado* (1950). D: William Witney. Roy Rogers, Dale Evans, Pat Brady. An undercover investigator looks into the theft of a wagon-load of ore and finds that the mastermind of a certain "foreign power" is trying to smuggle uranium overseas in a submarine.

*Bells of San Angelo* (1947). D: William Witney. Roy Rogers, Dale Evans, Andy Devine. An investigator for the Border Patrol teams up with a novelist who writes Westerns in order to solve a murder linked to silver miners smuggling precious metal across the border.

*Big Jake* (1971). D: George Sherman. John Wayne, Richard Boone, Maureen O'Hara. A gunfighter is enlisted by his estranged wife to rescue their grandson, who has been abducted for ransom by a gang of kidnappers.

*Bite the Bullet* (1975). D: Richard Brooks. Gene Hackman, James Coburn, Candice Bergen. Adventures and interplay among contestants during a 700-mile horse race across the West.

*Blazing Saddles* (1974). D: Mel Brooks. Cleavon Little, Harvey Korman, Gene Wilder. A broad spoof ("politically incorrect" in today's terms) of the entire Western genre of the 1950s, full of jokes and gags for those who understand the movies and characters they refer to.

*The Bravados* (1958). D: Henry King. Gregory Peck, Joan Collins, Steven Boyd. A rancher seeks revenge on the four outlaws that he thinks killed his wife, only to find out that they did not do it, and that he has become as bad as they were.

***Breakheart Pass*** (1976). D: Tom Gries. Charles Bronson, Richard Crenna, Ben Johnson. An undercover secret service agent tries to find out who is smuggling illegal guns to the Indians on a train, and has to thwart the evil-doers before the train arrives at a fort captured by renegades.

***Broken Arrow*** (1950). D: Delmer Daves. James Stewart, Jeff Chandler, Debra Paget. Indian chief Cochise and an express agent try to understand each other's viewpoint and make the first steps towards peace between Indians and whites during the Apache Indian conflicts in the Southwest.

***Buffalo Bill and the Indians*** (1976). D: Robert Altman. Paul Newman, Joel Grey, Kevin McCarthy. Presents the viewpoint that Buffalo Bill Cody was a magnificent showman, while at the same time being a bit of a fraud.

***Butch Cassidy and the Sundance Kid*** (1969). D: George Roy Hill. Paul Newman, Robert Redford, Katharine Ross. Semi-humorous view of the rise and fall of real-life outlaw Butch Cassidy and his Hole-in-the-Wall gang.

***Calamity Jane*** (1953). D: David Butler. Doris Day, Howard Keel, Allyn McLerie. Musical, sanitized rendition of the life of Calamity Jane in Deadwood, South Dakota, and her eventual fictional marriage to Wild Bill Hickok.

***Cat Ballou*** (1965). D: Elliot Silverstein. Jane Fonda, Lee Marvin, Michael Callan. This story of fictional schoolteacher Catherine "Cat" Ballou, who is forced to become a train-robbing outlaw, has elements that satirize Butch Cassidy and his outlaw gang.

***Chisum*** (1970). D: Andrew McLaglen. John Wayne, Forrest Tucker, Geoffrey Deuel. Though loosely based on the Lincoln County, New Mexico, cattle war, this tale gives cattle baron John Chisum the focus and lead role in resolving the dispute.

***Cowboy*** (1958). D: Delmer Daves. Glenn Ford, Jack Lemmon, Brian Donlevy. A hotel desk clerk dreams of being a cowboy and gets his wish (and a tough education) on the trail under a stern boss during a cattle drive from Mexico to Chicago.

***The Cowboys*** (1972). D: Mark Rydell. John Wayne, Roscoe Lee Brown, Bruce Dern. An aging rancher cannot find experienced cowboys for a cattle drive and is forced to take on a group of youngsters, teaching them the ways of the trail while keeping an eye out for marauding rustlers.

***Dances with Wolves*** (1990). D: Kevin Costner. Kevin Costner, Mary McDonnell, Graham Greene. A soldier travels out West to a new posting after the Civil War and eventually becomes integrated into a Sioux Indian tribe, thus contrasting the Indian way of life with that of the incoming white settlers.

***Denver and Rio Grande*** (1952). D: Byron Haskin. Edmond O'Brien, Sterling Hayden, Dean Jagger. A fictional story based on the real Denver and Rio Grande railroad in Colorado, and their race to beat the competition while laying track through the Royal Gorge.

***Destry Rides Again*** (1939). D: George Marshall. James Stewart, Marlene Dietrich, Brian Donlevy. The mild-mannered son of a tough sheriff is summoned West to tame a raucous town, but he has a different way of controlling the wilder element, which includes a feisty saloon queen.

***Dodge City*** (1939). D: Michael Curtiz. Errol Flynn, Alan Hale, Olivia de Havilland. An ex-buffalo hunter comes to Dodge City, becomes the sheriff, and tames the town using an amalgamation of techniques found in other Westerns.

***El Dorado*** (1967). D: Howard Hawks. John Wayne, Robert Mitchum, James Caan. An aging gunfighter is hired to help a land baron take over the local range, but he refuses and joins his old pal the sheriff in tackling the gang of hired guns who come to do the job.

***Escape from Fort Bravo*** (1953). D: John Sturges. William Holden, Eleanor Parker, John Forsythe. Civil War prisoners being held at a fort in Arizona try to cross the desert ahead of Indian attacks but end up being caught in one.

***A Fistful of Dollars*** (1964). D: Sergio Leone. Clint Eastwood, Gian Maria Volonté, Marianne Koch. When a gunfighter is caught between two rival gangs fighting over the same town, he pits one against the other as everyone tries to outshoot each other.

***5 Card Stud*** (1968). D: Henry Hathaway. Dean Martin, Robert Mitchum, Roddy McDowall. After a lynching over a card game, a mysterious preacher comes to town and the ranks of the lynch mob thin out one by one.

*For a Few Dollars More* (1965). D: Sergio Leone. Clint Eastwood, Lee Van Cleef, Gian Maria Volonté. Two bounty hunters look for the same outlaw to claim the reward—though for different reasons—and end up pooling resources to catch him after a bank robbery.

*Fort Apache* (1948). D: John Ford. John Wayne, Henry Fonda, John Agar. A veteran frontier soldier is disgusted when his new colonel, arriving from the East to deal with the Indians, doesn't like the West or understand how to negotiate with the local natives.

*4 for Texas* (1963). D: Robert Aldrich. Frank Sinatra, Dean Martin, Charles Bronson. A con-man throws in with a girl who owns a gambling riverboat, but is pestered by a rival con-man who wants to take over all the gambling business. Meanwhile, a crooked banker hires a thug to take everything from both of them.

*The Good, the Bad, and the Ugly* (1966). D: Sergio Leone. Clint Eastwood, Lee Van Cleef, Eli Wallach. The American Civil War serves as the backdrop to this tale of the interaction between three undesirable characters as they gather clues and search for a cache of gold coins that was buried by a soldier from the Confederacy.

*Gunfight at the O.K. Corral* (1957). D: John Sturges. Burt Lancaster, Kirk Douglas, Rhonda Fleming. Retelling of the events leading up to the famous shoot-out that occurred between the Earps and the Clantons behind the O.K. Corral in Tombstone, Arizona, in 1881.

*The Gunfighter* (1950). D: Henry King. Gregory Peck, Millard Mitchell, Skip Homeier. A veteran gunfighter comes to town peaceably to see his young son and finds that his reputation has preceded him, as younger guns want to prove themselves against him.

*Hallelujah Trail* (1965). D: John Sturges. Burt Lancaster, Lee Remick, Jim Hutton. A crisis sparked by a whiskey shortage in Denver as winter approaches creates trouble for the commandant of a local fort when the cavalry, a temperance group, and the volunteer Denver Free Militia converge on the wagon train bringing in fresh supplies.

*Hang 'Em High* (1968). D: Ted Post. Clint Eastwood, Pat Hingle, Inger Stevens. A former lawman is almost wrongfully lynched for cattle stealing, so he takes up a badge again and becomes a marshal bringing in prisoners for the "hanging judge," as he seeks revenge on the group who almost killed him.

*High Noon* (1952). D: Fred Zinneman. Gary Cooper, Grace Kelly, Lloyd Bridges. A town marshal is ready to retire with his new bride when he finds out that a gunman has been released from prison and is coming back to settle an old score.

*High Plains Drifter* (1973). D: Clint Eastwood. Clint Eastwood, Jack Ging, Verna Bloom. A mysterious stranger comes to town and is hired to protect the townspeople from outlaws who have been released from jail and are returning to seek retribution, but with unexpected results.

*Hondo* (1953). D: John Farrow. John Wayne, Geraldine Page, Michael Pate. An ex-cavalry scout tries to protect a woman and her son who are living in Apache territory, a mission that is complicated by the interaction between the three and Apache leader Vittorio.

*How the West Was Won* (1962). D: John Ford, Henry Hathaway, George Marshall. Debbie Reynolds, Gregory Peck, Carroll Baker. This epic retelling of the story of the pioneering of the West follows three generations of settlers from their journey down the Ohio River to the closing of the frontier in Arizona in the early 1900s.

*Jesse James* (1939). D: Henry King. Tyrone Power, Henry Fonda, Randolph Scott. Romanticized account of how Jesse and Frank James take their revenge on trains and banks after an unscrupulous railroad agent kills their mother and oppresses the local farmers. It ends with Jesse's assassination by Bob Ford.

*Last Train from Gun Hill* (1959). D: John Sturges. Kirk Douglas, Anthony Quinn, Earl Holliman. A marshal whose Indian wife has been raped and murdered waits to leave town on the last train out with the chief suspect, who is the son of an old friend.

*The Law and Jake Wade* (1958). D: John Sturges. Robert Taylor, Richard Widmark, Patricia Owens. A marshal, who was previously an outlaw, rescues an old friend from jail to repay a debt, but is kidnapped by him and forced to go on a search for buried treasure.

*Lawman* (1971). D: Michael Winner. Burt Lancaster, Lee J. Cobb, Robert Ryan. A marshal goes to an unfamiliar town to arrest some men who shot up a nearby town and killed an old man, but he meets with defiance from the local land baron and the townspeople.

***Little Big Man*** (1970). D: Arthur Penn. Dustin Hoffman, Faye Dunaway, Richard Mulligan. An old, old man reminisces about how he was at every major event that took place in the Old West.

***Mackenna's Gold*** (1969). D: J. Lee Thompson. Gregory Peck, Omar Sharif, Camilla Sparv. A gang of bandits captures a world-weary marshal and finds that conflicts arise between all of them as they force him to lead them to a hidden canyon of lost gold in the desert.

***The Magnificent Seven*** (1960). D: John Sturges. Yul Brynner, Steve McQueen, Eli Wallach. Seven gunfighters are hired to aid Mexican villagers who are being oppressed by a gang of roving bandits.

***The Man from Laramie*** (1955). D: Anthony Mann. James Stewart, Donald Crisp, Arthur Kennedy. An army officer investigates the killing of his brother during a cavalry patrol and the associated theft of a shipment of rifles and their sale to the Indians, while he comes up against the land baron who controls the entire area.

***Man of the West*** (1958). D: Anthony Mann. Gary Cooper, Lee J. Cobb, Julie London. A reformed outlaw is forced to rejoin his old gang in order to protect others from harm by the gang, a situation that leads to a climactic shootout.

***The Man Who Shot Liberty Valance*** (1962). D: John Ford. James Stewart, John Wayne, Lee Marvin. The story of how Western legends are created, as a young lawyer who comes to a wild town gains a reputation for supposedly having killed the toughest outlaw in the territory.

***McCabe & Mrs. Miller*** (1971). D: Robert Altman. Warren Beatty, Julie Christie, Rene Auberjonois. A small-time con man opens a saloon and bordello in a growing Western mining town, then runs up against a syndicate who wants to buy him out.

***McLintock!*** (1963). D: Andrew McLaglen. John Wayne, Maureen O'Hara, Chill Wills. A light-hearted look at family interactions between a rich Texas rancher and his estranged wife, and their eventual reconciliation, complicated by their daughter who has returned home for a visit.

***My Darling Clementine*** (1946). D: John Ford. Henry Fonda, Victor Mature, Walter Brennan. This re-telling of the Earp-Clanton feud that led to the gunfight at the O.K. Corral is not historically accurate, but makes for good entertainment.

***The Naked Spur*** (1953). D: Anthony Mann. James Stewart, Robert Ryan, Janet Leigh. A rancher captures a wily outlaw wanted for murder and his girlfriend, but the two others who accompany him to try to collect the reward are not so sure about justice.

***North to Alaska*** (1960). D: Henry Hathaway. John Wayne, Stewart Granger, Capucine. Comic complications surround two partners mining gold in Alaska when one goes to Seattle to bring back the other's supposed fiancée, but finds her married and brings back another woman in her place.

***Once Upon a Time in the West*** (1968). D: Sergio Leone. Charles Bronson, Henry Fonda, Claudia Cardinale. Sprawling tale of the coming of the railroad in the West and the ruthless railroad baron who tries to take over the land that has the only water for miles around.

***Open Range*** (2004). D: Kevin Costner. Robert Duval, Kevin Costner, Anette Bening. A group of men are herding cattle and grazing on the open range when they tangle with a cattle baron who wants them out of the area, resulting in actions that lead to a full-scale range war and gory shoot-out.

***The Outlaw*** (1943). D: Howard Hawks, Howard Hughes. Jack Buetel, Walter Huston, Jane Russell. Fictional story of the semi-friendly rivalry between Billy the Kid and Doc Holliday over a horse they both claim to own, as they try to outdo each other for the affections of big-bosomed Rio.

***The Outlaw Josey Wales*** (1976). D: Clint Eastwood. Clint Eastwood, Chief Dan George, Sondra Locke. A peaceful farmer turns into an avenging angel as he tries to escape from a posse and find the man who burned his farm and murdered his family during the Civil War.

***Paint Your Wagon*** (1969). D: Joshua Logan. Clint Eastwood, Lee Marvin, Jean Seberg. Two prospectors team up in an unlikely partnership to dig gold and end up marrying the same woman, all set in a background of an instant town created during the early California gold rush.

***Pale Rider*** (1985). D: Clint Eastwood. Clint Eastwood, Michael Moriarty, Carrie Snodgrass. Miners struggling to pan enough placer gold to survive are being forced out by a large corporation when a mysterious stranger arrives to rally them and inspire them to fight back.

***The Professionals*** (1966). D: Richard Brooks. Lee Marvin, Burt Lancaster, Jack Palance. A team of mercenaries is hired to rescue a tycoon's young wife who has supposedly been captured by a bandit that they fought with in the Mexican revolution.

***The Quick and the Dead*** (1995). D: Sam Raimi. Sharon Stone, Gene Hackman, Russell Crowe. A gathering of gunmen challenge the tyrannical boss of a town to see who is the fastest on the draw in a contest consisting of a series of lethal shootouts between the gunfighters.

***Radio Ranch*** (1940), the edited theatrical release of ***The Phantom Empire*** (1935). D: Otto Brower, Breezy Eason. Gene Autry, Smiley Burnette, Betsy King Ross. A radio singer at a guest ranch finds a lost science-fiction civilization deep under the earth, while battling sinister villains trying to steal radium deposits from under the ranch.

***The Rare Breed*** (1966). D: Andrew McLaglen. James Stewart, Maureen O'Hara, Brian Keith. A cowboy attempts to improve cattle breeding on the Texas range with a new type of bull from Britain.

***Red River*** (1948). D: Howard Hawks. John Wayne, Montgomery Clift, Joanne Dru. Tension between young blood and the older generation amid the problems that occur during a classic cattle drive.

***Ride the High Country*** (1962). D: San Peckinpah. Randolph Scott, Joel McCrea, Mariette Hartley. An aging former federal marshal and his down-on-his-luck gunfighter partner take on one last job for a bank by transporting gold from a mining town in the high mountains.

***Rio Bravo*** (1959). D: Howard Hawks. John Wayne, Dean Martin, Walter Brennan. A sheriff, his drunken deputy, and an old coot try to hold a prisoner in jail while his older brother tries to break him loose by one method or another.

***Rio Grande*** (1950). D: John Ford. John Wayne, Maureen O'Hara, Claude Jarman. Strained relationships between a cavalry office, his estranged wife, and their enlisted son, who ends up in the fort under his father's command.

***Rio Lobo*** (1970). D: Howard Hawks. John Wayne, Robert Mitchum, Ed Asner. Two old saddle pals join forces to defeat a rancher who is trying to take over everybody's water rights.

***Rough Night in Jericho*** (1967). D: Arnold Laven. Dean Martin, George Peppard, Jean Simmons. A former marshal and his deputy come up against a ruthless town boss who wants to take over his former girlfriend's stage line.

***Saddle the Wind*** (1958). D: Robert Parrish. Robert Taylor, John Cassavetes, Julie London. An ex-gunman has settled down to a peaceful life of cattle ranching, but his younger brother is a wild one, which leads to an inevitable conflict and shoot-out between the two. The drama unfolds over the background of cattlemen versus homesteaders.

***The Searchers*** (1956). D: John Ford. John Wayne, Jeffrey Hunter, Ward Bond. A driven man and his adopted nephew search for years for his niece who has been captured by Indians, with the implication that he is going to kill her for being "tainted."

***Sergeants 3*** (1962). D: John Sturges. Frank Sinatra, Dean Martin, Peter Lawford. An ex-slave wants to join the army and fight Indians, while three boisterous sergeants are sent to find out why all the inhabitants of an entire town have disappeared.

***Shane*** (1953). D: George Stevens. Alan Ladd, Van Heflin, Walter (Jack) Palance. A drifting gunfighter comes to town hoping to settle down, but when he finds that local homesteaders are up against a ruthless land baron who wants to control the entire valley, he uses his gun skills to help them fight back.

***She Wore a Yellow Ribbon*** (1949). D: John Ford. John Wayne, John Agar, Victor McLaglen. An aging cavalry officer is ready to retire when he is assigned one last task to make peace as the Indians get ready to go on the warpath.

***The Sheepman*** (1958). D: George Marshall. Glenn Ford, Shirley MacLaine, Edgar Buchanan. A cowboy brings a herd of sheep he has won in a poker game to cattle country, where he faces antagonism from the local ranchers, headed by a rascally former saddle pal who appears to have suddenly gone respectable.

***The Sheriff of Fractured Jaw*** (1959). D: Raoul Walsh. Kenneth More, Jayne Mansfield, Henry Hull. Humorous account of a British aristocrat who journeys to the West to sell guns and is inadvertently appointed the sheriff of a town caught between two rival ranches, and how he resolves the situation.

***The Shootist*** (1976). D: Don Siegel. John Wayne, Lauren Bacall, Ron Howard. An aging gunfighter learns that he has cancer and decides to stage a shootout to settle the score with old enemies and finish it all in a hurry instead of waiting for his natural end.

*Silverado* (1985). D: Lawrence Kasdan. Kevin Kline, Scott Glenn, Kevin Costner. Four gunmen band together in an unlikely combination to defeat a corrupt sheriff and his henchmen.

*Son of Paleface* (1952). D: Frank Tashlin. Bob Hope, Jane Russell, Roy Rogers. When a recent Harvard graduate comes to the West to claim his father's inheritance, he finds that it is missing, but soon becomes mixed up with a singing lawman who is hot on the trail of a lady stage robber dubbed the Torch.

*The Sons of Katie Elder* (1965). D: Henry Hathaway. John Wayne, Dean Martin, James Gregory. The sons of Katie Elder have moved away from the old homestead, but return and are reunited for her funeral, after which they investigate the suspicious death of their father and the unexplained take-over of the family ranch.

*Stagecoach* (1939). D: John Ford. Claire Trevor, John Wayne, Andy Devine. Interactions among a motley group of characters who are brought together during a perilous stagecoach journey across New Mexico.

*The Stalking Moon* (1969). D: Robert Mulligan. Gregory Peck, Eva Marie Saint, Robert Forster. An ex-army scout helps a white woman, who was captured by Indians and bore a half-breed son, escape from the boy's Indian father who is relentlessly pursuing her.

*¡Three Amigos!* (1986). D: John Landis. Steve Martin, Chevy Chase, Martin Short. Three Western movie stars from the silent film era mistakenly go to help a Mexican village that is being terrified by a real Mexican bandit named El Guapo.

*3:10 to Yuma* (1957). D: Delmer Daves. Van Heflin, Glenn Ford, Felicia Farr. Suspenseful interplay between a farmer needing money and a captured outlaw, as they wait in a hotel for the train to take the outlaw to prison in Yuma, Arizona.

*3:10 to Yuma* (2007). D: James Mangold. Russell Crowe, Christian Bale, Ben Foster. Remake of the 1957 film with more emphasis on action, violence, and gore.

*Tom Horn* (1980). D: William Wiard. Steve McQueen, Linda Evans, Richard Farnsworth. The story of the final days of real-life Wyoming bounty hunter Tom Horn.

*Tombstone* (1993). D: George P. Cosmatos. Kurt Russell, Val Kilmer, Sam Elliott. This details the arrival of the Earp brothers and their wives in Tombstone, and the events that culminated in the gunfight at the O.K. Corral, then afterwards when Wyatt Earp takes his revenge as he hunts down his brother's attackers.

*The Train Robbers* (1973). D: Burt Kennedy. John Wayne, Ann-Margret, Rod Taylor. Six men and a woman go into Mexico to recover half-a-million dollars from a train robbery and are pursued by a Pinkerton operative who reveals a surprising twist at the end.

*True Grit* (1969). D: Henry Hathaway. John Wayne, Kim Darby, Glen Campbell. A 14-year-old girl teams up with an aging, overweight U.S. marshal to track down her father's killer in the rough world of the Indian Strip.

*True Grit* (2010). D: Joel Cohen, Ethan Cohen. Jeff Bridges, Haillee Steinfeld, Matt Damon. This remake of the 1969 version is more true to the original novel, but is also more graphic than its predecessor in terms of violence and bloodshed.

*Two Mules for Sister Sara* (1970). D: Don Siegel. Clint Eastwood, Shirley MacLaine, Manolo Fabregas. A drifter saves a nun from an attack in the desert, only to eventually find out that she is a prostitute and a revolutionary fighting with the rebels against the French.

*Unforgiven* (1992). D: Clint Eastwood. Clint Eastwood, Gene Hackman, Morgan Freeman. A former gunman who has settled down as a farmer comes out of retirement to earn money for his children by hiring out to kill two cowboys who have cut up a saloon woman.

*The Villain* (1979). D: Hal Needham. Kirk Douglas, Ann-Margret, Arnold Schwarzenegger. A handsome Stranger accompanies the voluptuous Miss Charming Jones to guard a chest of money, while Cactus Jack Slade tries to steal it and Indian Chief Nervous Elk has his own plan for getting the money (need one say more?).

*Wagon Master* (1950). D: John Ford. Ben Johnson, Harry Carey, Jr., Ward Bond. Two itinerant cowboys are hired to lead a wagon train headed for Utah, while bandits lurk behind them.

*The War Wagon* (1967). D: Burt Kennedy. John Wayne, Kirk Douglas, Howard Keel. Unjustly accused and imprisoned, a former ranch owner takes his revenge on the local mining company that stole his ranch for the gold on it by robbing a rich shipment of their gold that is being transported in a frontier-style armored wagon.

*Wild Bill* (1995). D: Walter Hill. Jeff Bridges, Ellen Barkin, David Arquette. A fictionalized account of some of the events in the life of Wild Bill Hickok, told in a series of episodes that happened during the years that led up to his murder by Jack McCall in Deadwood, South Dakota.

*The Wild Bunch* (1969). D: Sam Peckinpah. William Holden, Ernest Borgnine, Robert Ryan. Following a botched bank raid, an aging group of bank robbers and outlaws are hired by Mexican rebels with a villainous leader to pull off one last heist by stealing a shipment of guns from an American munitions train.

*Winchester '73* (1950). D: Anthony Mann. James Stewart, Dan Duryea, Stephen McNally. The story follows a prize Winchester rifle as it is stolen and passes through various unsavory hands before it makes its way back to its rightful owner.

*Wyatt Earp* (1994). D: Lawrence Kasdan. Kevin Costner, Dennis Quaid, Gene Hackman. This story of Wyatt Earp takes up and continues on where the gunfight at the O.K. Corral left off to follow Earp's vendetta against his remaining adversaries from the gunfight.

*Young Bill Hickok* (1940). D: Joseph Kane. Roy Rogers, George "Gabby" Hayes, Jacqueline Wells. Bill Hickok postpones his wedding when he is sent to guard a gold shipment, but loses it to Southern sympathizers and is wrongly accused of stealing it; he recovers it with the aid of Gabby and a singing Calamity Jane.

*Young Guns* (1988). D: Christopher Cain. Emilio Estevez, Kiefer Sutherland, Lou Diamond Phillips. A young Billy the Kid is taken under the wing of British rancher John Tunstall as the events that led up to the Lincoln County cattle war unfold.

# Chapter Notes

## Preface

1. McDonald, ed., *Shooting Stars*, 133.
2. Dmytryk, *On Screen Directing*, 132.
3. Fenin and Everson, *The Western*, 363.
4. Garfield, *Western Film*, 56.
5. Ibid., 130.
6. For example, see Calder, *There Must Be a Lone Ranger*; Sarf, *God Bless You Buffalo Bill*; and Garfield, *Western Film*.
7. Kitses and Rickman, *The Western Reader*, 26
8. Barra, *Inventing Wyatt Earp*, 347.
9. Ibid., 305.
10. Quoted in Barra, *Inventing Wyatt Earp*, 310.

## Chapter One

1. David Lavender. *The Great West* (New York: American Heritage Press, 1985), 240.
2. Ibid., 302.
3. The gold belt was eventually found to stretch for nearly seven hundred miles, starting in southwest Oregon and running almost to the Kern River, near Bakersfield, California.
4. The recovery of gold can be broken into two very general categories: placer gold mining and hard rock (or lode) mining. Placer gold is pure gold that exists in flakes and chunks in stream beds, where it has been washed down from veins of gold higher up in the mountains. This type of gold can be recovered quite simply by crude methods of separation, such as using a gold pan or some similar method of washing to separate the lighter gravel and sand from the heavier flakes of pure gold. This was the type of mining that took place in California in the 1850s. Gold panning and the use of a miner's rocker to recover gold is shown in *Pale Rider* (1985). The other general category, hard rock mining, requires sinking a shaft into solid rock to dig out the gold. This type of gold may be pure metal, in veins or chunks, or may be present as gold ore that has the gold chemically locked into it and requires smelting and other sophisticated chemical processes to separate the gold. This type of mining also requires large investments of capital for the men and machinery to dig tunnels and built a smelter. This was the type of mining that took place on the Com-

stock mining district in Nevada, Leadville, and later at Cripple Creek in Colorado.
5. A good historical example of the results of this type of mining can be viewed at Malakoff Digging State Historical Park near Nevada City, California.
6. "The Lost Adams Diggings," *Colorful Colorado*, Vol. 7, No. 5, March–April, 1972: 24–28, 30, 32.
7. Ray Stebbins, "Yellowstone Revisited," *Colorful Colorado*, Vol. 8, No. 1, July–August 1972: 2R-16R.
8. The gauge of a shotgun pellet represents the number of round balls that can be made from a pound of lead. Twelve-gauge, then, defines the diameter of a lead ball that is the appropriate size to make twelve round balls to the pound.
9. *Story of the Great American West* (Pleasantville: The Reader's Digest Association, 1977), 204.
10. The account of Buffalo Bill's service with the Pony Express comes from his autobiography published in 1879. Historian Louis Warren, however, has questioned whether or not Cody actually rode for the Pony Express and concluded that this story may have been part of Cody's re-invention of his show business personality after he had become famous. (Louis S. Warren, *Buffalo Bill's America: William Cody and the Wild West Show* [New York: Alfred A. Knopf, 2005].)
11. The first "transcontinental" railroad was the Panama Railway; it ran for forty-eight miles from the town of Aspinwall (now Colón) on the Atlantic side of the Isthmus of Panama to Panama City on the Pacific side. It was a very small, but profitable, railroad that carried passengers and freight bound for gold-rush California starting in 1855.
12. The modern myth of Tombstone started with the first annual Helldorado festival, which was held in 1929 to celebrate the town's wild past. The celebration included staged gunfights and a reenactment of the history of Tombstone. The Helldorado festival is still held annually at the end of October, with parades and reenactments of gunfights, including the famous one at the O.K. Corral.
13. Abbott, *We Pointed Them North*, 210.

## Chapter Two

1. Franz and Choate, *The American Cowboy*, 77.
2. Wichita *Eagle*, May 28, 1874.

3. *Daily Commonwealth*, Topeka, August 15, 1871.

4. *Frank Leslie's Illustrated Weekly*, December 1, 1883.

5. *Harper's Weekly*, October 16, 1886.

6. The dates after the names of these towns refer to the peak years of cattle shipping, not necessarily to other aspects of their history.

7. Dary, *Cowboy Culture*, 218.

8. *Manhattan Nationalist*, August 2, 1872.

9. Miller and Snell, *Great Gunfighters of the Kansas Cowtowns, 1867–1886*, 13.

10. Ibid., 5.

11. Lake, *Wyatt Earp*, 144.

12. Dykstra, *The Cattle Towns*, 113.

13. Riley and Etulain, eds., *Wild Women of the Old West*, 165–166.

14. Ibid., 159.

15. Ibid., 172.

16. Sennett, *Great Hollywood Westerns*, 255. Director Michael Cimino originally budgeted $12 million for the movie, but the cost escalated to an estimated $50 million, almost sinking United Artists studios (Garfield, *Western Film*, 7).

17. Robert L. Brown, *Colorado Ghost Towns—Past and Present* (Caldwell: Caxton, 1981), 121.

18. O'Neal, *Encyclopedia of Western Gunfighters*, 95.

19. Weston, *The Real American Cowboy*, 11.

20. Dykstra, *The Cattle Towns*, 144.

## Chapter Three

1. Simmon, *The Invention of the Western Film*, 3.

2. Kitses and Rickman, *The Western Reader*, 90–91.

3. Hamilton, *Thunder in the Dust*, 13.

4. This "Western" was actually made in Edison's "Black Maria" studio, built in 1893 in West Orange, New Jersey. This small, dark, cramped, overheated shed is credited as America's first movie studio. The name supposedly came from the studio's resemblance to a police wagon.

5. The actor underneath the dress was male, as men often played the parts of women in early films.

6. Shipman, *The Story of Cinema*, 36.

7. Quick and LaBau, *Handbook of Film Production*, 7.

8. Kitses and Rickman, *The Western Reader*, 115.

9. O'Neil, *The End and the Myth*, 206.

10. Simmon, *The Invention of the Western Film*, 68.

11. Etulain and Riley, eds., *The Hollywood West*, 2.

12. Ibid., 4.

13. Andrew B. Smith, *Shooting Cowboys and Indians*, 12–13.

14. Ibid., 30.

15. United Artists was formed by movie stars Mary Pickford and her husband star Doug Fairbanks, director D.W. Griffith, and actor Charlie Chaplin to give them more creative control over their movies. William S. Hart was part of the original discussions that eventually led to the formation of the company, but Hart dropped out after he found out that the others planned to finance their own productions.

16. McDonald, ed., *Shooting Stars*, 2.

17. Stebbins, J. R., "The Reluctant Badman," *Colorful Colorado*, Vol. 6, No. 6, May–June, 1971: 10–14, 16, 91.

18. McDonald, *Shooting Stars*, 17.

19. Reddin, Paul. *The Wild West Shows*. Urbana: University of Illinois Press, 1999, 199.

20. McDonald, *Shooting Stars*, 28.

21. George-Warren, *Public Cowboy No. 1*, 126.

22. Ibid., 129.

23. In 1938 Yates sold ARC to William Paley's Columbia Broadcast System to become Columbia Records.

24. David Rothel, *The Singing Cowboys* (New York: A.S. Barnes, 1978), 55.

25. Guy Logsdon, "The Cowboy's Bawdy Music," in Charles W. Harris and Buck Rainey, ed., *The Cowboy: Six-shooters, Songs, and Sex* (Norman: University of Oklahoma Press, 1976), 132.

26. Simmon, *The Invention of the Western Film*, 100.

27. Mascot's movie lot was the previous Mack Sennett studios, off Ventura Boulevard in the San Fernando Valley of Los Angeles. The Monogram Studios were on Sunset Boulevard in Silver Lake. Monogram survived the ups and downs of many of the other Poverty Row studios and changed its corporate name to Allied Artists Picture Corporation in 1953.

28. George-Warren, *Public Cowboy No. 1*, 160–161; Stanfield, *Horse Opera*, 82.

29. George-Warren, *Public Cowboy No. 1*, 138. Autry's second starring picture, *Tumbling Tumbleweeds* (1935), took one week to make at a cost of $18,801. The movie was named for the hit song written by Bob Nolan of the Sons of the Pioneers and recorded earlier in the year.

30. Garfield, *Western Film*, 36.

31. Autry, *Back in the Saddle Again*, 35.

32. And his real name was? Michael Munn claims that the name on Wayne's birth certificate was Marion Robert Morrison (Munn, *John Wayne*, 6). Pilar Wayne, John Wayne's third and last wife said that the name on his birth certificate was Robert Michael Wayne (Wayne, *John Wayne*, 8). The name under his picture in the 1925 Glendale High School yearbook was Marion Mitchell Morrison (Munn, 8). Perhaps the truth has become hazy in the legend. Incidentally, Wayne received his nickname "Duke" from his dog. He was Big Duke, the dog was Little Duke (Munn, 3)

33. Munn, *John Wayne*, 6–7.

34. Ibid., 191.

35. George-Warren, *Public Cowboy No. 1*, 2.

36. Ibid., 22.

37. *The Phantom Empire* (1935) was originally released as a twelve-part serial. The serial was edited into a movie called *Radio Ranch* for a 1940 theatrical release.

38. George-Warren, *Public Cowboy No. 1*, 131.

39. Ibid., 144.

40. The Internet Movie Database; *Gene Autry*.

41. George-Warren, *Public Cowboy No. 1*, 154.

42. McDonald, ed., *Shooting Stars*, 98.

43. Stanfield, *Horse Opera*, 95.

44. George-Warren, *Public Cowboy No. 1*, 174.

45. Ibid., 170.

46. Andrew B. Smith, *Shooting Cowboys and Indians*, 192–193.

47. The ranch was Placeritos Ranch, before it became Monogram Ranch. As part of Autry's business ventures, he bought it in 1953 and rented it for filming television series, including *Maverick* with James Garner, *Gunsmoke* with James Arness, and *The Life and Legend of Wyatt Earp* with Hugh O'Brien. Many of the Western movie buildings burned in a brush fire in August 1962, and the property was later sold. The ranch was restored as a movie set in 1990 and continued on as a movie location, being used, for example, for the HBO television series *Deadwood*.

48. White, *King of the Cowboys*, 9.

49. Trigger was a golden palomino stallion that appeared in all of Rogers' films. The horse was originally called Golden Cloud and was owned by Hudkins Stables, a company who rented horses to movie studios, before Rogers bought him in 1943.

50. Long before movie star Roy Rogers was given the title "King of the Cowboys" by Republic Studios in the 1940s, this title was used by Buck Taylor, a trick rider of exceptional skill who appeared in *Buffalo Bill's Wild West* in the late 1880s.

51. Sarsaparilla was a carbonated soft drink flavored with an extract from the dried roots of a series of fragrant climbing vines found in tropical Central America, which gave it an acrid, sweet taste.

52. Shipman, *The Story of Cinema*, 898.

53. Barbour, *Saturday Afternoon at the Movies*, 156.

54. Thomas G. Smith, *Industrial Light and Magic*, 190–191.

55. Scott Eyman, *Lion of Hollywood: The Life and Legend of Louis B. Mayer* (New York: Simon & Schuster, 2005), 397.

56. Griffith and Mayer, *The Movies*, 471.

57. Estimates of the number of weekly tickets sold vary by source. Griffith and Mayer, for example, state that a Gallup poll estimated that 55 million tickets were sold in 1941, down from a previous estimate by the Hays office of 85 million (Griffith and Mayer, *The Movies*, 365). The following estimates of the decline in sales seem reasonable:

    1941: 85 million (Griffith and Mayer, *The Movies*, 365).

    1946: 80 million (Eyman, *Lion of Hollywood*, 400) or 90 million (Quick and LaBau, *Handbook of Film Production*, 9).

    1947: 87 million (Shipman, *The Story of Cinema*, 898).

    1951: 54 million (Eyman, *Lion of Hollywood*, 452).

    1960: 40 million tickets (Quick and LaBau, *Handbook of Film Production*, 9).

    1969: 15 million (Shipman, *The Story of Cinema*, 898).

58. Jackson, *Classic TV Westerns*, 17.

59. George-Warren, *Public Cowboy No. 1*, 192.

## Chapter Four

1. Andrew B. Smith, *Shooting Cowboys and Indians*, 48–49.

2. Metro-Goldwyn-Mayer, *How the West Was Won*, 25.

3. Those readers wanting further insight into the practical intricacies of making movies will benefit from reading *The Big Picture* by Tom Reilly.

4. Munn, *John Wayne*, 309.

5. With consummate satiric typecasting "El Guapo" in Spanish means "the brawler" or "the bully."

6. Movie actors in the silent period of the mid-1920s wore film make-up that consisted of a chalk-white face-powder, heavy red lipstick, and an outline of heavy black mascara around the eyes. This created a high degree of contrast to delineate the actor's facial features and compensate for the low-contrast of the film stock used at the time.

7. Parks, *The Western Hero in Film and Television*, 30.

8. McDonald has commented that screenwriter Carl Foreman was blacklisted as a result of testimony before the House Un-American Activities Committee (HUAAC) investigating Communist infiltration in Hollywood. Foreman supposedly wrote the screenplay for *High Noon* (1952) as a parable of contemporary Hollywood, which he found to be complacent, divided, and indifferent (McDonald, ed., *Shooting Stars*, 79.)

9. Interestingly, whether a coincidence or a nod of tribute to the real West, a real-life woman named Kate Elder (otherwise known as "Big Nose" Kate) was the girlfriend and common-law wife of Doc Holliday.

10. Blake, *Code of Honor*, 113.

11. Ibid., 19.

12. Ibid., 42.

13. Reilly, *The Big Picture*, 56.

14. For an entertaining view of what it was like during the transition from the silents to talking pictures, the plot of the MGM musical *Singin' in the Rain* (1952) delightfully satirizes the difficulties that two of the main characters undergo during the change, including problems with the sound pick-up, the synchronization of voices with image, and the realization that not all actors had voices suitable for the talkies.

15. Blake, *Code of Honor*, 77.

16. An example of a budget that spiraled out of control was *Heaven's Gate* (1980), a story set against the background of Wyoming's Johnson County War. The film was originally budgeted for $10 to $12 million — in itself an exorbitant amount — but costs rapidly grew to an estimated $36 to $50 million. For this the studio got an overblown original 225-minute running length that was later re-cut to 148 minutes. Critics did not feel that the re-editing helped.

17. Barbour, *Saturday Afternoon at the Movies*, xviii.

18. Ibid., xv.

19. Garfield, *Western Film*, 76.

20. O'Neil, *The End and the Myth*, 201.

21. Ibid.

22. Stanton, *Where God Put the West*, 77.

23. Stanfield, *Hollywood, Westerns and the 1930s*, 58.

24. Fenin and Everson, *The Western*, 292.

25. Blake, *Code of Honor*, 167.

26. Lloyd, ed., *They Went That-A-Way*, 35.

27. O'Neil, *The End and the Myth*, 227. This stunt is still spectacular today, and was reprised under a French carriage to good effect in the sword swashbuckler *The Musketeer* (2001), and under a German Nazi truck in *Raiders of the Lost Ark* (1981).

28. McDonald, ed., *Shooting Stars*, 115.

29. Thomas G. Smith, *Industrial Light and Magic*, 145.

30. Digital images need to be at least the equivalent of twelve megapixels or more to avoid a grainy look. As technology advances, as it inevitably will, higher and higher resolutions will be commonly used.

## Chapter Five

1. Quoted in Stanton, *Where God Put the West*, 1.

2. Hamilton, *Thunder in the Dust*, 155.

3. Andrew B. Smith, *Shooting Cowboys and Indians*, 10.

4. George-Warren, *Public Cowboy*, 46.

5. Smith, *Shooting Cowboys and Indians*, 54.

6. Ibid., 136.

7. Ibid., 45.

8. Ibid., 219.

9. Simmon, *The Invention of the Western Film*, 56.

10. Ibid., 36.

11. In the early days of movie distribution, prints of films were purchased by exhibitors. "Exchanges" were businesses where exhibitors traded or sold films to others who needed new material, after they had already shown them. Later, copies of films were rented instead of purchased, and exchanges became wholesalers who purchased films from production companies and then rented copies to theaters.

12. McDonald, ed., *Shooting Stars*, 6.

13. The Miller Brothers show opened in Norfolk, Virginia, on May 20, 1907. Later they added cowboy stars of the silent screen, such as Tom Mix and Buck Jones, to the show.

14. Andrew B. Smith, *Shooting Cowboys and Indians*, 115.

15. George-Warren, *Public Cowboy No. 1*, 51.

16. According to local Navajo legend, these towers of rock help to hold up the sky.

17. Ford was born in Portland, Maine, in 1894 as John Martin Feeney, not as Sean Aloysius O'Feeney in 1895 as some sources claim. He worked as a stuntman, propman, and occasional actor before becoming a movie director. During World War II, Ford had a distinguished career as the head of the Field Photographic Branch for the Office of Strategic Services (OSS). He died in 1973.

18. D'Arc, *When Hollywood Came to Town*, 208.

19. Lloyd, ed., *They Went That-A-Way*, 35.

20. Mitchell Butte and Merrick Butte were named for two soldiers who served under Kit Carson. They were killed while trying to mine silver in an area sacred to the Navajo Indians.

21. Munn, *John Wayne*, 56–57.

22. Some of the images, particularly the sky and background clouds, were exceptionally dramatic as cinematographer Archie Stout filmed them on infrared film stock, which had been recently developed for World War II.

23. Military installations in the West often started out as temporary facilities with the title of "Camp" until they were later replaced by more elaborate permanent installations and their names were changed to "Fort."

24. Moon, *Tall Sheep*, xiv.

25. Ibid., 150–151.

26. Cowie, *John Ford and the American West*, 186.

27. Sennett, *Great Hollywood Westerns*, 253.

28. Mount Whitney is the highest mountain in the continental United States at 14,494 feet above sea level.

29. Lawton, *Old Tucson Studios*, 59.

## Chapter Six

1. Parks, *The Western Hero in Film and Television*, 1.

2. O'Neal, *Encyclopedia of Western Gunfighters*, 5.

3. It is thought that the real Hickok might have contracted gonorrhea that affected his eyesight later in life (Schoenberger, *The Gunfighters*, 86).

4. This film was also notable for being the first Western filmed in Technicolor.

5. O'Neal, *Encyclopedia of Western Gunfighters*, 5.

6. John Mack Farragher, "The Tale of Wyatt Earp," in Mark C. Carnes, ed., *Past Imperfect*, 154.

7. Barra, *Inventing Wyatt Earp*, 346.

8. Carnes, ed., *Past Imperfect*, 160; Sarf, *God Bless You Buffalo Bill*, 53.

9. Another brother, Warren Earp, did not accompany them. Warren was killed in a drunken saloon fight in Willcox, Arizona, on July 6, 1900.

10. Wyatt eventually abandoned his common-law wife Mattie Blaylock, who ended up as a prostitute in Pinal, Arizona, and died of an overdose of laudanum on July 3, 1888.

11. Barra, *Inventing Wyatt Earp*, 304. Doc has often mistakenly been credited with attending dental college in Baltimore.

12. Ibid., 75. Kate was born in Budapest, Hungary. She changed her name to Fisher after she ran away from home.

13. Miller and Snell, *Great Gunfighters of the Kansas Cowtowns, 1867–1886*, 194.

14. O'Neal, *Encyclopedia of Western Gunfighters*, 5.

15. Schoenberger, *The Gunfighters*, 113.

16. Later in life she wrote in a pamphlet, which she sold while on the lecture circuit, that she was named Marthy Cannary and was born in 1852, but the spelling "Canary" is the correct family name and her birth date of 1856 has been verified by careful researchers.

17. The most widespread existing picture of Billy the Kid, which was believed to have been taken in Fort Sumner, New Mexico, in 1879 or 1980, is a full-length portrait that shows him with a Winchester carbine and wearing one holstered Colt single-action revolver gun in the conventional fashion, butt backwards, beside his left hip. Because of this photograph, he has been supposed to have been left-handed, which was the inspiration for the title of *The Left-Handed Gun* (1958). The photograph, however, is a tintype, an early form of photograph that created an original image on a metal plate. As part of the tintype process, the image becomes reversed, and Billy was actually right handed. In addition, firearms expert Robert Wilson (Wilson, *Winchester*, 46) has pointed out that the loading gate for the Winchester carbine in the photograph is shown as being on the left, whereas in reality it would be on the right side of the gun, thus also proving that the image is reversed.

18. O'Neal, *Encyclopedia of Western Gunfighters*, 5.

19. For reasons that were never completely clear, Annie changed the family name from Moses to Mozee and her own surname to Oakley.

20. Wilson and Martin, *Buffalo Bill's Wild West*, 142.

21. How "Butch" Cassidy received his nickname has been the subject of some dispute. Turner claimed he got it because he worked at one time in a butcher's shop (George Turner, *George Turner's Book of Gunfighters* [Amarillo: Baxter Lane, 1972]). Drago has stated that Cassidy worked as a butcher in 1889 in Rock Springs, Wyoming, and that is where he received the name (Gail Drago, *Etta Place: Her Life and Times with Butch Cassidy and the Sundance Kid* [Plano: Republic of Texas Press, 1996]). Warner (1940), however, a friend of Cassidy's, stated that he gave Cassidy the nickname after Cassidy fired a heavy hunting rifle nicknamed "Butch" that had such a powerful recoil that it knocked him over (Matt Warner, *The Last of the Bandit Riders* [Caldwell, IO: Caxton, 1940]).

22. Harry Longabaugh received his nickname "The Sundance Kid" after he spent time in the jail at Sundance, Wyoming, for horse-stealing when he was a teenager.

23. Bob B. Bell, "High Doom in the Andes," *True West*, Vol. 55, No. 11, November/ December 2008, 66–69.

## Chapter Seven

1. In an ironic turn of fate, the Lee company later removed the rivets on the hip pockets because of complaints that they were scratching the leather of saddles.

2. Beard, *100 Years of Western Wear*, 34.

3. George-Warren and Freedman, *How the West Was Worn*, 44.

4. Beard, *100 Years of Western Wear*, 34.

5. Enss, *How the West Was Worn*, 10.

6. George-Warren and Freedman, *How the West Was Worn*, 9.

7. Ibid., 63–65.

8. Enss, *How the West Was Worn*, 40.

9. Fenin and Everson, *The Western*, 183.

10. George-Warren, *Public Cowboy No. 1*, 125.

11. Fenin and Everson, *The Western*, 184.

12. Autry, *Back in the Saddle Again*, 37.

13. Enss, *How the West Was Worn*, 69.

14. Rattenbury, *Packing Iron*, 194.

15. Bianchi, *Blue Steel & Gunleather*, 27.

## Chapter Eight

1. The word cartridge is derived from *carta*, the Latin word for paper, because the cases of some early cartridges were made from paper.

2. Humorous as this may seem, a company named Moores Patent Firearms Co. of Brooklyn, New York, actually made a small .32 caliber rimfire belt revolver in 1861 that had a cylinder that took seven cartridges. The seven-shot examples given in the text, however, refer to the six-shot Colt Model P Peacemaker commonly used in Western movies.

3. Rifles have barrels that are typically twenty-two to twenty-four inches long to produce reasonable accuracy at a long distance. A carbine is a rifle with a barrel that is several inches shorter, which gives it better maneuverability at short distances, such as when shooting from a horse, but results in poorer accuracy at long distances.

4. Semi-automatic pistols, such as those used by police today, were not developed in the United States until around 1900, and were not popular until after the introduction of the Colt Model 1911. They did not enter into widespread usage among law enforcement agencies until the 1980s.

5. Dragoons were mounted troops, organized in 1833, who were trained to fight either on horseback or on foot like the infantry. Typically they fought on foot, only using their horses as a means of rapid transportation to a battle site. After the Civil War, the Dragoons were absorbed into the cavalry.

6. Bullets are defined by their caliber, which is the diameter of the bullet in inches (though some modern bullets are specified in millimeters). Thus .45 caliber firearms use a bullet that is nominally 0.45 inches in diameter, though in practice the diameter is slightly bigger in order to seal the bullet tightly inside the barrel when the gun is fired.

7. This revolver was known as "The Navy" because the cylinders were engraved with a scene of a battle that occurred in May of 1843, when the three ships of the Texas navy (at that time the Lone Star Republic) were victorious over the Mexican navy.

8. Schwing, *Standard Catalog of Firearms*, 7th ed., 244.

9. Wilson, *Colt*, 190.

10. Remington Arms Company of Ilion, New York, was founded by Eliphalet Remington in 1816, making it the oldest firearms manufacturing company in the United States.

11. Ironically, Schofield shot himself with one of

his own revolvers at Fort Apache, Arizona, on February 17, 1882, in what was reported to be a temporary fit of insanity brought on by worry.

12. Warner, *The Last of the Bandit Riders*, 43.

13. Wilson, *Winchester*, 47–48.

14. Warner, *The Last of the Bandit Riders*, 43.

15. Not commonly known is that the first model of firearm from Colt was a rifle with a revolving cylinder, manufactured in 1832, with the first revolver following in 1834 (Wilson, *Colt*, 5).

16. Wilson, *Colt*, 262; and Wilson, *Winchester*, 77.

17. Each pellet of size 00 (double-ought) buckshot is one-third of an inch in diameter.

Shotgun shells were typically loaded with one to one and a half ounces of lead, so ten or so of these lead balls could do some serious damage at short range.

18. The name "derringer" had its origin in a small pocket pistol manufactured by Henry Deringer, Jr., of Philadelphia. Note the different spelling of Deringer's proper name with only one "r." Eventually the name "derringer" became a generic term for small guns that were intended for easy concealment.

## Chapter Nine

1. Calder, *There Must Be a Lone Ranger*, 105.

2. Nash, *Encyclopedia of Western Lawmen & Outlaws*, 83.

3. Agnew, *Smoking Gun*, 245–246.

4. O'Neal, *Encyclopedia of Western Gunfighters*, 147.

5. *Abilene Chronicle*, August 17, 1871.

6. Agnew, *Smoking Gun*, 69.

7. Wilson, *The Peacemakers*, 163.

8. Leo Milligan, "Pistol Aces of a Past Era," *Guns Review*, Vol. 3, No. 3, March 1963: 18–19.

9. Miller and Snell, *Great Gunfighters of the Kansas Cowtowns, 1867–1886*, 178–179.

10. Milligan, "Pistol Aces of a Past Era," 18–19.

11. O'Neal, *Encyclopedia of Western Gunfighters*, 328.

12. Ibid., 113.

13. Bianchi, *Blue Steel & Gunleather*, 16.

14. Maria C. Janis, *Gary Cooper Off Camera* (New York: Harry N. Abrams, 1999), 143.

15. Munn, *John Wayne*, 233.

16. Wichita *Eagle*, October 30, 1873.

17. *Globe Live Stock Journal*, May 12, 1885. The reporting of this fight is a good example of possible minor inaccuracies in primary sources. The *Globe Live Stock Journal* gives the initials of Camp as C.P., Wall's first name as James, and Mather as Mathers. The Dodge City *Democrat*, on the other hand, reported Camp's initials as C.C., and Wall's first name as John.

18. Rosa, *Guns of the American West*, 136.

19. Seeing screen heroes perform these shooting feats has led people to believe that this is possible in real-life. There was an incident in Denver, Colorado, in the 1990s where an individual with a knife, crazed on illegal drugs, attacked a policeman. The outcome was that the police had no choice but to shoot and kill the man. After the incident, however, critics complained that the police should have shot the knife out of his hand.

20. Nash, *Encyclopedia of Western Lawmen & Outlaws*, 1.

21. Wichita *Weekly Beacon*, January, 1876.

22. Lake, *Wyatt Earp*, 37–38.

23. O'Neal, *Encyclopedia of Western Gunfighters*, 5.

24. Wilson, *The Peacemakers*, 200.

25. Lucius Beebe, and Charles Clegg, *The American West* (New York: E.P. Dutton, 1955), 425.

26. "The Wild Bunch," *Colorful Colorado*, Vol. 2, No. 4, Spring 1967: 36–40, 42, 43, 108–110.

27. O'Neal, *Encyclopedia of Western Gunfighters*, 29.

28. Francis M. Forster, *Synopsis of Neurology* (St. Louis: C.V. Mosby, 1962), 152.

29. Agnew, *Smoking Gun*, 106.

## Chapter Ten

1. Randy Roberts, and James S. Olson, *John Wayne: American* (New York: Free Press, 1995), 439.

2. Maria C. Janis, *Gary Cooper Off Camera* (New York: Harry N. Abrams, 1999), 154.

3. Curiously *tonto* is a Spanish adjective that means "foolish" or "stupid."

4. Wilson Rockwell, ed., *Memoirs of a Lawman* (Denver: Sage Books, 1962), 263.

5. The description "Tom-Horned" became a common one for victims who were ambushed without warning.

6. For those who like Western trivia, Rooster Cogburn wore his eye patch on different eyes in the 1969 and 2010 versions of *True Grit*. In the 1969 version, John Wayne wore his eye patch over his left eye; in the 2010 version, Jeff Bridges wore his over his right eye.

7. Rosa, *The Gunfighter*, 66.

8. Because Cochise Country was newly-created from Pima County, the governor selected the first county officials to serve until the next election, instead of using the normal election process.

9. Eyewitness accounts of John Behan in the Tombstone *Daily Nugget*, November 3, 4, & 5, 1881.

10. There are various expert opinions as to what took place at the O.K. Corral and arguments over the "facts" can become quite heated. For a more-detailed thoughtful analysis of what probably happened, see Barra, *Inventing Wyatt Earp*, 178–227.

11. Varner, *Western*, 48.

12. John Mack Farragher, "The Tale of Wyatt Earp," in Mark C. Carnes, ed., *Past Imperfect*, 160.

## Chapter Eleven

1. Boyd Magers, and Michael G. Fitzgerald, *Westerns Women: Interviews with 50 Leading Ladies of Movie and Television Westerns from the 1930s to the 1960s* (Jefferson: McFarland, 1999), 1.

2. Ibid., 25.

3. Simmon, *The Invention of the Western Film*, 112.

4. McDonald, ed., *Shooting Stars*, 196.

5. Correctly speaking, "Victorian" refers to the time period between 1837 and 1901 when the English monarch Victoria was on the throne; however, the term "Victorian" is also used here in a wider sense to designate the characteristic moral and social climate that existed during the years of Queen Victoria's reign.

6. It was not until the 1920s that the sales of cosmetics became popular. What had been disreputable in the late 1800s became fashionable and quite acceptable sixty years later.

7. Tuska, *The American West in Film*, 228.

8. Ramon F. Adams, *The Cowman & His Code of Ethics* (Austin, Encino Press, 1969), 13.

9. Robert L. Brown, *Colorado Ghost Towns — Past and Present* (Caldwell: Caxton, 1981), 119.

10. *Cripple Creek Citizen*, December 7, 1899.

11. O'Neal, *Encyclopedia of Western Gunfighters*, 61.

12. Ibid., 264.

13. Vestal, *Queen of Cowtowns*, 60.

14. James R. Peterson, *The Century of Sex: Playboy's History of the Sexual Revolution* (New York: Grove Press, 1999), 100.

15. Tom Hickman, *The Sexual Century: How Private Passion Became a Public Obsession* (London: Carlton Books Limited, 1999), 43.

16. Peterson, *The Century of Sex*, 116.

17. Ibid., 101.

18. Hickman, *The Sexual Century*, 50.

19. Peterson, *The Century of Sex*, 120.

20. Hickman, *The Sexual Century*, 49.

21. Stanfield, *Hollywood, Westerns and the 1930s*, 171.

22. Scott Eyman, *Lion of Hollywood: The Life and Legend of Louis B. Mayer* (New York: Simon & Schuster, 2005), 189–190.

23. John Heidenry, *What Wild Ecstasy* (New York: Simon & Schuster, 1997), 51.

24. Shipman, *The Story of Cinema*, 903.

## Chapter Twelve

1. Agnew, *Life of a Soldier on the Western Frontier*, 11.

2. For a view of the Mandan ceremony, see the representative painting by Karl Bodmer in *America's Fascinating Indian Heritage* (Pleasantville: The Reader's Digest Association, 1978), 164.

3. Sennett, *Great Hollywood Westerns*, 198.

4. Tuska, *The American West in Film*, 52.

5. Ibid., xix.

6. D'Arc, *When Hollywood Came to Town*, 92.

7. Topeka *Commonwealth*, June 4, 1873.

8. Agnew, *Life of a Soldier on the Western Frontier*, 180–181.

9. An abbreviation of the inventor's name "Gatling" led to the later slang gangster term "gat" for a semi-automatic pistol.

10. The name "howitzer" is derived from a Czech word that means "catapult."

11. This type of projectile was known as "case shot" and was painted red to distinguish it from other rounds in the field. Case shot was developed by Henry Shrapnel of the British army, thus was named "shrapnel" after him. The modern meaning of the word shrapnel includes the shell fragments.

12. Calder, *There Must Be a Lone Ranger*, 39.

13. Simmon, *The Invention of the Western Film*, 74.

14. Anne B. Eales, *Army Wives on the American Frontier* (Boulder: Johnson Books, 1996), 159.

15. Richard I. Dodge, *The Plains of the Great West and Their Inhabitants* (New York: G.P. Putnam's Sons, 1877), 395.

16. A brevet was a temporary commission to a higher rank, without the formal authority consistent with the rank. Brevet ranks were commonly awarded during the Civil War for outstanding bravery or other distinguished service. Brevet officers were allowed to use their highest brevet rank, hence George Armstrong Custer was addressed as General Custer, although he was only a lieutenant-colonel in the regular army.

17. Varner, *Western*, 40.

18. Alvin M. Josephy, Jr., "They Died with Their Boots On," in Mark C. Carnes, ed., *Past Imperfect*, 146.

# Bibliography

Abbott, Edward C., and Helena H. Smith. *We Pointed Them North*. New York: Farrar & Rinehart, 1939.

Adams, Andy. *The Log of a Cowboy*. Boston: Houghton Mifflin, 1903.

Agnew, Jeremy. *Brides of the Multitude: Prostitution in the Old West*. Lake City: Western Reflections, 2008.

_____. *Entertainment in the Old West: Theater, Music, Circuses, Medicine Shows, Prizefighting and Other Popular Amusements*. Jefferson: McFarland, 2011.

_____. *Life of a Soldier on the Western Frontier*. Missoula: Mountain Press, 2008.

_____. *Medicine in the Old West: A History, 1850–1900*. Jefferson: McFarland, 2010.

_____. *Smoking Gun: The True Story About Gunfighting in the Old West*. Lake City: Western Reflections, 2010.

Aikman, Duncan. *Calamity Jane and the Lady Wildcats*. Lincoln: University of Nebraska Press, 1987.

Aitchison, Stewart. *A Traveler's Guide to Monument Valley*. Stillwater: Voyageur Press, 1993.

Asbury, Herbert. *Carry Nation*. New York: Alfred A. Knopf, 1929.

Askins, Charles. *Gunfighters*. Washington, D.C.: National Rifle Association, 1981.

Autry, Gene. *Back in the Saddle Again*. Garden City: Doubleday, 1978.

Barbour, Alan G. *Saturday Afternoon at the Movies*. New York: Bonanza Books, 1986.

Barra, Allen. *Inventing Wyatt Earp: His Life and Many Legends*. New York: Carrol & Graf, 1998.

Beard, Tyler. *100 Years of Western Wear*. Salt Lake City: Gibbs-Smith, 1993.

Bianchi, John E. *Blue Steel & Gunleather*. North Hollywood: Beinfeld, 1978.

Blake, Michael F. *Code of Honor: The Making of Three Great American Westerns*. Lanham: Taylor Trade, 2003.

Brant, Marley. *Jesse James: The Man and the Myth*. New York: Berkeley, 1998.

Breihan, Carl W. *The Complete and Authentic Life of Jesse James*. New York: Frederick Fell, 1953.

_____. *Lawmen and Robbers*. Caldwell: Caxton, 1986.

Calder, Jenni. *There Must Be a Lone Ranger: The American West in Film and in Reality*. New York: Taplinger, 1975.

Cameron, Ian, and Douglas Pye, eds. *The Book of Westerns*. New York: Continuum, 1996.

Canary, Martha J. *Life and Adventures of Calamity Jane*. Original 1893 pamphlet reprinted in Aikman, Duncan. *Calamity Jane and the Lady Wildcats*. Lincoln: University of Nebraska Press, 1987.

Carmichael, Deborah A., ed. *The Landscape of Hollywood Westerns*. Salt Lake City: University of Utah Press, 2006.

Carnes, Mark C., ed. *Past Imperfect: History According to the Movies*. New York, Henry Holt, 1995.

Carter, Samuel. *Cowboy Capital of the World*. Garden City: Doubleday, 1973.

Cowie, Peter. *Seventy Years of Cinema*. Cranbury: A.S. Barnes, 1969.

_____. *John Ford and the American West*. New York: Harry N. Abrams, 2004.

Culhane, John. *Special Effects in the Movies: How They Do It*. New York: Ballantine, 1981.

Cunningham, Eugene. *Triggernometry: A Gallery of Gunfighters*. Caldwell: Caxton, 1941.

D'Arc James V. *When Hollywood Came to Town: A History of Moviemaking in Utah*. Layton: Gibbs Smith, 2010.

Dary, David. *Cowboy Culture: A Sage of Five Centuries*. Lawrence: University Press of Kansas, 1989.

DeArment, Robert K. *Bat Masterson: The Man and the Legend*. Norman: University of Oklahoma Press, 1979.

Dmytryk, Edward. *On Screen Directing*. Boston: Focal Press, 1984.

Dorsey, R. Stephen. *Guns of the Western Indian War*. Eugene: Collector's Library, 1995.

Drago, Gail. *Etta Place: Her Life and Times with Butch Cassidy and the Sundance Kid*. Plano: Republic of Texas Press, 1996.

Drago, Harry S. *The Great Range Wars: Violence on the Grasslands.* New York: Dodd, Mead, 1969.

_____. *The Legend Makers: Tales of the Old Time Peace Officers and Desperadoes of the Frontier.* New York: Dodd, Mead, 1975.

DuBoff, Leonard D. *The Performing Arts Business Encyclopedia.* New York: Allworth Press, 1996.

Dykstra, Robert R. *The Cattle Towns.* New York: Alfred A Knopf, 1968.

Eisele, Wilbert E. *The Real Wild Bill Hickok.* Denver: William H. Andre, 1931.

Elman, Robert. *Badman of the West.* Secaucus: The Ridge Press, 1974.

Enss, Chris. *How the West Was Worn: Bustles and Buckskins on the Wild Frontier.* Helena: Two Dot, 2006.

Eppinga, Jane. *Tombstone.* Charleston: Arcadia, 2003.

Erdoes, Richard. *Saloons of the Old West.* New York: Alfred Knopf, 1979.

Estergreen, M. Morgan. *Kit Carson: A Portrait in Courage.* Norman: University of Oklahoma Press, 1962.

Etulain, Richard W., and Glenda Riley, eds. *The Hollywood West: Lives of Film Legends Who Shaped It.* Golden: Fulcrum, 2001.

Everson, William K. *A Pictorial History of the Western Film.* New York: The Citadel Press, 1969.

Faulk, Odie B. *Dodge City.* New York: Oxford University Press, 1977.

_____. *Tombstone: Myth and Reality.* New York: Oxford University Press, 1972.

Fenin, George N., and William K. Everson. *The Western: From Silents to the Seventies.* New York: Grossman, 1973.

Fradkin, Philip L. *Stagecoach: Wells Fargo and the American West.* New York: Simon & Schuster Source, 2002.

Franz, Joe B., and Julian E. Choate, Jr. *The American Cowboy: The Myth and the Reality.* Norman: University of Oklahoma Press, 1955.

Frayling, Christopher. *Once Upon a Time in Italy: The Westerns of Sergio Leone.* New York: Harry N. Abrams, 2005.

French, Philip. *Westerns: Aspects of a Movie Genre.* New York: Viking, 1973.

Garavaglia, Louis A., and Charles G. Worman. *Firearms of the American West 1866–1894.* Niwot: University Press of Colorado, 1997.

Garfield, Brian. *Western Film.* New York: Rawson Associates, 1982.

George-Warren, Holly. *Cowboy: How Hollywood Invented the Wild West.* Pleasantville: The Reader's Digest Association, 2002.

_____. *Public Cowboy No. 1: The Life and Times of Gene Autry.* New York: Oxford University Press, 2007.

_____, and Michelle Freedman. *How the West Was Worn.* New York: Harry N. Abrams, 2001.

Griffith, Richard, and Arthur Mayer. *The Movies.* New York: Simon & Schuster, 1970.

Hamilton, John R. *Thunder in the Dust: Classic Images of Western Movies.* New York: Stewart, Tabori & Chand, 1987.

Hitt, Jim. *The American West from Fiction (1823–1976) into Film (1909–1986).* Jefferson: McFarland, 1990.

Horan, James D. *The Authentic Wild West: The Gunfighters.* New York: Gramercy Books, 1994.

_____. *The Authentic Wild West: The Lawmen.* New York: Gramercy Books, 1996.

_____. *The Authentic Wild West: The Outlaws.* New York: Gramercy Books, 1996.

Hughes, Howard. *Once Upon a Time in the Italian West.* London: I.B. Taurus, 2004.

Jackson, Ronald. *Classic TV Westerns.* New York: Carol, 1994.

Jacobsen, Joel. *Such Men as Billy the Kid.* Lincoln: University of Nebraska Press, 1994.

Jahns, Pat. *The Frontier World of Doc Holliday.* New York: Indian Head Books, 1957.

Kelly, Charles. *The Outlaw Trail: The Story of Butch Cassidy.* New York: Bonanza Books, 1959.

Kitses, Jim. *Horizons West.* Bloomington: Indiana University Press, 1969.

_____, and Gregg Rickman. *The Western Reader.* New York: Limelight Editions, 1998.

Lake, Stuart N. *Wyatt Earp: Frontier Marshal.* Boston: Houghton Mifflin, 1994.

Langford, Nathaniel P. *Vigilante Days and Ways.* Chicago: A.C. McClurg Press, 1912.

Lawton, Paul J. *Old Tucson Studios.* Charleston: Arcadia, 2008.

Lenihan, John H. *Showdown: Confronting Modern America in the Western Film.* Urbana: University of Illinois Press, 1985.

Lloyd, Ann, ed. *They Went That-A-Way.* London: Orbis, 1982.

Lubet, Steven. *Murder in Tombstone: The Forgotten Trial of Wyatt Earp.* New Haven: Yale University Press, 2004.

Maltin, Leonard. *Movie and Video Guide.* New York: Penguin-Putnam, 1998.

Marks, Paula M. *And Die in the West: The Story of the O.K. Corral Gunfight.* New York: William Morrow, 1989.

McChristian, Douglas C. *The U.S. Army in the West, 1870–1880: Uniform, Weapons and Equipment.* Norman: University of Oklahoma Press, 1995.

McDonald, Archie P., ed. *Shooting Stars: Heroes and Heroines of Western Film.* Bloomington: Indiana University Press, 1987.

McGrath, Roger D. *Gunfighters Highwaymen & Vigilantes.* Berkeley: University of California Press, 1987.

McLaird, James D. *Calamity Jane: The Woman and*

*the Legend*. Norman: University of Oklahoma Press, 2005.

McLoughlin, Denis. *Wild and Wooly: An Encyclopedia of the Old West*. Garden City: Doubleday, 1975.

Metro-Goldwyn-Mayer. *How the West Was Won*. Culver City: Metro-Goldwyn-Mayer, 1963.

Metz, Leon C. *The Encyclopedia of Lawmen, Outlaws, and Gunfighters*. New York: Facts on File, 2003.

_____. *The Shooters*. New York: Berkley, 1976.

Miller, Nyle H., and Joseph W. Snell. *Great Gunfighters of the Kansas Cowtowns, 1867–1886*. Lincoln: University of Nebraska Press, 1963.

_____, and _____. *Why the West Was Wild*. Topeka: Kansas State Historical Society, 1963.

Mognahan, Jay, ed. *The Book of the American West*. New York: Bonanza Books, 1963.

Moon, Samuel. *Tall Sheep: Harry Goulding, Monument Valley Trader*. Norman: University of Oklahoma Press, 1992.

Munn, Michael. *John Wayne: The Man Behind the Myth*. New York: New American Library, 2003.

Murdoch, David H. *The American West: The Invention of a Myth*. Reno: University of Nevada Press, 2001.

Murray, John A. *Cinema Southwest: An Illustrated Guide to the Movies and Their Locations*. Flagstaff: Northland, 2000.

Myers, John M. *Doc Holliday*. Lincoln: University of Nebraska Press, 1955.

Nachbar, Jack, Jackie R. Donath, and Chris Foran. *Western Films 2: An Annotated Critical Bibliography from 1974 to 1987*. New York: Garland, 1988.

Nash, Jay R. *Encyclopedia of Western Lawmen & Outlaws*. New York: Da Capo Press, 1994.

Nolan, Frederick W. *The Lincoln County War*. Norman: University of Oklahoma Press, 1992.

O'Neal, Bill. *Cattlemen vs Sheepherders*. Austin: Eakin Press, 1979.

_____. *Encyclopedia of Western Gunfighters*. Norman: University of Oklahoma Press, 1979.

O'Neil, Paul. *The End and the Myth*. Alexandria: Time-Life Books, 1979.

Parks, Rita. *The Western Hero in Film and Television: Mass Media Mythology*. Ann Arbor: UMI Research Press, 1982.

Patterson, Richard. *Butch Cassidy: A Biography*. Lincoln: University of Nebraska Press, 1998.

Pinteau, Pascal. *Special Effects: An Oral History*. New York: Harry N. Abrams, 2004.

Poling-Kempes, Lesley. *The Harvey Girls*. New York: Marlowe, 1991.

Quick, John, and Tom LaBau. *Handbook of Film Production*. New York: Macmillan, 1972.

Rattenbury, Richard C. *Packing Iron: Gunleather of the Frontier West*. Milwood: Zon International, 1993.

Reilly, Tom. *The Big Picture*. New York: Thomas Dunne Books, 2009.

Resnik, Gail M., and Scott Trost. *All You Need to Know About the Movie and TV Business*. New York: Simon & Schuster, 1996.

Rickey Don, Jr. *Forty Miles a Day on Beans and Hay*. Norman: University of Oklahoma Press, 1963.

Riley, Glenda, and Richard W. Etulain, eds. *Wild Women of the Old West*. Golden: Fulcrum, 2003.

Roberts, Gary L. *Doc Holliday: The Life and Legend*. New York: John Wiley & Sons, 2006.

Robinson, David. *From Peep Show to Palace: The Birth of American Film*. New York: Columbia University Press, 1995.

Rollins, Peter C., and John E. O'Connor, eds. *Hollywood's West: The American Frontier in Film, Television, & History*. Lexington: University Press of Kentucky, 2005.

Rollins, Philip A. *The Cowboy*. New York: Charles Scribner's Sons, 1936.

Rosa, Joseph G. *The Gunfighter: Man or Myth?* Norman: University of Oklahoma Press, 1969.

_____. *Guns of the American West*. New York: Exeter Books, 1988.

_____. *They Called Him Wild Bill: The Life and Adventures of James Butler Hickok*. Norman: University of Oklahoma Press, 1974.

_____. *Wild Bill Hickok: The Man and His Myth*. Lawrence: University Press of Kansas, 1996.

Russell, Don. *The Lives and Legends of Buffalo Bill*. Norman: University of Oklahoma Press, 1960.

Sarf, Wayne M. *God Bless You Buffalo Bill*. East Brunswick: Associated University Presses and Cornwall Books, 1983.

Schoenberger, Dale T. *The Gunfighters*. Caldwell: Caxton, 1983.

Schwing, Ned. *Standard Catalog of Firearms*. 7th ed. Iola: Krause, 1997.

Sennett, Ted. *Great Hollywood Westerns*. New York: Harry N. Abrams, 1990.

Settle, William A., Jr. *Jesse James was His Name*. Columbia: University of Missouri Press, 1966.

Shipman, David. *The Story of Cinema*. New York: St. Martin's Press, 1982.

Simmon, Scott. *The Invention of the Western Film: A Cultural History of the Genre's First Half-Century*. Cambridge: Cambridge University Press, 2003.

Sinyard, Neil. *Clint Eastwood*. Avenel: Crescent Books, 1995.

Slatta, Richard W. *The Cowboy Encyclopedia*. Santa Barbara: ABC-CLIO, Inc., 1994.

Smith, Andrew B. *Shooting Cowboys and Indians: Silent Western Films, American Culture, and the Birth of Hollywood*. Boulder: University Press of Colorado, 2003.

Smith, Duane A. *Rocky Mountain Mining Camps*. Lincoln: University of Nebraska Press, 1967.

Smith, Thomas G. *Industrial Light and Magic: The Art of Special Effects*. New York: Ballantine, 1986.

Sollid, Roberta B. *Calamity Jane*. Helena: Montana Historical Society Press, 1995.

Speed, F. Maurice. *The Western Film Annual*. London: MacDonald, 1954.

Stanfield, Peter. *Hollywood, Westerns and the 1930s*. Exeter: University of Exeter Press, 2001.

Stanfield, Peter. *Horse Opera: The Strange History of the 1930s Singing Cowboy*. Urbana: University of Illinois Press, 2002.

Stanton, Bette L. *Where God Put the West: Movie Making in the Desert*. Moab: Canyonlands Natural History Association, 1994.

Steele, Philip W. *Outlaws and Gunfighters of the Old West*. Springdale: Heritage, 1991.

Stiles, T.J. *Jesse James*. New York: Alfred A. Knopf, 2002.

Streeter, Floyd B. *Prairie Trails and Cow Towns*. New York: Devin Adair, 1963.

Sullivan, James. *Jeans: A Cultural History of an American Icon*. New York: Gotham Books, 2006.

Tefertiller, Casey. *Wyatt Earp*. New York: John Wiley & Sons, 1997.

Tripplett, Frank. *The Life, Times and Treacherous Death of Jesse James*. Chicago: J.H. Chambers, 1882.

Tuska, Jon. *The American West in Film*. Westport: Greenwood Press, 1985.

Utley, Robert M. *Frontier Regulars: The United States Army and the Indian, 1866–1891*. New York: Macmillan, 1973.

Utley, Robert M. *Billy the Kid*. Lincoln: University of Nebraska Press, 1989.

Varner, Paul, ed. *Western: Paperback Novels and Movies From Hollywood*. Newcastle, England: Cambridge Scholars, 2007.

Verhoeff, Norma. *The West in Early Cinema*. Amsterdam: Amsterdam University Press, 2006.

Vestal, Stanley. *Queen of Cowtowns: Dodge City*. New York: Harper and Brothers, 1952.

Walker, Janet, ed. *Western: Film Through History*. New York: Rutledge, 2001.

Warren, Louis S. *Buffalo Bill's America: William Cody and the Wild West Show*. New York: Alfred A. Knopf, 2005.

Wayne, Pilar. *John Wayne: My Life with The Duke*. New York: McGraw-Hill Book Company, 1987.

Weston, Jack. *The Real American Cowboy*. New York: Schocken Books, 1985.

Wetmore, Helen C. *Buffalo Bill: Last of the Great Scouts*. Stamford: Longmeadow Press, 1994.

White, Raymond E. *King of the Cowboys, Queen of the West*. Madison: University of Wisconsin Press, 2005.

Wilson, Robert L. *The Book of Colt Firearms*. Minneapolis: Blue Book, 1993.

_____. *Colt: An American Legend*. New York: Abbeville, 1985.

_____. *The Colt Heritage*. New York: Simon & Schuster, 1979.

_____. *The Peacemakers: Arms and Adventure in the American West*. New York: Random House, 1992.

_____. *Winchester: An American Legend*. New York: Random House, 1991.

_____, and Greg Martin. *Buffalo Bill's Wild West*. New York: Random House, 1998.

Wilstach, Frank J. *The Plainsman Wild Bill Hickok*. Garden City: Doubleday, Page, 1926.

Wright, Will. *Six Guns and Society: A Structural Study of the Western*. Berkeley: University of California Press, 1975.

# Index

Numbers in **bold italics** indicate pages with photographs.